The Dowaliby Family's Encounter with Murder and the Law

by DAVID PROTESS
and ROB WARDEN

Published by
Delacorte Press
Bantam Doubleday Dell Publishing Group, Inc.
1540 Broadway
New York, New York 10036

Library of Congress Cataloging in Publication Data

Protess, David.
Gone in the night : the Dowaliby family's encounter with murder and the law / by David Protess and Rob Warden.
p. cm.
ISBN 0-385-30619-9
1. Dowaliby, David—Trials, litigation, etc. 2. Trials (Murder)—Illinois—Chicago. I. Warden, Rob. II. Title.
KF224.D68P76 1993
345.773'1102523—dc20
[347.7311052523] 92-27231
CIP

Manufactured in the United States of America
Published simultaneously in Canada

May 1993

10 9 8 7 6 5 4 3 2 1

RRH

To Joan and Jennifer

and in memory of
Jaclyn and John

AUTHORS' NOTE

Most of the quotations that appear in our book are verbatim from the official record or tape-recorded interviews, although we occasionally have made slight alterations for intelligibility and have corrected grammar, spelling, and punctuation.

The dialogue that is not in the public record, or that we did not hear ourselves, has been reconstructed from the memory of the participants.

We are indebted to:

Our wives, Joan Protess and Jennifer Alter Warden, and several friends—Flora Skelly, Terry Stephan, Grace Mark, and Joanne Alter—who read and commented on our continually evolving manuscript.

David and Cynthia Dowaliby, who cooperated fully at every stage of our research and writing.

Law enforcement officials who granted us candid interviews—Chief Paul Dennis Greves of Blue Island, Chief William Fischer and Captain John Bitten of Midlothian, Illinois State Police Director Jeremy D. Margolis, and other officials who spoke with us but requested anonymity.

Charlotte Waters, the widow of Chicago Police detective John Waters, for giving us access to her husband's detailed diaries and supplementing those with her own recollections.

Judge Richard E. Neville, who granted us extensive interviews.

Illinois Appellate Court Justice Alan J. Greiman, who shared his recollections of what went on behind the scenes during the appeal. (We obtained, from sources other than Greiman, various internal documents pertaining to Appellate Court deliberations.)

Illinois Chief Justice Benjamin K. Miller, who explained little-known practicalities of the appellate review process.

Lawyers who shared their insights—Robert L. Byman, Robert J. Clifford, Edward M. Genson, Jo-Ann Della-Giustina, Daniel L. Franks, Lawrence H. Hyman, Stephen M. Komie, Daniel Lynch, J. Kevin McCall, Ralph E. Meczyk, Patrick T. Murphy, Catherine M. Ryan, Janet J. Trafelet, and Terrence J. Truax.

(The trial prosecutors, Patrick W. O'Brien and George M. Velcich, declined to be interviewed for the book, but they did answer some of our questions during an on-the-record session at Northwestern University after the trial. O'Brien also read the first twenty-seven chapters of our manuscript; he disagreed with our interpretation of certain events but did not point out any factual errors.)

Journalists who filled gaps in our knowledge of events that they covered—Marsha Bartel, Paul Hogan, Peter Karl, Douglas Longhini, Phil Rogers, and Mary Ann Williams.

Thomas N. Sannito, professor of psychology at Loras College, who gave us insights into the jury selection process, and six members of the Dowaliby jury, who spoke candidly with us upon the condition of anonymity.

Prosecution witness Everett Mann, who helped us understand how witnesses evolve.

Customers of the Park Avenue Restaurant in Harvey, Illinois, especially Kenneth Blomlie and Ronald (Rocky) Ohrt.

Illinois Department of Corrections officials Nic Howell and Dorothea Green, who facilitated our frequent visits to Stateville and Pontiac penitentiaries.

Relatives, neighbors, and supporters of the Dowalibys on whose privacy we often intruded—Holly Deck, Ann Dowaliby, Michelle and John Goldrick, Diane Grandchamp, Mary and Thomas Malia, Rose and John Medema, Peggy and Gene O'Connor, Trisha Rickard, Beverly Robinson, Julie Schedin, Mary and Robert Tolbert, and Victoria and Daniel Verble.

Students at Northwestern University's Medill School of Journalism who provided valuable research—particularly J. Carl Ganter (who also took many of the photographs in this book), as well as Cindy Eberting, Gina Nolan, Eric Weiner, and Ian Zack.

Medill Dean Michael Janeway and Center for Urban Affairs and Policy Research Director Burton Weisbrod, whose support made the project possible.

Our literary agent, Molly Friedrich.

Finally, our editors, Brian DeFiore and Shawn Coyne, for believing in the project and helping it come to fruition.

This tale will not be told in vain, if it shall be found to illustrate the great truth, that guilt, though it may attain temporal splendour, can never confer real happiness; that the evil consequences of our crimes long survive their commission, and, like the ghosts of the murdered, forever haunt the steps of the malefactor; and that the paths of virtue, though seldom those of worldly greatness, are always those of pleasantness and peace.

—Sir Walter Scott,
The Heart of Midlothian,
1818

MISSING

As darkness fell on the middle-class Chicago suburb of Midlothian, seven-year-old Jaclyn Dowaliby donned her purple and white nightgown, said good night to her family, and headed for bed, clutching a Christmas catalog filled with wishes.

Sometime before morning, she vanished.

At 10:26 A.M. on Saturday, September 10, 1988, the Midlothian police received a call from a man who said in a steady voice, "There's been a break-in in my house. I live in Midlothian."

"What's your address, sir?" the police dispatcher, Sally Crowley, asked.

"Thirty-six, thirty-six West 148th Place," the man said. "There's been a break-in, and my daughter is missing."

"What's your last name?" Crowley asked.

"Dowaliby."

"And when do you think it happened, overnight?"

"Yes."

In the background, a woman screamed, "Oh, my God!"

"Okay, I'll have an officer right by," Crowley said.

"Thank you."

"Um, hmm."

Midlothian Patrol Officer Donald Woodark, who was cruising the area in a squad car, arrived at the home five minutes later.

Woodark was met by David Dowaliby, Jaclyn's adoptive father, a wiry, thirty-one-year-old construction foreman with deep-set eyes and a bushy mustache.

David's wife, Cynthia, a strikingly pretty woman of twenty-six with long, raven hair, was pacing back and forth, crying. Their four-year-old son Davey was watching cartoons on television, and David's fifty-seven-year-old mother, Ann Dowaliby, was sitting on a couch with her head in her hands.

Woodark asked when they discovered Jaclyn missing.

"About nine o'clock this morning," David replied.

The Dowalibys said that they searched the neighborhood, contacting persons who might know where Jaclyn was. David called the police when Cynthia discovered that a basement window had been broken.

The only thing that appeared to be missing, other than Jaclyn, was her printed, purple and white bedspread bearing the image of a little girl called Lady Lovely Locks.

David led Woodark outside to look at the broken basement window, which opened into Ann Dowaliby's living quarters. The window was at the southeast corner of the house, directly beneath Jaclyn's bedroom. The screen had been ripped back from left to right and the window smashed. Several pieces of glass were still in the frame. Other pieces were on the ground.

David and Woodark next went into Ann's basement bedroom to examine the window from the inside. The room was dimly lit even now, at midmorning on a sunny day. Directly beneath the window was a towel rack, on top of which was a basket. There was broken glass in the basket and scattered about the floor.

Woodark asked to see Jaclyn's bedroom. He noticed that her bed had no sheets, only a mattress pad. On the bed was a small, open suitcase. The dresser drawers were open, with clothes hanging out of them. A Sears, Roebuck & Company Christmas "Wish Book" lay open on the night table.

Woodark and David then went to the front door, which David said he had found ajar at about 8:00 A.M. Woodark asked if the door had been locked the previous night. David said that it had been, adding that he was careful to bolt it because Jaclyn had gone out one morning by herself without permission.

Woodark asked if David had any idea who might have taken Jaclyn.

"Yes," David said. "Jim Guess."

James Guess was Jaclyn's biological father; he and Cynthia had been married briefly when he was twenty-two and she was eighteen.

Shortly after their divorce, David told Woodark, Guess had tried to snatch Jaclyn by going through a window at Cynthia's family's home.

Guess had had no contact with Jaclyn since then, but his mother, Jackie Guess, had seen her from time to time, David said. In fact, Jaclyn had stayed overnight at the Guess home a couple of weeks earlier.

Woodark asked for a description of Jaclyn. David said she was about four feet tall, had brown hair and blue eyes, and was last seen wearing a purple and white nightgown. Woodark went to his car, radioed Jaclyn's description to police headquarters, and asked that detectives be sent to the home.

Without waiting for the detectives, Woodark returned to the window and picked up several pieces of the broken glass. Then he went to the basement, where he parted the curtains on the window and picked up more glass, stacking it on a plywood bench.

Shortly after noon, Hayden Baldwin, a state police evidence technician, arrived. Told by Woodark that the disappearance probably involved a domestic dispute, Baldwin casually processed the scene.

He took several photographs, but no close-up of the broken window or of an apparent shoe scuff mark on the wall beneath the window. He dusted for fingerprints on the window and front door, but not on the rear door or on a sliding patio door. Inside Jaclyn's room, he failed to dust her dresser, bed, or night table. He did not even ask to see the missing sheets, which he was told had been washed.

After about two hours, Baldwin departed, leaving behind such potentially significant evidence as the torn window screen, the broken glass, and Jaclyn's mattress pad, sheets, and pillows.

As Woodark took additional details, Jackie Guess drove up, having been called by Cynthia about half an hour before David called the police. Woodark asked Jackie the whereabouts of her son, James. She said he was in a Florida prison —a fact she had withheld from the Dowalibys.

As the day wore on, several Midlothian detectives and FBI agents arrived. One detective verified that James Guess indeed was in prison in Florida, serving a seven-year sentence for sexual battery.

Another detective asked for a picture of Jaclyn. From the living room mantel, Cynthia grabbed the first handy photograph. It was Jaclyn's kindergarten picture, now two years old.

The FBI set up telephone-monitoring equipment in case there was a ransom demand. If Jaclyn's disappearance turned out to be an interstate crime, the FBI would have jurisdiction to take over the investigation. Meanwhile, however, the Midlothian Police Department was in charge.

Despite the growing number of investigators at the scene, the official attitude was nonchalant.

"We got missing-child reports all the time," Midlothian Police Chief William Fischer would explain. "The kids always turned up, so we weren't approaching this as a major criminal investigation."

Fischer's twenty-two-member police department had little trouble maintaining order in the southwest suburb of fourteen thousand. Crime had risen slightly in recent years as low-income families had moved into the fringes of the town, but the trend had not noticeably affected the Dowalibys' quiet neighborhood in the heart of Midlothian.

The neighborhood was filled with young, first-time homeowners with children. Most of the homes were frame bungalows, built to meet the post-World War II demand for low-cost, single-family housing. The Dowaliby home, however, was distinctive—a tan-brick ranch, the largest home on the block.

Fischer had known Ann Dowaliby for many of the thirty years that she and her late husband had owned the home. Fischer recalled David as "a good kid," whose record was marred only by two youthful marijuana arrests.

Since David, Cynthia, and their two children had moved into the home in 1986, they had seemed to be just a typical middle-American family in a typical middle-American suburb.

The summer of 1988 had been hot and humid, and the Dowalibys' neighborhood was filled with the sounds of children at play. The willowy Jaclyn, clad in tank top and shorts, was among the more noticeable of the children. She was outgoing and giggly, and her brown hair flowed as she rode her bicycle, turned cartwheels, and practiced baton twirling up and down the block.

Jaclyn's bedroom, the largest in the house, was decorated in purple, pink, and white. She had a canopy bed, with Lady Lovely Locks sheets that matched her bedspread.

David and Cynthia had a smaller bedroom just down the hall, with an adjoining bath. Davey had the remaining bedroom, once occupied by David's younger brother, Brian. The walls and interior of the door bore fist marks that Brian had inflicted in a fit of temper as a teenager. Cynthia had covered the largest hole with a Teenage Mutant Ninja Turtles poster.

Ann Dowaliby owned the house but had agreed to sell it to

David and Cynthia. Until they could arrange financing, Ann was living in the basement.

Cynthia and David had settled comfortably into their seven-year relationship, which was a far cry from their brief, stormy previous marriages—Cynthia's to James Guess, David's to a fiery eighteen-year-old named Windy Jones.

In David, Cynthia had found someone on whom she could rely, a faithful, hardworking husband who shared her devotion to Jaclyn, whom he had adopted as an infant. Cynthia was a dream come true for David, a beautiful, loving wife with strong family values.

Their personalities were different but complementary. She was temperamental and strong-willed. He was steady and easygoing. What they shared was a vision of the American dream—upward mobility, a home of their own, and the good life for themselves and their children.

David worked for a company that built shelving and conveyor systems at warehouses and factories. He had begun as a carpenter and had risen to foreman, supervising crews of up to thirty men and earning twenty-one dollars an hour.

In nine years with the company, David had missed only one day of work—the day he went to court to adopt Jaclyn.

Cynthia supplemented the family income with a part-time job in the food service department of a hospital and was pursuing a junior college degree in medical administration. Mostly, however, she took care of Jaclyn and Davey.

She was a room mother at Jaclyn's school and a volunteer at Davey's preschool. After school, she made it a point to do something with the children—taking them out for "fun food," going to a park, or teaching them to dance.

Cynthia groomed and dressed the children meticulously, shopping secondhand stores for stylish bargains. She and Jaclyn delighted in the time they spent together in front of a makeup mirror; they always painted their toenails to match.

David engineered frequent family fishing and camping trips. He taught Davey to ride a two-wheeler and took Jaclyn to the annual father-daughter Brownie dance. In the backyard, David built a jungle gym that was a magnet for neighborhood children. Jaclyn loved to swing on it with her friends. Davey pretended that it was a fort, defending the home from imaginary enemies.

The household was not without tension, however. Cynthia and David had difficulty finding time to be together, and there were the predictable problems of a mother-in-law and daughter-in-law living under one roof.

Tempers flared when Ann accused Cynthia of pampering the children and when Cynthia complained about Ann's habit of going out and drinking to excess, which occurred about once a month.

During the summer of 1988, Cynthia and Ann had a fateful clash over, of all things, Jaclyn's Lady Lovely Locks sheets.

Cynthia had removed the sheets to wash them. Ann noticed that the bed had been stripped and, in an effort to be helpful, made it with a set of plain brown sheets.

"Jaclyn doesn't like those sheets," Cynthia said. "She only likes her Lady Lovely Locks sheets."

"But they're in the wash," Ann objected.

"That's okay," Cynthia said. "She can sleep on the mattress pad."

Ann huffily removed the brown sheets.

"It's your house, kid," she said. "If you want Jaclyn to sleep without sheets, it's okay with me."

Ann vowed never to make Jaclyn's bed again.

Three days before Jaclyn disappeared, a postcard arrived at the Dowaliby home. On it were photographs of two little boys and, in large black type, the word "MISSING."

Jaclyn noticed the card and asked her grandmother, "Does that say 'missing'?"

"Yes, that's what it says," Ann Dowaliby replied.

"Did somebody take them?" Jaclyn wanted to know.

That was possible, Ann answered, leading Jaclyn to the living room couch, where they sat and talked.

"Who would have taken them?" Jaclyn asked.

"Maybe some bad men," Ann said. "That's why you always have to be careful of strangers."

"What should I do if someone took me?"

"You have to do everything you can to get away."

* * *

Without broadening the search for Jaclyn beyond Midlothian, investigators spent Saturday afternoon, September 10, piecing together the Dowalibys' initial version of the events leading up to David's call to the police:

The preceding day, Friday, David went to work at about 8:00 A.M., as usual. Cynthia drove Jaclyn to school, returned home, and put laundry on the clothesline—including Jaclyn's Lady Lovely Locks sheets. Cynthia then went to several rummage sales with Ann Dowaliby.

In the afternoon, Cynthia was called unexpectedly to work at her part-time hospital job. She left Davey in Ann's care. After school, Jaclyn came home and played with Davey and neighborhood friends.

David arrived home about 5:00 P.M., changed clothes, and left to go bowling in the adjoining suburb of Blue Island.

On her way home, Cynthia bought Jaclyn a new school dress at a local thrift shop. When Cynthia got home, shortly after David left, the children were playing outside. She took them out for Kentucky Fried Chicken.

At about 7:30 P.M., David's sister, Michelle Goldrick, stopped by to pick up some clothes that Ann had bought at the rummage sales for Michelle's four-year-old daughter, Marissa.

Michelle, Cynthia, and Ann talked in the living room and then went to the basement to look at the clothes. Jaclyn went along to show off her new dress.

As the women sorted through the clothing, Jaclyn went upstairs and returned with a red dress trimmed with lace that she called her Christmas dress. She said that she was about to outgrow the dress and that her cousin, Marissa, could have it.

With Christmas on her mind, Jaclyn asked if she could pick out gifts from a Sears "Wish Book" that recently had come in the mail. Cynthia told her that it was bedtime but that she could look at the book in her room. It was about 9:00 P.M.

Since Jaclyn's sheets had not been replaced, she would sleep on the mattress pad. Jaclyn was wearing a purple Lady Lovely Locks nightgown, gold-cross pierced earrings, and Roger Rabbit underwear.

David returned home from bowling at about nine-thirty, went into Jaclyn's room, and kissed her good night. When Michelle left a little later, he bolted the front door.

As David and Cynthia prepared for bed, Ann told them she was going out drinking with friends from the Eldorado, a restaurant where she worked as a waitress. She left through the rear door and would not return until the next morning, spending the night with a man she knew only as "Big Mike."

David set the alarm clock for 7:30 A.M. because he planned to practice golf before playing in an afternoon tournament. He soon fell asleep, but Cynthia got up and watched television.

Before returning to bed, Cynthia checked the children, finding Jaclyn asleep, propped up on two pillows, with the Wish Book on her bedside table.

That was the last time Cynthia saw her daughter.

When the alarm rang on Saturday morning, Cynthia shut it off. David decided to forgo practicing in advance of the golf tournament, and he and Cynthia went back to sleep.

A few minutes later, Davey came into the bedroom. David got up to fix breakfast and, on the way to the kitchen, found the front door ajar. David assumed that Ann must have returned during the night and failed to close it when she went out again. He looked for her car, which was not there. Annoyed, he shut the door. It did not occur to him to check on Jaclyn.

Davey ate breakfast and watched *Pee-wee's Playhouse,* while David read a magazine and smoked cigarettes. Cynthia awoke at about 9:00 A.M., and David poured her a cup of coffee. She sipped the coffee in bed and got up at "around nine-thirty."

Cynthia called her sister-in-law, Sylvia Borrelli, with whom she had planned to begin a ceramics class that morning. Cynthia said she probably would be unable to attend because Ann was not home to baby-sit.

Cynthia then went to wake up Jaclyn.

Finding the bed empty, she called out, "Where's Jaclyn?"

David did not know.

After they looked around the house, Cynthia called the home of Jaclyn's friend Sarah Haseman. Jaclyn was not there.

David went to two neighboring homes, where Jaclyn often played. Jaclyn was not there either. When David returned, he and Cynthia again checked Jaclyn's room; that is when they noticed the bedspread missing and became concerned that Jaclyn might have been kidnapped. Cynthia, suspecting her ex-husband, called Jackie Guess.

Cynthia, David, and Davey scoured the neighborhood, first on foot, then in David's pickup truck. Ann arrived home, hung over, and joined in the search.

As Cynthia paced on the front lawn, looking up and down the street, she saw the broken window and screamed for David.

He ran to her, led her into the house, and called the police.

In the afternoon, David Dowaliby took a break from hours of increasingly repetitive questioning to call Peggy O'Connor. Peggy and her husband, Gene, were the Dowalibys' closest friends.

Peggy was taken aback when she heard David's voice, since he was supposed to be playing in the golf tournament that afternoon with her husband.

"Why aren't you golfing?" she asked.

"Peggy, you're not going to believe this, but Jaclyn's been kidnapped," David said.

After a pause, Peggy said, "Jim's probably got her. She'll be okay."

Peggy immediately went to the Dowaliby home, where she was astonished to find that Jaclyn's room had not been cordoned off. Relatives, friends, and investigators walked freely in and out of the room and about the house.

Mary Malia, Cynthia's mother, choked back tears but managed a smile when she saw Peggy. Ann Dowaliby was sitting in the living room, staring into space. Cynthia was almost delirious.

"Cyndi," Peggy said, "we've got to stay strong to bring Jaclyn home."

An FBI agent took Peggy aside and asked, "Who do you think did this?"

"Jim Guess," she replied. "He tried to do it once before—this time he got her."

As FBI agents made plans to interview James Guess in prison, Midlothian officers asked the Dowalibys if they could suggest any other suspects.

Cynthia said that James had an emotionally disturbed younger brother, Timothy, who might have taken Jaclyn.

Three officers went to the Guess home in south suburban Harvey and interviewed Timothy. He was a scrawny twenty-seven-year-old with bad teeth and stringy shoulder-length hair who had been diagnosed as psychotic—a paranoid schizophrenic.

Timothy said that he had spent the entire previous night working at a nearby restaurant, the Park Avenue. Jackie Guess added that she "saw him" at the Park Avenue at about 5:30 A.M.

A few hours after the officers left, two FBI agents arrived and searched the Guess home with Jackie's permission, finding nothing of relevance to the investigation. Jackie Guess told the agents that Timothy had just left for the Park Avenue, where he spent most of his nights. She said she knew he had been at the restaurant the previous night because she "called him" there at about 5:00 A.M. and asked him to bring home her car—which, she said, he did.

The agents went to the Park Avenue, where they found Timothy. He claimed that he had been at the restaurant from 9:00 P.M. Friday until 5:00 A.M. Saturday. Three employees, whom the agents interviewed on the spot, said that Timothy indeed had been there during those hours.

That, the agents concluded, made two false suspects provided by the Dowalibys.

The first reporter on the story was Dick Johnson, a tall, athletic, sandy-haired man with glasses, who worked for the Chicago ABC television station, Channel 7.

Johnson called the Dowaliby home and spoke with David,

who declined to be interviewed, saying that his wife was "very upset" and they had too much on their minds to bother with the media.

"I was just trying to see if we could help," said Johnson, but David remained firm.

David's attitude struck Johnson as strange. "If my kid were missing," he said later, "I'd be shouting it from the rooftops."

That night, David Dowaliby's golf buddies and their families gathered at the O'Connor home for what was to have been a posttournament celebration.

At ten o'clock, they somberly watched Channel 7 as Jaclyn's kindergarten photograph flashed across the screen.

"The Midlothian police have spent most of the day searching for seven-year-old Jaclyn Dowaliby, apparently abducted out of her bed last night," said Dick Johnson.

The camera cut to the Dowalibys' broken window with the torn screen as Johnson continued, "Police say it's possible someone could have broken in this basement window and kidnapped her, though they're puzzled that no one in the house or next door heard anything—not even a sound from the little girl."

Midlothian Police Captain John Bitten then was asked by Johnson, "So what do you think right now?"

"Well," said Bitten, "there's a lot of unanswered questions in it."

"Tonight," Johnson concluded, "with so little evidence and so few leads, police are at a loss to explain what happened to Jaclyn and where she might be."

McDEVITT TAKES CHARGE

Daniel S. McDevitt entered the investigation a day late.

When he arrived at the Midlothian police station at 7:30 A.M. on Sunday, September 11, chaos reigned. There was an urgent need for order—his specialty.

McDevitt, a powerfully built man with bushy eyebrows, sandy hair, and a jutting jaw, held the rank of captain in the Illinois State Police. He headed a special unit designed to prevent small police departments from botching major criminal investigations.

After nearly fifteen years with the state police, McDevitt had seen almost everything. A veritable rock of cynicism, he peppered his speech with irreverent barbs and epithets, from which no one was immune.

With his forceful style and stature, McDevitt immediately eclipsed Midlothian Chief William Fischer, the reserved, softspoken leader of the investigation. Fischer knew when he was in over his head and, the previous day, had asked McDevitt for help.

After Fischer briefed him, McDevitt was curious about Ann Dowaliby's alibi. He wanted to meet "Big Mike." Big Mike turned out to be Michael T. Healy, a forty-four-year-old former body builder who lived with his mother. McDevitt found him at home.

Healy said that at about midnight on Friday, September 9, he had gone to one of his regular haunts, the Eldorado Restaurant. There he joined a group, including Ann Dowaliby, at a table. He knew Ann because she worked at the Eldorado.

They drank until about 4:00 A.M., when a waitress suggested that Mike drive Ann home, Ann being in no condition to drive herself. As it turned out, Ann also was in no condition to tell Mike where she lived. He took her to his apartment and helped her into his bed. He slept on the couch. When they awoke about 9:30 A.M., he took her to the Eldorado, where she got into her car and drove away.

After hearing all this, McDevitt wrote Big Mike off as a big disappointment and returned to the Midlothian police station. "Well," he told Fischer, "we've got a drunken grandma who sleeps around, but I don't think she took Jaclyn."

Fischer smiled. He and John Johnson, the head of the FBI's southwest suburban office, had big plans for McDevitt: They wanted him to take charge of the investigation to find out who did take Jaclyn.

McDevitt resisted, but it was hard for him to refuse Johnson, with whom he had worked on many cases. Johnson pulled all the right strings. McDevitt's leadership was desperately needed, Johnson said. The case was about a seven-year-old girl. McDevitt had a young daughter.

Then McDevitt saw Jaclyn's kindergarten photo. His resistance melted. He agreed to head a task force headquartered in Midlothian to investigate Jaclyn's disappearance.

"Your first challenge is right outside that door," said Fischer, ushering McDevitt toward a horde of reporters who shouted questions.

"One at a time," McDevitt barked.

"Do you have any suspects?"

"Several."
"How many is several?"
"Several."
"Is several fewer than ten?"
"Several."

As McDevitt stonewalled reporters, clues at the crime scene were vanishing rapidly.

At the Dowaliby home, women anxiously awaiting word of Jaclyn occupied themselves—by thoroughly cleaning the house. They mopped floors, vacuumed rugs, polished furniture, and scoured counters and mirrors.

Cynthia's mother, Mary Malia, dutifully made Jaclyn's bed—having slept in it the previous night. In the basement, Ann Dowaliby picked up the broken glass, a possible hazard to Davey, and threw it into the trash. Ann also folded Jaclyn's sheets, which had been in a basket in the kitchen, and put them into a closet.

FBI agents and Midlothian police officers, who had been stationed around the clock at the Dowaliby home since the previous day, sat by idly as the house became spotless.

David and Cynthia Dowaliby were not at home for the cleaning, having agreed to take "routine" FBI lie-detector tests.

As they left in separate FBI cars, Cynthia noticed that a neighbor appeared to be moving.

"Stop the car!" she screamed, demanding that FBI agent T. Scott Hendricks find out who was moving and why.

Hendricks radioed the Midlothian police and asked that someone check to see if the move could be related to Jaclyn's disappearance.

When Cynthia arrived at FBI headquarters, she was distraught. "Right now I'm here, and Jaclyn's out there," she said. "I should be trying to help find her."

The polygraph examiner, Peter J. Flanagan, concluded that Cynthia was too upset to take the test. "It wouldn't be fair for you to take it now," he told her. Hendricks drove her home.

David had no trouble taking his test, which comprised four

"relevant" questions—whether he helped plan the disappearance of Jaclyn, whether he caused it, whether he knew who caused it, and whether he knew where Jaclyn was. David responded "no" to each question.

Flanagan concluded that his responses were "not indicative of deception." David had passed.

After the test, David elaborated on his answers in an FBI interview. He said he strongly suspected that someone in the Guess family had taken Jaclyn and that she probably was safe. After the interview, David signed a form consenting to a search of his pickup truck. Agent Alfred Hardman drove David home.

While David and Cynthia were downtown, Midlothian Detective Neal Caauwe had missing-person posters made up from Jaclyn's kindergarten photograph. That afternoon, Caauwe, a squat, heavyset man with compressed facial features that made him look like a bulldog, returned to the Dowaliby home to interview four-year-old Davey.

Caauwe was joined by Kevin Shaughnessy, a state police sergeant with chubby cheeks, thinning brown hair, and a mustache. Shaughnessy was McDevitt's man on the scene. His assignment was to observe the Dowaliby family and relay what he saw and heard directly to McDevitt.

Caauwe and Shaughnessy asked Cynthia's permission to question and fingerprint Davey. They said it would be good to have Davey's fingerprints on file. Cynthia agreed. "When Jaclyn comes home, you can fingerprint her, too," she said.

The officers then took Davey to the patio behind the house. After taking his fingerprints, they asked him if he had heard anything during the night that might help his sister.

Davey said he did, and then gave two versions of events, both of which the officers discounted as fanciful. At first, Davey said that he awoke during the night to the sound of breaking glass, but he went back to sleep without doing anything. Then he changed the story, saying that he went downstairs after hearing the glass shatter, saw a man in his grandmother's bedroom, and went back upstairs to bed.

When asked why he did not wake up his parents, Davey said that disturbing them would have gotten him "in a lot of trouble." Without further probing, Caauwe and Shaughnessy thanked Davey and "swore him in" as a junior policeman, giving him a badge.

While Davey was being deputized, David went to pick up some of the missing-child posters at the Midlothian police station. He posted some of them in stores in the Midlothian business district and others at the toll plazas on Interstate 294, which runs near the western and southern edges of Midlothian.

When David returned home, his friend Gene O'Connor suggested it would be a good idea to distribute the posters around the Guess neighborhood in Harvey, particularly to several cheap motels on 159th Street.

"Let's do that," David said.

Gene was expected home to eat, but told David he would hurry back and go with him to Harvey. After Gene left, however, David decided not to wait. By the time Gene returned from dinner, David already was back from Harvey. He was depressed.

David told Gene and FBI Agent Timothy Eley about a disturbing conversation with an attendant at a filling station, where David had stopped to drop off a poster.

"Is this the little girl missing in Midlothian?" the attendant asked, unaware that he was addressing her stepfather.

"Yes, it is," David replied.

"I think the stepfather did it," said the attendant.

David went directly home.

"I thought about talking to the guy," David said, "telling him who I was, what kind of father I am—but I thought, what the hell, he's just one guy. There may be thousands of people like that out there, and I can't convince them all."

Moving away from Eley, David told Gene, "You know what? The cops are treating me like a suspect."

"Dave," said Gene, "look at it this way—if they didn't try to make sure, they wouldn't be doin' it the right way."

A little later, David asked Eley if they could talk privately. They went into the master bedroom, where David asked whether he had passed the FBI lie test.

"What did the examiner tell you?" Eley asked.

"He said I passed."

"Then you passed."

In that event, David wanted to know, was he still considered a suspect in Jaclyn's disappearance?

"No one can be totally ruled out as a suspect until an apprehension is made," Eley said.

Daniel McDevitt, unhappy that he had allowed himself to become sidetracked by an imbibing grandmother and pushy reporters, finally turned to the tasks at hand—finding Jaclyn and whoever took her.

Since daybreak Sunday, police canine units and a U.S. Coast Guard helicopter had been searching forest preserves, woods, railroad tracks, and other nearby areas where a child might wander. About forty officers from various law enforcement agencies were involved in the search.

McDevitt ordered investigators to canvass the Dowaliby neighborhood door to door. When they came up with nothing, he ordered them out to look harder. To keep them focused, McDevitt posted an enlargement of Jaclyn's kindergarten picture on the inside door of the task force headquarters.

"Jaclyn's face is the last thing they'll see when they leave to look for her," McDevitt told a reporter.

McDevitt also had dozens of wallet-sized copies of the photo made and gave one to each investigator to carry during the search.

As the hours passed, McDevitt and his team grew increasingly frustrated.

There was no trace of Jaclyn.

On Monday, September 12, the Dowalibys' neighbors tied yellow ribbons on trees up and down 148th Place. Jaclyn's second-grade classmates made a large sign. "We're praying for Jaclyn," it said.

Early that morning, Timothy Eley drove David and Cynthia to the Midlothian police station, promising them they could be together.

They were fingerprinted by police, and nurses took blood and urine samples to check for the presence of illegal drugs.

After the samples were taken, an officer led Cynthia into another room, separating her from David. She would not see him again for several hours.

After waiving his rights to remain silent and to have a lawyer present, David was interrogated by Kevin Shaughnessy of the state police and Alfred Hardman of the FBI.

Shaughnessy asked David once again to describe the events of Friday night, in as much detail as possible. Shaughnessy even wanted to know David's bowling scores, which David said he thought were 139, 157, and 158.

When he got home from the Anchor Bowl, David said, he found Cynthia and Davey watching TV. He hugged Davey, watched TV for a few minutes, and went to bed at about ten-fifteen.

Although David previously had said that he went into Jaclyn's room and kissed her, he now said he did not do that because she was picking out Christmas gifts and had asked not to be disturbed. Asked if he made love to Cynthia Friday night, David said he could not recall.

When Shaughnessy asked about illegal drug use, David acknowledged that he had been arrested for selling marijuana in 1975 and for simple possession in 1979. He said that he still occasionally smoked marijuana and sometimes sold small quantities to friends. His only other involvement with illegal drugs, he said, had been the previous July, when he and Cynthia tried cocaine that a friend brought to a music festival.

Cynthia, who was not read her rights, was interviewed by Agent Eley and Thomas N. Walsh, a state police investigator. Like David, Cynthia once again went over the events leading up to Jaclyn's disappearance.

She said that when David arrived home at about nine-thirty, the children "welcomed him with open arms"—contradicting earlier statements that Jaclyn was in bed when David came home. She also said that she and David made love that night—an event that David had claimed he could not recall.

She acknowledged occasionally using marijuana and once trying cocaine, but said she no longer used illegal drugs.

The interview ended when it became apparent that Cynthia, to quote Eley's report, "was under a tremendous amount of emotional discomfort and stress, as evidenced by the intermittent periods of crying and sobbing."

Walsh next interviewed Ann Dowaliby, asking her a series of questions about Jaclyn. On a notepad Walsh wrote, "The night she went to bed." That phrase was followed by a doodle resembling an S, the significance of which would be debated later. After the doodle, Walsh wrote the words "Brat. Typical seven-year-old. Refused to mind. Spank. She has."

That evening, Shaughnessy and Walsh told McDevitt about the day's interviews. McDevitt raised his bushy eyebrows. He was growing increasingly suspicious of the Dowalibys.

Preoccupied with coordinating the search for Jaclyn, McDevitt steered clear of the press that afternoon. However, in an interview with the *Chicago Tribune,* Midlothian Police Captain John Bitten questioned whether the Dowalibys were telling the truth about Jaclyn's disappearance.

"We can't really call it a kidnapping," Bitten said. "We can't rule out a family member being involved yet. If there was physical evidence that the girl was grabbed, then we might call it a kidnapping."

David and Cynthia were expressing frustration with the investigation. David's brother, Brian, suggested that they call in a psychic. He knew of one, a woman named Linda Petrine. "I didn't believe in psychics, but I was willing to try anything," David said later.

At Brian's request, Petrine came to the Dowaliby home on Monday evening. A wall-eyed bleached blonde with a melodramatic voice, Petrine could have been sent by Central Casting.

The Dowalibys invited investigators to sit in on the session, but they declined, even though Petrine had worked—successfully, she claimed—with the FBI and several police departments on other missing-persons cases.

Petrine tape-recorded the session. After the Dowalibys

showed Petrine the broken window and she touched the glass, she described two men, one "a black youth with medium skin tone," the other "a thin white man, dingy light brown hair that needed to be washed, light-colored eyes—blue or green, bad teeth."

She added that the latter was "spacey—like he was on drugs. He had very nervous habits. He has a tattoo on his right arm. It's in blue ink. It's not a very well-done tattoo." She then described "feelings" she said she was having about Jaclyn.

A little later, when Petrine repeated the description of the white man, Cynthia said it sounded like her former brother-in-law, Timothy Guess. "He has the worst teeth you've ever seen and very dirty hair, and he's spacey," Cynthia said. "It's Tim!"

"Why did he take her?" David asked.

"Something to do with a child he had that was taken from him somehow," Petrine replied.

Petrine asked to talk to David in private. When they were alone, she said, "I feel I have to tell you that your daughter has been strangled."

As she said this, David recalls, she put her hands around her throat and her face turned red.

"Stop it," David said, and she released her hands.

"Where is she?" he asked.

"I keep seeing all these tall fields, very high, like dry straw, like wheat, yet behind the wheat there's green trees," Petrine said. "Something about water crossing in that area, two streams of waterbeds that crossed over."

"All I ask is that you just try to think of how we can get her back," David said.

Petrine drew a sketch of a field with high grasses in front of billowing trees with intersecting streams in the background.

"Is it far from here?" David asked.

"Possibly Indiana."

David told her, "Don't mention any of this to Cyndi."

"That's why I wanted to talk to you alone," Petrine said.

Petrine then added that the abductor might have dropped a piece of yellow paper in front of the house.

As Petrine left, she asked Cynthia to provide her with an article of Jaclyn's clothing—preferably an undergarment—and something Jaclyn had written.

Cynthia gave her a coloring Jaclyn had made to enter in a contest for a trip to Disney World and promised to provide the undergarment the next time they met.

The next morning, David went out to look for the yellow paper Petrine thought the intruder might have dropped.

Directly in front of the house, he found a yellow receipt from a store in Merrillville, Indiana.

He tried to make out the name, but it was illegible.

PRIME SUSPECTS

On Tuesday, September 13, Hayden Baldwin, the state evidence technician, told Daniel McDevitt something that, if correct, would be devastating evidence against the Dowalibys.

Baldwin said that he had been thinking about the broken window and was troubled that several large pieces of glass had been found on the ground outside. When a window is broken, Baldwin said, most of the glass usually falls with the direction of the force. The large pieces found outside the home might indicate that the window had been broken from the inside.

Baldwin also questioned whether an intruder could have squeezed through the window without disturbing the objects directly beneath it, particularly in the dark.

McDevitt dispatched Baldwin to retrieve the window. When he arrived at the Dowaliby home, however, Baldwin discovered that much of the broken glass had been thrown into the trash—and the torn window screen had disappeared. Some jagged glass remained in the window frame, which Baldwin removed with the Dowalibys' permission. He retrieved other pieces of broken glass from a bag of trash in the basement.

Baldwin took the frame and broken glass to the state crime laboratory for forensic tests. Although the results would not be available for three months, for now McDevitt thought Baldwin's theory about the window made sense.

Other snippets of fact and speculation heightened McDevitt's suspicion of the Dowalibys. For instance, on Sunday, Sergeant Kevin Shaughnessy had asked David Dowaliby whether any of the neighbors had mentioned hearing or seeing anything unusual. According to Shaughnessy, David responded, "After the accident?"—a possible Freudian slip.

Could it be, McDevitt wondered, that the Dowalibys had accidentally killed Jaclyn and then broken the window to make it appear that there had been an intruder? Might they have broken the window from inside to avoid being seen by neighbors?

McDevitt also questioned whether an intruder could have taken Jaclyn without awakening David or Cynthia. The intruder would have passed on a hardwood floor within a few feet of their bedroom.

In addition, McDevitt found it suspicious that David did not check on Jaclyn when he found the front door open, particularly in view of David's statement that Jaclyn recently had gone out by herself without permission in the early morning hours.

Then there was the failed attempt by the Dowalibys to cast suspicion first on James Guess and next on Timothy Guess.

The Dowalibys, moreover, did not appear to be model citizens. They had admitted smoking joints and once using cocaine, and David had two pot convictions—"two priors," in cop talk.

There was ample cause, McDevitt concluded, to regard the Dowalibys as prime suspects in Jaclyn's disappearance.

McDevitt mentioned his suspicion that there had been an accident to FBI Agent Steven Kashirsky, who, it turned out, already had been thinking along similar lines. Kashirsky further speculated that, if there in fact had been an accident, Cynthia most likely was responsible; she had told FBI agents that she was the children's primary disciplinarian.

"Jaclyn's her kid," McDevitt agreed. "If the stepfather was responsible, she would have turned him in by now."

McDevitt, however, had not yet rejected the possibility that Jaclyn had been abducted, and he deployed investigators to check out leads pointing in that direction.

One of the most intriguing leads involved a break-in at an apartment less than a mile from the Dowaliby home at 2:00 A.M. on Friday, September 9, the night before Jaclyn disappeared.

The apartment was occupied by Erzsebette Sziky and her seven-year-old daughter, Nicole. Sziky told police that she was lying on the couch in her living room when she heard a noise. She assumed it was her cat and did nothing, but a few minutes later she saw a man in her kitchen. He ran out a rear door.

According to the police report of the burglary, Sziky was unable to describe the intruder other than to say that he had a bandanna tied around his head. The report indicated that the man had entered a bedroom after tearing back a screen, a mode of entry similar to that described by the Dowalibys. However, Sziky told police that Nicole appeared to have been undisturbed.

Investigators also were dispatched to Trail Creek, Indiana, to interview the family Cynthia had seen moving out of Midlothian on Sunday. Other investigators interviewed an African-American man who had been seen playing basketball in a park near the Dowaliby home and an elderly man whom neighbors characterized as "strange." After the interviews, investigators concluded there was no reason to suspect these persons knew anything about what happened to Jaclyn.

The thoroughness with which the initial leads were explored, however, would be questioned by the Dowaliby family. For instance, John Goldrick, the husband of David's sister Michelle, was upset that investigators seemed to ignore an apparent shoeprint on the basement wall beneath the window. Goldrick, a shoe salesman, thought the print had been left by a size seven or eight athletic shoe.

Other relatives thought it unusual that no family members other than David, Cynthia, and Ann were asked to account for their whereabouts the night Jaclyn disappeared.

David Dowaliby asked Agent Kashirsky if it might be a good idea to issue a public plea for Jaclyn's safe return.

Kashirsky replied that there was no reason for the Dowalibys to say anything at the moment because the case already was receiving massive publicity. "If the coverage ever starts dying down, you could boom it back up again with a plea," he said.

David and Cynthia, mistrustful of Kashirsky but not up to facing a barrage of reporters' questions, turned to family members for advice.

The consensus was that someone should say something to the media. David's twin sister, Rose Medema, was the logical choice for the job. She was attractive and articulate, as well as being the family member with the most formal education, a master's degree.

David and Cynthia helped draft a statement, which Rose read to the reporters clustered outside the home. The statement said that the family was praying for Jaclyn's safe return, thanked the volunteers who had been looking for her, and urged them to continue the search.

Chicago television stations used none of the prepared statement, but instead carried stories based on Rose's response to questions—stories that raised doubts about whether a stranger could have abducted Jaclyn.

Reporter Phil Walters, of Channel 5, the Chicago NBC station, said: "The parents are too distraught to speak, but speaking for them, Jaclyn's aunt said the family believes the child may have been taken by a relative because it is unlikely that someone would break into an occupied home at random and take a child, but they have no specific suspects to suggest to police."

On the 10:00 P.M. news, Channel 2, the CBS station, carried a brief clip of Rose—misidentified in a caption as "ROSE

MEEMA''—saying, ''It's odd that someone would break into a house just to take a child, but who it is we don't know.'' Reporter Jim Avila concluded the Channel 2 report, ''The aunt is just as puzzled as everyone else.''

''They're making it look like we're hiding something,'' David lamented.

''I told you not to talk to the press,'' said Kashirsky.

At Daniel McDevitt's request, David and Cynthia agreed on Tuesday to take polygraph tests the next day at the Midlothian police station.

Although David already had passed an FBI polygraph test, Wednesday's test would be administered by McDevitt's man, Thomas N. Walsh, a state police polygraph examiner.

Ann Dowaliby advised David against taking the test or cooperating further without consulting a lawyer, since it was evident he was being treated as a suspect.

''Mom, if I don't go they won't look for Jaclyn,'' David told her. ''They'll just look at me.''

''They're not going to believe you anyway,'' said Ann.

''If I don't go, it'll just give them another reason to think I'm guilty,'' David replied.

MURDER IN THE WORST DEGREE

Wednesday, September 14, dawned warm and sunny—a day of hope that would end in despair.

"Missing-girl searchers frustrated," said a headline in the morning *Chicago Tribune*. The story said investigators retraced their steps Tuesday in the search for Jaclyn and quoted Midlothian Captain John Bitten as saying the efforts "came up a big zero."

Bitten continued to sound puzzled by Jaclyn's disappearance. "We have no indications from neighbors and teachers that Jaclyn led anything but a happy life," he was quoted as saying.

As a gesture of hope, Mary Malia and Ann Dowaliby decided to spruce up their granddaughter's room. On Wednesday morning, they bought pink paint, brushes, and rollers.

David and Cynthia promised to help Mary and Ann paint the room in the afternoon, after returning from taking their polygraph tests at the Midlothian Police Department.

Daniel McDevitt, however, had a different agenda for the balance of David and Cynthia's day: further interrogation.

David and Cynthia had agreed to take the polygraphs on the condition that they not be separated. FBI Agent Timothy Eley, who assured them that they could be together, except while actually taking the tests, drove them to the police station shortly before noon.

The state police polygraph examiner, Thomas Walsh, asked each the same questions—whether they knew where Jaclyn was, whether they did anything to cause her disappearance, whether they harmed her Friday night or Saturday morning, and whether they broke the basement window.

Walsh found Cynthia's test results inconclusive because of her "emotional state during her examination."

Although Walsh's questions of David were basically the same as those asked in the FBI polygraph test, which David had passed three days earlier, Walsh concluded that David was not telling him the truth. However, Walsh added, his opinion was tentative "due to the subject's noncooperation during parts of his polygraph examination."

David later offered an explanation for his alleged uncooperativeness: "As we began, Walsh asked me to answer a series of questions untruthfully, so that he could see how lies registered on the polygraph. I agreed to do that, and I had no problem denying that my name was David Dowaliby or that I lived in Midlothian. But then he asked me if I killed my daughter. I just couldn't answer 'yes' to that question. Walsh became very upset with me. If that's what he considered uncooperative, I was definitely uncooperative."

After the tests, David and Cynthia were taken into an adjoining office to be fingerprinted. Cynthia's prints were taken first, with David by her side.

While David's prints were being taken, Agent Eley asked Cynthia if she would like something to drink. She said she would, and the officer led her into an adjoining room.

Cynthia and David would not see each other again until nightfall.

As Cynthia sipped a soda, Eley told her that investigators wanted to ask David a few questions. "How would you like to go for a ride—maybe to a shopping mall?" Eley asked.

Cynthia agreed to go for a short drive, but said she was not interested in going shopping. She went along, she said later, in the hope of catching sight of Jaclyn.

The excursion lasted several hours, during which Eley asked her questions that she had already answered repeatedly. When he took her home in the midafternoon, he led her to the patio and they sat across from each other at the picnic table.

"Cynthia, we feel David knows something he's not telling us," Eley asserted. "Accidents happen, and we think David may know something about that."

"No," Cynthia said. "I would know if he knew something."

Eley then gave her a little speech about Christian faith. "God always forgives," he said.

In the early afternoon, Daniel McDevitt received the laboratory results on David and Cynthia's blood and urine tests, which eliminated the possibility that either had used illegal drugs within the previous ten days. Only caffeine was detected in Cynthia's samples; only nicotine in David's.

Disappointed, McDevitt ordered the samples retested specifically for marijuana or cocaine, but the results again proved negative.

McDevitt nevertheless later told the FBI that David probably was high on drugs when he passed the FBI test.

As a result of McDevitt's incorrect assertion, the FBI prepared a case summary saying that, although David's FBI polygraph had indicated no deception, "it was later learned that these test results may have been affected by his use of drugs."

* * *

Shortly after 6:00 P.M., Agent Steven Kashirsky received two telephone calls in rapid succession. The first was from the Midlothian police, the second from the state police.

The purpose of each was to relay grim news: The body of a little girl believed to be Jaclyn had been found in Blue Island, about four miles from the Dowaliby home.

Kashirsky interrupted Timothy Eley, who was speaking of God and forgiveness to Cynthia on the patio. Kashirsky and Eley asked Mary Malia to step outside with them.

On the front steps, they told her they believed Jaclyn had been found. She was dead.

"We're sorry," Kashirsky said. "Who should tell Cyndi?"

"I'll tell her," said Mary tearfully.

Cynthia was in the living room when Mary and the agents walked back into the house.

"Cyndi, they've found Jaclyn," Mary said.

"Where is she?" Cynthia screamed.

"Cyndi, she's dead."

Cynthia burst into tears and collapsed. Mary and Eley carried her to the living room couch. They put their arms around her, but Cynthia pushed Eley away, screaming, "Where's David? I want David. Who could do this? Who would do this?"

David was in the midst of a five-hour interrogation at the Midlothian Police Department.

At 3:00 P.M., Kevin Shaughnessy and Alfred Hardman again advised David of his right to an attorney and his right to remain silent. Again, David waived his rights.

Shaughnessy and Hardman then hammered him with questions for five hours, concentrating on what Hardman described as "apparent inconsistencies in his previous statements."

The actual degree of inconsistency is difficult to assess, since the session was not tape-recorded and the investigators did not take notes. A day later, Shaughnessy and Hardman made handwritten notes from memory. Five days after that, Hardman typed a report based on the handwritten notes.

Hardman's report quoted David as saying that he sometimes had given "the right answers as opposed to the truthful answers" in previous interviews because he was concerned about his "stepfather image"; that if he had realized that the investigation would go into such detail, he would have given different answers.

David admitted, the report claimed, that he "had lied or withheld information" concerning two matters—the extent of his involvement with illegal drugs and whether he had kissed Jaclyn good night on September 9.

Concerning drugs, the report said: "Dowaliby described himself as 'a one-pound reefer dealer.' Dowaliby stated that he sells marijuana because he needs the money and that he sells more than just enough to pay for his personal use."

Concerning kissing Jaclyn, it said: "Dowaliby stated that he had not answered this question truthfully in the previous interviews, and knew at the time that he was lying. Dowaliby stated that he lied because he thought that he should have checked on Jaclyn before he went to bed."

When Shaughnessy asked David if he knew where Jaclyn was, according to the report, he answered, "I didn't do it."

"At one point during the interview," the report added, "Dowaliby became emotionally upset and began crying and rubbing his face. Dowaliby then sat up straight in his chair and said, 'You think you've got me broken down, you think I'm going to confess, but I'm not.' "

Shaughnessy and Hardman were informed shortly before 6:00 P.M. that the body tentatively identified as Jaclyn had been found, but they withheld the news from David for an hour and a half.

In the interim, they persuaded David to sign a form consenting to a search of his home and vehicles and to allow the police to photograph him. However, the police had no film. Two officers had to be dispatched to a nearby drugstore to buy some before the photographs—standard mug shots—could be taken. Only then did Shaughnessy and Hardman tell David that Jaclyn had been found.

According to Hardman's report, David's first asked if she had been found in a field, and then asked whether she was alive.

When told that she was dead, according to Hardman, David said, "You're lying to me just to get me to confess. I guess you guys think I should cry now."

David later provided quite a different version of the interrogation.

He denied ever saying that he intentionally provided false or misleading information to investigators.

David said he told Shaughnessy and Hardman that he had been forthright on the subject of drugs from the beginning of the investigation. When they pressed him for additional details, he said, he told them that when he was a teenager he once had been paid $10 for carrying a pound of marijuana to a friend's house; Shaughnessy and Hardman twisted that to make it look as if David currently was "a one-pound reefer dealer."

David said his initial claim that he had kissed Jaclyn good night had been a mistake, which he had corrected as soon as he realized it was wrong. He said he made the mistake because it had been his habit to kiss her good night.

As the interrogation continued, according to David, Shaughnessy became increasingly heavy-handed.

"Your wife told us she thinks you took Jaclyn," David quoted Shaughnessy as saying. "Your family believes that. They all think you took her."

Fearing that his family might have abandoned him, David said, he cried. When he regained his composure, he told the investigators, "You think you've got me broken down, you think I'm going to confess, but I'm not."

At this point, David said, the investigators asked him to sit for photographs; he was reluctant because he wanted to leave, but relented when Shaughnessy told him, "If you're really innocent, like you claim, these pictures can't hurt."

When the investigators finally told him that they believed Jaclyn had been found, David said, he first asked whether she was alive and then asked where she was.

He said that he did not recall asking whether she had been found in a field, although he acknowledged that he might have, since he knew that investigators were searching fields;

also, Linda Petrine had said that Jaclyn would be found in a field.

At the end of the interview, David said, he accused Hardman and Shaughnessy of lying to try to get him to confess, and that is when he told them, sarcastically, "I guess you guys think I should cry now."

The body had been found by Michael Chatman, who lived at the Islander Apartments, a complex of eighteen three-story brick buildings mostly occupied by African-Americans.

Chatman said that when he came home from work, he parked his car on the north edge of the complex's parking lot, near a Dumpster. When he got out of the car, he smelled a foul odor that did not appear to be coming from the Dumpster. He checked the weeds behind the Dumpster and discovered the body, which was in an advanced state of decomposition. He immediately went into his apartment and called the police. It was 5:46 P.M.

Blue Island Detectives Douglas Hoglund and Joseph Kosman arrived at the scene within minutes. They saw the decomposed body of a small girl in a purple and white nightgown partially wrapped in a matching bedspread, only three feet from the edge of the paved parking lot. A rope had been wound several times around her neck, and a pair of white cotton underpants lay two feet from her body.

The officers secured the area and requested help.

Blue Island Police Chief Paul D. Greves had just gotten into his car after having a cup of coffee at a fast-food restaurant in Blue Island when he heard Kosman's voice on the radio: "I've got a body down here at 1924 Canal!"

Greves raced to the scene, where Kosman told him that there was little doubt that the body was Jaclyn's because the bedspread bore the image of Lady Lovely Locks.

Reporters and photographers soon arrived in droves. According to Greves, some of them slipped five- and ten-dollar bills to residents of the apartments to take photographs from their balconies. "You guys are animals!" Greves shouted. "You'd do anything for a story. Have some respect." To hide the body from the cameras, Greves ordered it covered with a sheet.

Greves, a well-groomed ex-military man of fifty-four with deep-set brown eyes and thinning gray hair, set up a temporary headquarters in a fire station adjacent to the apartment complex. Daniel McDevitt soon joined him. They organized ten teams of two officers each to canvass the apartment complex, asking residents if they had seen anything or suspected that anyone in the area was capable of murdering a little girl.

At nightfall, a score of police searched the area with flashlights as dozens of tenants of the apartment complex watched from their windows and balconies.

Hayden Baldwin processed the area for physical evidence. When he finished, the body was put in a white plastic body bag and taken to nearby St. Francis Hospital, where death was pronounced.

Daniel Collins, of the Cook County medical examiner's office, accompanied the body and wrote a report stating: "Police indicated that they have a prime suspect in mind."

Ann Dowaliby went to the Midlothian Police Department, a two-minute drive from the Dowaliby home. Someone drove her, but she does not recall who. "I was too shaken," she said.

She went inside and demanded to see David, but an officer told her that David could not be disturbed.

"His daughter has been found murdered, and he needs to know!" Ann shouted at the officer.

The officer told her to stop yelling. When she refused to quiet down, he took her by the arms and started pushing her out the back door of the station.

"Take your hands off me," Ann said. "I can walk by myself."

"Well then, get out," the cop said.

Ann stood outside the back door, crying.

Midlothian Chief Fischer pulled into the parking lot. "Bill, they won't let me see my son," Ann said.

"Wait a minute, Ann," Fischer told her. "I'll find out what's happening."

Fischer did not return. Two officers came out the back door and returned a few minutes later, carrying rolls of film.

Then Cynthia's brother, Michael Borrelli, drove up. Ann told him, "They found Jaclyn dead, and they won't let me see David. I've got to get home. He needs a lawyer."

Michael drove Ann home.

Only later would Ann wonder why Michael was at the police station.

At about 8:00 P.M. Alfred Hardman finally drove David home, with Kevin Shaughnessy sitting in the backseat.

As the car turned into the driveway, according to David, he was overcome by a "sinking feeling" that they were telling the truth about Jaclyn being found.

He ran into the house, where Cynthia was sitting on the living room couch, sobbing softly.

David put his arms around her. "Cyndi, I'm so sorry I couldn't be here," he said. "They promised us we could be together, but they lied."

A policeman in street clothes entered the living room.

Ann asked what he wanted.

"I just want to ask Dave and Cyndi a few questions," the policeman said.

"Get out of my house," Ann ordered. "Get out, all of you!"

The remaining law enforcement agents filed out of the house. A few minutes later, FBI Agent Steven Kashirsky came to the door. "We need our recording equipment," he told Ann. "I'd like to come in and get it."

"You stay outside," Ann said. "We'll get your equipment. You can't come into my house without a warrant."

Ann handed him the recording equipment.

In the living room, as David and Cynthia held each other and cried, family members were stunned to overhear David whisper, "Cyndi, I swear I didn't do it."

"I know, I know," Cynthia said.

ARRANGEMENTS

The Dowalibys faced two urgent realities Wednesday night: making funeral arrangements for Jaclyn, and getting legal help for David.

"They had to put mourning on hold," Ann Dowaliby said later.

Before David returned from the police station, Ann said, she realized that he needed a criminal lawyer, but she had no idea how to find one.

John Medema, the husband of David's twin sister, Rose, called a friend, Ted Kostiuk, and asked if he could recommend a lawyer. Kostiuk, a former Chicago police detective, recommended Ralph Meczyk.

Kostiuk had known Meczyk for twenty years. They had been in the same National Guard unit during the Vietnam War. They had remained good friends, even though Meczyk, as an assistant public defender, wound up representing several defendants whom Kostiuk had arrested.

At Medema's request, Kostiuk called Meczyk at his home. Meczyk immediately called the Dowaliby home and spoke with Rose Medema.

After consulting briefly with her husband and Ann Dowaliby, Rose made a tentative appointment for David and Cynthia to see Meczyk the next morning. Meczyk said he would call the Midlothian police, inform them that he represented the Dowaliby family, and demand that they stop interrogating David without a lawyer. By this time, however, the interrogation was over and David was on his way home.

Late Wednesday night, John Medema and Ann took David aside. "The police are trying to blame you for this, and you need a lawyer," Ann said. John told David, "Look, I heard of somebody good. Let's try him."

David agreed.

John and Rose Medema picked up David and Cynthia early Thursday morning and drove them to Meczyk's office in downtown Chicago. The trip was an ordeal. Cynthia was so upset, according to John, that he had to stop the car several times while she vomited.

They arrived at Meczyk's office on the sixteenth floor of a building across the street from Chicago City Hall promptly at 8:30 A.M. Meczyk was late. Lawrence Hyman, a lawyer who shared offices with Meczyk, welcomed them.

Meczyk arrived a few minutes later. He and Hyman were a study in contrasts. They had begun their careers on opposite sides—Meczyk as an assistant public defender, Hyman as an assistant prosecutor. Meczyk was a short, pudgy man of thirty-eight with rimless glasses and Woody Allen–like hair. His office was cluttered with papers and files. Hyman, thirty-seven, was tall and trim, with a decidedly coiffeured look. His office was immaculate and tastefully decorated.

While Cynthia and the Medemas spoke with Hyman, David followed Meczyk into his office. At Meczyk's request, David described the events of the past several days, insisting that he knew nothing more than he had told investigators about Jaclyn's disappearance and death.

Meczyk told David it was almost inevitable that he would be arrested. "The police are under tremendous pressure to solve this crime," Meczyk said. "They need to pin it on someone."

After David's arrest, Meczyk said, he could expect the police to "pull out all the stops" to get him to confess. They might even beat him, putting a telephone book over his head to prevent bruising.

"No matter what they do to you, you can't give in to them," Meczyk said. "You've probably talked too much already. Under no circumstances are you to tell them anything further without me being present."

When David and Meczyk returned to Hyman's office, Meczyk apologized to Cynthia and the Medemas for excluding them from his conversation with David. Turning to Rose, Meczyk said, "I believe your brother. I believe he's innocent, and I would be happy to represent him."

Rose asked how much Meczyk's services would cost. "A case like this typically will run $30,000 or $40,000, plus expenses," he said. "I'm not worried about the money, but Larry will want to make sure we have a retainer. We'll need $6,000 by Saturday."

David and Cynthia nodded. They could raise the money.

Meczyk said he thought it unlikely that Cynthia would be arrested, but that she nonetheless needed separate legal representation. Lawrence Hyman could represent her.

As the Dowalibys and Medemas prepared to leave, Meczyk told them, "I want to warn you that you may hear some stuff about me. I had a tax problem, and there were charges against me. I was set up, so I know how you feel."

No one asked Meczyk to elaborate on his tax problem or the disposition of the charges, but Meczyk had been a target of Operation Greylord, a recently completed federal investigation into Cook County judicial corruption.

One phase of the Greylord investigation focused on a group of lawyers, known as hustlers, who represented clients for their bail bond slips—which could be turned in for cash at the office of the clerk of the Circuit Court. The investigation documented how judges steered defendants to the hustlers in return for kickbacks on the bond refunds.

Meczyk was not charged with paying kickbacks, but rather with submitting a federal tax return underreporting his bond-slip income by at least $15,000 for 1980. He pleaded guilty, saying he was "contrite and very ashamed." In 1987 he was sentenced to thirty days' work release, four years' probation, five hundred hours of community service, and a $5,000 fine.

The Attorney Registration and Disciplinary Commission wanted to yank Meczyk's law license temporarily, but two weeks after he took the Dowaliby case the Illinois Supreme Court let him off with a censure—a public scolding.

In the car on the way home, David told Cynthia and the Medemas, "Ralph says it's inevitable I'm going to be arrested." David said he was favorably impressed with Meczyk. "I want to hire Ralph," David said. "I think he's good."

Cynthia and the Medemas agreed. "It wasn't like we could go lawyer-shopping," John Medema recalls. "We had Ralph. He came highly recommended by a friend who used to be a cop."

While the Dowalibys and Medemas were meeting with Meczyk and Hyman, Cook County Medical Examiner Dr. Robert J. Stein performed an autopsy on Jaclyn's body, which by this time had been identified through dental X rays.

Dr. Stein's postmortem examination report said: "Subject is seen to wear a pink purplish-like short nightgown with figures as well as lettering that states, 'Lady Lovely Locks.' Also present is a rope which appears to be wound a number of times around the neck, extending over the upper portion of the chest. The rope is consistent with a clothesline in appearance.

"The body is almost completely covered with maggots, mostly in the head and neck area. Further examination of the head shows that it is almost completely disarticulated at the level of the third cervical vertebra.

"Based upon the gross anatomic findings, death is ligature strangulation. The manner of death is homicide.

"Multiple sections taken for microscopic studies to rule in or rule out sexual abuse proved to be negative. The negative does not mean that the subject was or was not sexually abused."

In a telephone conversation Thursday afternoon, Ralph Meczyk informed David Dowaliby of Dr. Stein's finding that Jaclyn apparently had been strangled.

David told Meczyk that he would spare Cynthia that fact.

The finding of Jaclyn's body in Blue Island thrust Chief Paul Greves into a leadership position in the investigation. With a forceful personality and nineteen years of law enforcement experience, he was ready to assume the role.

However, Greves wanted to avoid a turf war with Daniel McDevitt, the head of the task force. The two quickly reached an accommodation. McDevitt would continue to run the investigation out of the Midlothian Police Department, and Greves would become a member of the task force.

McDevitt asked Greves to take primary responsibility for the continuing canvass of the Islander Apartments, concentrating first on the six buildings bordering on the parking lot behind which Jaclyn's body had been found.

Greves and an aide prepared a preprinted form containing standard questions to ask the tenants—where they parked, whether they had smelled anything strange, whether they had seen any strange cars or anyone unusual in the area between September 9 and September 12, and whether they knew the Dowalibys.

In Thursday's interviews, five tenants reported that during the period in question, they had seen unfamiliar persons and cars near the location where Jaclyn's body had been found. None of the descriptions matched the Dowalibys or their vehicles.

While the interviews were being conducted, other officers carrying evidence bags combed the overgrown field and woods behind the middle Dumpster, looking for anything that might have evidentiary or forensic value. In particular they were looking for the gold-cross earrings that Jaclyn's parents said she wore to bed but that were not found with the body.

The investigators found nothing, but Greves and Hayden Baldwin wanted reporters to think otherwise. They decided to stage a little scene for the media.

Greves and Baldwin got down on their hands and knees a few feet from where the body had been found and pretended to put something into evidence bags.

Reporters wanted to know what they had found. "We found something that might be significant," Greves said. When pressed on what the evidence was, Greves responded, "No comment."

The purpose of deceiving the news media, according to Greves, was to get stories published and broadcast that might lead the killer, thinking that his arrest might be imminent, to confess or make a mistake.

The discovery of the "potentially significant evidence" was reported prominently on that evening's newscasts.

The *Chicago Tribune* quoted Greves as saying that he and Baldwin had found something that was "really going to help" in the investigation. "Greves declined to say what the evidence was," the story said, "but state crime lab technicians put whatever they found into two small brown paper bags to remove it from the scene."

Paul Greves later said that he began to suspect that David and Cynthia were hiding something when he called the Dowaliby home Thursday afternoon and they refused to talk to him.

Greves said he could not understand why innocent parents would refuse to cooperate. "I think, if I were the Dowalibys, I'd be sitting outside the door of the police station," he said. "I can't imagine anything you could do that would offend me. I'd say, 'Look, I understand that you consider me a suspect, but I didn't do it. I'll cooperate in any way I can, but I want to find out who did this.' "

McDevitt told reporters that the Dowaliby family no longer

was cooperating with investigators. "They're pleading the Fifth Amendment now," he said.

Ralph Meczyk denied McDevitt's charge, saying, "All we know is the family is in mourning, and they want the killer caught."

All through the day, friends and relatives visited the Dowaliby home to offer condolences.

Mary Malia selected items to be buried with Jaclyn—Minnie Mouse jewelry Jaclyn had bought with her own money, pictures of the family, a doll Jaclyn had had since she was a toddler, and Jaclyn's "Purry Furry," a small stuffed cat.

Because Jaclyn's body was so badly decomposed, clothes could not be put on it—a detail Mary thought Cynthia need not know for now. They sent Jaclyn's favorite dress—her Christmas dress—and a new pair of red and white tights to be put into the casket. As far as Cynthia knew, Jaclyn would be dressed in the garments.

Late in the day, Mary went to Hickey Memorial Chapels in Midlothian to make arrangements for Jaclyn's funeral. Blue Island Mayor Donald E. Peloquin, a close friend of Chief Greves, was part owner of the funeral home.

Four years earlier, while Greves was still a sergeant on the Blue Island police force, he had been the manager of Peloquin's mayoral campaign. As a reward, Greves was appointed chief of police after Peloquin won.

As soon as Mary left the funeral home, Peloquin called Greves. "Guess what?" Peloquin said. "We're handling the Dowaliby funeral. The family was just in here."

It was a connection Greves soon would exploit.

After all the relatives and friends left the Dowaliby home late Thursday night, Cynthia wrote a good-bye letter to be buried with Jaclyn:

Dear Jaclyn,

I knew when you grew up you wanted to be a cheerleader. You wanted to be a mother and be married. I loved you for this. You were a great reader and you wrote your name and letters beautifully. I loved you because you always wanted to wear a dress or skirt to school. You were a beautiful roller-skater and bike-rider. You were friends with everybody and I loved you for that. You were a good-hearted, sweet, loving, precious angel. I liked it when you dressed up with the dress clothes. Little Davey loved to pretend with you. You taught him well. He will always know you in his heart and we will tell him more about you when he's old enough to understand. Davey looked up to you Jaclyn and he always will.

Jaclyn, I wish you could come to us and tell us you're okay and safe and loved. We were so sad when we couldn't find you and even sadder when you left us for God. Our hearts cried out to you. We want you to know that we will be with you again in Heaven and we are no longer afraid to die. We know you will be there waiting for us with open arms. Our hearts ache out of love for you.

Our hearts cried out for you everyday. I am still aching inside because I miss my little girl and want her back. So, if you can somehow give yourself back to me in any way, like my dreams, I will be at total peace in my heart. I will do my best. You're my angel. I know you liked that movie, "Date With an Angel." You were that angel sent up to God for eternal peace.

I love you and miss you so very much, words cannot express. I will never give up on you Jaclyn. I'm sorry this happened to you. You will still be a cheerleader and anything else you ever wanted to be in life in my heart. My love for you just grows and grows.

Love you,
Daddy, Mommy, and Davey

On Friday morning, September 16, the telephone rang at the Dowaliby home. Ann Dowaliby answered it.

"Tonight David dies," said a male voice.

Jaclyn's wake was that afternoon and evening at the Hickey Memorial Chapels. David called Ralph Meczyk. "Do you think someone might come to the wake and try to kill me?" David asked. "Ralph, I'm scared to go to my own daughter's wake."

Meczyk borrowed a bulletproof vest from one of his private investigators and gave it to David, who wore it at Jaclyn's funeral on Saturday. More than two hundred friends and relatives attended the funeral mass at St. Christopher Catholic Church in Midlothian.

Reporters and television cameras were positioned outside on the sidewalks as David and Cynthia entered the church arm in arm at 11:15 A.M. The service lasted about an hour.

"As we sit here," said the Reverend Daniel Brady, "each of us is troubled by the tragic death of this little girl. We know she is safe in God's hands. But we're still shocked. We've been made numb. There really are no words, no answers. All we can do is put our arms around each other and know we are not alone."

Before the casket was taken to St. Mary's Cemetery for burial, Blue Island Mayor Donald Peloquin, the funeral director, granted Chief Paul Greves a final request.

Greves had heard a rumor that the Dowalibys had placed a diary into the closed casket. He asked Peloquin to check it out. Peloquin opened the casket, finding Jaclyn's Christmas dress draped over her body, Cynthia's farewell letter, family photos, costume jewelry, a doll, and a stuffed animal—but no diary.

The evening of Jaclyn's funeral, McDevitt sent a state police investigator, Vincent Schavone, to the home of Gene and Peggy O'Connor. Schavone had not been involved in the investigation, but was selected for the mission because he had grown up in Midlothian and knew Gene O'Connor.

"I'd like you to come in and talk to McDevitt," Schavone told Gene. "I want you to know everything we know."

Gene agreed, and the next day, Monday, September 19, he met McDevitt at state police headquarters.

McDevitt told him, "I think there was an accident. I'll tell you this, people shouldn't go to jail for the rest of their lives over an accident."

Gene replied, "There's no way an accident happened and then he threw her in a field like a piece of garbage."

"She wasn't thrown in a field like a piece of garbage," McDevitt replied. "She was carefully placed a couple of feet from a parking lot where she could be easily found. It was like she had been tucked in."

McDevitt added, "I think their worst fear has come to pass—that Jaclyn wasn't found right away. They thought she would be found and they would have a nice, neat little funeral."

McDevitt went on, "If you care about these people, go to them and tell them to come in here and tell me the truth, and I'll do everything I can to help them."

McDevitt said there was conclusive evidence that David and Cynthia were involved in the murder.

"What's the evidence?" Gene wanted to know.

McDevitt did not tell Gene that he believed the window had been broken from the inside. "I can't reveal the evidence now," he said, "but when they go to trial and that evidence is revealed, I'm going to turn around and look at you, and you'll know what I was talking about."

McDevitt gave Gene his card. "Call me anytime," he said.

Gene immediately went to David's house. "Let's go outside," he said. They went for a walk. "Dave, I just talked to McDevitt, and he says he's got proof that you did this."

"How could he have any evidence at all?" said David, looking Gene straight in the eye. "I'm innocent."

"That's what I wanted to hear," said Gene, hugging David.

WITNESSES EVOLVE

Investigators under the direction of Blue Island Chief Paul Greves continued the canvass of the Islander Apartments.

Late Friday afternoon, during Jaclyn's wake, two officers knocked on the door of Everett Channing Mann, a thirty-five-year-old Chicago Transit Authority ticket-taker who lived on the third floor of one of the buildings adjoining the parking lot.

Using the interview form they had developed the previous day, the officers asked Mann, among other things, if he had seen any "strange cars" in the area between September 9 and 12. Mann said that he had—a "dark-colored" one a little after 2:00 A.M. on Saturday, September 10.

Mann said that he saw the car near the "middle Dumpster," one of three large garbage receptacles serving his portion of the apartment complex. Jaclyn's body had been found near that Dumpster.

Greves, intrigued by Mann's sighting, sent two Blue Island investigators to ask Mann if he recalled anything more. In this interview, Mann added that he had caught a glimpse of the driver's profile—someone "with a large, straight nose" who appeared to be Caucasian.

The officers showed Mann photographs of five men, all frontal views, and asked if he could identify any of them. Mann said that he could not be sure, but that one of the men in the photographs had a nose structure resembling that of the occupant of the car. It was a photograph of David Dowaliby.

The officers took Mann to the Blue Island police station, where Greves told them to take Mann's formal statement—and to tape-record it.*

On the tape, Mann said that he had gotten off work at 10:30 P.M. on Friday, September 9, and then took Latricia Wood, whom he described as his "best friend," for a drive along Chicago's lakefront. They went to her apartment on the South Side of Chicago at about 1:30 A.M. on Saturday, September 10, and he spent about fifteen minutes there before heading home.

As he pulled into the Islander Apartments parking lot, Mann continued, the headlights of a car came on. He saw the car for roughly ninety seconds as it pulled out of the parking lot.

"Did you observe any occupants in the car?" one officer asked.

---

* Unlike the vast majority of law-enforcement officials, Greves was a believer in audiotaped statements. Law enforcement officers and prosecutors avoid taping statements because, if a case comes to trial, the law requires the prosecution to turn over any tapes to defense lawyers. If there are inconsistencies between a taped interview with a witness and that witness's testimony at trial, the tapes can be used to discredit the witness. Thus, police rarely use tape recorders in criminal investigations. The Mann interview was the only known audiotaped interview by police during the Dowaliby investigation.

"I saw one head, like a male head with a large nose, large straight nose," Mann said.

"Sir, could you tell if that male was a black male or a white male?"

"He looked, well, from looking at him, it looked more like a Caucasian male from the hair type. It didn't look like he would have what most blacks call a black hairstyle. But he did have a large, German-type nose. That's why I believe it to be Caucasian, because of the nose configuration."

"What were the lighting conditions in the parking lot at that time?"

"Well, there was one streetlamp on. I mean one light on near my building. Nothing on in the middle area because it was dark. Then there was some, like the building lights were on down at the far end, near the fire station. So it was light, dark, light."

"Approximately how far—you said both cars were more or less parallel?"

"Parallel, correct."

"How far apart?"

"I don't know the exact distance, but I'd say it's about seventy-five yards."

"Do you think you'd be able to recognize this car if you see it again, or the occupant?"

"I might, but I don't know about the occupant because all I saw was a silhouette. I saw a man facing forward driving his car facing the direction the car was moving and I saw a large, straight nose. It looked to be a dark-colored, midsize car. Like, the closest thing I could think of to parallel it would be the latest seventies version of the Chevy Malibu."

"Like a late seventies Malibu?"

"Yes, that's the design."

"Could you tell if it was a two- or a four-door car?"

"Not offhand, no."

"In no way you could tell the color at this point?"

"No, I don't know whether it was dark blue, navy blue, black, dark brown."

At this point, Mann was again shown the photo array and asked, "The nose most resembles which subject?"

"Subject number four here," Mann said, indicating the photograph of David Dowaliby.

Mann then was taken to the Midlothian police station, where he retold his story to Kevin Shaughnessy, of the state police.

According to Shaughnessy's report, "Mann said the vehicle was a dark-color, midsize car, which he thought to be about a 1979 Chevrolet Malibu." Mann said he was familiar with Malibus because, when he was in the Air Force in the mid-1970s, he had served under a sergeant who drove one.

Thus, in each successive interview, Mann told police more and more of what they seemed to want to hear. Originally the car was merely "dark-colored." Then it became "midsize." Then it evolved into a car paralleling "the latest seventies version of the Chevy Malibu." Finally it became "about a 1979 Chevrolet Malibu."

Similarly, Mann's recollection of the driver seemed to improve. Originally he was unsure even of the driver's race or gender. By the final interview of the day, according to a report by Shaughnessy, he "observed one male white occupant" driving the car and indicated he could "identify the subject." A separate report prepared by Blue Island detective Douglas Hoglund on the final interview asserted flatly that Mann "identified David Dowaliby as being seen in the area."

However, none of the police reports mentioned a crucial detail—that Mann had observed the car and driver from no closer than three quarters of the length of a football field.

When Paul Greves told Daniel McDevitt that a witness had claimed to have seen a dark-colored, late-seventies Chevrolet Malibu in the Islander Apartments parking lot, McDevitt became extremely excited.

"Jesus Christ," McDevitt said, "that's the Dowalibys' car!"

Cynthia Dowaliby owned a 1980 Chevrolet Malibu. Although it was light blue, McDevitt speculated that it might have appeared dark under the lighting conditions.

The news of the Mann sighting coincided with the discovery by McDevitt's investigators that David Dowaliby had bowled in Blue Island the night before he reported Jaclyn missing. The bowling alley was only about a mile from the Islander Apartments.

For McDevitt, the latest developments were confirmation that David and Cynthia were involved in their daughter's death—a view Greves soon came to share.

Daniel McDevitt ordered his investigators to check out Everett Mann's background.

Mann seemed to be clean. However, the investigators found something that troubled McDevitt—Mann aspired to be a cop. Between 1981 and 1986, he had applied to join the Chicago Police Department, the Illinois State Police, and the FBI, but was rejected each time.

McDevitt realized that the objectivity of a witness whose life's goal was to become a police officer could reasonably be questioned by a defense lawyer or a jury.

On the other hand, Paul Greves reasoned that Mann had a strong motive not to become a witness: Mann, who was married, could not avoid acknowledging that he had been out with another woman before he saw the car.

"By telling us what he saw, Everett Mann exposed his liaison," Greves said. "That gave him credibility."

The member of the Cook County state's attorney's staff first assigned to the investigation was Robert Clifford, the supervisor of criminal prosecutions in the south suburban area. Clifford had worked on many cases with Paul Greves.

Clifford and Greves decided to conduct an experiment to test Everett Mann's reliability as an eyewitness: They went to the Islander Apartments to reenact his identification.

Clifford stood where Mann said he parked. Greves drove a two-door blue Pontiac out of the spot next to the middle Dumpster. Clifford could see no nose structure whatsoever. Then Greves stood at Mann's location, and they repeated the experiment. Greves could not see a nose structure either.

They decided to keep their observations to themselves.

* * *

When Robert Clifford learned that there was a tape recording of Everett Mann's ambiguous statement to Blue Island police, he was upset.

"Who decided to do that?" Clifford demanded at a meeting with Greves.

"I did," Greves said. "I thought it was appropriate."

"That's not going to be very helpful to us," Clifford said. "It would be a shame if that tape disappeared."

Greves said he looked on Clifford's suggestion as improper and did not destroy the tape. He put it into his desk drawer and, he said, "I honestly forgot about it."

State Police Sergeant Shaughnessy and Blue Island Detective Joseph Kosman, continuing the canvass of the Islander Apartments, interviewed Derrick L. Darling and Gloria J. Lake, who lived together in the building where Everett Mann lived.

Darling and Lake said they had seen a Chevrolet Malibu near their apartment on September 13, the day before Jaclyn's body was found. Based on this statement, they were taken to the Midlothian police station, where Kevin Shaughnessy interviewed them separately.

Darling said he and Lake went for a walk to the corner grocery store at about 1:30 P.M. on September 13. On the way, they walked through the Islander Apartments parking lot.

In the rear of the lot, Darling claimed, he saw a blue four-door 1980-to-1982 Malibu backed into a parking space behind 1950 Canal. Describing himself as a Chevrolet enthusiast, Darling said he was certain of the make of the car.

Darling recalled saying to Lake, "If I had that car I would fix it up." The car had a few rust spots and the lenses on the front turn-signal lights were different, one being dull, the other shiny.

When shown pictures of various cars, according to Shaughnessy's report, Darling "positively identified Dowaliby's Chevy Malibu that he observed on Tuesday, September 13, parked unoccupied behind 1950 Canal."

Lake was unable to identify the car but was certain that the sighting occurred at 1:30 P.M. because she had gone to the store to use the pay telephone to make an important call.

Shaughnessy knew that if Darling and Lake were right about the time, the car they saw could not have been Cynthia Dowaliby's Malibu. Shaughnessy himself had been interrogating David Dowaliby at precisely the time that Darling and Lake claimed to have seen the car, and other officers had been with Cynthia at home in Midlothian, where her Malibu was parked.

While Kevin Shaughnessy was interviewing Darling and Lake, Blue Island detectives interviewed Melvin and Lavern Buckley, who lived in one of the Islander Apartment buildings bordering on the parking lot.

The detectives did not show the Buckleys an array of actual photographs, as they had shown Everett Mann, but only photocopies of photographs of David and Cynthia and their vehicles. From the photocopies, the Buckleys identified David as having been at their building "on several occasions in the past month." Melvin Buckley also claimed to have seen David's pickup in the area, and Lavern Buckley claimed to have seen the Malibu there within the past month.

The Buckleys accompanied the detectives to the Midlothian police station, where they were interviewed further. This time they were shown the actual photographs, and they repeated the identifications.

The Buckleys became more precise about where they had seen David Dowaliby: He had been a frequent guest at an apartment on the first floor of their building. The Buckleys added that a strong odor of marijuana regularly emanated from this apartment, which only recently had been vacated by a couple who occupied it.

Police tracked down the couple, who claimed that they had never seen David Dowaliby.

On Sunday, September 18, the *Tribune* carried a story about the case on the front page of its local news section. The news coverage in recent days had been unfavorable to the Dowalibys, saying that they were refusing to cooperate with police.

The Sunday story, however, indicated there was no solid evidence that the Dowalibys were involved in the crime.

"The only thing police know for sure is that seven-year-old Jaclyn Dowaliby was strangled," the story began.

Gene and Peggy O'Connor read the paper and took it to show David and Cynthia, thinking it would raise their spirits. David read the story and passed it to Cynthia. After reading the first sentence, Cynthia jumped up, screamed, and ran into Jaclyn's bedroom, slamming the door behind her.

Stunned, Peggy asked David, "What's the matter?"

"She didn't know," David said.

"Didn't know what?"

"How she died."

Meanwhile, Midlothian Detective Otto Soyk made a 10:00 A.M. appearance before Circuit Court Judge Jeffrey A. Malak to request search warrants for Cynthia's Chevrolet Malibu and the Dowalibys' home, yard, garage, and "the person of David Dowaliby."

The complaint for the warrants, written by Assistant State's Attorney Clifford, summarized the evidence, which the police contended constituted probable cause to justify the search. The complaint said there was no evidence of a forcible entry other than the broken window, that when police arrived there were no sheets on Jaclyn's bed, and that a witness, Everett Mann, had "identified David Dowaliby" as the driver of a car he saw in the Islander Apartments parking lot between 2:00 and 2:30 A.M. on September 10.

Judge Malak signed the warrants at 10:12 A.M. Half an hour later, seven cars carrying about twenty officers from Midlothian, Blue Island, Crestwood, the Illinois State Police, and the FBI converged on the Dowaliby home. They shut off the street to traffic as curious onlookers gathered.

Midlothian Police Chief William Fischer knocked on the door, with Blue Island Chief Paul Greves at his side. When David opened it, Fischer said, "I have warrants to search your home and cars." Two officers frisked David, while the others began searching the premises. Cynthia, Ann, and Davey watched.

At about 1:00 P.M., the searchers emerged with five paper shopping bags filled with items from the house and garage, including pillowcases, the mattress pad, a pillow, and sheets from Jaclyn's room; a triple-beam scale (a device sometimes used to weigh drugs) from the master bedroom; pieces of rope from the garage; and a pink blanket from the basement. In the master bedroom police found a bulletproof vest but did not remove it.

The Malibu was towed to a garage for processing by Hayden Baldwin. However, police accidentally locked the keys in the trunk of the car. The tow-truck driver had to return to the Dowaliby home to get another set before Baldwin could begin.

From the Malibu, Baldwin removed a roll of twine, a hairnet, and the trunk liner, and took them to the Joliet Crime Laboratory for microscopic analysis.

McDevitt hoped the analysis would reveal evidence that Jaclyn's body had been transported in the car. He told reporters, "We're not letting up. We're all plugging away. I hope the person who's responsible for this little girl's death knows that."

Keeping the heat on the Dowaliby family, McDevitt sent Kevin Shaughnessy to interview Michael Borrelli, Cynthia's oldest brother. Shaughnessy told Michael that David was the prime suspect.

"I knew it, goddamn it," Michael responded. "I knew he was involved. We gotta get that son-of-a-bitch locked up."

Michael not only became an ongoing source of information to Shaughnessy and McDevitt but also served a counterintelligence function.

Specifically, police used him to carry disinformation designed to break down David and Cynthia's resolve. Michael would return from his meetings with McDevitt to share with family members "new evidence" allegedly implicating his brother-in-law.

Cynthia, infuriated by Michael's behavior, asked Ralph Meczyk to find out where Michael had been when Jaclyn disappeared.

Meczyk, however, chose not to do that, concerned about offending Michael's wife, Sylvia Borrelli—a potentially important witness whom Cynthia had called the morning that Jaclyn was reported missing.

On Monday, September 19, David, Cynthia, and family members visited Jaclyn's grave. On it, they found a red silk rose that had not been there the day of the funeral.

Who put it there was a mystery, since the grave was still unmarked.

Later, Cynthia asked a florist if a red rose had any special meaning.

"It means 'I love you still,' " the florist told her.

While the Dowalibys were at the cemetery, state police investigators continued interviewing neighbors.

Sergeants Steven Reilly and Kevin Shaughnessy went to the home of Jeffrey and Constance Koleczek, who lived two houses west of the Dowalibys. The Koleczeks had two children, one of whom, eight-year-old Jennifer, often had played with Jaclyn.

According to Shaughnessy's report, Jeffrey Koleczek said that "he had to tell Davey, Jaclyn's brother, not to play with rope." On several occasions, Davey had tied himself up and swung the rope around, which Koleczek thought was dangerous.

Constance Koleczek said that the night before Jaclyn was reported missing, she stayed up watching television until she joined Jeffrey in bed at about eleven-thirty. At 12:17 A.M.—she remembered the time because she had looked at a digital clock—she was awakened by a "moan" outside the bedroom window. She looked out the window and awakened Jeffrey. He got up and turned on the porch light. Seeing nothing out of the ordinary, he returned to bed. A little later, their children came into their bedroom, frightened, but did not indicate why.

Reilly and Shaughnessy interviewed Jennifer Koleczek, but, unaccountably, did not ask her why she had been frightened. Jennifer told them that Jaclyn never gave any indication that her parents abused her. Jennifer said that "Jaclyn was a happy girl and never cried for anything other than a good reason."

Reilly and Shaughnessy next interviewed Susan E. Haseman, the recently widowed mother of Sarah Haseman, one of Jaclyn's best friends.

Haseman said she was up until ten-thirty or eleven the night before Jaclyn was reported missing and heard nothing out of the ordinary. At ten or ten-thirty the next morning, Haseman said, she had just gotten out of the shower when her daughter told her Cynthia Dowaliby had called and asked if Jaclyn were there.

Haseman was "not concerned" immediately but "became concerned" a few minutes later when another neighbor called and told her that Jaclyn was missing; Haseman then went to the Dowalibys' home to see if she could help.

The police report of the interview focused on Haseman's negative assessment of Jaclyn. "Jaclyn was a different person around adults, more timid, reserved, than she was around the children," Haseman was quoted as saying. "On several occasions, Jaclyn's friends would all hide from her."

Seven-year-old Sarah Haseman told Reilly and Shaughnessy that Jaclyn had been spanked "once or twice" by her parents, but nothing major or out of the ordinary.

The report said that both Sarah and Susan were "positive that neither David nor Cyndi came by that morning to see if Jaclyn was here." The implication was that the Dowalibys had not bothered even to look for Jaclyn at the home of one of her best friends. In fact, Susan had told the officers that Cynthia had telephoned the Haseman home that morning and asked whether Jaclyn was there.

Reilly and Shaughnessy also interviewed Erin Bell, the mother of Kyle Bell, a playmate of Davey Dowaliby. "Bell commented that she considered the Dowaliby children somewhat unsupervised," Reilly and Shaughnessy's initial report stated. The report quoted Bell as saying that Davey had been allowed to cross the street by himself and once had walked around the neighborhood "clad only in a T-shirt."

In a supplemental report of the interview, written the following week, Reilly and Shaughnessy asserted that Bell also had described the "emotional condition" of David Dowaliby on the morning of September 10. "Dowaliby was acting in a normal manner and did not appear overly distraught," said the supplemental report. "Bell indicated that she thought it was unusual for someone to walk home slowly when their child was missing."

However, Reilly and Shaughnessy's handwritten notes on the Bell interview contained no such quotation. In fact, the handwritten notes said that Bell described both David and Cynthia as "serious and concerned" on September 10.

On September 20, Blue Island Chief Paul Greves questioned why the Dowalibys had stopped talking to investigators. "It's unimaginable to me that anyone could stand by and have a family member dead and not cooperate," he told reporters.

In response, Meczyk and Hyman released a brief typed statement. "The Dowaliby family is innocent of any wrongdoing. They have cooperated fully with law enforcement," the statement said. "This investigation has become accusatorial. It is an outrage that police and others are compounding their tragedy by inferring that members of the Dowaliby family are suspects or have withheld any information in the death of their daughter."

Greves then responded to the response. "I haven't accused anyone," he said. "I'm trying to solve this crime. I'm frustrated and I want to ask questions. At least seventy-five percent of my time is spent tracing leads I feel confident the family could answer."

Most news accounts treated the banter perfunctorily, but Paul Hogan, of Channel 5, the Chicago NBC station, was critical of the police, accusing them of using "pressure tactics" to get the Dowalibys to talk.

The lanky, bearded Hogan, a frequent champion of unpopular causes, spoke in a tone reminiscent of a high school civics teacher: "It's clear tonight the Dowalibys strongly assert their innocence and portray themselves as victims of police badgering, and only evidence strong enough to lead to arrests, charges, and convictions can remove that presumption of innocence."

On September 21, Daniel McDevitt and Paul Greves told reporters that the Illinois Crime Laboratory had made the case "a top priority" and that a breakthrough was expected soon. For public consumption, McDevitt and Greves would not elaborate, but, off the record, they told reporters that the evidence pointed to David and Cynthia's guilt.

As reporters were leaving, Channel 5's Paul Hogan approached McDevitt and asked, "Confidentially, what makes you think they're guilty?"

According to Hogan, McDevitt answered with a question: "What if I were to tell you that the basement window was broken from the inside?"

"I would know they were guilty," said Hogan.

"Well, it was," McDevitt asserted.

"Case closed," said Hogan.

Believing McDevitt, Hogan lost interest in the story.

McDevitt had succeeded, for the time being, in neutralizing a potential nemesis.

The same day, Sergeant Reilly drove to the Joliet crime lab and picked up the rope found around Jaclyn's neck. He took it to show to Jeffrey Koleczek.

According to Reilly's report, Koleczek looked at the rope and said without hesitation, "That's the rope Davey used to play with."

Reilly asked if Koleczek was sure.

"Yes," Reilly quoted Koleczek as saying, "that's the rope."

The crime lab, as Daniel McDevitt and Paul Greves had told reporters, was hard at work on the case.

Joseph V. Ambrozich, a state forensic scientist, analyzed the fingerprints from the broken glass recovered from the Dowaliby home.

Ambrozich found one latent print. He compared it with fingerprints of David, Cynthia, Ann, and Davey Dowaliby—but found no match.

The rest of the physical evidence was turned over to another forensic scientist, Jennie Hahn.

One of Hahn's findings was particularly intriguing: On the rope Hahn observed two hairs, only one of which appeared to be Jaclyn's. The other was a Negroid head hair.

Hahn also examined numerous other hairs. On the panties that were found two feet from the body, Hahn observed a light brown head hair visually similar to Jaclyn's and a brown pubic hair that obviously could not have come from the prepubescent victim. On the trunk liner from the Malibu, Hahn noticed one Caucasian pubic hair and seven light brown hairs that were consistent with Cynthia's head hair.

Ten pieces of Jaclyn's fingernails had been clipped during the autopsy and sent to Hahn. Hahn found blood stains under seven clippings. She typed the blood from the largest nail, finding it to be Type O; Jaclyn and Cynthia both had Type O blood, David Type A.

Hahn observed that the mattress pad and sheets seized during the search were unstained with blood or bodily fluids.

On the pillow from Jaclyn's bed, Hahn found two bloodstains, but they appeared to be old. On the bedspread in which Jaclyn was wrapped, Hahn found five faint stains that appeared to be blood, although she was unable to determine the type or even if they were human blood.

Hahn visually examined a white medicine bottle cap that had been found with Jaclyn's body when it was unwrapped at the morgue. She noted that the cap bore the instruction "reclose tightly," but she did not test it for fingerprints or medicinal residue.

Finally, Hahn analyzed the Malibu trunk liner and Jaclyn's maggot-covered bedspread and nightgown for fiber evidence. She excluded the possibility that any fibers on the trunk liner came from the bedspread or nightgown, and vice versa; in other words, there was no physical evidence that Jaclyn's body had been transported in the Malibu.

On the afternoon of September 22, FBI Agent Steven J. Kashirsky interviewed Sylvia Borrelli, Cynthia's sister-in-law.

Kashirsky wrote a report quoting Borrelli as saying that, when Cynthia had called her to cancel their plans to attend the ceramics class on September 10, Cynthia had mentioned that she was "going to wake up the children."

The report piqued Daniel McDevitt's interest. Telephone records showed that Cynthia's call to Sylvia had been made at 9:46 A.M., yet David initially had said that Jaclyn was discovered missing at "about 9:00 A.M." Moreover, Kashirsky's report referred to waking up "the children," although David had told police that Davey had been awake since 8:00 A.M.

The seeming inconsistencies bolstered McDevitt's cover-up theory, which he had begun to develop after learning that the Dowalibys' window appeared to have been broken from the inside.

McDevitt now speculated that David and Cynthia had hoped that Ann would discover the broken window but that they needed to buy time when she failed to arrive home to play her unwitting role.

In McDevitt's view, the call to Sylvia had been designed to create a witness who would believe that, as far as Cynthia knew, the children were just fine at that time.

Then David and Cynthia could stage the neighborhood search, pretend to discover the window, and finally call the police.

A month into the investigation, law enforcement officers were generating a paper trail leading in one direction—toward implicating the Dowalibys.

On October 6, Hayden Baldwin prepared a Crime Scene Report claiming that when he initially had examined the Dowaliby home twenty-six days earlier, he had noticed evidence strongly indicating that no one had entered through the basement window.

Baldwin now asserted that there had been a layer of "undisturbed dust" on the inside windowsill and spider webs around the window frame. Further, he claimed, the area just outside the window had been partially covered with dead leaves and soil that "showed very little sign of disturbance."

Beneath the window on the inside, Baldwin's report continued, there had been a metal towel rack, a plywood stand, and a cardboard box. "None of the items showed signs of disturbance," the report said.

Months later, Baldwin would claim that he had made handwritten notes of these observations during his initial examination of the crime scene but had destroyed the notes after completing his report.

Baldwin never would explain why, although he took dozens of photographs, he took none of the layer of dust on the windowsill, the spider webs, or the leaves outside the window. Nor would he explain why he failed to preserve the dust with evidence tape or an electrostatic dust-lifter he had with him on September 10.

Meanwhile, Midlothian Chief William Fischer asked Donald Woodark, the first officer to arrive at the Dowaliby home, to write a new report including any details he had failed to note on September 10.

Woodark then wrote a report claiming that he, too, had noticed the undisturbed dust.

On the afternoon of October 10, Ann Dowaliby called Paul Greves and said she would like to talk to him. "Every other police official had had a chance to talk to the family, but he hadn't," Ann said later. "I thought Greves was a very dedicated man. I thought there was a small hope that what I said to him could lead to the person who killed Jaclyn."

Greves agreed to see her immediately. When she arrived, he told her up front, "I have to tell you, in all fairness to you, I'm convinced your son and daughter-in-law are guilty."

"I'm certain you're wrong," Ann responded.

Greves asked whether she thought it was possible that Cynthia killed Jaclyn accidentally and David hid the body.

"Anyone can have an accident," Ann said, "but I know Cyndi as a mother. If Cyndi had killed Jaclyn accidentally, she couldn't have hidden it from me. She would have gone to pieces. I would have seen it. Her face would have been the evidence."

"Well then, that only leaves one person," Greves told her—meaning David.

"That's not true," Ann said. "There are many suspects."

Greves asked her who she had in mind, and she mentioned several, most of whom the police already had eliminated. Nonetheless, Greves assured her he would check further into the suspects she had named.

The next morning, Greves called Ann and asked her to come to the station. She said she went to see him immediately, thinking he might have turned up something on the possible suspects. That was not the case, however. Greves and Assistant State's Attorney Norma Reyes wanted to interrogate her.

The session lasted almost four hours, after which Reyes prepared a three-page report and asked Ann to sign it.

Most of the report was a neutral recitation of information Ann had provided in interviews with various officers after Jaclyn's disappearance, but there were three points that went beyond police versions of her earlier statements:

First, the report indicated that Ann had found no sign of an intruder in her basement bedroom. When she returned home on the morning of September 10, the report said, "She noticed glass on the floor and boxes. Nothing else was disturbed, except a makeup mirror that she had on a table. She looked all around but only noticed the mirror out of place."

Second, the report supported the contention that the murder weapon had come from the Dowaliby home. When Ann was shown an evidence bag containing the coiled rope recovered from Jaclyn's body, according to the report, she said that it looked "like the type of rope Davey played with" and that she had not seen the rope since Jaclyn's disappearance.

Third, the report suggested that illegal drugs somehow might have been connected to the crime, stating that Ann "knows David smokes marijuana. She heard that he sells marijuana, but doesn't know for sure."

After reading the report, Ann refused to sign it. According to Ann, it twisted what she said or meant. According to Reyes, however, Ann would not sign it because "she did not want to implicate her son."

Reyes's explanation was accepted by her colleagues in the state's attorney's office.

David Dowaliby's mother, unwittingly, had just become a key witness for the prosecution.

POWER STRUGGLE

The Cook County state's attorney's office was headed by Richard M. Daley, a Democratic politician whose ambition was to win the job that his late father had held for more than two decades: mayor of Chicago.

Daley had cultivated a tough-on-crime image, portraying his office as the last bulwark against disorder. He had based promotions on convictions, sending an unmistakable message: Win at any cost.

In 1985, Daley had named thirty-eight-year-old career prosecutor Patrick W. O'Brien to head the Felony Trial Division. To get the job, O'Brien had beaten out a good friend of Robert Clifford, the prosecutor assigned to the Dowaliby case.

O'Brien was a boorish, humorless, mistrustful man with a sunken chin, receding hairline, and flushed complexion. Thick glasses and a narrow mustache gave him a milquetoast appearance that could not have been more misleading. O'Brien was as hard-nosed as they come in a job where gentility is rare.

Clifford did not get along with O'Brien, whom he regarded as a "geek" and once invited to "step outside" to settle their differences with their fists.

Against this backdrop, in mid-October, Daniel McDevitt arranged a meeting with prosecutors at the Blue Island police station to discuss bringing charges against David and Cynthia Dowaliby.

At the meeting, Patrick O'Brien took the seat at the head of the table, making it clear that he—not Clifford—would be calling the shots.

McDevitt laid out the evidence—the recollection by Baldwin and Woodark of the supposedly undisturbed layer of dust, the Everett Mann identification, and the purportedly inconsistent statements made by David.

The prosecutors were unimpressed.

"You can't tell us who did it," O'Brien said. "You've got to come up with more."

"Come on, you guys," McDevitt said. "What do you want?"

"More evidence," O'Brien replied.

David Dowaliby, meanwhile, acquired a watchdog, a brown Labrador retriever. He also changed the locks on the doors and started sitting up nights holding a shotgun across his lap. Gene O'Connor kept him company as Cynthia and Davey slept.

As the weeks wore on, the strain began to take its toll on Davey Dowaliby. "He couldn't sleep without the light on," Cynthia said later. "He was terrified that someone would break into the house and abduct him."

Cynthia and David carried Davey's mattress into their room and put it on the floor next to their bed. "He knew no one could get him if we were there," said Cynthia. "I would reach down and hold his hand until he fell asleep."

* * *

In late October, Cynthia Dowaliby learned that she was pregnant. The baby would arrive in early summer.

"It was totally unplanned," said Cynthia. "Looking back, I feel like God had to find a way to save me. Because I had to be strong for the baby, I found the strength to keep going."

In early November, Daniel McDevitt, Paul Greves, and William Fischer went to the state's attorney's office in Chicago and again met with Patrick O'Brien.

For three weeks, the task force had searched for additional evidence but had come up with nothing new. O'Brien still insisted there was not enough evidence to bring charges.

McDevitt stood up, slammed his fist, and told O'Brien, "Goddamn it, I don't understand this! What do you want us to do? We're tearing our guts out on this case. We know who's responsible."

Greves supported McDevitt, but with a calmer tone: "Pat, this is all we got. I don't see any evidence here that points to anyone except Cynthia and David."

O'Brien indicated that he had discussed the case with his boss, State's Attorney Daley, but still was noncommittal. "We'll let you know," O'Brien said.

McDevitt and Greves met for coffee the next morning at a Burger King and discussed their frustrations. "I've got seventeen years to go before I retire, and I'm going to work on this case every day until then," McDevitt vowed.

They talked about the politics of the case. They thought maybe Daley was holding back on the indictments until after the state's attorney's election a few days hence, on November 8. Another possibility was that Daley was not being given the facts by O'Brien.

They knew that prosecutor Robert Clifford shared their view that the Dowalibys had committed the crime, but they were not sure about O'Brien.

As Richard Daley prepared to announce his mayoral candidacy in mid-November, shortly after winning his third term as state's attorney, the Dowaliby case was grabbing headlines but going nowhere.

No significant evidence had been developed since mid-October, when Patrick O'Brien first had told Daniel McDevitt and the police chiefs that the evidence was insufficient to charge the Dowalibys.

Nonetheless, on the advice of his top political aide, Frank Kreusi, and against the advice of several career prosecutors in the office, Daley ordered the case to proceed.

"Let's charge them and let a judge worry about it," Daley told O'Brien and other prosecutors.

On November 21, the day before Daley planned to announce his intention to run for mayor, O'Brien called McDevitt and the police chiefs to yet another meeting.

When they arrived, O'Brien told them of Daley's decision on the Dowaliby case. "We're gonna go," O'Brien said. "We're charging them both." The charges would be first-degree murder and concealment of a homicide.

McDevitt, Paul Greves, and William Fischer were elated. Although they believed that Jaclyn's death probably had been an accident, the murder charges would be a hammer for producing confessions to lesser charges.

With O'Brien, they planned a strategy to achieve that result. David would be arrested first, since it was presumed that he would be more likely to confess. The theory was that David was "less guilty"—that Cynthia, the disciplinarian, had caused Jaclyn's death and David had concealed it.

O'Brien suggested that Greves arrest David, since the two had had little contact during the investigation. "He won't know where you're coming from," O'Brien said.

As soon as David was in custody, prosecutors would offer him a deal: If he admitted what happened, they would go easy on him.

Fischer would arrest Cynthia after, it was hoped, prosecutors had obtained David's confession. Other officers would take Davey Dowaliby to the Illinois Department of Children and Family Services and question him away from his family.

The arrests would be made the next morning, November 22. With Thanksgiving two days away, the timing might weaken the Dowalibys' resolve, enhancing the pressure to confess.

When the meeting in O'Brien's office ended, Greves, McDevitt, and Fischer arranged to go to the home of Judge Cornelius J. Houtsma, Jr., to get him to sign arrest warrants. They knew Houtsma from having testified in his courtroom. "We knew he'd be friendly," Greves explained.

When they arrived at Houtsma's home on the far Southwest Side of Chicago, Houtsma's daughter answered the door.

Houtsma, wearing a polo shirt and slacks, shook the officers' hands and asked, "Who's going to testify?"

"I am," Fischer said.

After being sworn, Fischer briefly summarized the evidence against the Dowalibys. Houtsma signed the arrest warrants, ordering the Dowalibys held without bond.

That night O'Brien called Robert Clifford at the state's attorney's office in Markham. "Something's going to happen in the Dowaliby case tomorrow," said O'Brien. "Hang loose between Markham and Midlothian."

"What are you going to do, send me a smoke signal?" Clifford snapped. "Call me back when you can be more specific."

O'Brien did not call back.

Clifford had been aced out of a sensational case by the office heavyweight.

ARREST AND SEPARATION

At 6:00 A.M. on Tuesday, November 22, officers involved in the investigation met with Patrick O'Brien at state police headquarters to go over final details before executing the plan worked out the preceding day.

Forty minutes later, a state trooper pulled over David in his pickup truck four blocks from the Dowaliby home, while Paul Greves waited in an unmarked car nearby.

Greves could see the flashing lights of the trooper's car and hear his radio transmission. "Excuse me, sir," Greves heard the trooper say, "may I see your driver's license?"

The trooper asked David to get out of the truck.

Greves approached and asked, "Are you David Dowaliby?"

"Yes, I am," David answered.

"I have a warrant for your arrest on a charge of murder."

As soon as Greves radioed that David was in custody, Nancy Dollarhide, a state police investigator, called David's boss, Ronald Patterson. Dollarhide impersonated Cynthia, saying, "Ron, we just woke up and Dave is going to be a little bit late."

The call was a ploy to prevent Patterson from calling the Dowaliby home when David did not arrive on time, possibly alerting Cynthia to his arrest; Cynthia no doubt would have contacted Ralph Meczyk and Lawrence Hyman, who would have blocked any interrogation.

The ploy worked.

Greves drove David to the Blue Island police station and took him into a conference room. Daniel McDevitt, whom David had not previously met, joined them. While Patrick O'Brien waited in an adjoining room, Greves and McDevitt questioned David.

"Listen, David, what's done is done," Greves said. "If it was an accident, just tell us. It changes the whole complexion of this case."

David burst into tears. After regaining his composure, he told Greves, "I have nothing to say to you."

McDevitt showed David the kindergarten photograph of Jaclyn and, putting his hand over his heart, said, "I keep this right here."

David asked if he could have the picture.

Without answering, McDevitt spread out several other photos on the table—color shots of Jaclyn's decomposed body.

"This is what you did," he said. "Take a look at these."

David turned his head away.

After a few moments of silence, Greves called a young prosecutor into the room and asked, "If we were to charge him with concealing a homicide, how much time would he get?"

"Three years, tops," said the prosecutor.

David said nothing.

Frustrated, Greves and McDevitt ended the interview.

"We almost had him," Greves told O'Brien as David was

taken to a cell. "It looked like he was going to say something. He was weeping and vulnerable, but then he pulled back."

A little after 8:30 A.M., Ronald Patterson called the Dowaliby home to find out why David had not arrived at work.

When Cynthia answered, Patterson asked, "Cyndi, is Dave still there?"

"No."

"What time did he leave?"

"I don't know, Ron, I guess he left at the regular time."

"Cyndi, didn't you call me?"

"No."

"You'd better call your lawyer."

Cynthia called Ralph Meczyk. As they were talking, William Fischer, flanked by Neal Caauwe and Kevin Shaughnessy, knocked on the Dowaliby front door. Ann opened it, and Fischer asked, "Where's Cyndi?"

"Why?" Ann responded.

"We have a warrant for her arrest," Fischer said.

"She's in the kitchen," Ann said.

Fischer went into the kitchen. Cynthia, wearing blue jeans and a flannel shirt, was still on the phone.

"I'm talking to my lawyer," she told Fischer.

Fischer asked for the phone. "This is Chief Bill Fischer," he told Meczyk, "and I'm about to arrest your client."

"I'll be right down," Meczyk said.

Fischer then read the warrant to Cynthia, his hands trembling. Cynthia put on a green corduroy jacket and, taking only a handbag, was led away in handcuffs.

Caauwe and Shaughnessy stayed behind.

"We're taking Davey into protective custody," Detective Caauwe told Ann Dowaliby as the car pulled away. "Where is he?"

"Follow me," said Ann, leading them through the bathroom into Cynthia and David's bedroom, where the four-and-one-half-year-old was asleep on the mattress on the floor.

Davey cried when Ann awakened him. He was fully

clothed but wet. Ann put him on the bed and began to change his clothes. Suddenly she stopped. "You're not taking him," she said.

"Please, Ann, there's enough going on now," Caauwe said. "I will arrest you if you stand in my way."

Ann reluctantly resumed changing Davey's clothes. It would prove significant later that, although Davey was completely naked in Caauwe's presence, Caauwe noticed no marks or bruises on Davey's face and nothing unusual about Davey's body.

"You know these guys?" Ann asked Davey.

"Yes," Davey answered, apparently recalling that they had given him a deputy's badge shortly after Jaclyn disappeared.

"Do you want to go with them?" Ann asked.

"No," Davey replied, clinging to Ann.

Caauwe persuaded him to come for a "short ride" in the police car, taking him by the hand.

During the thirty-minute drive to the headquarters of the Department of Children and Family Services on Chicago's South Side, Caauwe asked Davey if he could remember what happened the night his sister disappeared.

Davey said he could not remember. Caauwe asked why, and Davey said he could not hear anything. Caauwe asked him to explain, and Davey said he was wearing earplugs.

Thinking Davey might mean earphones, Sergeant Shaughnessy asked, "You mean the kind you put over your ears to play music?"

"No," Davey said, "earplugs like when you're swimming."

Caauwe asked if he knew what happened to Jaclyn. Davey said, "The Lord wanted her up in Heaven."

Caauwe noted that it was getting close to Christmas, and asked Davey what he wanted from Santa Claus.

"I want my sister home," he said.

A little later, Davey asked, "We're going kind of far, aren't we?"

When Caauwe said yes, Davey asked if he would be back home for Thanksgiving.

Caauwe said he did not think so.

They arrived at Children and Family Services at about 10 A.M. and were met by Marlon C. Daniels, a caseworker. Caauwe took Daniels aside and told him that Davey's parents had been arrested that morning for the murder of Davey's sister, that the parents use drugs, that Davey's grandmother drinks a lot, and that Davey "says he has to wear earplugs at night."

Caauwe added that the Dowalibys might be part of a devil-worshiping cult engaged in ritualistic child abuse. He said that David Dowaliby had a bright red rose tattooed on his right arm and that Jaclyn had once colored a picture of a cow, making its tongue purple. The tattoo and purple cow tongue could be demonic symbols, he opined.

After Caauwe and Shaughnessy left, Daniels asked Davey if he had any brothers or sisters. Davey said that he used to have a sister but that she had "gone to God." He explained that two men had come into the house, wrapped Jaclyn in her blanket, and taken her away; he did not see the men, but heard glass breaking.

Daniels wrote a report saying that he noticed a red mark on the left side of Davey's face and a bruise on his right lower lip. When asked how he got the marks, Davey said, "My parents don't beat me."

Daniels concluded his report, "Parents charged in connection with murder of sibling. Child at risk of physical injury."

At about 12:30 P.M., a tearful Davey was taken a few blocks to Mount Sinai Hospital, where doctors checked his vital signs and took a full set of X rays. He was admitted to the hospital's Pediatric Ecology Unit, where he would have no contact with family members for five days.

David Schneidman, a Children and Family Services spokesman, told reporters that Davey had been hospitalized because he was "emotionally distraught."

Cynthia Dowaliby was taken to the Blue Island police station, where an officer handed her a piece of paper to read. It was her Miranda rights.

"Book her," the officer snapped.

Officers took mug shots of Cynthia, and Paul Greves told

her that she could make one call. She called Ann Dowaliby, who told her that Davey had been taken away. When Cynthia finished the call, Greves led her upstairs to Sergeant Joseph Baskeys's office.

According to Cynthia, she told Greves only, "This is unreal," and Greves replied, "This *is* real." She said that she turned her back to Greves, saying nothing further.

Greves would remember the encounter differently, claiming that he had told Cynthia, "If you're responsible for your daughter's death, it will come out," and Cynthia responded with hostility, "I want my lawyer. I have nothing to say." Greves said that her attitude convinced him of her guilt.

Whatever was said, there is no dispute that Greves then threw an envelope of Jaclyn's autopsy photos in front of her.

"If you want to look at how your daughter ended up, here are the pictures," he said.

Greves then left. According to Cynthia, another officer came into the room and told her, "We'll have to use the tarantula." She said the officer pointed to a terrarium in which she indeed saw a tarantula. "By the way," Cynthia quoted the officer as saying, "its name is 'Confess.' "

"My back was turned to the officer, and for a moment I thought he might put the tarantula on me," said Cynthia. "Then I thought, there was no way they were going to do that. I was scared, but I'm not stupid."

Greves acknowledged that there was a tarantula named "Confess" in a terrarium in Baskeys's office; it had been a gift from fellow officers when Baskeys was promoted to detective.

However, Greves said, he doubted Cynthia's claim that she was threatened with Baskeys's pet. "I don't see how it could have happened," he said. "I was with her for all but a couple of minutes."

Greves could not explain how, if it did not happen, Cynthia came to know the creature's name.

Ralph Meczyk and Lawrence Hyman arrived at the Blue Island police station at about 10:00 A.M.

Meczyk angrily confronted Greves, "You guys pulled a midnight raid here. You know better than that."

"I'm not obligated to contact lawyers before an arrest," Greves told Meczyk.

Meczyk and Hyman were permitted to confer briefly with their clients, who were then taken to the Midlothian police station—for no other purpose, Greves would concede, than to share the media spotlight with Midlothian officials.

Camera crews from five television stations and reporters from a score of area radio stations and newspapers were waiting. "It was a circus," Greves would admit.

David and Cynthia were led into the station in handcuffs, providing ample photo opportunities, and then were promptly returned to Blue Island.

At a press conference that evening, McDevitt pointed to a large photograph of Jaclyn that had been posted on the wall of the task force office.

"We did it for her," he declared.

TWO BIG STORIES

The Wednesday, November 23, *Chicago Sun-Times* devoted its entire tabloid front page to two stories: the Dowalibys' arrest and State's Attorney Daley's mayoral plans.

"Parents Accused," said one headline. "Daley D-Day Set," said the other. Three photographs accompanied the headlines—one of the Dowalibys in handcuffs; one of Jaclyn; and, between them, one of Daley with law books in the background.

The Dowaliby case and Daley's mayoral campaign would compete for media attention in the months that followed.

On Wednesday morning, the Dowalibys were taken separately to the Cook County Jail, a sprawling complex adjacent to the Criminal Courts Building at Twenty-sixth Street and California Avenue in Chicago.

Paul Greves drove David to the jail, still hoping to

finagle a confession. Greves thought David was weakening because he cried on and off during the ride.

When they arrived, Greves accompanied David into a processing area. They spent about a half hour together, giving Greves an opportunity to work on him.

"If this was an accident, now's the time to tell the truth," Greves said. "You still have this one last shot."

"I have nothing to say," said David.

David was taken to a cell that was adjacent to an area where two transvestites were being held. Naively assuming that they were women, David provided a rare moment of levity for the guards by inquiring if his wife would be brought there.

In fact, Cynthia was being processed in a separate women's area of the institution.

As she was led into a cellblock, a prisoner shouted, "There she is! That's her green coat!"

"Oh, you're just as pretty as you look on TV," said another prisoner.

"Baby-killer!" shouted another.

There were several threats. "I'll get you!"

"Get me out of here!" Cynthia pleaded with a guard.

The guard led her to an isolation cell.

Later in the day, two hearings pertaining to the Dowalibys were held in Cook County Circuit Court—one on a request by the Department of Children and Family Services for temporary custody of Davey Dowaliby, the other on a petition filed by Ralph Meczyk and Lawrence Hyman requesting that bail be set for David and Cynthia.

At the first hearing, Juvenile Court Judge Robert M. Smierciak found that it was in Davey's best interest to grant temporary custody to the state. However, Smierciak said he would review the arrangement on December 7. He ordered Children and Family Services to report at that time on the possibility of placing Davey with John and Rose Medema, his uncle and aunt.

At the second hearing, Judge Michael B. Bolan heard arguments for low bail by the defense and no bail by the prosecution.

Meczyk and Hyman argued that their clients had shown themselves to be "good risks" by not fleeing during the investigation, even though they knew that they were likely to be arrested.

Patrick O'Brien responded that bail should be denied for two reasons: First, Jaclyn's murder was a potential capital offense; in Illinois, the murder of a child under age twelve carries the death penalty when the death results from "exceptionally brutal or heinous behavior indicative of wanton cruelty." Second, the evidence against the Dowalibys was strong; in Illinois, bail may be denied only if proof of guilt "is evident or the presumption great."

To support his second contention, O'Brien flatly asserted that the rope found around Jaclyn's neck belonged to the Dowaliby family and that a witness, whom he did not name, had placed "a man believed to be David Dowaliby" at the scene of the crime.

"That's weak, very weak," Bolan told O'Brien. "All you've shown is that a homicide occurred. If you want them held on no bond, offer me some evidence."

"That's all I'm prepared to say," O'Brien responded.

Judge Bolan called a recess, saying he wanted to review the law, and went into his chambers—with O'Brien. They returned a few minutes later and, in a turnabout, Bolan proclaimed that he would need no further evidence in order to deny bond, since "another judge found sufficient evidence." He was referring to Judge Cornelius Houtsma, who two days earlier had signed the Dowalibys' arrest warrants and denied bond.

Hyman protested, "There's nothing directly linking my client, Cynthia Dowaliby, to the crime."

"When you strangle a seven-year-old with a rope, it's heinous conduct and wantonly cruel," Bolan shot back, ducking Hyman's point. Jaclyn's murder, Bolan said, was "depraved" and "an act bereft of mercy."

With that, Bolan scheduled a preliminary hearing for December 2 and adjourned court for the Thanksgiving weekend.

David and Cynthia would continue to be held without bail.

While the custody and bail hearings were in progress, Davey Dowaliby was examined at Mount Sinai Hospital's Pediatric Ecology Unit, known by the acronym PEU.

The unit was established in 1986, when Mount Sinai, like many hospitals, was struggling for survival. The next year, the hospital signed a lucrative contract with the state of Illinois under which the PEU would evaluate and treat suspected child-abuse victims.

Patrick T. Murphy, the public guardian of Cook County, whose office represents abused and neglected children, had been critical of the PEU almost since its inception.

"It is a bureaucracy that was set up to find child abuse and, typical of bureaucracies, it becomes a self-fulfilling prophecy," Murphy charged. "Mount Sinai finds just about everyone abused, and in a lot of cases they've really blown it. If you sent a bowling ball there, they would find it had been abused—look, three holes!"

Murphy assigned Jeanette Volpe, an attorney in his office, to represent Davey. This was a routine action to assure that Davey's legal rights were protected, since the Dowalibys' lawyers represented only David's and Cynthia's interests.

Because of the impending Thanksgiving holiday, however, Volpe would not see Davey until Friday. Meanwhile, Davey was left to the devices of the Mount Sinai staff.

Dr. Sharon Ahart, a Mexico-educated physician, gave Davey a genital and rectal examination. Afterward she wrote a report claiming that he showed signs of both sexual and physical abuse.

Although there were "no lacerations, lesions, marks, or tenderness" in Davey's genital area, Ahart found his rectal tone "moderately lax"—a possible sign of sexual abuse. "While doing a rectal exam, I asked him if anyone had put anything in his butt," Ahart wrote. "He spontaneously replied, 'My momma didn't put anything in my butt.' He then became anxious and asked me if I was done."

To support her claim that Davey had been physically abused, Ahart prepared a chart indicating that there were seventeen bruises, scars, sores, and scabs of various sizes on Davey's body, several on his back and shoulders. "I asked him how he got the marks on his shoulders," Ahart wrote. "He stated, 'My momma hit me with a belt.' "

Dean Morask, an assistant state's attorney assigned to juvenile cases, was informed of Ahart's conclusions. Taking what Ahart said at face value, Morask arranged for the Chicago Police Department to photograph Davey's body from various angles.

The police photos showed that all of the marks described by Ahart either had been grossly exaggerated or did not exist. Mount Sinai personnel, unaware that the photos contradicted Ahart's findings, continued their evaluation of Davey.

Noel Kalinowski, a Mount Sinai child development specialist, gave Davey a test assessing his personal and social skills, fine motor-adaptive skills, language ability, and gross motor development. Kalinowski found Davey's performance on each area of the test was "age-appropriate" and "well developed."

Then Detective Caauwe appeared on the scene. In a meeting with Kalinowski and Stanley Luke, a Mount Sinai psychologist, he presented "evidence" supporting the view that David and Cynthia had killed Jaclyn.

Caauwe claimed that both parents had failed polygraph tests. He said that when Cynthia was taken into custody, "she showed no reaction and never asked about Davey." She had a pair of Jaclyn's underwear in her purse—"a strange thing to carry around as a remembrance of your dead child." When David had learned that Jaclyn's body had been found, he had said, "I suppose you want me to cry now."

Caauwe added, "When we found Jaclyn's body, we had to pull possums away from it. From the waist up, she was mostly a skeleton and her hair fell off like a wig."

After Caauwe's briefing, Kalinowski conducted an hour-long "child-development interview" with Davey in a room containing a large dollhouse and dolls.

From a small observation room, Assistant State's Attorney

Dean Morask, several police officers, including Caauwe, and Helene Schaefer, a Children and Family Services caseworker, watched portions of the interview through a two-way mirror. The interview was not electronically recorded, but Kalinowski wrote a report on her version of the session.

After a few background questions, Kalinowski asked, "Does Mom drink beer, wine, or booze?"

"She drinks wine," Davey answered.

"How does she act when she drinks?"

"She acts just fine."

"Does Mom use drugs, smoke pot?"

"She cooks with a pot."

"What happens at home when you are naughty?"

Davey gave no response.

"What happened to Jaclyn if Mom got mad at her?"

"Spank her."

"With what?"

"My dad's belt."

"Were her clothes on or off when she got spanked?"

"Hit her here," Davey said, pulling down his pajama bottom and pointing to his bare buttocks.

"What would Dad do when he got mad at Jaclyn?"

"I don't know."

"Can you tell me what happened when Jaclyn died?"

"God wanted her. That's why they broke in. The men were gonna take her to Heaven."

"Did anyone tell you not to talk about what happened that night?"

"No."

At this point Kalinowski showed Davey a pair of so-called anatomically correct dolls. He inserted his finger into the vaginal area of the female doll.

Using the male doll, Kalinowski asked him to show her places where he liked to be touched.

"I don't like to be naked," he said.

Davey undressed the dolls, and Kalinowski asked him, "Did you ever get all naked at home?"

"Yeah."

"Who would get all naked?"

"Me, Mom, and Jaclyn. Dad was gone. We were in the bedroom all naked. We would play a game."

"What kind of game?"

Davey gave no response.

Kalinowski wrote a report concluding "patient's statements are consistent with a history of sexual abuse, and physical abuse to his sister, Jaclyn."

Helene Schaefer, the caseworker who watched the interview, wrote a report drawing no such conclusion. Her report contained several details that were not in Kalinowski's report. In fact, Schaefer made it clear that some of the things that Davey said were fanciful. She quoted Davey as saying, for instance, that his father worked at a White Castle restaurant and that Jaclyn slept in the kitchen.

Schaefer's report was supported by contemporaneous notes, which she preserved. There was no such corroboration for Kalinowski's report; she destroyed her notes.

Shortly after the interview, Mount Sinai radiologists completed a report on the X rays taken of Davey, finding "no evidence of fracture or bony destruction"—conditions associated with abuse.

At 9:15 P.M., a Mount Sinai nurse put Davey to bed crying. "I want to go home," he pleaded as the nurse hugged and coddled him until he fell asleep.

That night, Cynthia dreamed that she heard Davey calling her. She sat up in bed and looked around until she realized that she was alone, in an isolation cell, at the county jail.

On Thanksgiving evening, Channel 7's Dick Johnson broke an anonymously sourced story on what he described as a "disturbing side of this family tragedy."

Channel 7 had learned exclusively, Johnson reported, that Davey Dowaliby allegedly had been "physically and possibly sexually abused." Johnson said that the "shocking" findings had been made by hospital personnel.

David Dowaliby was watching the Channel 7 news that night with a guard at the county jail. When Johnson concluded the report, the guard glared at David, kicked a chair, and stalked out of the room.

The *Tribune* picked up Johnson's story, reporting that the Dowaliby family "may have more trouble around the corner" because of allegations that Davey had "a number of bruises on his body."

On the day after Thanksgiving, caseworker Marlon Daniels interviewed Rose and John Medema, David's sister and brother-in-law, and Ann Dowaliby at the Medema home in Midlothian.

The Medemas, junior high school special education teachers and the parents of two young sons, told Daniels that Davey could stay with them while his parents were in jail. Davey could have his own room, the Medemas said, and Ann Dowaliby would baby-sit in their home while they were at work.

Daniels then interviewed Ann. He told her that marks had been found on Davey's body, giving rise to concern that he might have been physically abused. Ann told him there had been no marks on Davey's body when she dressed him in the presence of two police officers the morning he was taken away.

As Daniels left, he told the Medemas that a decision on Davey's placement would be made soon and he would notify them. That afternoon, Children and Family Services concluded that Davey would not be placed with the Medemas. Instead, the agency arranged for him to be discharged on Monday to a not-for-profit child-welfare organization known as Hephzibah.

Hephzibah—the name is a biblical term meaning "comforting mother"—operates a temporary shelter for children in the western suburb of Oak Park, about twenty miles from Midlothian.

On Friday afternoon, while Daniels spoke with the Medemas, Noel Kalinowski again interviewed Davey at Mount Sinai. This time Jeanette Volpe, the watchdog from the public guardian's office, was present, as was Assistant State's Attorney Dean Morask. Volpe and Morask observed the interview through the two-way mirror.

Kalinowski gave Davey a black marker and paper and suggested that he draw. After watching for a few minutes, she opened a book titled *Children Don't Lie* and turned to a "physical-abuse chart" that depicted such items as a coat hanger, a knife, a broom, a belt, a rope, an electric cord, and an iron.

Kalinowski asked if he knew what the items were, and he identified all of them. When he identified the knife, he said, "My mom didn't spank me with a knife."

"Did she spank you with anything?" Kalinowski asked.

"She used to spank me with a belt," Davey answered.

"What part of your body would she spank?"

He pointed to his buttocks.

"Were your clothes on or off?"

"Like, pull them down."

"Which part of the belt did Mom use, the strap or the buckle?"

He pointed to the strap and said, "My sister is always the one that always gets spanked so much."

"Where was she when she got spanked?"

"In her room."

"What would Mommy spank her with?"

Davey's response would be disputed. According to Kalinowski, he pointed to the broom, the belt—and the rope. According to Volpe, Davey paid no attention to Kalinowski and merely "scribble-scrabbled" on the chart.

Kalinowski next asked about the night Jaclyn disappeared, and Davey said that his mother said a "magic word" to make Jaclyn go to sleep.

"When she made Jaclyn go to sleep, did she wake up again?" Kalinowski asked.

"No, you can't come back from Heaven," Davey said. "I'm not gonna be mad at the men that stole her."

"Was she asleep before the men stole her?"

"Yeah."

"How do you know?"

"That's right, I had a dream last night. Castles came here full of mean kings."

Kalinowski then asked him about other family members, specifically John and Rose Medema.

Davey said they were his aunt and uncle and the parents of his cousins, Johnny and Matt. He quickly added, "Nobody should have told you their names. I don't want nobody to know those names."

"Why?" Kalinowski asked.

"Because," Davey answered, banging his marker on the chart as his voice trailed off.

Kalinowski ended the interview, and concluded in her report that Davey's statements were "consistent with a history of physical abuse to himself and Jaclyn."

Volpe disagreed. "Davey didn't understand what was happening to him," she would say. "The Mount Sinai worker questioned him over and over again about his parents and his sister. He was being pressed for information that he clearly didn't have."

The next day, Mount Sinai psychologist Stanley Luke spoke with Davey, who said he wanted to go home to his parents. Luke told him that would not be possible because his parents were "with the police to get more information from them regarding Jaclyn's death."

"Are they in jail?" Davey asked.

"Yes," Luke replied.

Davey broke into tears, but, according to Luke's report on the session, "seemed to accept this news fairly well."

After Luke left, however, a nurse wrote on Davey's chart that he was hysterical and required constant comforting. After the nurse settled him down, she noted, he washed his hands compulsively. When he finally went to sleep, according to the chart, he repeatedly kicked off his covers and tossed around in the bed with his arms flailing.

Throughout Sunday, according to a report by Mount Sinai social worker Toni Brucato, Davey cried continuously, saying he missed his parents and wanted to go home.

That night, the Medemas, Ann Dowaliby, and Cynthia's mother, Mary Malia, arrived at Mount Sinai; it was the first time since his hospitalization five days earlier that Davey had been allowed visitors.

Brucato, however, refused to allow Mary to see her grandson because her name was not on the approved visitors' list. Brucato wrote on Davey's chart that Mary was "tearful, angry, and defensive" and quoted her as saying that "this entire situation is wrong."

John, Rose, and Ann, whose names were on the approved list, were allowed to see Davey separately in the PEU on the eleventh floor. They were told they each could spend no more than fifteen minutes with Davey.

John went up first. "Hi, Davey," he said as Brucato ushered him into the room. Davey, wearing a hospital gown, sat straight and motionless on a chair.

"I know you," Davey said.

"Yes, I'm your Uncle John."

Davey said nothing. "He seemed like he was in shock," John would say later. "That was not Davey."

Rose went up next. "Would you like a hug?" she asked Davey. He clung to her. "That was not normal behavior for him," Rose would say. "He was not a cuddly kid. He didn't sit on people's laps."

Rose sat beside him and could see that his lower lip was quivering and his shoulders were drawn in. "I could only think, 'My God, what have they done to him?' " she said.

Rose said she was afraid to say anything because Brucato was taking notes. "I was worried that I might say something wrong and she would write it down," Rose recalled.

After Rose returned to the lobby, Ann went upstairs. She noticed that Davey was wearing the same pair of socks she had put on him five days earlier.

Ann bent over to hug him, knowing he thought she was responsible for sending him to Mount Sinai, and told him, "Oh, I missed you so much."

Hands by his side, Davey told her, "I want to go home. When I come home, I'm not going to do bad things. I'm not going to hit Jaclyn."

Then, wringing his hands, he said, "They told me Mommy and Daddy are in jail."

"Don't worry," Ann said, "they'll be out soon."

"You're not allowed to tell him that," Brucato interrupted.

Ann attempted to change the subject. "Just think of all the

nice things we're going to do when you come home," she said.

"You shouldn't make him any promises," Brucato declared.

When it was time for Ann to leave, Davey cried uncontrollably.

"Davey thought it was within my power to bring him home," Ann would say. "I told him to go with the police, and I lied when I said they would bring him right back. I betrayed him. He'll hold it against me for a long, long time."

On Monday, Mary Anne Brown, director of Hephzibah, went to Mount Sinai to pick up Davey. A nurse took him to change his shirt and to say good-bye to Sharon Ahart. Then Brown and Davey left in Brown's car for the half-hour drive to Hephzibah.

In the car, Davey talked about such things as the neighborhoods they passed, the children he would meet at Hephzibah, and whether she knew that his sister had died. Davey assured her he always ate all of his vegetables.

When they arrived at Hephzibah, according to Brown, Davey was relieved to discover that there was a chimney for Santa Claus.

Once inside, Brown introduced Davey to the other children living there. Brown then spent a little time alone with Davey. She asked Davey what he would like to do. He said he would like to see his parents. She promised to talk to the judge about that, not realizing Davey did not know what a judge was. He asked her to draw a picture of one, which she tried to do.

At dinner, after the children said grace, Davey asked if they also would say a prayer for his sister, Jaclyn, who, he told them, was dead. The children promptly agreed, and repeated grace. Davey thanked them and began eating.

During the meal, he asked if any of the children had moms and dads in jail. Several hands went up.

"Whew," Davey said, "now I don't need to be embarrassed."

THE INDICTMENTS

On Monday, November 28, a three-judge panel of the Illinois Appellate Court acted on an emergency petition filed by Ralph Meczyk and Lawrence Hyman requesting bail and an immediate preliminary hearing for the Dowalibys.

The appellate panel ordered Judge Michael Bolan to hold the preliminary hearing "forthwith" and, if he found that there was enough evidence to prosecute the Dowalibys, nevertheless to reconsider his denial of bail.

The next day, Meczyk and Hyman presented Judge Bolan with the Appellate Court order and asked that the hearing, previously scheduled for December 2, be held immediately. Prosecutor Patrick O'Brien, however, told Bolan that he needed several more days to interview key witnesses.

Bolan lofted *Black's Law Dictionary* and proclaimed

that "forthwith" meant only "as soon as practical." That would be Friday, December 2, Bolan announced—the same day he had set for the hearing before the Appellate Court intervened.

The November 30 *Chicago Tribune* carried a prophetic story by its criminal courts reporter, Matt O'Connor.

"It is possible that the state could go before the Cook County grand jury on or before Friday and announce indictments in court before Judge Bolan," O'Connor wrote. "If that happens, there would be no preliminary hearing."

For the prosecution, there was an advantage to obtaining grand jury indictments at this point: Indictments cut off the right to a preliminary hearing, which would be open to the public and would expose the circumstantial nature of the evidence. Grand jury sessions are, by law, secret.

Moreover, prosecutors have more control over a grand jury than over a preliminary hearing. A grand jury hears only the evidence that prosecutors choose to present. Defense lawyers do not cross-examine witnesses, as they do at a preliminary hearing. Given the one-sided nature of grand jury proceedings, indictments are returned in virtually all cases that prosecutors present.*

On Friday, O'Brien appeared before the November Cook County grand jury just hours before its term was to expire. He called two witnesses, Daniel McDevitt and Assistant State's Attorney Dean Morask.

Despite the requirement of secrecy, a transcript of the session would find its way into the hands of journalists, but not until after the trial.

The transcript showed that O'Brien and his witnesses led the grand jurors to believe that there had been no intruder at the Dowaliby home, that five eyewitnesses had linked David Dowaliby or the Malibu to the Islander Apartments, and that the Dowalibys were child-abusers.

---

* In November 1988, according to figures released by the Cook County state's attorney's office, 837 cases were presented to the grand jury—and indictments were returned in all but 1 case.

McDevitt was up first. After a few preliminary questions, O'Brien turned to the evidence, asking leading questions that would elicit affirmative responses. Referring to the basement window, he asked, "At the time that this window was examined, it was found that dust on the inside windowsill was not disturbed?"

"Yes, sir," McDevitt replied, omitting the fact that there was no contemporaneous record of any dust.

"Did you learn in your investigation that the Dowalibys stated that at the time they went to bed on Friday night all the doors to the house had been closed and locked?" O'Brien asked.

"Yes, closed, locked, and bolted," said McDevitt. In fact, police reports quoted David as saying that he locked and bolted only the front door; Ann Dowaliby had gone out the rear door after David went to bed, and police reports did not refer to the sliding patio door.

McDevitt next testified that the medical examiner had ruled that Jaclyn's death resulted from strangulation and that a rope had been found wrapped around her neck. However, McDevitt was not asked and did not volunteer that a Negroid hair had been found on the rope.

Turning to the Islander Apartments, O'Brien asked whether Everett Mann had seen a Chevrolet Malibu—the kind of car owned by Cynthia Dowaliby—pulling away from the area where Jaclyn's body later was found.

"Yes, sir," McDevitt answered, although Mann had claimed only that the car he saw resembled a Malibu. McDevitt did not mention that Mann consistently had described the car as dark-colored, while Cynthia's Malibu was light blue.

"And was Everett Mann shown a photo array and did he pick out the picture of David Dowaliby?" O'Brien asked.

"Yes, sir, he selected Mr. Dowaliby's picture," McDevitt answered, incorrectly suggesting that Mann had been positive in the identification. The grand jury was not told that

Mann had claimed only that David's nose structure resembled that of the driver.*

O'Brien asked if, on the trunk liner of Cynthia's Malibu, head hairs had been found "which were visually similar to Jaclyn Dowaliby's head hairs."

"Yes, sir," McDevitt answered, suggesting that Jaclyn's body might have been in the trunk—a possibility virtually excluded by the State Crime Laboratory's finding that no fibers on the trunk liner had come from Jaclyn's bedspread or nightgown.

"Did the crime lab determine that Jaclyn's pillow showed two areas which turned out to be human blood?" O'Brien asked.

"Yes," McDevitt answered, not mentioning that the stains were tiny and predated Jaclyn's disappearance.

O'Brien asked whether investigators had located two witnesses, Gloria Lake and Derrick Darling, who "on the late evening of September 13" saw a four-door blue Chevrolet Malibu in the Islander Apartments parking lot.

"That's correct," McDevitt said, although Lake and Darling had told investigators that they saw the blue Malibu not "in the late evening" but in the early afternoon—when the Dowalibys were in the company of police.

Turning to David's allegedly self-incriminating statements, O'Brien asked, "In an interview on September 11, was David Dowaliby asked by the investigators if any of the neighbors had heard or observed anything on Friday, September 9, and into Saturday morning, September 10?"

"Yes, he was," McDevitt answered.

"And was his response to that statement, 'After the *death*?'?"

"Yes, sir." In fact, the police report on which these questions were based quoted David as responding, "After the *ac-*

---

* In a sworn statement on October 26, 1990, McDevitt would admit, "I didn't take Mr. Mann's identification to be a positive." *In Re: In the Interest of David Dowaliby*, Cook County Circuit Court, Juvenile Division, No. 88 J 20093, McDevitt deposition, p. 61.

cident?" (David later claimed that he actually said, "After the *incident*?")

When David was informed that Jaclyn's body had been found, O'Brien asked, "Did he ask if it was found in a field?"

"Yes," McDevitt said. The grand jurors were not told either that David knew investigators were searching for Jaclyn in fields, or that Linda Petrine, the psychic, had told David that Jaclyn would be found in a field.

O'Brien also asked about allegedly inconsistent statements attributed to Cynthia—that she first had claimed to have been the person who discovered Jaclyn missing, but later said that David was searching for Jaclyn before she, Cynthia, got up.

The question was based on an apparent error in a police report of an interview with Cynthia. Contrary to the report, the handwritten notes of the interview quoted Cynthia as saying that the search began "before Ann returned home"—not before Cynthia got up.

Nonetheless, McDevitt unhesitatingly answered that Cynthia had made the inconsistent statements.

Finally, O'Brien asked, "From the time the body was found until the arrest of David and Cynthia Dowaliby, did either of them inquire of the police regarding the status of the investigation?"

"Never," said McDevitt. The answer was misleading, since the Dowalibys' lawyers had inquired about the status of the investigation repeatedly during that period.

O'Brien then showed the grand jurors twenty photographs of Jaclyn's decomposed body and twenty-one autopsy photographs.

"At this time, I would have no further questions of this witness," he said.

However, the grand jurors had questions of their own, most pertaining to Everett Mann's sighting.

"Was it Mr. Mann who saw the car and the defendant, Mr. Dowaliby, in the car?" one grand juror asked.

"Yes, ma'am," McDevitt said.

"He identified him from photos?"

"He initially described the vehicle and then described the driver of the vehicle."

"It's well lit?"

"That section you have to drive through was fairly lit." In fact, in the audiotaped interview with police, Mann had said that the area was poorly lit. Moreover, the grand jury was not told that Mann had been seventy-five yards away when he allegedly saw the car and the driver's nose structure.

Another grand juror asked McDevitt, "Did you learn from your canvass of the building in the area that David Dowaliby had actually been seen in that area, in and around those buildings?"

"We had a couple identify a photo of David Dowaliby, indicating that they had seen him in an apartment near where the body was found," McDevitt said. "They identified him, as well as his automobile and his pickup truck."

McDevitt was referring to statements by Melvin and Lavern Buckley, residents of the Islander Apartments, who had claimed, after prompting by police, that they had seen David Dowaliby visit an apartment in their building. McDevitt failed to mention that the couple who lived in the apartment said that they had never seen David.

The grand jurors' remaining questions dealt with whether the Dowalibys could be subpoenaed to testify. O'Brien declined to respond, but asked McDevitt, "Did you receive any notification from the attorneys of the Dowalibys whether they would invoke their Fifth Amendment rights?"

"That's exactly what they told us, sir," McDevitt answered.

A persistent grand juror suggested calling David Dowaliby as a witness, even if it meant holding the matter over for a new grand jury. "I am just trying to find out how can we get him here and have another grand jury because our time limit will be out," the grand juror said.

Before O'Brien responded, the grand juror added, "Today, you are asking for an indictment?"

"Yes," O'Brien pressed.

There were no further questions, and McDevitt was excused.

O'Brien called Dean Morask, who, along with Jeanette

Volpe, of the public guardian's office, had observed the November 25 interview of Davey Dowaliby at Mount Sinai Hospital.

O'Brien asked Morask whether Davey had said, "My sister's always the one that always gets spanked so much."

"He said that," Morask said.

"Was he further asked, 'What would Mommy spank her with?' and did he point to a book that contained pictures of a broom, a belt, and a rope?"

"That's correct," Morask replied, although Jeanette Volpe would strongly dispute the contention that Davey pointed to any pictures in the book.

O'Brien asked several questions about Dr. Sharon Ahart's physical examination of Davey, showing him the body chart on which Ahart had indicated evidence of injuries.

Morask testified that he had seen Ahart's report and the body chart, but he did not reveal the existence of police photographs showing that there had been no unusual marks on Davey's body—photographs Morask himself had ordered.

"I have no further questions of this witness," O'Brien said.

A grand juror asked whether Davey ever had been asked whether his parents whipped him.

"I believe he was asked that question," Morask said.

"Do you know his answer?"

"I don't remember the answer." In fact, Davey had been asked that question in Morask's presence and had denied ever being whipped by his parents.

Morask was excused.

The grand jury then voted indictments, charging Cynthia and David Dowaliby with first-degree murder and concealment of a homicide.

The indictments would be kept secret until, as Matt O'Connor's *Tribune* story suggested, they were announced on December 2, just before the preliminary hearing would have begun before Judge Bolan.

Regardless of the validity of the evidence presented to the grand jury, the indictments served the short-term purposes of the police and prosecutors, bringing the state into compliance with the Appellate Court order.

There would be no messy preliminary hearing, and the indictments increased the psychological pressure on the Dowalibys—a key element in the police strategy to break their resolve.

On December 1, Catherine Ryan and Janet Trafelet, lawyers whom the Dowalibys had hired for the juvenile case on Ralph Meczyk's recommendation, appeared before Judge Robert Smierciak. They asked that Davey be allowed to visit his parents in jail and move in with his uncle and aunt, John and Rose Medema.

Assistant State's Attorney Revelle Peritz opposed both requests. She said that the Dowalibys might "pressure" Davey during visits and, if he were placed with the Medemas, he might hear conversations about the murder of his sister.

Faith Salsburg, representing Children and Family Services, argued that visitation should be permitted because Davey "needs to know his parents are alive," but opposed placing him with the Medemas. Davey should continue to live in the "neutral environment" of Hephzibah, Salsburg said, adding that his mood had brightened since he was moved there the previous Monday.

Mary Anne Brown of Hephzibah testified in favor of visitation, saying, "He wants to see his parents. He's lost his sister and now he's lost his parents."

Judge Smierciak ordered that Davey be permitted to visit his parents and said he would rule later on whether Davey should be allowed to live with the Medemas.

After the hearing, Public Guardian Patrick Murphy publicly accused police, prosecutors, and Mount Sinai personnel of mistreating Davey. "What they did to the kid, I think, was unconscionable," Murphy told reporters. "They questioned him like a defendant. They were trying to get him as a witness."

On Friday, December 2, Cynthia and David Dowaliby were led into Judge Michael Bolan's courtroom from separate holding areas behind the bench.

They had not seen each other since leaving the Blue Island

Police Department for the Cook County Jail eight days earlier. Now they were not permitted to touch but, as they took seats at the defense table beside Meczyk and Hyman, each whispered "I love you" to the other.

Patrick O'Brien and his assistant George Velcich were seated at the prosecution table, and the courtroom was packed with reporters and relatives and friends of the Dowalibys.

The purpose of the session was purely perfunctory: to have the indictments read in open court.

Minutes later, the Dowalibys were arraigned before Judge Richard J. Fitzgerald, the presiding judge of the Criminal Division of the Circuit Court. They pleaded not guilty, and the case was assigned to Judge Richard E. Neville.

Neville was chosen randomly by computer from a group of ten Criminal Court judges whom Judge Fitzgerald had deemed eligible to handle "heater cases"—cases that would receive widespread news media attention. Other judges did not hear such cases for a variety of reasons, ranging from inexperience to temperament that might embarrass the system.

Ralph Meczyk and Lawrence Hyman had mixed feelings about drawing Neville. He was a former prosecutor and son of a Chicago police officer but was regarded as an iconoclast—capable of tough decisions that might not be to the liking of the state's attorney's office. His sympathies might lie with the prosecution, but less so than many other judges who might have been assigned the case.

After the arraignment, Meczyk told reporters that the Dowalibys "are ready for their day in court." Referring to the scores of relatives and friends who had been in the courtroom, Meczyk added, "They are here for support. They think it's terrible what's happening. They think it's an outrage that they took a little boy away and locked up the mother and father, while the real killer is going unpunished."

Chicago's weekend newspapers carried major stories about the developments in the case, but another story received greater play—Richard Daley's press conference to announce formally his candidacy for mayor of Chicago.

LOOKING THROUGH THE GLASS

With Judge Smierciak's blessing, Davey visited his parents at Cook County Jail.

Mary Anne Brown, the executive director of Hephzibah, took him to see his mother first and then his father. The initial visit to each was a "contact visit," meaning that they were permitted to touch each other.

Brown described the first time Davey saw his mother since her arrest: "It was very heartfelt. He sat on his mom's lap and stroked her face. She said she loved him, and he said he loved her. There were a lot of hugs and kisses. Cynthia reminded Davey to say his prayers—and that he should pray for Jaclyn.

"Davey tried to reassure her that he was okay. We brought pictures of him at Hephzibah, so that she could visualize where he was. Cynthia asked him what he had been eating, and he said, 'Yogurt.' She said that was good. She gave him a package of crackers that she had saved from one of her meals. We had brought some cookies but weren't allowed to give them to her.

"We spent an hour. The visit ended abruptly because the time seemed to go so quickly. He didn't cry. He was prepared, and he knew he was going to see his dad next. When we left, Cynthia waved until we were out of sight. Davey kept turning around and waving."

Brown then led Davey to the men's section of the jail. "A funny thing happened on the way," she said. "Davey decided to hide the cookies in his pockets and try to sneak them in to his dad. When the guards searched him, he told them, 'Don't crumble the cookies.' They laughed and let him take them inside.

"The visit was very playful. You could tell that there were a lot of things that they did together. They shared the cookies, and David laughed when Davey said, 'I'm a cute little boy, aren't I, Dad?' David drew a picture of himself and wrote, 'I love you.' Davey put it up on the wall of his bedroom and saved it the whole time he was at Hephzibah.

"The visit was supposed to be an hour, but the guard gave us some extra time. When we finally had to leave, David helped him put on his coat and said he had grown taller. When Davey whispered 'I love you,' his dad cried. It was a tearful good-bye, very emotional, but Davey handled it pretty well.

"Both parents helped him adjust to the situation. They tried to demystify where they were. They told him that they could watch TV and that they watched some of the same things he watched."

Contact visits normally are not allowed at the jail. They were permitted initially for the Dowalibys only because Brown was insistent, incorrectly believing that Smierciak had ordered them. After the first visits, however, jail officials checked with Judge Smierciak and learned that he had ordered no departure from the jail's routine.

During subsequent visits, Davey and his parents were separated by a plate glass panel and bars. They spoke through louvered devices like those in ticket booths at movie theaters and drive-through banks.

"It was difficult because they obviously were used to touching each other, but David and Cynthia made the best of it," Brown said. "They weren't about to waste the visits.

"Cynthia and Davey pretended that they were in a spaceship, like it was something out of a movie they had seen together. She read him a book. She had to hold it up to the glass so that he could see the pictures while she turned the pages.

"Both parents focused a lot on him. They would ask what he ate and what he did. They were very concerned that he would see the media coverage and that it would add to his anxiety.

"During the first visit, David gave Davey an Oreo cookie that one of the other prisoners had saved for him. Davey carried it around in his pocket for a long time, and we finally had to throw it away."

For Brown, the jail visits confirmed a conclusion that other Hephzibah staff members had begun to draw—that Davey did not appear to be an abused child; Mount Sinai had been wrong.

"Davey had wonderful rapport with his mom and dad," Brown said. "This was one of the most conclusive pieces of evidence. To have his sister die and his parents disappear was pretty alarming to him, but he was on target for a four-year-old—just a regular kid."

On December 5, Ralph Meczyk and Lawrence Hyman renewed their effort to have bail set for the Dowalibys. Appearing before Judge Richard Neville, they argued that bonds of $100,000 each would be sufficient to ensure that David and Cynthia would appear in court.

Meczyk called the evidence against David "merely conjectural and certainly circumstantial." Against Cynthia, Hyman said, "the state has produced not a scintilla of evidence."

Patrick O'Brien abandoned his earlier demand that bail be denied, thus avoiding a dispute over whether the evidence of guilt was "great," the requirement for denying bail in Illinois. O'Brien argued instead for high bail—$1,000,000 each.

After listening to the arguments, Neville set bail at

$800,000 for David and $300,000 for Cynthia. That did not mean they actually would have to post $1,100,000 to be released. Under an Illinois bail reform measure enacted in 1963, defendants are required to post only 10 percent of the bail amount, but are liable for the balance if they fail to appear in court.*

Thus the Dowalibys could be released by posting $110,000. That was more than they had. In an effort to bring the amount within reach of the family's resources, Meczyk and Hyman filed a motion to reduce bail with the Illinois Appellate Court.

On Thursday, December 15, the Appellate Court granted the defense motion without explanation. Having previously ordered Judge Bolan to hold a preliminary hearing "forthwith," the Appellate Court now was intervening for the second time with an order favorable to the Dowalibys. Cynthia's bond was cut to $100,000, meaning that she could be released by posting $10,000, and David's to $500,000, meaning that he would need $50,000.

Cynthia's bond was posted that afternoon, thanks to gifts and loans from family members and friends. Meanwhile, money was pouring in to secure David's release.

Cynthia learned from a 5:00 P.M. television newscast that she was to be released. A few minutes later, a guard appeared. "Get your stuff," said the guard. "You're outta here."

Outside the jail, Meczyk, Hyman, and a horde of reporters and camera crews waited. When Cynthia came out, wearing

---

*Until 1963, private bail bondsmen posted collateral for the full amount of defendants' bail, charging a 10 percent fee for the service. If a defendant failed to appear in court, the collateral was forfeited, at least theoretically. The Illinois General Assembly changed the system in response to newspaper disclosures that judges were not requiring the forfeitures. The change eliminated private bondsmen and put the state into the bail bond business, allowing defendants to secure their release by posting 10 percent of the amount set by the court. The "reform" soon led to abuses exposed in the federal investigation known as Operation Greylord. As detailed on pages 41–42, Ralph Meczyk was convicted in 1987 of failing to pay taxes on money he received through refunds of clients' bail bonds.

her green corduroy jacket, she stood silently beside Hyman as he made a brief statement.

"Cynthia Dowaliby would like to tell you that she and her husband are innocent," he said. "They are grieving over their loss, and she wishes to go home."

Seconds later, Cynthia climbed into a BMW that Hyman had borrowed for the occasion, and he drove her around the block where her mother, Mary Malia, was waiting. They embraced and headed for the Dowaliby home.

When they arrived, Ann Dowaliby was sitting at the kitchen table, counting piles of cash and checks, mostly in small denominations. The total fell just short of the $50,000 needed for David's bail. With a few calls to friends who were willing to dig deeper, they made it.

The next morning at the jail, David anxiously awaited a daily ritual—the opening of the cells and the ensuing dash of prisoners to three telephones. That morning would be his first chance to talk to Cynthia in the twenty-four days since their arrest.

David's cell was on the upper level of a two-level tier. The telephones were on the lower level. When the cells were opened, he jumped over the upper level railing, landing on his feet, and was first to the phones.

He immediately got through to Cynthia, who told him that the family had raised enough money to make his bail. David was astounded; he had no idea that his family and friends would respond with so much so quickly.

Late that afternoon, Ann Dowaliby and Rose Medema met Hyman at the county jail to post the bond with $50,000 cash. It took quite some time to count out the money, most of it in tens and twenties, which Ann had hidden in a bag under her blouse.

When David finally was brought to the jail lobby, he was disappointed that Cynthia was not there, but he appreciated the reason: She had gone to Hephzibah to see Davey for the first time since her release.

After embracing his mother and sister, David left with Hyman through a rear door, abetted by a friendly deputy sheriff. Ann and Rose, in an effort to distract reporters and television crews, went out the front door.

One camera crew, however, captured glimpses of David and Hyman's exit. That night, television viewers saw a defendant and his lawyer speeding off in a BMW.

On December 19, Ralph L. Meyer, Jr., a forensic scientist for the Illinois State Police, shattered Daniel McDevitt's belief that the Dowalibys' basement window had been broken from the inside.

By analyzing how the broken pieces of the window fit together, Meyer determined the direction of the force that broke it: "The window was broken from the outside in, and not the inside out," he concluded.

McDevitt's illusion had been based on the presence of several large pieces of glass outside the home. It is true that, when a window breaks, large pieces tend to fall in the direction of the force. However, glass is resilient and pieces may fall in either direction.

Moreover, McDevitt had not allowed for another possibility—that an intruder, after breaking the window, might have enlarged the opening by removing pieces that remained in the frame and placing them on the ground outside.

All in all, it had not been Daniel McDevitt's best week.

First, the Dowalibys had been released from jail without the expected confession. Then the state's own forensic report on the window disproved the centerpiece of McDevitt's theory of the case—that the Dowalibys, needing to create evidence of an intruder but not wanting to risk being seen, had broken the window from the inside.

After their release, David and Cynthia visited Davey regularly at Hephzibah, an expansive, homey, two-story red brick building in Oak Park, a forty-five-minute drive from Midlothian.

On Christmas they arrived with arms filled with gifts. The Hephzibah staff provided others from a list supplied by David and Cynthia while they were in jail. For Davey, however, the best present, a GI Joe airplane, came from Santa Claus.

David and Davey sat on the floor, assembling the plane. Then Davey helped Cynthia prepare a breakfast of scrambled eggs, biscuits, and gravy, which they shared with Mary Anne Brown.

After a tearful parting, David and Cynthia drove to St. Mary's Cemetery. Approaching Jaclyn's still-unmarked grave, they saw a wreath on a tripod stuck into the frozen ground. At the top of the wreath, taped to a red bow, was a quarter.

Like the red silk rose found on the grave shortly after Jaclyn's burial, the appearance and message of the wreath were mysteries that family members would struggle endlessly to understand.

In mid-January, the Department of Children and Family Services finally completed its investigation of John and Rose Medema and recommended that they be awarded temporary custody of Davey.

Judge Smierciak promptly accepted the recommendation.

Davey left Hephzibah on January 20 to join the Medemas, who lived near the Dowalibys. The home had a large yard, where Davey could play with his cousins, Matthew and John, Jr.

The change was a vast improvement for Davey, but still disappointing. Under Judge Smierciak's order, Davey was permitted to see his parents only twelve hours a week and was not allowed to be alone with them.

The following month, Richard Daley vanquished two opponents in the Democratic mayoral primary, guaranteeing his election over token Republican opposition. He would be replaced as state's attorney by Cecil A. Partee, an African-American Democratic machine politician.

Partee would pursue the politically safe course that Daley had set for the Dowaliby case—to leave it in the hands of the courts.

* * *

On February 7, Ralph Meczyk and a defense investigator, Patrick Daugherty, approached Everett Mann at a downtown Chicago Transit Authority ticket booth where he was working.

Meczyk wanted to ask Mann about the car he claimed to have seen in the Islander Apartments parking lot. Mann was busy but agreed to meet them two days later.

Over bowls of soup at the Mall Restaurant in downtown Chicago, Mann told Meczyk and Daugherty why he believed that the car was a late seventies Chevrolet Malibu: His Air Force sergeant, Ralph Styer, had driven a 1976 Malibu.

About half an hour into the discussion, Mann agreed that Daugherty could turn on a tape recorder, and Mann then repeated the gist of what he had just said.

Inexplicably, Meczyk failed to follow up on Mann's statement about the Malibu with a more basic question—how he was able to identify David Dowaliby's photograph. Meczyk also failed to ask anything about the distance from which Mann observed the car and the lighting conditions at the time.

However, Meczyk did elicit one tidbit that would call Mann's identification of the Malibu into question: "You told me that you had a sergeant in the Air Force who had the *exact* car as the one you identified, is that correct?" Meczyk asked.

"Correct," Mann answered.

In fact, the defense would discover, Ralph Styer's 1976 Malibu and Cynthia Dowaliby's 1980 Malibu were strikingly different.

On February 16, Meczyk and Hyman asked Judge Neville to dismiss the indictments of David and Cynthia on the grounds that Patrick O'Brien had engaged in "prosecutorial misconduct" and "serious due process violations" before the grand jury.

"The things that were said in that grand jury room misled the grand jurors into voting the indictment against David Dowaliby," Meczyk told Neville.

Hyman contended that the grand jury heard "not one iota" of evidence connecting Cynthia Dowaliby to Jaclyn's death—

essentially the same argument that Neville had rejected at the bond hearing.

The chance that Neville would dismiss the indictments was near zero because Meczyk and Hyman simply were not in a position to challenge the most misleading statements presented to the grand jury.

Since Meczyk had failed to ask Everett Mann about his so-called identification of David Dowaliby, the defense was unaware that it was not nearly as positive as the grand jury might have assumed from Daniel McDevitt's testimony. Moreover, the defense did not know that Assistant State's Attorney Dean Morask's testimony concerning child abuse was contradicted both by police photographs and by Assistant Public Guardian Jeanette Volpe.

Instead, the defense was reduced to arguing that the indictments should be dismissed because O'Brien had given the grand jury deceptive legal advice.

First, Meczyk claimed, O'Brien had improperly implied that the Dowalibys would refuse to answer questions if summoned to testify. Second, said Meczyk, it had been "absolutely misleading" for O'Brien to suggest that the grand jury might not have the power to compel David Dowaliby to provide a pubic hair sample.

Countering the defense arguments was a cinch for the prosecution.

Assistant State's Attorney George Velcich, whom O'Brien had selected to "second-chair" the case with him, asserted that the grand jury had not been misled about the likelihood of the Dowalibys testifying, since they had refused to cooperate with the police after Jaclyn's body was found.

Velcich added that O'Brien's advice to the grand jury on the question of a pubic hair sample had been "accurate because there is no Illinois case that says that is permissible." He comfortably concluded that "there is nothing in the grand jury transcript at all, anywhere, that is false, that is misleading, or that in any way prejudices these two defendants."

When it was O'Brien's turn to speak, he seized the opportunity to lay out, for the first time publicly, the most damaging allegations that had been presented to the grand jury.

O'Brien said that there was no evidence of a forced entry at the Dowaliby home, other than the broken window, which he called "false information" that the Dowalibys gave to police in an effort to divert attention from themselves.

"It can be concluded," said O'Brien, "that the only people who had an opportunity to kill Jaclyn Dowaliby were her own parents, David and Cynthia Dowaliby."

O'Brien then claimed that an eyewitness had seen David in a Chevrolet Malibu in the Islander Apartments parking lot at about 2:15 A.M. Saturday, September 10.

As McDevitt had done before the grand jury, O'Brien exaggerated what Everett Mann had seen. Referring to Mann without naming him, O'Brien boldly asserted: "He saw one white male in that car. He identified later in a photo array that white male as being David Dowaliby. The Chevy Malibu is owned by the defendants. A photo of that car was shown to that witness and identified."

O'Brien knew, of course, that Mann never had been so positive. This did not trouble O'Brien, since identification testimony usually improves over time. Indeed, Everett Mann's identification of David and the Malibu had gotten better over the course of his conversations with police and prosecutors.

However, what O'Brien did not know was that hard evidence of Mann's initial uncertainty about the identification had been preserved. Locked in Blue Island Chief Paul Greves's desk was a tape recording of the September 16 police interview in which Mann was tentative about everything but the driver's nose.

To O'Brien's horror, the recording eventually would find its way into the hands of the defense. For now, however, O'Brien was on a roll.

Continuing, he asserted that the state crime laboratory had found "human blood" on Jaclyn's pillow but did not specify the amount of blood or its age. Since Meczyk and Hyman had not seen the crime lab report, they could not counter the false implication that the blood was related to Jaclyn's death.

Finally, O'Brien turned to the Mount Sinai report of the November 25 interview with Davey Dowaliby, quoting Davey as saying, "My sister is the one who always gets spanked so much. She was spanked with a broom, a belt, and a rope."

"Judge," O'Brien concluded, "I believe from the evidence that was placed before the grand jury and the fact that we don't have to present all of our evidence to the grand jury that counsel's motion to dismiss should be denied."

Neville agreed. He said that the defense, in essence, had asked him to accept the inferences they drew from the grand jury evidence and to disregard the prosecution's inferences. "I don't believe I can do that," said Neville.

The indictments would stand.

Neville concluded with a civics lesson for reporters. "I believe that it is important for the press to indicate that this hearing has not been a presentation of competent evidence about the guilt or innocence of the defendants," he said. "At a trial, the evidence will be presented in an orderly fashion and someone will determine whether or not it's believable."

The "someone" Neville referred to would be himself or a jury, but his comments recognized that the fourth estate also would play an influential role in the case.

Notwithstanding Neville's admonition, reporters jumped on O'Brien's disclosures of the grand jury evidence.

"Prosecutors reveal Dowaliby evidence," said a February 17 *Tribune* headline over a story reporting O'Brien's sensational references to blood on Jaclyn's pillow and to Davey's statement that Jaclyn "was always the one who got spanked so much."

"The new details were unveiled at a hearing in which defense attorneys sought dismissal of the murder charges," said the story, which prominently quoted O'Brien's line: "The only people who had an opportunity to commit the murder were David and Cynthia Dowaliby."

The story ran twenty-six paragraphs, only three of which quoted the defense lawyers.

Since the Dowalibys were under continuing orders from their attorneys not to talk to reporters, they were unable to tell their side of the story.

The defense point of view was not getting across.

DETECTIVE FOR THE DEFENSE

Sitting in the living room of their condominium in the Hegewisch neighborhood on the far South Side of Chicago, police detective John J. Waters and his wife, Charlotte, had watched the television coverage of the Dowalibys' arrest in November 1988.

As the parents of four children, three of them daughters, John and Charlotte Waters had been horrified by Jaclyn's death. Based on what John Waters saw on television, he confidently told his wife of twenty-eight years, "Oh, they're guilty."

Charlotte Waters accepted her husband's view. He was regarded as an excellent judge of character, whose first impressions usually proved correct. He had honed his judgment both through formal education—he held a degree in social science from DePaul University—and through frontline experience as a hostage negotiator, expert on con games, and burglary detective. Now, at age fifty, John Waters had spent exactly half his life as a Chicago police officer.

A few weeks after Waters had voiced his initial impression of the case, he and Charlotte watched a Channel 7 account of a court appearance by the Dowalibys. Charlotte remarked that Cynthia, now out on bond, looked very different than she looked in handcuffs the day of her arrest. Her long hair freshly permed, she was wearing a stylish black and white dress under a white gabardine coat.

"Oh, yeah," Waters said, "the good old Catholic Church takes care of that." Being a devout Catholic himself, Waters was not being disparaging. He merely was noting the church's reputation among cops for helping members accused of crimes look their best for court.

On the side, Waters worked for a detective agency, Special Operations Associates, which employed moonlighting cops as investigators.

In the first week of April 1989, Ralph Meczyk and Lawrence Hyman turned to the agency for help in the Dowaliby case.

The agency referred the lawyers to Waters, a strapping man, six feet, one inch tall, with hazel eyes and graying dark brown hair receding at the part. Waters was wary about getting involved—his career had been devoted to convicting defendants, not helping them—but he agreed at least to meet with Meczyk and Hyman.

At a meeting in their offices on Saturday, April 8, they briefed him on the facts, telling him why they believed their clients were innocent. They asked him to look at the Dowalibys' broken window, in light of what he knew about burglary. Waters agreed, with the caveat that he would immediately end his involvement if he concluded that the police were correct that there could not have been an intruder.

Waters asked if there had been any similar break-ins in the area. In response to a subpoena a few days earlier, Meczyk and Hyman had received a police report about the burglary at the Midlothian home of Erzsebette Sziky that occurred the night before Jaclyn Dowaliby disappeared.

The report contained several facts that seemed similar to

the Dowalibys' version of what happened at their home: Entry had been made through a bedroom window at about 2:00 A.M., and a screen had been cut. Although there unquestionably had been an intruder, no fingerprints were found. Most important, Sziky had a seven-year-old daughter, Nicole.

Waters, however, was skeptical of a link between the crimes because the report said that Nicole had not been disturbed. It also said that the intruder had taken several things from the home—jewelry, a large glass bottle containing coins, and a radio with a cassette tape player. Nothing of that sort had been taken from the Dowaliby home.

That afternoon, Waters went to the Dowaliby home with a pen and legal pad. He introduced himself to the Dowalibys, who led him through the house and showed him the window. He quickly concluded that there was no doubt—"absolutely no doubt," he would tell his wife that night—that an agile intruder easily could have gone through the window. An intruder would not have crawled through the broken windowpane but instead would have swiveled the window upward and crawled under it.

Waters also noted that what the police had described only as a "smudge" on the basement wall beneath the window was clearly a footprint. An intruder coming through the window feet first on his stomach could have pushed off the wall, leaving the footprint, and avoided disturbing the objects beneath it.

On his legal pad, Waters noted that the police search for fingerprints was deficient. "Police did not dust Ann's bedroom, did not dust mirror, never dusted basement door, Jaclyn's room," he wrote.

During his brief tour of the home, Waters noted the fistmarks on the walls of Davey Dowaliby's room. David explained that his younger brother, Brian, had inflicted the marks several years before David and Cynthia moved into the home.

That evening, Waters visited the Sziky home. He noted several facts not in the police report that seemed to strengthen the possibility of a link between the Sziky and Dowaliby crimes. For one thing, the Sziky home turned out to be a basement apartment, and the window through which the intruder entered was about the same size as the Dowalibys' broken basement window. The window swiveled upward, just like the Dowaliby window.

Waters also discovered that while the police report described the Sziky window only as a bedroom window, it was in fact seven-year-old Nicole's bedroom window. Nicole happened to be sleeping in another bedroom the night of the break-in.

Most interesting, Erzsebette Sziky told Waters that the intruder might have been preparing to take her daughter. She said that after the intruder fled, she immediately checked Nicole and found her asleep beneath blankets that she had not been covered with earlier.

Sziky said she thought nothing of the covers initially. The possible significance occurred to her only after she learned that Jaclyn Dowaliby had been found wrapped in a blanket. She said she had not contacted the police after her discovery because she wanted to stay out of the glare of publicity surrounding the Dowaliby case.

Waters thanked Sziky for the information and then drove to the Dowaliby home, measuring the distance on his odometer. The homes were only seven tenths of a mile apart.

Based on his initial discussions and a day of gumshoeing, Waters thought it was possible that the Dowalibys might indeed be innocent. After church on Sunday, he began combing police reports and court transcripts; what he found strengthened that possibility in his mind.

Waters wrote on his legal pad that the Negroid hair on the rope found around Jaclyn suggested that Jaclyn's killer might be nonwhite. He also noted that there was lime green paint on the rope and that the police obviously had not been able to link the paint to the Dowaliby home. Waters was struck by the shoddiness of the police investigation. "Why was nothing collected from the mattress pad?" he scribbled. He regarded Patrick O'Brien's contention before the grand jury that no one could have entered the Dowalibys' window as "easy to discredit."

Some of what Waters read troubled him, however. Why

weren't the sheets on Jaclyn's bed? Did David really mention Jaclyn's "death" before her body was found? Why was there blood on Jaclyn's pillow? What were the Dowalibys doing with a triple-beam scale? Were the hairs on the Malibu trunk liner Jaclyn's?

Waters discussed the case with Charlotte. He told her that his initial impression of their guilt could have been wrong, but he remained uneasy about getting involved. "My investigations are for prosecutors," he said. "I'd be on the opposite side here." He indicated, however, that he was less concerned about working for the defense than about another possibility he still entertained: "What would I do if I got into this and decided that they're guilty?" Charlotte replied, knowingly, "You'll do what's right. You'll tell the truth."

There was an even stronger reservation in Waters's mind, one that had nothing to do with the merits of the case: Waters was dying of cancer of the colon.

Two years earlier, he had been given only one year to live. Although, for the time being, he had no trouble working a full shift at the police department and devoting time to outside investigative work, he had no way of knowing how long his strength would hold out.

The next day, Waters told Meczyk and Hyman about his illness. They were stunned, given his healthy appearance. They had no hesitancy, however, about having him continue on the case and agreed to pay him $10,000 plus expenses.

Meczyk and Hyman explained that another investigator, Patrick Dougherty, was working on the case, but he would be leaving soon because he had accepted a job in another state.

Two general kinds of investigation were needed. One was the tedious task of checking every aspect of the prosecution's case. The other, more compelling for Waters, was looking into leads and developing evidence that could solve the case—in other words, trying to find out who killed Jaclyn.

In the tedious category, the most important task at hand was investigating Everett Mann. Waters immediately ran a computer check to see if Mann had a criminal record. He learned that Mann had been charged with aggravated assault for threatening someone with a gun on a Chicago Transit

Authority platform in 1985; he pleaded guilty to a reduced charge of carrying an unregistered weapon and was fined $200.

Checking other public records, Waters discovered that Mann's voter registration record falsely indicated that he lived in Chicago at a time when he actually lived in Blue Island. Waters instinctively suspected the reason: Mann in all likelihood had applied for a job with the city of Chicago, which required its employees to live in the city. (Mann's employer, the Chicago Transit Authority, was separate from city government and had no such requirement.)

Waters went to Mann's apartment. Mann was not home, but his wife, Melvon, was quite forthcoming. When Waters asked if her husband had applied for a city job, she said yes, he had applied twice to the Chicago Police Department but had been rejected.

This tidbit prompted Meczyk and Hyman to subpoena Mann's police employment applications and related materials. The documents showed that Mann had used the same false Chicago address he had given on his voter card. More important, the files showed that he had been rejected both times on the basis of psychological tests indicating that he suffered from cyclothymia—a condition characterized by marked mood swings.

In his quest to find Jaclyn's killer, Waters began making regular visits to her grave. The Dowalibys had told him about the red rose and the wreath that had been left anonymously on the grave. Both incidents had occurred while the grave was unmarked. Waters thought he might encounter the killer in the cemetery.

As Waters sat there, he alternatively pored over records and contemplated theories about who might have committed the crime. Although he had not yet ruled out David and Cynthia, he was concentrating on other possibilities. Various scenarios ran through his mind, and he made notes on how to check each one. He speculated that the killer knew the Dowalibys or was familiar with the house.

Foremost in his mind was Timothy Guess, Cynthia's former brother-in-law and Jaclyn's uncle. Guess was psychotic and had seen Jaclyn shortly before she disappeared—when she stayed overnight at the Guess home.

Waters's suspicion of Guess was heightened when Patrick Dougherty, the soon-to-depart defense investigator, learned that Guess had a possible connection to the apartment complex where Jaclyn's body had been found.

On April 11, Dougherty interviewed a woman who, at the time Jaclyn disappeared, lived at the Islander Apartments and worked with Guess at the Park Avenue Restaurant. The woman, Margaret Murphy, told Daugherty that Guess sometimes picked her up at the apartment complex and drove her to work.

Waters made notes to himself to recheck Guess's alibi and further investigate his familiarity with the Islander Apartments.

Before he did those things, however, he wanted to see the area where Jaclyn's body was found under conditions similar to those of the night Jaclyn vanished. Shortly after midnight on April 19, he went to the Islander Apartments. He parked his car in the spot where Everett Mann parked and scribbled, "total darkness, impossible to see."

From the apartment complex, Waters drove to the Dowaliby home. It was four and seven tenths miles. He noted that 148th Place was pitch black and that the window was a logical point of entry—the "most darkened area of house."

The next morning, John Waters drove Cynthia to Jaclyn's graveside. He wanted to observe her reactions. From his experience with con artists, he looked for any hint of insincerity. But after chatting with her for hours at the cemetery, he found none.

After dropping Cynthia off at home, Waters drove downtown to meet with Ralph Meczyk. He was persuaded that Cynthia was no con artist, but he wanted to discuss some of the things that still troubled him about the case.

He began by asking about the sheets. Meczyk explained that Cynthia had been called to work after washing the sheets and had not found time to replace them. There was, after all, a "fluffy" mattress pad on the bed.

Waters asked about David's statements to police. Meczyk said that many of the statements had been distorted or taken out of context. For instance, David had denied that he referred to Jaclyn's "death" before her body was found. David claimed that he had used the word "incident," the police quoted him as saying "accident," and Patrick O'Brien embellished it before the grand jury, claiming that David said "death."

Finally, Waters asked about the triple-beam scale that had been found in the police search of the Dowaliby home. Meczyk said that it belonged to David's older brother, James, who had drowned years earlier; it had been stored in a closet and forgotten.

In succeeding days, Waters looked closely at Timothy Guess. He found that Guess had no criminal record. On April 22, Waters went to the Park Avenue restaurant to check Guess's alibi. Park Avenue employees stuck to what they had told the FBI—that Guess had been at the restaurant at the time Jaclyn disappeared. Some of the employees acknowledged, however, that Tim was such a fixture in the place that they might not have noticed if he had left for a while.

Waters told Meczyk that it would be a good idea to obtain Guess's fingerprints and have them compared with the unidentified print on one of the broken pieces of glass from the Dowalibys' basement window. In an effort to do that, Meczyk and Hyman went to the Park Avenue. Under the guise of interviewing Guess, they hoped to pocket a drinking glass he touched.

When they arrived at the restaurant, however, Guess was not there. Meczyk and Hyman offered a waitress $100 to obtain a glass Guess handled. A few days later, the waitress delivered a tumbler and collected her $100. Unfortunately, the tumbler was made of rough plastic, and prints could not be lifted from it.

As part of the investigation of Guess, Waters tried to determine if he might have traveled the previous winter to Arlington, Texas, where an intruder had entered a home through a window and abducted a five-year-old girl. The girl had been found strangled to death. Someone already had been charged in that case, but Waters wanted to check anyway, because Guess's sister lived forty miles from Arlington. An exhaustive check of airline and car-rental records, plus interviews with family members, turned up no indication that Guess had been there.

Meanwhile, Waters began tracking down Margaret Murphy, Guess's co-worker who lived at the Islander Apartments. She dodged him for several days. When he finally found her, she was not very cooperative. She now claimed, contrary to what she had told defense investigator Patrick Dougherty, that Timothy Guess never had picked her up at the Islander Apartments.

"Does she think Tim is implicated and is protecting him?" Waters wondered in his notes. "Is she following his request not to say that he picked her up and dropped her off to keep himself away from the scene?" Waters added a note to himself to check telephone records to see if Timothy Guess and James Guess might have spoken before the murder.

Waters also considered other possible suspects in the immediate family—Ann and Brian Dowaliby on David's side, and Michael Borrelli on Cynthia's.

Ann Dowaliby obviously had access to the house and part of her time was unaccounted for on the night Jaclyn disappeared. Police reports indicated that she left home "about 10:30 P.M." and that the man with whom she spent the night, Michael Healy, had not joined her until "after midnight."

Waters's suspicion of Ann was heightened by an interview with a former baby-sitter the Dowalibys had used in Riverdale. The baby-sitter told Waters that when she heard about Cynthia and David's arrest she thought, "How could anybody think they did this?" When Waters asked about other members of the Dowaliby family, the baby-sitter told him, "Ann was cold to Jaclyn but gave Davey a lot of love." Waters noted, "Suspects Ann—interesting."

His interest in Ann was further piqued by Ann's October 10, 1988, statement taken at the Blue Island police station. State's Attorney Norma Reyes's report had quoted Ann as saying that her basement room apparently had not been disturbed, that David had used marijuana, and that the rope thought to have killed Jaclyn was similar to the one with which Davey Dowaliby had played. "Is she that dumb?" Waters wrote.

He wondered if Ann might have been trying to protect herself with the statement, but his suspicion was allayed somewhat when he interviewed her on May 7. She told him that she went to the Blue Island police station in an effort to persuade Chief Paul Greves that David was innocent. She said that Norma Reyes distorted what she actually said. "It's her statement, not mine," Ann told Waters.

Waters related his conversation with Ann to Ralph Meczyk, who said she drank quite a bit and, according to Waters's notes, "He is considering making her unavailable for court." Waters made a note to check her alibi further.

Brian Dowaliby was familiar with the house, had lived there, and, judging from the fist marks on the wall, apparently had a violent temper. Police reports indicated he had been out with a girl until 1:45 A.M. on September 10, 1988, but he had no alibi after that. "Check him out," Waters wrote on his legal pad.

Michael Borrelli, the oldest of Cynthia's three brothers, also was familiar with the house. He had been largely estranged from his family until a few months before Jaclyn disappeared.

When Borrelli and Sylvia Sinks began dating in late 1987, they occasionally socialized with the Dowalibys. Their wedding reception had been held in the Dowalibys' basement in March 1988. The following summer they frequently were at the Dowaliby home for barbecues. Borrelli had taken Jaclyn out for frozen yogurt a couple of days before she disappeared.

The key reason that Waters suspected Borrelli, however, was his vigorous cooperation with the police effort to implicate David. Waters wondered if Borrelli might have been trying to divert attention from himself.

In a month of investigating, Waters had grown increasingly confident that David and Cynthia were innocent. He wanted his wife, who he thought had a "sixth sense" about people, to meet the Dowalibys and assess their demeanor. He arranged for them to have dinner on May 12 at a south suburban restaurant.

As they waited in the cocktail lounge, Charlotte noticed that Cynthia, now more than seven months pregnant, unconsciously caressed the unborn child. "She was looking forward to having this child," Charlotte would recall.

David seemed nervous, however. His eyes darted back and forth, and he ordered beers in rapid succession. "He wouldn't be finished with one beer when he would order another," she said.

The conversation was entirely small talk. Among other things, they talked about Cynthia's pregnancy and John's intention to go to Florida at the end of the next week to interview James Guess in prison. Ralph Meczyk had learned that Patrick O'Brien had been to see Guess a few days earlier, and he wanted Waters to find out what they had talked about.

After dinner, John asked Charlotte, "Well, what do you think?"

"She seems very sweet, very loving," Charlotte said of Cynthia. "I can't picture her killing this child."

Mentioning David's nervousness, she said, "Maybe he's hiding something, but I don't believe it's murder." One possibility, she said, was that he was simply self-conscious, aware that she was there to size him up. Other possibilities were that he blamed himself for not awakening when Jaclyn was abducted or that he might have been covering for someone else.

Charlotte strongly suggested that, before meeting with James Guess, John learn more about David and Cynthia's relatives and past relationships. "You don't know nearly enough about these people's lives," she said.

John agreed. He decided to spend the next several days pulling together background information on the Dowaliby and Borrelli families, both of which, he would discover, were star-crossed.

STAR-CROSSED LIVES

Ann Dowaliby was born Anna Rogers, a coal miner's daughter. She was the third of seven children raised in Harlan County, Kentucky, a depressed Appalachian area. Her personality reflected her roots. She was earthy, plainspoken, and sarcastic, with little capacity for subtlety.

In 1948, after graduating from high school, Ann moved to Detroit and married a Greek-American named James Damas. He was working as a bartender in Detroit but was from Cicero, Illinois, a Chicago suburb that had become famous a quarter century earlier as the headquarters of Al Capone. Soon after they were married, Ann and James migrated to Chicago, taking an apartment in the Kenwood neighborhood on the city's South Side.

Ann and Damas had two children, Christine, born in 1950, and James, Jr., in 1954. One year after James, Jr., was born, Ann and Damas separated. So that Ann could work, the children stayed with their paternal grandmother, Penelope Damas, in Cicero.

This arrangement worked out fine, according to Ann, until her estranged spouse threatened her with a gun. "If I can't have you, no one will," she quoted Damas as saying. Fearful that he meant it, Ann moved, switched jobs, and obtained an unlisted telephone number. She took James, Jr., with her, but left Christine with Penelope Damas.

Ann's new apartment was in an ethnic neighborhood southwest of Kenwood. She worked as a waitress in a restaurant, where she met Ernest Dowaliby, a housepainter thirteen years her senior. He was a descendent of Lebanese Maronites (Christians in communion with the Pope); the family name meant "wheelmaker" in Arabic.

When the divorce was granted in 1956, Ann won custody of both children, but she allowed Christine to continue living with Penelope Damas. One day Penelope and Christine vanished. Ann later discovered that they had gone to Greece. She would never see her daughter again.

After a brief courtship, Ann and Ernest Dowaliby were married in a civil ceremony on Friday the thirteenth of April 1956. Ernest adopted James Damas, Jr.

On Valentine's Day 1957, Ann gave birth to twins. Twins had not been expected. Although Ann had gained a lot of weight during the pregnancy, the doctor heard only one heartbeat and put her on a diet.

Before going to the hospital, the parents-to-be selected one name for a girl and one for a boy. Now they could use both—for the girl, Rose, after Ernest's mother; for the boy, David, after Ann's youngest brother, David Rogers.

A year earlier, when David Rogers was eleven years old, he had been hit by a car and instantly killed—one of an endless stream of tragedies in Ann's life.

After the twins, the Dowalibys had three more children: Laurine, born in 1958; Michelle, in 1959; and Brian, in 1964.

In his youth, David Dowaliby was cast as the hero-protector of his sisters, according to family members. When David was five years old, his twin sister, Rose, jumped into water over her head in a swimming pool. Rose bobbed several times, swallowing water, until David grabbed her hair and pulled her to the ladder. He was credited with saving her life.

David's early casting as a hero-protector carried over into his relationship with Cynthia, family members said. They speculated that it may have contributed to the police suspicion that he was the kind of guy who would take a fall for a murder committed by his wife.

The family suggested that other traits David developed in his youth had returned to haunt him.

When he was in the first grade, for instance, David got lost on Chicago's South Side. A stranger offered to help him. David had been warned about strangers, but he unhesitatingly climbed into the stranger's car. They drove around for a few minutes looking for his house and finally went to the neighborhood police station. "I've got a kid who's lost," the man told a policeman on the station steps. "What's his name?" the officer asked. "David," the man answered. Ann already had reported David lost, and a police officer took him home.

Ann believed it was David's naive faith in the goodwill of others that led him to submit to days of repetitive grilling by the police after Jaclyn's disappearance, even though he had been warned that everything he said could be used against him.

David developed a penchant for flippant sarcasm, a trait Ann said he probably inherited from her. During questioning, David had made remarks that investigators thought inappropriate, coming, as they did, from someone whose child was missing. For instance, when asked in an obviously hostile context whether he had any enemies, he had replied, "Everybody loves me. You love me, don't you?" Later, after receiving a Miranda warning, he had snapped, "Don't you think if I did it I could have made up a better story?"

In high school, David started smoking marijuana, resulting in his two pot convictions. As minor as the offenses seemed, they fueled Daniel McDevitt's suspicion that drugs might have had something to do with Jaclyn's murder.

By and large, David's early years seemed typical for the

time, place, and his family's situation. His hardworking father managed to save enough money to buy a modest home in Hazel Crest, a fast-growing suburb south of Chicago. David said his childhood memories were mostly idyllic—visiting his maternal grandmother in the country, swimming, building rafts on which he floated on lazy summer afternoons.

In 1969, when David and Rose were in the seventh grade, the Dowalibys had accrued enough home equity to buy a better house. They chose the tan brick ranch in Midlothian.

The Dowaliby children were enrolled at the public Spaulding School. David did not read much, but his class went to the library one day and each student was told to select a book. David picked George Orwell's *Animal Farm.* When his teacher explained the socio-political significance of the book, he was fascinated. He next read *Nineteen Eighty-four.*

When David began the eighth grade, he met Gene O'Connor, a heavyset lad with reddish-brown hair who became his best friend. "If you were his friend, you were his friend for life," Gene said of David. "He never pulled shit on you. He was the one guy you could count on."

Gene and David attended Midlothian's Breman Township High School. David was on the swim team and track team as a freshman and sophomore, but he gave up organized athletics in his junior year. "I learned to swim as good as I was going to," he said. "I wasn't going to get any better." He added that he gave up track for the same reason.

In early 1973, during David's junior year, Ernest Dowaliby suffered a heart attack. Discharged after a brief hospital stay, the elder Dowaliby was recovering at home when he suffered a second heart attack while Ann was running an errand. Too frugal to call an ambulance, Ernest drove himself to the hospital.

David wanted to drive, but Ernest would not allow it because David did not yet have a driver's license. Ernest drove, and David rode on the passenger side. They arrived safely at South Suburban Hospital in Hazel Crest, but Ernest died a few days later of a myocardial infarction. He was fifty-five.

After David's graduation, college was not an option. His

twin sister, who had been a member of the Student Council, speech team, Thespians, and French Club, was the most academically talented of all the Dowaliby children. She was collegebound, and Ann could not afford tuition for more than one child.

David got a job lugging beef at a meat-packing company near the then-active Chicago stockyards. He soon discovered that the business was not on the up and up. One night the owners instructed him and three other trusted employees to stay late and cut Mexican stamps off a truckload of beef roasts so they could be sold as U.S. beef. David faithfully kept their secret, but began looking for more honorable employment.

He worked as a welder and as a meatcutter before landing a cushy position managing sixty apartments in Riverdale, not far from Midlothian. He received a salary and a rent-free apartment.

As soon as David was earning his own money, he fulfilled his childhood longing for outdoor sports. He bought fishing tackle, and a bow and arrow for the deer season. He also took up golf, and soon was shooting in the mid-nineties.

In 1979, seven years after Ernest's death, the Dowaliby family suffered another tragedy. David's half brother, James, age twenty-five, drowned in a swimming accident near Kankakee, Illinois. David was now the man of the family.

Faced with adult responsibilities, David responded appropriately. He had been planning to buy a new car, but his employer persuaded him that a house would be a better investment. David found a two-bedroom bungalow in Riverdale for only $34,000. At age twenty-two, he became a homeowner.

A few months later, David met Windy Jones. "She was a wild thing, real young, with a bad temper," Gene O'Connor said. "She was thin, tall, and real pretty."

After dating for several weeks, Windy moved in with David in Riverdale. Ann did not approve of the arrangement, and told them they either should get married or stop living together. David and Windy got married.

Less than a year later, according to David, Windy became

disenchanted with monogamy. "Being married is no fun," David quoted her as saying. She left, taking everything except David's bed. She even took the sheets. A few weeks later, she wanted to return, but David would not hear of it. "You made your choice," he said. Ann advised David to get a divorce and lent him the money to pay a lawyer.

At the time of David's breakup with Windy, Gene O'Connor was living with his mother, but he wanted to be out on his own. David asked him, "Hey, why don't you come and live with me? I could use the company—and somebody to help pay the mortgage."

Gene moved in with David in Riverdale. David got a job at Rax Erecting, where Gene worked, and soon advanced to foreman, the position he held at the time of his arrest. David and Gene spent their off-hours golfing, bowling, bass fishing, and dating.

In November 1980, Gene met Peggy Belavich, a tall, slender, blue-eyed blonde who happened to be the best friend of Cynthia Borrelli Guess. Two weeks after Gene and Peggy met, they decided they wanted to live together. Gene asked David if Peggy could move into the Riverdale house with them. David was cool to the idea, according to Gene, but agreed. "If you really care about her, okay," David said.

A few days before Christmas, Cynthia stopped by the Riverdale house to drop off presents for Peggy and Gene, but they were not home. David answered the door and accepted the gifts.

When Peggy returned, David excitedly inquired, "Who's your girlfriend?"

"Forget it," Peggy said. "She's married—and she's pregnant."

Cynthia was the fifth and youngest child of Mary and Daniel Borrelli, natives of the Southwest Side of Chicago and members of the Gage Park High School class of 1952. "In those days," Mary Malia said, "you finished high school, got married, had a house with a flower garden and a bunch of kids."

The Borrellis did what was expected. Married in 1953, their

first child, Michael, arrived in 1954, and their second, David, in 1955. The house came in 1958, a cozy three-bedroom in the burgeoning south suburb of Country Club Hills. A month after they moved in, their third child, Gary, was born, followed by Julianne in 1960 and, finally, Cynthia in 1962.

Daniel Borrelli was an architectural draftsman and naval reservist. Mary worked as a waitress for banquets at a local restaurant, but mostly she was a wife and mother. True to her image of life, she became an avid gardener, turning their half-acre lot green and fragrant in the warm months.

According to Mary, Cynthia was a shy, unassuming child who loved to play outdoors. Family friends from those days described Cynthia as polite and pleasant, with an endearing smile and a large vocabulary that came from competing with older siblings.

At Southwood Elementary School, Cynthia made average to above-average grades and excelled at sports, winning ribbons in track and field. She was one of the best baton-twirlers in the school and marched in several parades in downtown Chicago.

Despite the semblance of normalcy, Cynthia's youth was far from idyllic. The Borrelli marriage was stormy. According to Mary, Daniel was a perfectionist who had little tolerance for imperfection in his children. "Sometimes his relationship with the older boys was like World War Three," Mary said, "but he treated the younger children, particularly Cynthia, much better."

Thinking a change of scenery might help their relationship, the family moved to Aurora, Colorado, in June 1975. Cynthia had trouble adjusting. Her grades, which had been good at Southwood, plummeted. The Borrellis' marital situation did not improve, and Daniel left home that winter.

In December 1975, Mary and the children moved back to the Chicago area. Mary found an apartment in south suburban Matteson and took a job at Oak Forest Hospital. Cynthia finished the eighth grade at Southwood that spring and enrolled at Rich Central High School.

Mary divorced Daniel in January 1976, ending twenty-three years of marriage. At about the same time, Cynthia started dating James Guess, an itinerant construction worker. Mary disliked James, whom she described as rude. Cynthia's friends shared that judgment. "He was good-looking but no good," said one.

Later that year, at a function of a singles group called the Thirty-Fifty Club, Mary met Thomas Malia. He was divorced and, like Mary, had five children. Mary and Thomas were married two years later. Daniel also remarried, but his second marriage ended in divorce as well.

Meanwhile, Cynthia dropped out of high school and got a job grilling hamburgers at a White Castle restaurant in Midlothian. There she met Peggy Belavich (later to be Peggy O'Connor), who was one of the supervisors. When Cynthia started the job, according to Peggy, some of the other workers perceived her as aloof, moody, and cold. Peggy did not share that perception. She said that the other workers mistook Cynthia's shyness for aloofness and resented her because she was pretty and hardworking.

Shortly after Cynthia went to work at White Castle, one of her closest childhood friends, Denise Malik, suffered a crippling injury. Denise and several companions had been riding a snowmobile alongside a train track. When a barreling freight appeared, they decided to race it. The draft pulled Denise's snowmobile under the train wheels, severing her arm.

Cynthia spent many hours at Denise's bedside following surgery to reattach the arm. Denise eventually regained use of the scarred limb but never recovered emotionally. She became an alcoholic.

Cynthia did not drink much herself, but alcohol was a problem for James Guess, the man she was dating. Peggy O'Connor said that Guess womanized in saloons, got into barroom brawls, and routinely drove his Pontiac Trans-Am wildly while under the influence—activities that often brought Cynthia to tears. "Jimmy was Cyndi's first love," said Peggy. "She was blind to the kind of guy he was."

When Cynthia was eighteen years old, she became pregnant by James. Wanting the child to have a father, she decided to marry him, against her better judgment and that of her mother. James, who was working fairly steadily, promised to reform and behave like a good husband and father.

When Cynthia and James told Mary of their plans, Mary said she turned to James and said, "You know I don't like you, but Cyndi says it is going to be different." Cynthia and James were married with Mary's blessing in January 1981, in a nondenominational service.

Julianne, the sister of the bride, was the maid of honor, and Denise Malik, who had been like a sister, was a bridesmaid. Cynthia selected bridesmaids' dresses with long sleeves to make Denise feel more comfortable.

Peggy, who also was a bridesmaid, moved in with Gene O'Connor and David Dowaliby in Riverdale the following November. Shortly after Cynthia dropped off the Christmas presents and met David for the first time, David saw her at a party with James Guess. A few days later, David saw Guess in a bar with another woman.

David recalled Guess asking, "Don't I know you?"

"I'm a friend of Gene and Peggy," David answered.

James turned away, embarrassed.

As Cynthia's due date approached, Mary Malia recalled her waiting outside a bar one night while James was inside drinking. By this time, Mary said, it was obvious James had not changed.

When the baby was born on May 17, 1981, Mary said the doctor came to the waiting room and told James, "Mr. Guess, you have a beautiful baby girl."

"A girl?" Mary quoted Guess as saying. He was disappointed because he had wanted a boy, and did not participate in selecting a name. Cynthia chose "Jaclyn," a name that, to quote Mary, "she thought was beautiful, like her newborn child."

Two weeks later, Cynthia left James. She moved back home with the Malias, who were living in Markham. She sued for divorce and child custody on the grounds of "extreme and repeated mental cruelty." She refused to see James or allow him to see Jaclyn.

While the suit was pending in Cook County Circuit Court, James allegedly tried to break into the Malia home. One night around midnight, while Cynthia was out with friends, he climbed onto the roof and tried to enter through a window in a bedroom where Cynthia's stepsister, Karen Malia, was sleeping.

Karen awakened and caught a glimpse of James, who ran away. The Malias called the police. Officers found James walking through the parking lot of a nearby shopping center. He denied the attempted break-in and was not arrested.

When Cynthia returned home that night, family members told her about the incident. They sat around the kitchen table, speculating about why James would break into the house. They concluded he was trying to snatch Jaclyn to get back at Cynthia.

At her divorce hearing in 1981, Cynthia testified that Guess repeatedly drank to excess and stayed out at night. Guess did not show up for the hearing, and the judge signed an order granting the divorce and giving Cynthia custody of Jaclyn.

Cynthia was finished with men—until she got to know David Dowaliby.

SHADOWING THE STATE

John Waters wanted to find out more about Cynthia Dowaliby's ex-husband. On May 19, 1989, Waters flew to Orlando, Florida. The next morning, he drove to the Avon Park Correctional Institution—home to James Guess.

The trip was intended to do more than satisfy Waters's personal curiosity. He had two important reasons for going. First, Ralph Meczyk wanted him to find out if Guess had told Patrick O'Brien anything that could damage the Dowalibys at trial. Second, Waters wanted to look for any hint, perhaps an unguarded gesture or intonation, that someone in the Guess family might have taken Jaclyn.

Waters described Guess as "short, thin, stringy blond hair, piercing blue eyes, long face, mustache." The crime for which Guess had been convicted, he told Waters, was "a date rape."

Guess related that the FBI had interviewed him on September 11, 1988, the day after Jaclyn was reported missing. When the agents left, he said, he broke down crying, and was put into solitary confinement. A few days later, he learned that Jaclyn had been murdered.

Guess said he wrote Cynthia a letter, telling her, "I still love you." He sent the letter in care of his mother, who decided not to deliver it. Twice after that, Guess said he called the Dowaliby home, hoping to speak to Cynthia, but hung up when David answered.

Waters asked if Guess thought there was any possibility that Cynthia could have killed Jaclyn. "No way," Guess answered. "She couldn't hurt anybody. She's sweet and caring." Next Waters asked if Guess thought Cynthia would protect David if he had committed the crime. "No way," Guess again said.

Guess said he "felt bad" about Jaclyn's adoption. "At first, it hurt my pride," he said, although he eventually came to believe it was best for Jaclyn. Since the adoption, he had seen Jaclyn only once—in 1985, when she was visiting Jackie Guess. "I never told her who I was," he said. "It broke my heart."

Waters asked if Guess could think of anyone who would be capable of committing the crime. "Maybe a pervert, or someone who knew her through the neighborhood or school," he replied. As for his younger brother, Timothy, Guess said, "No, Tim is a child himself. He's been on drugs, but he couldn't hurt a fly."

Guess described Patrick O'Brien's recent visit. O'Brien had asked him what kind of person Cynthia was, Guess said, but had shown no interest in hearing anything favorable. O'Brien, said Guess, was "a real asshole."

O'Brien had asked about Cynthia's drug use, and Guess acknowledged that he and Cynthia had "experimented with drugs for a couple of years when we were growing up." He said he told O'Brien, "We went through a lot of kid stuff," adding that they were divorced because Cynthia "outgrew the relationship."

When O'Brien had asked if Cynthia could have killed Jaclyn, Guess said he told him the same thing he told Waters—absolutely not. Nor, Guess said he stated emphatically, would she have protected David if he committed the crime.

At first, Guess said, O'Brien had implied that he might help Guess in some way if he cooperated with the prosecution. By the end of the interview, however, O'Brien had indicated that he had no interest in calling Guess as a witness.

"People think I'm bad," Guess told Waters. "It really pisses me off. This was my daughter. All I ever wanted was the best for Jaclyn and Cyndi. I love them with all my heart."

Waters returned home to find Cynthia packing the family belongings to move. Ann Dowaliby had just sold the house to raise money to pay legal fees. David and Cynthia were moving in with her mother and stepfather, Mary and Thomas Malia, who now lived in a two-bedroom condominium in nearby Tinley Park.

Cynthia was frantic that the trial date was only five weeks away—about the time her baby was due—and there was much investigating still to be done. "We're not going to finish in time," she told Waters.

"We'll get it done," he assured her.

The night before the move, at the suggestion of Ralph Meczyk and Lawrence Hyman, David and his next-door neighbor Robert Tolbert conducted a videotaped experiment. The purpose was to test Waters's theory about how an intruder could have entered the home through the basement window.

Tolbert played the role of intruder, dressed appropriately in a dark T-shirt, jeans, and sneakers. At one hundred seventy-five pounds and standing six feet, Tolbert was no elf, yet he comfortably slipped through the window feet first on his stomach. He pushed off the basement wall with his right foot and easily avoided the towel rack and other objects below.

David captured it all on videotape, showing that someone could have broken into the home exactly the way Waters suspected.

In anticipation of a June 1989 trial date, the prosecutors gave a list of their prospective witnesses to the defense. On it was a name neither Waters nor the defense lawyers recognized, Roy Padecky. His address was given as the Islander Apartments.

From the manager of the apartment complex, Eileen Blaylock, Waters learned that Padecky recently had moved to the nearby suburb of Alsip. Blaylock said that Padecky, a small-time drug dealer, had told the police that Cynthia Dowaliby had had an affair with a man who lived in the Islander Apartments the winter before Jaclyn's murder. Padecky claimed that he was present when Cynthia used drugs with the man, according to Blaylock.

Waters immediately went to ask Cynthia, as delicately as possible, whether there was any truth to the story. She assured him it was not true. She agreed that Waters could take a Polaroid photograph of her to put into an array of photographs of other women to show to Padecky.

On May 15, Waters tracked down Padecky in Alsip. Padecky said that he was painting an apartment in the Islander complex in January 1988 when a brown-haired woman rapped on the window and asked him to help her. Her car, a white Oldsmobile Cutlass, was stuck in a snowbank in the parking lot. She introduced herself as "Cynthia" and said she was waiting for her boyfriend, whose name Padecky recognized. Padecky pushed the car out of the snow and, in gratitude, the woman gave him a line of cocaine.

When Jaclyn's body was found nine months later, Padecky said, police questioned him about whether he knew or ever had sold drugs to David or Cynthia Dowaliby. Padecky told them no, and agreed to take a lie detector test, which he passed.

Daniel McDevitt, however, was not satisfied and gave Padecky a test of his own. "He got up very close to my face and said he would kick the fuck out of me if I wasn't telling the truth," Padecky told Waters. "McDevitt said if he found out I was lying he would tell the Herreras I was a narc." (The Herreras were notorious Chicago drug dealers.)

About a month later, Padecky was arrested on a drug charge. In jail, he saw television coverage of the Dowaliby case and claimed to recognize Cynthia Dowaliby as the woman whose car he had pushed out of the snowbank several months earlier. Padecky then called Blue Island Police Chief Paul Greves and told him about the alleged affair. Greves said he was interested in the story but already had heard it—from Eileen Blaylock.

Waters pulled out the photo array and asked Padecky if any of the women looked like the "Cynthia" he saw in January 1988. Padecky picked the bottom left photo. It was not Cynthia Dowaliby's.

Prosecutors shared Waters's assessment that Padecky's credibility was zero, and they would not call him to testify. Padecky, however, would figure into the case after the trial, when it was revealed that, at the time of Jaclyn's murder, he bore a striking physical resemblance to David Dowaliby.

In late May, John Waters interviewed all of the Dowaliby neighbors who had given statements to the police. He found that the police accounts of what the neighbors had said were one-sided, focusing on the purported poor quality of parenting by the Dowalibys while omitting or glossing over favorable opinions.

Waters began with Robert Tolbert, who said it was "impossible" that the Dowalibys were guilty. Although Tolbert had not known the Dowalibys well before Jaclyn's murder, he said that they seemed "very family-oriented" and that he had never seen them strike the children.

Waters asked Tolbert if he heard any unusual noises around the time Jaclyn disappeared, since his bedroom was only a few feet from the Dowalibys' broken window. Tolbert said that although he slept with his bedroom window open, he did not hear the window break.

Waters asked if there was a chance that the window had been broken before September 9, if it might have been unrelated to Jaclyn's disappearance. Tolbert said he did not think that was possible because he had just sown new grass in his yard and had watered it daily in early September because of the heat. He felt certain that he would have noticed if the window had been broken.

Later, Waters interviewed Tolbert's wife, Mary, going over

most of the same questions, with the exception of anything she might have heard. Mary is deaf. She, too, expressed confidence that the Dowalibys were innocent. She said that she had seen laundry on the Dowalibys' clothesline on September 9, 1988, although she did not specifically recall seeing Jaclyn's sheets.

Mary, a hospital X-ray technician, added that when she had gone to work at 5:30 A.M. on September 10, she noticed Cynthia's car in an unusual position—overhanging the driveway.

From the Tolbert home, Waters walked across the street to the Naughton residence. "We didn't see anything unusual that night," Thomas Naughton said. "You don't see much because the street is so dark." Naughton said the Dowaliby children always seemed "happy."

Next, Waters visited Bruce Beatty, who lived to the east of the Naughtons. Beatty said that Jaclyn "seemed like a normal little kid" but that she and Davey had a reputation "for running out in the street." Asked if he thought the Dowalibys killed Jaclyn, he answered, "I'll give them the benefit of the doubt."

Waters walked around the corner to the home of Francis Lasky, who said he had known the Dowalibys "for many, many years." Lasky's son had been with James Dowaliby, David's older brother, when he drowned. Lasky said, "Cyndi and Dave are good parents who never laid a hand on the kids."

Lasky's wife, Betty, described Cynthia's blue Malibu as "a real beater" that often broke down, adding that it was unlikely that anyone would use it on a desperate mission when a well-functioning vehicle—David's truck—was available. "Would you take a body in a car that barely would make it around the block?" she asked.

Waters went to the home of Lori Oyervides, a back-fence neighbor of the Dowalibys. She said that they had cut an opening in the fence so their children could play together. She said she had "never heard Dave or Cyndi speak harshly to the children." The Dowalibys "never spanked them," she said. "Discipline was for them to go to their room." She added that the Dowalibys were innocent, and "I wish they'd catch the one who did it."

Holly Deck, the Dowalibys' next-door neighbor to the west, told Waters she felt strongly that the Dowalibys did not kill Jaclyn. She said that between 11:00 P.M. and midnight on September 9, her three dogs barked at her kitchen door, which faced the Dowaliby home. She said the dogs knew the Dowalibys and would not react to them "with that kind of nasty bark." Her husband, Delmar, looked out at the time but saw nothing. Nonetheless, one of the dogs, a Chihuahua named Dolly, would not be quieted. Dolly was Jaclyn's favorite.

"Cyndi is a good mom," Deck told Waters, adding that David showed "no partiality" toward his biological son over his adopted daughter. However, Deck described Ann Dowaliby as "very cold to Jaclyn," adding that Ann "couldn't believe" that her former bedroom had been given to Jaclyn.

Daniel Verble, who lived to the east of the Tolberts, also professed a strong belief in the Dowalibys' innocence. "I know what David did for the kids," Verble said. "He took them fishing and camping, and built a fort and a swing set for them."

Renee Verble said she left for work at 10:30 P.M. Friday, September 9, and returned at 5:30 A.M. the next day. She noticed that Cynthia's Malibu had remained "in the same place," although she did not recall whether it was overhanging the driveway.

Waters asked Daniel Verble about the view of Susan Haseman, as expressed in police reports, that the Dowaliby children were poorly supervised.

"Dead wrong," said Verble.

Haseman, who lived farther to the east, told Waters that she thought Cynthia was incapable of hurting the children but that she did not know David well enough to express an opinion about him. Waters wrote of Haseman, "She's very influenced by the evidence the state says they have."

Haseman referred to "the witness," meaning Everett Mann, and to the allegations that Davey Dowaliby had been abused. She said she would be a witness for the prosecution concerning the lack of supervision, adding that she was "upset" that certain neighbors would no longer speak to her.

Waters tried to interview Jeffrey and Constance Koleczyk, neighbors two doors to the west of the Dowalibys, both of whom were prospective prosecution witnesses. Constance answered the door. She told Waters she heard "a moan" just as she was going to bed at about 12:30 to 1:00 A.M. on September 10. "It was loud enough to seem like it was in the same room," she said. She looked out but saw nothing.

Jeffrey Koleczyk then came to the door. "We don't want to talk to anybody about this, especially a private detective," he said. He asked Waters to leave. "Of course, I'm sorry if I bothered you," Waters said.

Later, Waters returned to the home, left his card, and asked Constance to ask her husband to reconsider. Waters also asked neighbors "to try to pry Koleczyk loose." Koleczyk agreed to be interviewed a few days later.

Waters mainly wanted to find out what Koleczyk had told the police about the rope found wrapped around Jaclyn. A state police report indicated that Koleczyk had been shown the rope on September 21 and had said without hesitation, "That's the rope Davey used to play with."

Koleczyk told Waters, however, that he never said the rope was the same, but "only similar."

At Ralph Meczyk's request, John Waters set out to find Ralph Styer, the Air Force sergeant under whom Everett Mann had served in the mid-1970s. Meczyk wanted to know if Styer really owned a Malibu resembling Cynthia Dowaliby's, as Mann had claimed.

Styer had left the Air Force, so tracking him down was not easy. In early June, however, Waters learned that Styer was managing a fast food restaurant in Marquette, Michigan. Waters went to see him on June 7, 1989.

Styer told Waters that in late 1975 he had bought a new 1976 Chevrolet Malibu, a red one with a black vinyl top.

Waters showed Styer a photograph of the Dowaliby Malibu.

"It's not even close to my car," Styer said.

When Waters asked what he recalled of Everett Mann, Styer answered, "I don't recall him at all. If this guy would have impressed me, I'd have remembered him."

Styer promised to look for a photograph of his 1976 Malibu and mail it to Meczyk. Several days later, Meczyk received a photo showing Styer standing in front of his car, which was a bright red two-door with a sloped back. In silhouette it bore virtually no resemblance to Cynthia's 1980 Malibu, which was a light blue four-door with a longer, more traditional trunk sandwiched between its rear fenders.

Still concentrating on the car, Waters interviewed Derrick Darling and Gloria Lake, the couple who had told police they had seen a light blue Malibu in the Islander parking lot on September 13, the day before Jaclyn's body was discovered. The police theory was that David might have driven the car to the apartment complex to see why the body had not been discovered.

Darling had told the police that the car he had seen had rusted panels, but Waters had found that the Dowaliby Malibu had "not a bit of rust."

Waters noted on his legal pad that Darling at first had placed the time when he and Lake saw the car at 1:30 P.M. Waters knew that David could not have been there at that time because he was being interviewed by the police. A few days later, Darling claimed that the time was between 3:00 and 3:30 P.M., when David was not with the police. "Probably coached by Shaughnessy," Waters wrote.

Darling and Lake had moved, but Waters traced them through voter records and interviewed them. Darling acknowledged that he initially had told police that the sighting occurred at about 1:30 P.M. He claimed, however, to have recalled later that the show *Win, Lose, or Draw* had come on television shortly before he saw the car; the show had begun at 3:00 P.M.

Just to make sure that Darling could not become a credible witness, Waters returned to ask the Dowalibys' neighbors if they recalled seeing the car move on September 13. Several neighbors assured him that the car had not left the front of the Dowaliby home between September 10 and 17, when police towed it away.

In the course of his interviews, Waters found two additional witnesses, Eileen and Brian Anderson, who said they noticed the Malibu overhanging the drive on September 9. They distinctly recalled that it was still in the same unusual spot the next morning.

After two months of investigation, Waters was puzzled about what the prosecution conceivably had that might persuade a judge or jury that the Dowalibys were guilty.

In his view, there was evidence that an intruder took Jaclyn, that David and Cynthia were loving parents, that Jaclyn was a happy child, that the Malibu had not been moved from in front of the home, and that Everett Mann and Derrick Darling were not credible identification witnesses.

Referring to the prosecution, Waters mused on a legal pad, "Are they desperate? Is their whole case going to be that it couldn't have happened the way Cyndi and Dave say it did?"

By early summer, Waters's health began to deteriorate. He was in and out of the hospital for chemotherapy. He grew weaker by the day, but he felt that Meczyk and Hyman had the ammunition they needed to destroy the prosecution case.

He thus wanted to spend his remaining energy on the search for Jaclyn's killer. In recent weeks, both because of the press of other matters and his illness, he had not had time to stake out the cemetery, as he had earlier in the investigation. He resumed that practice, still hoping the killer might visit Jaclyn's grave.

His notes indicate that his cemetery visits at this point were more than routine stakeouts—that they were occasions to contemplate his own mortality and to pray.

After a two-hour visit to the cemetery on June 21, he wrote, "Said a prayer for Jaclyn and asked for her help."

On July 1, Waters tried to call Cynthia at the Malias'. It had become his habit to talk to her every day at about 10:00 A.M., and she always awaited his call. There was no answer this morning, however, and Waters correctly suspected why: David had taken her to Olympia Fields Osteopathic Hospital to give birth.

After nearly eight hours in labor, the obstetrician induced the delivery. A seven-pound, four-ounce daughter was born at 6:20 P.M. They named her Carli Marie, the latter having been Jaclyn's middle name.

When Waters spoke to Cynthia later, she said that Carli had been born with a slight heart murmur, which the doctors thought would heal naturally. Otherwise, Carli was healthy. "God has brought back my little girl," Cynthia said. "She looks almost like Jaclyn. I know it's not Jaclyn, but I feel maybe it's her spirit or something."

The joy soon turned to panic, however, when a tearful nurse appeared in Cynthia's room. The nurse, clutching Cynthia's hand, told her and David that someone from Children and Family Services had called. "They're coming to take your baby," the nurse said, sobbing.

"That can't be," Cynthia said. "It's all arranged through the court. My mother has temporary custody."

David called Ralph Meczyk. Under the court-approved arrangement, the Dowalibys' juvenile attorneys had agreed to notify Children and Family Services immediately of the birth. They had done that, but it turned out that the caseworker who took the call either chose to ignore the agreement or was unfamiliar with it, and had set the bureaucracy in motion to seize the infant.

While Meczyk frantically tried to straighten out the situation, an intern who was sympathetic with the Dowalibys' plight advised them, "Take your baby and get out of here."

As much as they appreciated the intern's sentiment, the Dowalibys chose a more prudent course. Cynthia "stood guard" at the door of the nursery while David waited by a public phone to hear from Meczyk. About ninety minutes later, Meczyk called and told them the mix-up had been straightened out.

"It was a harrowing one and a half hours," David told Waters.

The next day, Cynthia's mother, Mary Malia, came to the

hospital to accept custody of Carli. A Children and Family Services caseworker came into the room, picked up Carli, and officially placed her into Mary's arms as the Dowalibys stood by.

Because of the possibility that someone had alerted reporters to the departure, hospital personnel arranged for the Dowalibys to leave through a service elevator.

That night, in a cathartic effort to come to grips with the events of the previous thirty-six hours, David put his feelings in writing:

"Yesterday, our child was born. Today, her name is Carli Marie, and she is as beautiful as her name. It would be wrong for me to think she is a replacement for Jaclyn. But I do.

"All she knows of our world is the comfort and warmth of her mother's breasts. How wondrous it must be to only know the warmth in life, and not the pain. It hurts me to think how I'll have to change all that someday. 'Beware of strangers. They steal little children from their parents, and sometimes never let them go home. They're very scary, and they're for real!'

"My wife and I are delighted about our new daughter. She doesn't know it yet, but she's given us new hope and faith.

"Carli is asleep. The nurse comes in the room, a look of horror in her eyes. 'What's wrong?' I ask. 'Please sit down.' Suddenly my thoughts are flooded with fear. She could have told us there was a bomb in the room, and we would not have been as frightened as we were to hear those three words.

"I sit next to my wife, and I hold her hand. And she's trembling. The nurse is nervous and trembling herself. 'We just received a call from a man from DCFS. He told us he's on his way to take your daughter back with him.'

"Beware of strangers. They take little children from their parents and sometimes never let them go home."

The trial had been postponed for Carli's birth and now was scheduled to begin in two months. John Waters knew he could not check every fact about every possible suspect by then.

He decided that the probability was low that either Ann Dowaliby or Brian Dowaliby were involved in Jaclyn's death. Their time was fairly well accounted for—not beyond question, but well enough that Waters thought his time was better spent on other suspects.

Timothy Guess remained a strong suspect, in Waters's view, even though he had failed to crack Guess's alibi. Waters mused about ways to confirm Guess's possible connection to Margaret Murphy and the Islander Apartments.

Waters also regarded Cynthia's oldest brother, Michael Borrelli, as a strong suspect, because Borrelli had actively cooperated with the police effort to pin Jaclyn's murder on David.

Waters knew the subject was touchy with family members, but he casually inquired about Borrelli in the context of gathering more complete family background. He learned that Borrelli had not been close to the family from his teenage years until the summer before Jaclyn disappeared.

Borrelli had drifted from state to state, living in Colorado, Texas, and California. Once, when he had been locked out of a family cottage near Kankakee, Illinois, he had ripped a screen and broken a window to get inside.

Waters obtained Borrelli's criminal record, which showed that, by age twenty-two in 1976, he had been arrested ten times for property crimes. He had four convictions, and he had served time in Cook County Jail. In 1975 the FBI opened a file on him after he was arrested for interstate credit card fraud, but Waters was unable to obtain the FBI file.

After Jaclyn's murder, family members told Waters, Borrelli had become "remote and strange." Waters also noted that Borrelli had not attended Carli's recent christening.

Borrelli was five feet, eight inches tall, slender, and agile. He drove a dark-blue, late-model, midsize car. He was familiar with Blue Island, having lived there at one time.

Family members described Borrelli as "hyper, loud, and pushy." Waters wrote on a pad that Borrelli "immediately hit it off with McDevitt—they were both pushy and hard." When David was released on bond, Borrelli had angrily called McDevitt, demanding to know why David got out of jail.

"I am suspicious," Waters wrote, indicating that he wanted to find out where Borrelli was when Jaclyn disappeared. However, a startling development intervened to prevent Waters from further checking Michael Borrelli, or Timothy Guess.

"I GOT STOLED"

On September 6, 1989, Blue Island Police Chief Paul Greves called a press conference to announce that a twenty-four-year-old man, Perry Hernandez, had been arrested the previous day for two crimes: a brutal assault of a woman in the Blue Island Metra commuter train station, and the abduction and sexual assault of a Blue Island girl.

Greves gave few details of the crime against the child, whom he did not identify, but focused instead on the Metra crime, which had occurred the previous April 21. News organizations would play the story accordingly; crimes on public transportation had become big news in the wake of several highly publicized assaults.

After the press conference, a Channel 5 reporter, Phil Walters, lingered and asked Greves specifically how the police had linked Hernandez to the Metra crime.

"By the videotape," Greves answered, explaining

that a surveillance camera on the platform had recorded the crime.

Walters asked to see the tape. After checking with a south suburban prosecutor, Greves showed Walters the tape and allowed him to copy it. "I thought this was going to be a bullshit assignment," Walters gleefully told Greves, "and now look what I got."

Channel 5 aired the tape on its evening newscasts. It showed a stocky, black-haired man repeatedly striking a woman with his fists and trying to drag her away by the hair as she clung desperately to a turnstile in the empty station.

Walters's only mention of the child abduction was a passing comment that Hernandez had been "arrested for the attack after being picked up on separate charges of abducting and molesting a six-year-old girl over this past weekend."

The child abduction was reported only incidentally by other media as well, but it alerted the Dowalibys, their attorneys, and John Waters that it might be related to Jaclyn's disappearance.

Waters called the Blue Island police and asked for details of the abduction. He learned that the abductor climbed through a kitchen window late at night at the home of David and Carline MacRand and carried their six-year-old daughter, Rory, out of the house.* The abduction occurred on September 2, 1989, just a few days short of one year after the Dowaliby crime.

Rory MacRand told police that she was molested under a railroad trestle near the Cal-Sag Channel in Blue Island.

"I got stoled," she said.

When reporters disclosed the MacRand abduction on September 6, Waters called Cynthia at home. His notes indicate that he expected her to be excited about the development, but instead he found her "sick over the thought" of Jaclyn being with the brutal man she had seen on television.

Cynthia said that the Metra victim had wandered into the

---

* To protect the privacy of the victim, these names have been changed, as have the names of other sexual-abuse victims and their family members mentioned later in this book.

Anchor Bowl the night of the attack, where Gene O'Connor had seen bite marks on her nose and legs. The victim once had lived on the Dowalibys' block in Midlothian, although Cynthia did not know her.

The next day, Waters served a subpoena on the Blue Island police for a copy of the MacRand file, but they refused to surrender it immediately. Waters drove to the MacRand home and noted that it was visible across an alley from the apartment building where Hernandez lived. Waters then drove to the railroad trestle where Rory MacRand had been molested, noting it was less than a mile from the Islander Apartments.

On September 9, Waters went to see Erzsebette Sziky, the woman whose Midlothian home was burglarized the night before Jaclyn vanished. Waters showed her a photograph of Perry Hernandez that had been published in a community newspaper.

Sziky said she already had seen Hernandez on television, and told Waters, "It looks just like him." She said she could be more certain if she could see a profile photo, since she had seen only a side view of the man. Waters said he would obtain one.

At a hearing before Judge Neville on September 11, the Blue Island police turned over a copy of the MacRand file. It contained a copy of a statement signed by Perry Hernandez, who denied the Metra beating but admitted the MacRand abduction.

In the statement, Hernandez also confessed to trying to break into a home "where I thought a little girl lived" just before he abducted Rory MacRand. However, someone was awake in the first home and Hernandez fled after opening the window.

Hernandez said he then went to the MacRand home, where he "had seen a little girl playing before." He removed a screen from a window, climbed inside, carried Rory out, took her to the Cal-Sag Channel, and molested her.

The statement concluded, "I knew I had a problem with fantasizing about little girls. I am sorry for anything I did."

A report in the file said that the mother, father, four other children, and a dog all were in the house when Rory MacRand was abducted, yet were not awakened.

After reading the file, Neville again postponed the trial, tentatively rescheduling it for late November. He said the Dowalibys' lawyers were entitled to investigate the MacRand case further and indicated that another trial delay was likely.

Outside the courtroom, Lawrence Hyman told reporters, "There are uncanny similarities here." Ralph Meczyk added, "Everyone said it was implausible that this could happen, that someone could break in and abduct a child from under your nose. Yet a year later, it happens."

However, police and prosecutors adamantly asserted that there were strong dissimilarities between the cases. The MacRand intruder left fingerprints at the point of entry, knocked several tomatoes and pieces of silverware onto the floor, turned off the electric power, dropped a cigarette pack in the house, and, most important, released his victim alive.

"We can put this to rest—there's no connection," proclaimed Assistant State's Attorney Patrick Quinn, who was in charge of the Hernandez prosecution.

Hernandez's attorney, Ronald A. Rodger, besieged by media inquiries, invited reporters to his office for a briefing. He said Hernandez denied the Dowaliby crime, while making admissions concerning Rory MacRand. In Rodger's view, the MacRand admissions strengthened the credibility of the Dowaliby denial. By Rodger's side was Julie Oster, who said she was Hernandez's girlfriend. "He wouldn't hurt anybody," Oster said.

Although the official line was that there was no link between the cases, reporters were skeptical. Channel 7 described them as "remarkably similar," and the next morning's *Chicago Tribune* emphasized the "apparent similarities."

Patrick O'Brien was upset. He called Greves and chastised him for announcing the Hernandez arrest and prompting public speculation that Hernandez might have killed Jaclyn Dowaliby.

"It's unfortunate for the Dowaliby case that this came up," Greves told O'Brien, "but I can't help that."

* * *

On September 12, John Waters measured the distance from the Dowaliby home to Julie Oster's apartment, where Hernandez had been staying at about the time of Jaclyn's disappearance. It was nine tenths of a mile. Waters was stunned to see that the apartment was just across an alley from the Sziky home.

Waters knocked on Erzsebette Sziky's door and asked whether anything belonging to her daughter might have been taken during the burglary the night before Jaclyn disappeared. In reading the Hernandez file, Waters had noticed that several personal items belonging to Rory MacRand had been taken, including underwear and bathing suits. Sziky revealed that her daughter had pierced ears and that the intruder had taken her earrings. Sziky said she had not mentioned this to the police because the earrings were not valuable.

Jaclyn's ears also were pierced, and the earrings she was wearing the night she vanished had never been found.

John Waters interviewed Perry Hernandez's girlfriend Julie Oster on September 13.

Oster said she had met Hernandez two years earlier, in the summer of 1988, and that he occasionally had stayed with her that September. However, she could not recall if he had been there the night Jaclyn disappeared.

Oster suggested that another man, who sometimes stayed with her during that period, was more likely than Hernandez to have committed the Dowaliby crime. That man, she said, had worked on a tugboat on the Cal-Sag Channel and had attempted suicide shortly after Jaclyn was found.

At the end of September 1988, Oster said, the lease on her apartment expired. She moved in with her parents, and Hernandez eventually moved into the Blue Island apartment near the MacRand home. He was living there when he was arrested. Rodger, who was present for the interview, told Waters that Hernandez steadfastly denied the Dowaliby crime.

Despite Hernandez's confession to the MacRand abduction, Rodger said, the police had not bothered to search his apartment for evidence that might link him to the Dowaliby murder. According to Hernandez, the police had not even questioned him about the Dowaliby case.

At a hearing before Judge Neville on September 15, Patrick O'Brien announced that the unidentified fingerprint on the Dowaliby broken window was not Perry Hernandez's.

As Meczyk left the courtroom, he told reporters, "There are still uncanny similarities between the two cases. We believe, in fact, that this is the person who committed the Dowaliby crime, and the jury is going to hear about it."

On September 16, John Waters, Ralph Meczyk, and Lawrence Hyman went to the MacRand home. Carline MacRand went over the crime in detail, adding information that was not in the police reports.

Most stunning, MacRand quoted her daughter as saying that Hernandez had threatened her with a rope. Under the trestle, said MacRand, Hernandez approached Rory with a rope stretched between his hands, made a threatening gesture with it, and threw it into the canal.

The morning after the crime, MacRand said she discovered that the screen had been cut before it was removed from the window—the same thing that had happened to the Sziky screen. She also discovered that all of the doors in the house had been unlocked, apparently providing escape routes.

MacRand volunteered that the police initially separated her from her husband, David, and questioned him as a suspect. Only after finding Rory's underpants near the Cal-Sag Channel did the police begin to believe that she had been abducted by a stranger.

At the end of the interview, Meczyk and Hyman gave MacRand $30 in cash, telling her to "buy something for the kids." They indicated that they would put her comments in writing and return with a statement for her to sign.

That evening, Carline MacRand questioned Rory more carefully about the rope, showing her a piece of twine and a roll of white string. Rory said the string was the closest to that with which she was threatened.

Carline MacRand immediately called Waters and told him that the statement that the lawyers were preparing should reflect that Rory's attacker threatened her with string. Waters's notes indicate that he was impressed that MacRand was so concerned with precision. "I think it confirms her story," he jotted. "It might explain why he didn't strangle her. String is not strong enough."

On September 22, Waters returned and obtained a handwritten statement from Carline MacRand explaining the string. The statement said, in part, "I showed Rory a roll of string and asked her if the rope was like that, or like another piece of twine I had in the house. She said it was just like the string. I explained to her that she must tell the truth or she could get in trouble. She said she was telling the truth."

When he finished taking MacRand's statement, Waters went to an ice cream parlor and returned with a quart of ice cream for the children. Waters was developing a close relationship with the MacRands, as he had with the Szikys and the Dowalibys. He called or visited all of them almost daily. This yielded information about what the police and prosecutors were doing. He learned, as a matter of fact, that the prosecutors were growing increasingly interested in John Waters.

At one point, two assistant state's attorneys showed up at the Sziky home and, according to Erzsebette Sziky, asked for a description of the Dowalibys' private investigator. Sziky was guarded. "He's a man," she responded. They asked how old he was. "Middle-aged." Is he thin? "Yes." Is his name John? "Maybe." John Waters? "Maybe." When did he become involved in the Dowaliby case? "I don't know."

At an appearance before Judge Neville on October 10, Patrick O'Brien said he wanted to subpoena Waters's notes. Meczyk said he would oppose turning them over to the prosecution. Neville took no action on O'Brien's request at that time, but later ordered them produced. When Neville issued the order, Waters recopied portions of his notes, eliminating most of the substantive information, and surrendered the sanitized version to O'Brien.

* * *

Despite his serious health problems, John Waters seemed to take on new energy with the discovery of Perry Hernandez.

He was interested in details of Hernandez's confession of an attempted entry into another home the night of the MacRand abduction. One of the police reports identified the head of the household as Enrique Arias.

Waters went to the address and interviewed Arias, who said that at about 3:00 A.M. on September 2 his wife heard a noise in the kitchen area. She discovered that the kitchen window and screen were open and that there were two holes in the window screen. Arias then went outside and found a chair beneath the window but did not see anyone. He called police, who took the chair as evidence.

The Ariases had three children, a son and two daughters. The younger daughter was five years old.

On October 23, Ralph Meczyk and Lawrence Hyman filed a motion asking Judge Neville to rule on whether they could present evidence relating to the MacRand, Sziky, and Arias cases at the Dowaliby trial. They argued that the three crimes were relevant because they "are startlingly similar to the kidnapping and murder of Jaclyn Dowaliby."

Neville said he would like to hear Erzsebette Sziky testify before deciding the motion, and set a hearing for November 20. He indicated that in order to introduce other crimes at the trial, the defense would have to demonstrate evidence of "substantial similarities" between those crimes and the Dowaliby case.

Two days after Meczyk and Hyman filed the motion, Midlothian detective Neal Caauwe went to Erzsebette Sziky's home and asked if the defense had "bribed or tricked" her in any way. Specifically, he wanted to know whether the defense had a hand in her belated contention that Nicole had been covered with blankets by the intruder. Sziky told Caauwe no, that she simply had recalled this fact after the police interview.

That evening, Sziky went to the Midlothian police station at the request of Patrick O'Brien and his assistant George

Velcich. She told Waters later that O'Brien and Velcich treated her "sweet at first, but then got tough."

She said they grilled her for two hours about her identification of Perry Hernandez and the changes in her account about the burglary. When she said at one point that her daughter's abduction was similar to the Dowaliby crime, O'Brien angrily jumped to his feet, yelling, "Whoa, whoa, whoa!" He demanded to know why she was helping the Dowalibys. "Because I think they are innocent," she said.

O'Brien asked her whether Meczyk and Hyman had given her money, saying they had "bribed" Carline MacRand with $30. "They didn't offer me anything," said Sziky. O'Brien also wanted to know how many times she had spoken to Waters. "I talked to a guy named John twice," she said.

Waters now realized that the state was fighting hard to keep evidence of Perry Hernandez's alleged and admitted crimes out of the Dowaliby trial. Waters knew he had until the November 20 court hearing to develop links that Neville would regard as "substantial."

He began by checking Hernandez's criminal record. It showed that Hernandez had not been arrested since 1985, but from 1982 to 1985 he had been arrested six times—three times for residential burglary, once for assault and battery, once for possession of marijuana, and once for auto theft. The auto theft occurred less than a mile from the Islander Apartments.

Waters took a mug shot of Hernandez to show to the manager of the apartment complex, Eileen Blaylock. She did not recognize Hernandez. Waters then took the photo to several nearby bars. One bartender recognized Hernandez as a regular patron. Waters also measured the distance from the complex to the bars where Hernandez said he drank the night he abducted Rory MacRand. Both were about a mile away.

Checking the three earlier residential burglaries for which Hernandez had been arrested, Waters found that a little girl lived in each home. In all three instances, Waters noted, Hernandez "attacked a window for entry, ripped a window screen, struck in the early-morning hours on a weekend, and lived within a mile of the crime scene." The pattern was the same as in the MacRand, Sziky, and Arias cases. "Every one applies to the Dowalibys," Waters wrote.

Next Waters decided to compare the screens in the MacRand, Sziky, and Arias cases. He found that the Sziky screen had been cut neatly but that holes had been poked in the MacRand and Arias screens. He was unable to make a comparison with the Dowaliby screen, which had disappeared.

Waters asked Cynthia Dowaliby if she was certain that none of Jaclyn's underwear or bathing suits had been taken. Cynthia double-checked and found that nothing was missing. He asked her if there was any chance that her electricity could have been turned off the night Jaclyn was taken. Cynthia said if that had happened, her digital clock would have started flashing. However, she told Waters that Ann Dowaliby's television set had gone on and off mysteriously the night Jaclyn disappeared.

Ralph Meczyk arranged through Ronald Rodger for Waters to interview two relatives of Perry Hernandez—Penny Hernandez, his older sister, and his cousin Jesse Hernandez, who lived near the MacRands.

Penny Hernandez said that her brother had had an argument with Julie Oster the night of the MacRand abduction. Perry then had gone to two taverns, where he got drunk.

Waters asked Penny whether her brother had any connection to the Islander Apartments. "Maybe Perry knew friends from work who lived at the Islander Apartments," Penny said. Waters asked her if she found any jewelry or girl's clothing in the home. She said no. Waters asked to search the basement, but Penny refused. She confirmed that the police had never searched the house.

Waters also checked a rumor, passed to him by Carline MacRand, that Perry Hernandez once had molested a young female relative. Waters interviewed the brother of the child in question, who said he once suspected that Perry "was after my little sister or her underpants." "I beat him up," said the brother. "If Perry had molested my sister, he would be dead." (Hernandez has since denied molesting the relative.)

Waters next met privately with Julie Oster, who now claimed for the first time that Perry Hernandez had been with her at the very time Jaclyn Dowaliby disappeared. She also told Waters that the Dowalibys' lawyers had offered her brother money to answer questions. Waters labeled that contention "bullshit" in his notes, although, at almost that very moment, Meczyk was delivering gifts of clothing to the MacRand children.

Waters wanted to interview Perry Hernandez, but Ronald Rodger would not allow that. However, Rodger gave Meczyk information from interviews that prosecutors had conducted with Hernandez after the publicity linking him to the Dowaliby case.

The prosecutors, according to Waters's notes, "told Rodger they believed Hernandez was innocent of Dowaliby because he didn't have a car or a driver's license." The logic apparently was that Hernandez would have had no means of transporting Jaclyn's body to the Islander Apartments—a view that Waters characterized as "ridiculous."

Meanwhile, Waters stumbled onto another possible connection between Perry Hernandez and Jaclyn. He asked Cynthia Dowaliby to drive past Julie Oster's former Midlothian apartment, where Hernandez had lived, to see if there was anything that might connect Jaclyn to the area.

Cynthia did that, noticing that the apartment was directly behind a fitness center where she had taken aerobics classes during the summer of 1988, often bringing along Jaclyn and Davey.

Waters interviewed the owner of the fitness center, Janet Balchristie, who vividly recalled the Dowaliby children.

She remarked that Jaclyn strongly resembled her own six-year-old daughter.

Ten months later, in a chilling development that Waters would not live to investigate, Balchristie's daughter, Jenny, by then Jaclyn's age, would be abducted from the family home by an intruder in the middle of the night and molested.

PRETRIAL JOCKEYING

Ralph Meczyk and Lawrence Hyman were elated by the information John Waters had developed on Perry Hernandez.

Having Hernandez as an alternative suspect, in the lawyers' view, was the perfect vehicle for creating reasonable doubt about the Dowalibys' guilt. Waters, on the other hand, wanted to do more than create reasonable doubt; he wanted to prove that Hernandez had committed the crime.

Meczyk and Hyman, frantically working on their strategy for the trial, needed Waters to look into other matters in advance of pretrial hearings, now scheduled to begin on November 20.

Waters protested, saying he might be close to solving the crime.

"Our job is to defend the Dowalibys," Meczyk reminded him, "not to prove who's really guilty."

Meczyk agreed that it would be ideal to nail the culprit. However, if Waters devoted most of his time to that effort and failed, more mundane but potentially crucial aspects of the defense case would go by the wayside.

Before every criminal trial, the defense and prosecution battle over what evidence will be admissible in court and what will not. The judge's pretrial decisions on evidentiary matters often are critical to the result—the difference between acquittal and conviction.

The pretrial work remaining to be done in the Dowaliby case was overwhelming. The prosecution had buried Meczyk and Hyman in more than three thousand pages of documents, and the list of prospective prosecution witnesses had grown to more than four hundred names.

Since it was not possible to investigate every person on the list, Meczyk and Hyman wanted Waters to focus on the ones who obviously stood to do the most damage to the defense case. There was no single witness who could inflict a decisive blow against Cynthia, but David's case was different because of Everett Mann.

Waters, who had uncovered the fact that Mann suffered from cyclothymia, suggested that Meczyk contact a psychiatrist to assess whether the condition might impair Mann's perception of reality. Waters recommended Dr. Jan Fawcett, chairman of the psychiatry department at Rush-Presbyterian-St. Luke's Medical Center, one of Chicago's major teaching institutions. Waters had seen Fawcett testify in several cases.

At Meczyk's request, Fawcett agreed to review Mann's psychological tests—Minnesota Multiphasic Personality Inventories—which had been the basis both for his military discharge and his rejections for employment by the Chicago Police Department.

Fawcett concluded that Mann's MMPIs were consistent with the diagnosis of cyclothymia, a form of manic-depression. Persons with the condition "experience swings in mood that sometimes cause them to dramatize or exaggerate events," he told Meczyk.

However, Fawcett added, since persons with cyclothymia have periods of normalcy, there was no way of knowing what Mann's mood might have been on September 10, 1988, when he claimed to have seen the late-model car pull out of the Islander Apartments parking lot.

Fawcett referred Meczyk to Dr. Frank Leavitt, director of the psychology department at Rush-Presbyterian-St. Luke's and an expert on interpreting the MMPI. Leavitt said that Mann's MMPIs were "extremely abnormal" and "very strongly suggestive" of cyclothymia. Asked how the condition might have affected Mann on the night Jaclyn disappeared, Leavitt agreed with Fawcett that there was no way of knowing for sure.

To fortify Fawcett and Leavitt's opinions, John Waters struck on a direct way to test the validity of Mann's perception: He would stage a reenactment of the event that Mann claimed to have witnessed in the Islander Apartments parking lot a year before.

Waters had developed a friendly relationship with Eileen Blaylock, the manager of the complex, whose help was needed to facilitate the experiment. He obtained her permission to photograph the lot, to control the lighting, and to arrange with tenants for cars to be parked where they had been at 2:00 A.M. on September 10, 1988.

At 10:00 P.M. on September 29, 1989, David Dowaliby sat in the driver's seat of his wife's Chevrolet Malibu at the precise spot where Mann claimed to have seen a similar car and driver one year, nineteen days, and twenty hours earlier. Donna Yarborough, a photographer hired by Meczyk, stood where Everett Mann said he had parked that night.

With every exterior light in that portion of the complex turned on, and with photographic floodlights positioned to illuminate the car, Yarborough videotaped David slowly pulling the Malibu out of its parking place.

Using a lens with twenty times the resolution power of the human eye, Yarborough captured the shape of the car and its color. However, the camera could not discern a nose structure or even the gender of the driver.

When the floodlights were turned off, producing lighting conditions approximating those described by Mann, the camera captured neither the shape of the car nor any image of the driver.

Waters beamed, thinking that the defense now had irrefutable proof that Mann could not have seen what he had claimed. Then he noticed that David Dowaliby's face had turned pale.

"What's the matter?" Waters asked.

"I feel sick," said David. "Despite what the cops believe, this is the first time I've been here. It's horrible to think that this is where Jaclyn ended up."

At about the same time, Blue Island Police Chief Paul Greves received an urgent call from Patrick O'Brien.

The conversation, as Greves later reconstructed it, went like this:

O'BRIEN—"Do we have all of the evidence in this case?"

GREVES—"Yes, you do."

O'BRIEN—"Sure there's nothing you haven't turned over?"

GREVES—"Why do you ask me that?"

O'BRIEN—"Was there a tape of the Everett Mann interview?"

GREVES—"Yes."

O'BRIEN—"Why didn't you turn that over?"

GREVES—"Because I was instructed by the prosecutor in charge to get rid of it."

Greves was referring to Robert Clifford, the former assistant state's attorney who had been in charge of the Dowaliby investigation—until O'Brien aced him out.

"Clifford's been talking to the defense," Greves quoted O'Brien as saying.

Greves said he thought that ironic, since Clifford had berated him for recording the interview in the first place. Now, in an act of sweet revenge, Clifford had told Lawrence Hyman, Cynthia Dowaliby's lawyer, about the tape.

Hyman, a former colleague of both O'Brien and Clifford in the state's attorney's office, promptly demanded that the prosecution surrender the tape.

Greves sent it to O'Brien, who had no choice but to turn it over to the defense.

The tape memorialized the weakness of Mann's parking lot

observations—and brought an abrupt halt to O'Brien's repeated claim that an "eyewitness" had placed David Dowaliby at the scene of the crime.

Ralph Meczyk and Lawrence Hyman hired an expert to check the state crime laboratory's finding that the unidentified fingerprint on the Dowaliby basement window glass was not Perry Hernandez's. The defense expert, George Bonbreak, former supervisor of the fingerprint section of the FBI crime laboratory in Washington, D.C., agreed with the state's finding.

Bonbreak used a photographic technique that was superior to the visual analysis performed by the state expert, Joseph Ambrozich. Unfortunately for the defense, the clearer image produced by Bonbreak's technique prompted Ambrozich to analyze the fingerprint evidence again. This time Ambrozich was able to determine who the print belonged to: It was Davey Dowaliby's.

Had it not been for the reexamination, the print would have remained unidentified at trial, and the defense could have argued that it was evidence of an unknown intruder.

On November 20, Judge Neville's courtroom was packed with reporters and spectators for a hearing on Perry Hernandez's possible connection to the Dowaliby crime. The question was whether the defense would be allowed to introduce evidence at the Dowaliby trial concerning the MacRand, Sziky, and Arias crimes.

Meczyk recited the numerous parallels that John Waters had discovered between those crimes and the Dowaliby case. "The fact in the Sziky home that the child was bundled in a certain way and ready to go is compelling circumstantial evidence that he was about to take that child out of the house," he said. "And if it wasn't for Mrs. Sziky being awake and looking at him, there but by the grace of God went Nicole, too."

Holding up photographs of Jaclyn Dowaliby and Nicole Sziky, Meczyk contended, "What's very, very striking here is that there is a tremendous resemblance between the children.

It's like a predator. He stalked Rory MacRand and wanted to get at the Arias child, almost got at the Sziky child, and unfortunately murdered the Dowaliby child. We are seeking to admit evidence of Arias, MacRand, and Sziky to show *modus operandi.* Your honor, this is all logically relevant evidence that disproves that David and Cynthia Dowaliby murdered their child."

Patrick O'Brien acknowledged that Hernandez did commit an assault on Rory MacRand and an attempted residential burglary at the Arias home. He argued, however, that "there is no evidence directly to link Perry Hernandez to the Dowaliby case."

He contended that there were "numerous distinctions" between the Dowaliby case and the Sziky and Arias cases. He noted that Erzsebette Sziky initially told police that her daughter had not been disturbed, arguing that there was no credible evidence that the burglary had been anything but a property crime.

"This guy had so much property he couldn't have carried a kid with him," said O'Brien. He added that Erzsebette Sziky's identification of Perry Hernandez, made more than a year after the incident, was unreliable. As for Arias, he said, despite Hernandez's confession to the attempted break-in, there was no evidence that he was attempting to take a child.

Foremost among the distinctions between the MacRand and Dowaliby cases, O'Brien continued, was the fact that Rory was released alive. However, O'Brien said he would not object to the defense raising the MacRand case at the Dowaliby trial. His reason, he said, had nothing to do with the law, but rather with the publicity surrounding Hernandez's possible link to the Dowaliby case.

"When Perry Hernandez was arrested, the defense took the opportunity to tell the media that he is the person who committed the Dowaliby crime," O'Brien said. "As a result of the intensive coverage, any jury that hears the Dowaliby case is going to be thinking about the MacRand case." This made it essential, he said, that the prosecution be allowed to disprove any connection to the Dowaliby jury.

After O'Brien sat down, Neville ruled that evidence relating to the MacRand case would be admissible, but not because of the media attention it had received. Rather, Neville accepted the defense argument that there were significant similarities between the MacRand and Dowaliby crimes.

The defense victory was incomplete, however. Neville indicated that he would not allow evidence concerning the aborted break-in at the Arias home. Despite Hernandez's explicit admission that he knew that a little girl lived there, Neville bought the prosecution's argument that there was no proof that Hernandez had intended to abduct her.

The Sziky case presented a different problem, having to do with Erzsebette Sziky's credibility, Neville continued. He wanted to determine that for himself, and ordered Sziky into court to testify on December 4.

When Erzsebette Sziky took the stand, she was wearing a new $145 dress that Meczyk had bought her at Marshall Field & Company for the occasion.

On direct examination by Meczyk, Sziky repeated what she had told John Waters. She had seen a dark-haired intruder, wearing jeans, flee her apartment. She found her daughter wrapped in blankets and later recalled the missing earrings, but did not report these facts to the police because she did not consider them important at the time.

Sziky explained how she had come to identify Perry Hernandez as the intruder. A year after the break-in, she had seen a television report of Hernandez's arrest for the Metra beating and MacRand abduction. When his photograph flashed on the screen, she screamed, "Oh, my God, it's him!"

Meczyk showed her a photograph of Hernandez, which she identified. "Is there any question in your mind today as to the person who was in your house on September the ninth, 1988?" he asked.

"No," Sziky replied. "No question at all."

On cross-examination, Patrick O'Brien established that Sziky had been unemployed since 1986, when she had worked at a tavern, and that her telephone service had been shut off because the bill had not been paid.

Sziky acknowledged that she did not contact the police

either after recalling that her daughter had been covered with blankets or after recognizing Perry Hernandez on television.

On redirect, Meczyk asked why she had not called the police after recognizing Hernandez on television. "I didn't want all the publicity," she said. "Everything was fine with us. I wanted to keep peace, you know. He was already in custody, being taken care of for other things."

"Now," Meczyk asked, "you never told, isn't it true, the Midlothian Police Department that your daughter had been covered in those blankets?"

"Right," she answered.

"Is there a reason why you didn't tell them she had been covered in those blankets?"

"It didn't have a meaning to me at the time."

Meczyk asked whether, when she was interviewed at the Midlothian Police Department on October 23, she was asked why she was helping the Dowalibys.

"Yeah, they did," said Sziky.

"What did you tell them?"

"I told them I wasn't helping anybody. I was just telling my story, what happened to me. I don't know the facts about anything else except what happened to me."

On recross, O'Brien asked whether she believed Hernandez committed the Dowaliby crime. His point was that such a belief might color her testimony in favor of the Dowalibys. Sziky acknowledged that, based on the similarities between the Dowaliby case and the break-in at her apartment, she thought Hernandez had committed both crimes.

O'Brien then called Midlothian Police Sergeant David Burke to the stand. Burke testified that he was the first officer at the scene of the Sziky crime and that Erzsebette Sziky did not tell him about the blankets or earrings, nor did she mention how the intruder was dressed or that he had long, dark hair.

O'Brien next called Midlothian Police Officer Robert L. Ufheil. He testified that two weeks after the break-in, Sziky had come to the police station to report additional property that the intruder had taken but did not mention the earrings.

Finally, O'Brien called FBI Agent Edward O'Malley to testify. O'Malley said he and another officer had interviewed Sziky on September 12, 1988, three days after the break-in at her home and two days before Jaclyn Dowaliby's body was found. She described neither what the intruder was wearing nor his hair, and mentioned nothing about her daughter having been covered with blankets.

After hearing the testimony, Neville declared a short recess. When he returned to the bench, he ruled that the defense would not be allowed to introduce evidence of the Sziky crime at the Dowaliby trial.

Neville found that Erzsebette Sziky's identification of Hernandez was unreliable because it was made a year after the crime and only after she saw his photograph on television. Even if the identification were reliable, Neville said, there would have to be "a whole trial" on whether the intruder disturbed Sziky's daughter. The Dowaliby jurors "would be spending all of their time on an issue that is unrelated to what they are really here for," said Neville, shaking his gray locks.

To make the record clear in the event the Dowalibys were convicted and had to appeal their case, Meczyk objected to the ruling. "Respectfully, your honor, I cannot quarrel with your decision," Meczyk began.

"Well," Neville interjected, "you can, but you won't change my mind."

"Just for the purposes of the record," Meczyk said, "I want to respond to your comments, and please don't take this to be a rebuke on our part, certainly not." He insisted that the Sziky evidence should be allowed because it would tend to raise reasonable doubt about whether the Dowalibys had killed Jaclyn.

Neville, true to his word, remained adamant.

The Dowalibys' lawyers, thus, would be able to raise only the MacRand case at trial. The jury would hear no testimony about the pattern of late-night break-ins, through windows, at nearby homes where little girls lived.

After inquiring about the attorneys' schedules, Neville said the trial would begin on March 26, 1990—and not later.

* * *

In mid-December, Peggy O'Connor told John Waters, "Cyndi is lashing out at everyone. People are saying terrible things about her, and she can't say anything back."

The strain was wearing on the defense team as well. Ralph Meczyk developed severe digestive problems, due to an ulcer. This was the biggest case of Meczyk's career—a case that could help restore his reputation after the disgrace of his Operation Greylord conviction. His stomach churned over the possibility that he might blow it.

Lawrence Hyman also was distracted because his wife was in her final month of pregnancy.

Waters wondered whether he would live to see the trial. On New Year's Day 1990, Meczyk asked if he felt up to continuing. "Are my efforts flagging?" Waters asked.

"No," said Meczyk, but Waters thought the answer was hesitant. Waters turned to the Dowalibys for moral support, but found them more in need of reassurance than he.

David told Waters he was worried about Cynthia. On December 16, Meczyk had told her, "Look, we might lose. Don't be too confident." Cynthia had been distraught since then.

"Tell Cyndi this is a bad time for her, with the holidays, Christmas without Jaclyn, and natural trepidation about the trial," Waters said. "Her reaction is normal."

Waters added, "Ralph gets pessimistic and down on himself. He worries about not being good enough—and that's good, because, if he was smug, he could get hurt. But he is so cautious and respectful of his opponent, and so hardworking, that he becomes a winner."

A little later, Waters called Cynthia. "Remember, you didn't do it, and you will be found not guilty," he told her. "Nothing is for sure, but the state can't prove a lie."

On March 7, 1990, Ralph Meczyk and Lawrence Hyman appeared before Judge Neville to ask for another delay. The Dowalibys were not present in court because no testimony was scheduled.

"We're not asking for that much more time, in light of everything that's transpired in this case," Meczyk told Neville. "We're asking for just a few more weeks."

Neville was unsympathetic. "I've been hearing since last November that we have a little more work to do. It is no—there's no more 'little more work' to do."

"We expect to be done within a very, very short time," Meczyk responded. "Our investigators are still doing certain things for us." He was referring not only to John Waters but also to Dr. Henry Lee, director of the Connecticut State Police crime laboratory, who was conducting experiments for the defense on glass breakage with windows similar to the Dowalibys'.

Meczyk pleaded for understanding. "We had to coordinate the entire effort in a small, two-man office," he said, adding that there were "just a few, few matters to zero in on."

Neville reluctantly relented. "I'm going to give you one more week," he said, delaying the trial from March 26 to April 3. "That is the last continuance," he proclaimed.

Meczyk and Hyman then announced the Dowalibys wished to be tried together before the same jury. This meant that David and Cynthia's defenses were compatible.

If their defenses had been in any way antagonistic—if evidence favorable to one reflected unfavorably on the other—the lawyers would have sought separate trials, or at least separate juries at the same trial. With separate juries, one jury can be excluded from the courtroom when evidence irrelevant to its defendant is admitted against another defendant.

Also, as a matter of right, the Dowalibys could have chosen to be tried by the judge, without a jury. Meczyk and Hyman had decided against that course. Cook County judges are elected and may have at least a subconscious tendency, in high-profile cases, to want to appear tough on crime.

"There was too much heat," Meczyk would reflect later. "It was not the type of case you would take in front of a judge."

O'Brien had an announcement of his own on March 7. "We are not going to *Witherspoon* the jury," he told Neville.

"Well, that solves that issue," Neville responded.

In lay terms, O'Brien's announcement meant that the prosecution had changed its position and would not seek the death penalty if the Dowalibys were convicted.

The term "Witherspoon" derives from a landmark 1968

case, *Witherspoon* v. *Illinois,* in which the U.S. Supreme Court voided a state law requiring judges to excuse prospective jurors who expressed "conscientious scruples" against the death penalty.

The Supreme Court held that mere scruples against the death penalty did not justify disqualifying jurors. However, jurors could be disqualified if their views on capital punishment would prevent them from making an impartial decision concerning the guilt or innocence of a defendant. Asking jurors about their views on the death penalty is known as "Witherspooning."

O'Brien did not explain why the death penalty would not be sought, but the legal reason was implicit: Under Illinois law, capital punishment is prescribed for the murder of a child under age twelve when "the death resulted from exceptionally brutal or heinous behavior indicative of wanton cruelty." Because of the decomposition of Jaclyn's body, there was no way to prove that her death resulted from brutal or heinous behavior.

Of course, prosecutors had known sixteen months earlier, when they proclaimed that they *would* demand the death penalty, that brutal behavior would be impossible to prove. Now, however, there was a strategic reason for announcing that they would not seek it: Jurors might be reluctant to convict the Dowalibys on circumstantial evidence if a death sentence were in the offing.

Moreover, the rationale for threatening the death penalty in the first place had disappeared. Originally it had been partly a psychological tool, designed to pressure the Dowalibys to confess in exchange for a lesser penalty. The Sword of Damocles was no longer useful, however, since it was now obvious that the Dowalibys were not going to confess.

When Meczyk called the Dowalibys to tell them that the death penalty would not be sought, he was surprised at the reaction. David answered the phone. "It doesn't matter," he said. "If you're innocent, dying isn't any worse than spending the rest of your life in jail."

* * *

On March 27, with a week remaining until the start of the trial, Judge Neville held a hearing to resolve two lingering disputes: whether defense experts would be allowed to testify at the trial about Everett Mann's mental condition, and whether the jury would be allowed to see the videotape of the defense reenactment at the Islander Apartments.

Neville was not asked to rule on whether the defense could use the videotape of Robert Tolbert climbing through the Dowalibys' basement window. Incredibly, the tape had been misplaced by the defense and would not be found until after the trial; another tape could not be made in the meantime because the home had been sold and the new owners refused to cooperate.

One legal question applied to both the psychiatric testimony about Everett Mann and the Islander Apartments videotape: Would their introduction at the trial invade the province of the jury? Courts permit such evidence only when it concerns matters that an average juror lacks the knowledge and experience to evaluate.

Judge Neville heard the psychiatric testimony behind closed doors, to the disappointment of reporters and over the vigorous objection of the defense. Ralph Meczyk and Lawrence Hyman had wanted the hearing open, so that the news media could report what Drs. Frank Leavitt and Jan Fawcett would say.

Neville would have none of that, however, ruling that there was "no compelling reason" to make the testimony public when it might never be used at the trial. "This information is barred," he told the lawyers. "It cannot be repeated to the press."

Leavitt testified first. On direct examination by Meczyk, he said that he had twenty-five years' experience evaluating MMPIs.

Mann's performance on the MMPIs was "extremely abnormal," Leavitt said. "I examine people daily in psychiatric units whose scores are not that abnormal."

Mann's tests, said Leavitt, showed a pattern that was "strongly suggestive" of cyclothymia, a disorder characterized by swings in mood between hypomania and depression.

Meczyk asked whether Mann's test results indicated that he was "still suffering from this particular pathology."

"He showed it over a twelve-year period," Leavitt answered. "I would assume he is still suffering from that disorder, yes."

"Can you state that this person was suffering from a bipolar disorder on September the tenth, 1988?" Meczyk asked.

"I would say that these data strongly suggest that diagnostic category, but I think you would want some additional proof," Leavitt answered.

On cross-examination, O'Brien asked a series of questions challenging the reliability of the MMPI. Leavitt countered that massive data gathered over almost a half century had established the test's reliability.

O'Brien asked if there would be times when cyclothymic persons were normal.

"That is correct," Leavitt allowed.

Next up was Jan Fawcett. He was even more certain in his diagnosis than Leavitt had been.

Mann's MMPIs "showed a definite pattern of manic mood states over a twelve-year period," he said. He called the pattern "rather remarkable," saying that it "adds validity to the diagnosis."

"What diagnosis is that?" Meczyk asked.

"Cyclothymic disorder," Fawcett replied firmly.

Fawcett explained that persons with the condition have "an exaggerated sense of their own importance, and they also exaggerate and dramatize things frequently. A whim or an initial observation might become in their minds an established fact very quickly, without much self-questioning or self-doubt." He concluded, "All of those factors could alter a person's perceptions or observations."

Meczyk asked, "Could you tell whether or not Mr. Mann on September the tenth, 1988, was suffering from cyclothymia?"

"Well," Fawcett answered, "I cannot tell whether he was or not, other than to say that cyclothymia is a chronic condition. He probably was suffering from cyclothymia."

On cross-examination, Fawcett said that persons suffering

from cyclothymia experience "short periods" where they are neither depressed nor hypomanic. In a depressed state, he acknowledged, a cyclothymic person might be less certain of observations than a normal person.

"You cannot tell in September 1988 whether Everett Mann was in the hypomanic state, mild depression stage, or in between either stage?" O'Brien asked.

"Based upon the information I have available to me, I cannot at this point, no," Fawcett answered.

Neville adjourned the hearing until the next morning. At that time, once again in chambers, he ruled that Leavitt and Fawcett would not be allowed to testify at the trial. Neville said that neither doctor could pinpoint what Mann's mental condition was—up or down—at the time he pulled his car into the Islander Apartments parking lot.

"The identification might be worse, or it might be better," Neville said. "There is no reason to bring all of this in before the jury. It proves nothing. All it does is cause confusion."

Noting that it is the jury's job to determine the credibility of witnesses, Neville added, "This testimony is dangerous to the jury's ability to make a decision unbridled by what I consider inappropriate attempts to have doctors invade their province."

Applying the same rationale, Neville also ruled that the jury would not be shown the videotape that the defense had made at the Islander Apartments.

The jury would have to make its own judgments on these issues by visiting the apartment complex and hearing the testimony of Mann and other witnesses.

Thus, through his pretrial rulings, Neville had halted John Waters's year-long assault on the prosecution's case.

Neville had foreclosed the defense from cross-examining Mann on an issue that went to the heart of his credibility.

Equally devastating, Neville had forbidden the defense from using the videotape showing that it would have been impossible for Mann to have seen what he had claimed.

These rulings, coupled with Neville's exclusion of the

Sziky and Arias evidence, severely undermined the defense's strategy for discrediting the prosecution's case.

The Dowalibys were still presumed innocent under the law, but, as a practical matter, the prosecutors had seized the momentum going into the trial.

A HOUSE OF CANARDS

Judge Neville's reputation was about as good as they get in the rowdy realm of the Cook County Circuit Court. He was described by lawyers as honest, bright, and blunt.

The forty-eight-year-old son of a Chicago police lieutenant harbored no illusions about the criminal justice system.

"We're just moving society along," he would say. "In a lot of cases, there's no way to know who's really guilty or innocent. The truth is, trials suffer from the same problems humans have—imperfection. They don't always reach a correct result, but they do end disputes and, whatever happens, life goes on."

The presumption of innocence, in Neville's view, was largely a pretense—as he put it, "If 'reasonable doubt' really meant 'reasonable doubt,' there would be a lot fewer convictions."

If Neville's pretrial rulings in the Dowaliby case seemed to favor the prosecution, perhaps they were predictable products of his roots.

He had grown up in a working-class neighborhood on the Northwest Side of Chicago, where the people, including his father, Lieutenant Edward ("Ace") Neville, tended to be patriotic, churchgoing Catholics, and anything but permissive.

Neville worked as a janitor to put himself through DePaul College of Law, graduating fourth in his class in 1965.

Naturally enough, he aspired to be a prosecutor—an ambition that, with Mayor Richard J. Daley at the height of his reign over the nation's last big-city political machine, he could realize only with the help of a political sponsor, or "Chinaman," in the local vernacular.

Neville's Chinaman was P. J. ("Parky") Cullerton, the county assessor, a powerful Daley ally and political boss of the ward in which Neville grew up. Cullerton landed Neville a job in the state's attorney's office in 1967.

First Assistant State's Attorney Louis B. Garippo became Neville's mentor. Garippo, who would later serve with renown on the circuit court and then become a well-known criminal defense lawyer, swiftly propelled Neville through the ranks to the office's Felony Trial Division.

In the next three years, Neville prosecuted some sixty jury cases, mostly murders. As a policeman's son, he took pride in winning the convictions of three men for killing police officers.

The victory that he regarded as his most important, however, was the case of Richard Schultz, who was put away for life for the rape-murder of a young northwest suburban girl. Jaclyn Dowaliby reminded Neville of the victim in that case.

In 1971 Neville left the state's attorney's office to enter private practice. He specialized in representing police officers accused of brutality, winning several high-profile cases.

Neville also successfully defended County Treasurer Edward J. Rosewell against federal bank fraud charges. Rosewell was a powerful Democrat—a connection that would help Neville later.

In the mid-1980s Neville went through a midlife crisis in

which he separated from his wife of twenty-one years after their children, a son and a daughter, were nearly grown.

Financially comfortable from his dozen years in private practice, he wanted to pursue new creative and professional challenges. However, his law partner, Matthew P. Walsh, wanted to continue working sixty to seventy hours a week and expected a comparable contribution from Neville.

Exploring alternative ways of earning a living, Neville struck on the idea of becoming a judge. Illinois judges are elected, but when vacancies occur between terms, the Illinois Supreme Court fills them by appointment.

Neville discussed a possible appointment with Supreme Court Chief Justice William G. Clark, who was encouraging enough that Neville sold his law practice. He began sculpting, writing a book on violence and cruelty, and working out daily at an exclusive fitness center, the East Bank Club, in preparation for annual mountain-climbing sojourns. The judicial appointment, however, was not forthcoming.

In 1986 Neville appeared before the Cook County Democratic Central Committee, seeking slating for election to a Circuit Court vacancy. Despite strong support from his former client, County Treasurer Rosewell, Neville did not make the slate.

Neville decided not to challenge the Democratic Party in the primary, since he did not have, as he put it, "a ballot name"—meaning a recognizable Irish surname. (In fact, although the name sounds English or Norman, Neville's father was Irish.)

A week before the ballots were to be printed for the 1986 primary election, however, Neville was notified by Cook County Democratic Chairman Edward R. ("Fast Eddie") Vrdolyak that one of the slated candidates had decided not to run.

"If you're still interested, you've got it," Vrdolyak said.

At the time, Chicago's reform Mayor Harold Washington was locked in a battle with Vrdolyak and other party regulars for control of the city government, a battle so bitter that *The Wall Street Journal* dubbed Chicago "Beirut on the Lake."

Washington fielded an independent judicial slate in the

election and managed to defeat several of the Vrdolyak-backed candidates. Washington, however, was on good terms with Rosewell and, as a favor, did not slate a candidate against Neville.

Two candidates did enter the race, but their ballot names, Pink and Bennett, were no better than his. Neville's election was assured when both Chicago daily newspapers, following the lead of the Chicago Bar Association and Chicago Council of Lawyers, recommended his election.

Neville was assigned to the Criminal Court building, where most of the judges, like him, were former prosecutors —a situation bemoaned by the defense bar.*

He decorated his inner sanctum at Twenty-sixth and California with a mixture of sophistication and whimsy, giving it the feeling of a cross between a museum and a college dormitory.

Neville dotted the chamber with sculpture, including his own creations, bearing some resemblance to the work of Henri Matisse, and, *inter alia,* a huge, stunning walnut relief of the Last Supper by a Serbian artist, Rade Bundalo. On the large shelf behind his desk, Neville placed a life-size birch bust of himself sculpted by Bundalo.

On the wall, near the Last Supper, he affixed a plaque—a memento of a trip to Yugoslavia mimicking the local accent: "Richer E. Novel, adovokat and konsellour att law."

"Urine Testing Pisses Me Off," proclaimed a yellow button on his desk, beside a brass penholder engraved with words of architect Daniel Burnham: "Make no small plans; they have no magic to stir men's blood."

Neville's courtroom, room 600, had a history that was both sentimental for Neville and significant in the annals of crime.

It was here that Neville's former mentor, Louis Garippo, had sat as a trial judge after leaving the state's attorney's office. It was here that, in 1980, John Wayne Gacy was con-

---

* Twenty-three of the thirty-four Criminal Court judges at the time the Dowaliby case arose were ex-prosecutors. Only three had been public defenders. Source: Administrative Office of the Illinois Courts.

victed by a jury and sentenced to death by Judge Garippo for the murders of thirty-three young men.

By a stroke of fate, two of the most sensational Cook County murder cases of the century—Gacy and Dowaliby—had found their way into the same courtroom.

Ralph Meczyk had been suspicious of Judge Neville from the beginning. Like Patrick O'Brien and George Velcich, Neville had roots in law enforcement and, like O'Brien and Velcich, was a Roman Catholic. Meczyk was, heart and soul, a defense lawyer and proud of his strong Jewish identity.

In recent weeks, Neville's pretrial rulings had further fueled Meczyk's mistrust. Meczyk, who had lost forebearers in the Holocaust, had come to view the judge as an arm of the state—a third prosecutor—and the case itself as an exercise in the power of established authority to crush guiltless citizens.

Meczyk suspected that, during the pretrial discovery process, the prosecution had cast out various "canards"—ruses designed to mislead the defense. The supposed canards ranged from listing hundreds of potential witnesses when only a handful actually would be called, to indicating that there would be no "bombshells" in the case.

The potential bombshell that Meczyk most feared was a last-minute positive identification of David Dowaliby by Everett Mann. Despite Mann's uncertainty at their restaurant meeting, Meczyk worried that the prosecution would get Mann to point to David in the courtroom and say, "That's the man I saw."

Even the police tape recording now in Meczyk's possession, showing that Mann had not made a positive identification, did not assuage this fear. Meczyk had seen tenuous identifications become certain in the past; the tape might be a canard.

As a result, Meczyk formulated trial tactics aimed at discrediting Mann with the dirt that John Waters had dug up (the false addresses on official documents) and attacking Mann's possible motive for testifying (his desire to land a job in law enforcement).

Unfortunately for the defense, Meczyk's strategy did not allow for the possibility that Mann's identification would remain indefinite—and that a ferocious attack actually would add unnecessary weight to his testimony.

Another potential bombshell, in Meczyk's mind, would be a surprise corroboration of dust on the windowsill.

In the hope of rendering the dust irrelevant, Meczyk asked John Waters if he could testify, as an expert, that an intruder could have avoided the dust—by entering the house through the hole in the window glass, rather than swiveling the window upward and sliding beneath it.

"I could not testify to that," Waters scoffed, pointing out that the hole was only nine inches top to bottom.

The through-the-glass theory, thus, was abandoned—quite fortunately, in Waters's view, both because it was implausible and because it would have been tantamount to a concession that the dust really was there.

Meczyk also worried about calling the Dowalibys to testify. Despite their assurances that no unknown skeletons were rattling in their closets, perhaps the prosecutors had held back some damaging tidbit with which David or Cynthia could be confronted and made to appear guilty.

Another element of Meczyk's strategy was to mount a counteroffensive that, in effect, would put Perry Hernandez on trial in the middle of the defense case. Meczyk's intent was not to accuse Hernandez directly of killing Jaclyn Dowaliby but rather to show that intruders do indeed snatch little girls in the middle of the night. Still, if the jury concluded that Hernandez did kill Jaclyn, so much the better.

To make the case against Hernandez and otherwise to help at the trial, Meczyk added a third member to the defense team—a thirty-nine-year-old former prosecutor named Daniel L. Franks.

During his nine years in the state's attorney's office, ending in 1985 when he entered private practice, the trim, bespectacled Franks had tried several cases opposite Meczyk. They had developed a grudging respect for one another. After Meczyk's guilty plea to tax charges in 1987, Franks had been a character witness for him in an ensuing disciplinary proceeding.

"I was impressed with Ralph's intensity and dedication," Franks would say. "While he was on work release, he left jail to defend a client in federal court."

With Franks rounding out the defense team—he, like Meczyk and Lawrence Hyman, being Jewish—Meczyk characterized the courtroom confrontation that was about to begin as a matter of "us against the *goyim*."

While Ralph Meczyk labored in fear that Everett Mann would exaggerate what he had seen in the parking lot, the prosecutors were taking precautions to assure just the opposite.

Having surrendered the tape recording of Mann's police statement to the defense, Patrick O'Brien and George Velcich assumed that Mann would be open to a devastating cross-examination if he went beyond that statement.

Thus, in the days leading up to the trial, the prosecutors put Mann through two "dress rehearsals" of his testimony—designed, ironically, to restrain him from becoming the eyewitness that O'Brien had been promising.

In an empty courtroom at the south suburban branch courthouse in Markham, Mann sat in the witness box. O'Brien played himself, asking the questions he would ask at the trial, while Velcich played defense lawyer, anticipating questions Meczyk might ask.

After the rehearsals, Mann seemed poised, confident, and, most of all, prepared to stay within the parameters of his tape-recorded statement.

In fact, the prosecutors had no bombshell. Their strategy was to weave the circumstantial threads together strand by strand, leading jurors to an inescapable conclusion that there had been no intruder. As O'Brien and Velcich saw it, their case would neither rise nor fall on any particular piece of evidence. If the jury disbelieved Mann, or even the dust, it would minimally affect the structural integrity of the whole.

Velcich, a graduate of the University of Notre Dame and Loyola University School of Law, was a logical choice to second-chair the case. Well-spoken, bright, and handsome, with a full head of dark brown hair, a mustache, and piercing brown eyes, he cut an especially impressive figure before juries.

The previous summer, Velcich had second-chaired O'Brien in winning life sentences against two men accused of raping and killing a medical student. A third defendant, labeled "scum" by Velcich, had plea-bargained for a twelve-year sentence in exchange for testifying against the other two.

Velcich's record in family murder cases was particularly impressive. In 1986 he had won an involuntary-manslaughter conviction against a father in the death of his two-year-old daughter, who, Velcich told the court, had been "shaken so badly that her brain was literally torn from her skull."

More recently, Velcich had secured guilty verdicts against a man accused of killing his two young sons, and a woman accused of killing an allegedly abusive husband.

The Dowaliby trial would be Velcich's last hurrah in the state's attorney's office before moving on to the more lucrative pursuit of defending insurance interests in civil cases.

He wanted to win this one—"for Jaclyn."

To complete the cast, Judge Neville ordered an even hundred prospective jurors—citizens drawn from the rolls of registered voters—brought into his courtroom over three days in early April 1990. From the pool, twelve jurors would be selected to hear the case, after a screening process known as the *voir dire.*

Neville began the *voir dire* by asking the prospective jurors to raise their hands if they had heard or read about the case.

Virtually every hand went up.

"Okay, almost everybody has heard about the case," said Neville. "That would be normal because of the publicity."

Next Neville asked, "Have any of you formed an opinion about the guilt or the innocence of the defendants?"

Those who raised their hands were asked individually whether they could set their opinions aside and judge the case solely on the evidence presented in court.

"I made up my mind from the newspapers and television that there was considerable guilt," said one would-be juror.

"I have the TV on at four o'clock, and I hear it over and over," another volunteered. "I have two grandchildren and it sort of physically and mentally upsets me."

"I'm pretty sure I got one way of thinking," said a third.

"I would like to say I could be fair, but I did form opinions up front, and first impressions are very difficult to overcome," said a fourth.

Neville excused those and twenty-one others, although several who said that they had formed opinions but still could be impartial remained in the jury pool. An additional nineteen were excused because of personal hardships.

On the third day, Neville allowed the lawyers to become involved in questioning the remaining fifty-six prospective jurors.* At this point the *voir dire* became a high-stakes game of wits as the lawyers jockeyed for advantage by eliminating jurors likely to favor the other side.

The Illinois Criminal Code allowed each side twelve peremptory challenges—the right to excuse prospective jurors without stating a reason. Peremptory challenges have to be exercised wisely because every time one person is excused there is a risk that he or she will be replaced with someone worse.

Prosecutors want to get rid of those who, for instance, have had negative experiences with law enforcement, have been active in liberal causes, or have strong tendencies to challenge authority. Defense lawyers want to dump those who identify with law enforcement, are politically conservative, or appear to have so-called authoritarian personalities.

The goal of each side is to exercise challenges against the twelve with the worst composite characteristics. The trick is to ask questions that will reveal those characteristics.

Before the questioning began, Neville divided the fifty-six

* By permitting lawyers to question jurors directly, Neville was bucking a national trend. In the federal courts and most state jurisdictions, judges conduct all the questioning. See *Ham* v. *South Carolina*, 409 U.S. 524 (1973).

prospective jurors into four panels of fourteen each. He ordered that the panels be questioned separately, first by the prosecution, then by the defense. Any person not challenged by either side would be sworn in as a juror before the next panel was questioned.

Patrick O'Brien probed the first panel on just four subjects —the organizations they belonged to, their reading habits, their experiences with police, and their military backgrounds.

Finding no one who admitted reading *Playboy* or *The New Republic,* belonged to the American Civil Liberties Union, or dodged the draft, O'Brien and George Velcich exercised no peremptory challenges.

To help the defense use its challenges wisely, Ralph Meczyk had retained Thomas N. Sannito, a nationally known trial consultant and professor of psychology at Loras College in Dubuque, Iowa.

Sannito had been reluctant to get involved in the Dowaliby case at first because, as he explained later, it was "messy and controversial." However, he said, he changed his mind partly because of Meczyk's passionate insistence that the Dowalibys were innocent and partly because he shared the defendants' roots: He had grown up in Riverdale, where the Dowalibys had met, and had an aunt who lived in Midlothian.

Sannito had helped select juries in five murder cases elsewhere. In four he was a defense consultant, helping to win either acquittals or guilty findings on lesser offenses. In the one case in which he was a prosecution consultant, the jury convicted the defendant of murder.

Sannito's system purported to measure authoritarianism in three ways: responses to questions, nonverbal clues, and demographic factors.

In addition to the information elicited by O'Brien, Sannito wanted to know if the prospective jurors controlled their family finances, if they had been honored for superior job performance, and if they were strongly religious—all bad signs for the defense.

During the questioning, he watched demeanor and body language. He wanted to exclude those who answered "Yes, sir" and "No, sir" to questions, sat stiffly erect, and put their thumbs and forefingers together in the shape of a steeple—further hints of authoritarianism.

Sannito took occupation into account, avoiding engineers, accountants, secretaries, or others whose jobs require following rigid rules.

Demographically, he preferred women jurors over men, believing women generally to be more tolerant and forgiving, and African-Americans over Caucasians, believing African-Americans generally to be more skeptical of police and prosecutors.

Meczyk, however, was wary of having African-Americans on the Dowaliby jury, fearing they might be offended by the attack he was planning on Everett Mann, who was black.

As Sannito took notes, Meczyk approached the first panel of prospective jurors, asking if anyone had "any quarrel at all that the prosecution has the burden of proof in a criminal case."

No one did.

Meczyk then attempted to ask individual jurors questions that Sannito had designed to identify authoritarianism.

Addressing Edward Chmura, who ultimately would be seated on the jury, Meczyk asked, "Mr. Chmura, do you own an automobile?"

"Yes," said Chmura.

"Who made the decision to purchase it, you or Mrs. Chmura?"

O'Brien objected, saying the question was irrelevant.

"Sustained," said Neville. "Let's get on to something else, Mr. Meczyk."

"Mr. Chmura, have you ever been recognized with an award for superior performance?"

"That is not a good question, Mr. Meczyk," Neville snapped.

"I'll rephrase it," said Meczyk. "Have you ever been awarded for anything—received any personal awards?"

With that, Neville ordered Meczyk and the other lawyers into his chambers.

"I am not going to let you spend an entire day asking questions so that your psychologist can decide who is strong and who is not," Neville told Meczyk. "It's a waste of my time."

"Let me state this—" Meczyk said.

"Ralph," Neville interrupted, "I don't care about the reasons."

"For the record, I'm trying to determine who has an authoritarian personality," said Meczyk.

"Mr. Meczyk, let me tell you something," Neville said with disdain. "I think to ask someone if they are superior is a stupid fucking question."

"Pardon me, your honor?" Meczyk sputtered.

"That is a stupid question," said Neville. "Now don't do it again."

"I won't," Meczyk promised.

After a pause, Meczyk added, "I have another request of the court. I have to go to the bathroom."

"No," said Neville. "Let's go, jurors are waiting. When we take a break, everyone can go."

Back in the courtroom, Meczyk tried a different tack. He asked juror-to-be Judith Hunt, who had indicated to Neville that she had a tentative opinion about the case, "At this time is your opinion for or against Mr. and Mrs. Dowaliby?"

O'Brien objected, since Hunt had said that she could be impartial.

"Sustained," said Neville.

With Meczyk foreclosed from eliciting any information that Sannito considered vital, the remaining questioning of the first panel went quickly.

Sannito was left to make his judgments from appearance, body language, and occupation. After one member was excused (having once been represented by Daniel Franks), Sannito recommended exercising peremptory challenges against seven others.

Since that would have exhausted more than half of the defense challenges on only one fourth of the jury pool, however, the defense lawyers wanted to save at least a couple of those challenges for later.

Four members of the panel clearly were unacceptable, three having close ties to law enforcement, one having been the victim of a major crime. Meczyk also wanted to challenge the one African-American on the panel. The remaining issue was whether to challenge the two others whom Sannito wanted to exclude.

One of these was Phyllis Halvorsen, a large woman with a pleasant smile and white hair that looked like spun glass. She was from the South originally and now worked as a claims supervisor for an insurance company. During the questioning, she had said that she was active in her church. "Religious people are often judgmental and unforgiving," Sannito said later, "but she had a sweet face and seemed very bright, so we thought maybe she would see the evidence."

The other was Richard Chmela, a technician for a computer company, a job requiring precision. As an eight-year Navy veteran, Chmela said that one of his favorite pastimes was reading about the Vietnam War. However, the defense thought Chmela had saving graces. He appeared intelligent, had never been a crime victim, and had long, curly hair that seemed anti-establishment.

On balance, the defense team reluctantly agreed to accept Halvorsen and Chmela, saving the challenges for a later panel.

As it turned out, however, the second panel was sufficient to complete the jury, with the prosecution and defense each using only five challenges.

Ironically, this left the defense with two unused challenges—but, under the procedure established by Neville, it was too late to challenge Halvorsen or Chmela.

"We have a jury," Neville exclaimed. "Imagine that!"

It comprised six men, six women, ten suburbanites, two Chicagoans—and no African-Americans.

A BANG AND A WHIMPER

On Tuesday, April 10, Judge Neville's courtroom overflowed with reporters, family and friends of the accused, crime buffs, and other spectators of various persuasions.

The huge rectangular room was the perfect stage for the drama that was about to unfold.

Behind the judge's bench were United States and Illinois flags and a massive bookcase filled with volumes of Illinois Supreme Court decisions dating back to Abraham Lincoln's time.

The witness stand was immediately to the judge's right. The jury box, farther to the right, extended almost to the spectator section, which consisted of seven long rows of pewlike seating dissected by an aisle.

The prosecution table was just a few feet in front of the jury box, with chairs for Patrick O'Brien and George Velcich facing the judge. The defense table was on the other side of the courtroom, with chairs for the Dowalibys and their lawyers facing the jury.

Journalists packed the front pews on both sides of the aisle. Behind the prosecutors sat Channel 7's bespectacled Dick Johnson, who had been first to report Jaclyn's disappearance and who later had broadcast the leak that Davey had been "abused." Behind the defense lawyers sat Channel 5's bearded Paul Hogan, who had abandoned the story earlier but now was filling in for a colleague who had taken a leave of absence.

The defendants' relatives and friends occupied the second and third rows on the defense side of the courtroom. Notably absent was John Waters, who was too ill to attend the opening session but promised to come later if his strength permitted.

The first scene was played outside the jury's presence.

Davey Dowaliby, now almost six years old, was summoned to the stand to determine whether the prosecution would be allowed to call him to testify.

"It would be our intention to ask him questions about what he remembers of Friday night before he went to bed and Saturday morning when he woke up, and what his parents were doing in those hours," O'Brien told Neville.

Regardless of how Davey answered the questions, the psychological impact of having him appear as a prosecution witness could be enormous. Even if he had nothing incriminating to say, the jury might infer that something so horrible happened that he had blotted it out of his memory.

Recognizing the potential prejudicial impact, Neville wanted to determine whether Davey was competent to testify and whether he had anything relevant to say.

Davey bounced to the stand, dressed like his father in a gray pinstriped suit, a cream-colored shirt, and a plain gray tie. From the spectator section, only his head was visible as he perched on the edge of the huge witness chair.

"Raise your right hand," said Neville.

Davey raised his left hand, and Neville told him, "The other one, the right hand."

Davey complied, taking the opportunity to wave to his

parents, seated a few feet away. He promised to tell the truth, the whole truth, and nothing but the truth.

"Do you know what it means to tell a lie?" Neville asked.

"Yeah," said Davey.

"What does it mean to you?"

"It means like if you really didn't do the thing, and you just tell them, it wouldn't be right. It would be a lie, because if you didn't do the thing and you just made something up, that would be a lie."

Neville led Davey through a series of questions—his name, who he lived with, how old he was. Davey answered clearly, confidently, without hesitation.

In an effort to determine what Davey knew about the time period relevant to the crime, Neville asked if he recalled his fourth birthday.

"No," said Davey.

Neville asked several additional questions about the summer of 1988, but Davey remembered virtually nothing, except that the family home was made of tan bricks and that he and Jaclyn once played in a nearby park.

As Neville excused Davey, Cynthia wiped away tears with a tissue. David put a comforting arm around her.

Neville called the lawyers into chambers. "The child appears to be articulate, well-adjusted, looks like a bright kid, well-spoken, at ease," he said. "So, for those reasons, I would believe he's competent. However, every time I asked him about what was happening when he was four, he told me he was not sure or he didn't know."

Although Neville did not rule immediately—"I'm going to think about this," he said—his remarks left little doubt that he would not permit Davey to testify.

It would be a rare victory for the defense.

When Judge Neville and the lawyers returned to the courtroom, the jurors filed in for the opening statements—Patrick O'Brien for the prosecution, Ralph Meczyk for David Dowaliby, Lawrence Hyman for Cynthia Dowaliby.

Neville told the jury, "Opening statements are made by lawyers to acquaint you with what they expect to prove, but opening statements are not evidence. Evidence comes in the form of testimony, exhibits, and stipulations."

As the Dowalibys held hands at the defense table, Neville told O'Brien to proceed.

Glancing at the defendants, O'Brien told the jury, "I believe what the evidence will show you is that there are some things in this courtroom that bind us tighter than hand-holding. I believe the evidence will show you that the defendants, David and Cynthia Dowaliby, are bound together by a chilling secret—that secret being that they are responsible for the murder of Jaclyn Dowaliby."

Pacing back and forth in front of the jury box, O'Brien neutrally recounted the time leading up to David's call to the Midlothian police on September 10.

Stopping, he faced the jury and said, "You will learn that this investigation, on the very day it began, was met with a roadblock. David Dowaliby lied to the FBI when he was interviewed by them, lied about when he had last seen his daughter, and, four days later, he changed his story and admitted he had lied. You will learn that the defendants presented the police with a mystery, but you will learn through the evidence that it was a mystery created by the defendants themselves. And you will learn why David Dowaliby lied."

The Dowalibys had claimed that an intruder entered the home through a broken window and abducted Jaclyn, O'Brien said, but investigators "drew the conclusion that no one came through that window."

Initially the Dowalibys tried to cast suspicion on James Guess, Jaclyn's biological father, O'Brien said, but that did not work because Guess was in prison. "He had been there since the summer," said O'Brien, "so the person who the defendants wanted to have as a suspect wasn't available to them."

O'Brien went into some detail on the discovery of Jaclyn's body. "The face was indistinguishable, eaten away by maggots," he said.

Much of the evidence would be circumstantial, he explained, saying, "There is no movie of what happened to Jaclyn Dowaliby in that house. The events from ten-thirty or eleven at night until ten-thirty the next morning were observed only by Jaclyn, the defendants, and the four-year-old brother, David. Jaclyn has been taken from us as a witness, but that doesn't mean we can't prove this case."

The Dowalibys' guilt would be shown, O'Brien said, by David and Cynthia's inconsistent statements to the police, by the missing sheets from Jaclyn's bed, by the blood on Jaclyn's pillow, by the connection between the rope found around Jaclyn and the Dowaliby home, and by Everett Mann's testimony.

As planned, O'Brien backed away from his earlier statements about the certainty of Mann's parking lot sighting. "You will hear that what he saw was a midsize car which, in that lighting, he described as dark-colored," he said. "You will hear that he saw one person in the driver's seat. All he could tell was that it was a male and that the one prominent feature he saw was a nose with a high bridge, or what he called a German nose."

Hinting at a motive for the murder, O'Brien claimed that Ann Dowaliby had told police that Jaclyn "was being a brat" before she was sent to bed—the suggestion being that Jaclyn might have died when discipline got out of hand.

"You will learn that Jaclyn Dowaliby, based upon degree of decomposition, was dead about four days," O'Brien said. "She was dead when she was dumped on Saturday at 2:00 or 2:15 A.M."

He concluded, "Obviously, you will learn of the horrible crime that was committed, and you will learn of the one thing which is more horrible than the crime itself—the attempts by the defendants to get away with it."

Ralph Meczyk was rattled. He opened with a stumbling, contradictory, and, at points, inaccurate statement that stunned even the judge.

"You couldn't pick up what the fuck he was doing," Neville would say later.

Meczyk began by comparing the actions of law enforcement officials to the murder itself: "There was one thing that was not as horrible as the murder of Jaclyn Dowaliby, but it was close to it. The real crime, or should I say the other crime in this case, was the fact that law enforcement charged David and Cynthia Dowaliby with the murder of their child. It's out of a Kafka novel."

While describing the Dowalibys as "a nice, average family" and "close, loving, and warm," Meczyk made them sound sleazy in almost the same breath. "Cynthia was married very, very briefly to Jim Guess," he said. "David was introduced a month before Cynthia had Jaclyn, was carrying Jaclyn, by their mutual friends, the O'Connors, and she was a very, very, of course, pregnant Cynthia Guess at the time. That was the first time David met her at a party."

The next time David Dowaliby saw James Guess, Meczyk continued, Guess "was in a bar with another woman, having a few drinks, and groping and kissing her at a side table."

At different points, Meczyk contradicted himself in describing David's demeanor after discovering Jaclyn missing. First, Meczyk claimed, "David walked calmly" to neighbors' houses looking for Jaclyn, acting "like the man he was, stoically." Moments later, however, Meczyk said that while David was searching for Jaclyn, "he ran down the street." He added that David "frantically knocks on that door" and was "panicky."

While searching the neighborhood, Meczyk said, the Dowalibys went to the home of a little girl named Rosa and asked if she had seen Jaclyn. "But Rosa didn't answer," said Meczyk. "All she had was a piece of bologna in her mouth, and shook it back and forth. That was the answer that they got. Now they are even more frantic."

Turning to Everett Mann, Meczyk remained inextricably bound to the strategy he had formulated before the trial, based on the fear that Mann's identification would be positive.

Ignoring O'Brien's opening statement, Meczyk flatly told the jury, "Mr. Mann says he sees, he describes to the police, the person as being David Dowaliby."

In keeping with his plan to attack Mann's character, Meczyk took a gratuitous slap that played right into the prosecution's hands. "Mann was coming home from work," Meczyk said. "I should say he wasn't coming directly home from work at the time. He had stopped beforehand and met someone else."

That was precisely the argument that the prosecution would use to enhance Mann's credibility: Mann was married, but by telling his story had to admit that he had been with another woman that night. Why would he do that, except out of duty to help solve a horrible crime?

At various points Meczyk even confused members of the Dowaliby family, referring to David's mother, Ann Dowaliby, as Cynthia's mother; to Cynthia's sister-in-law, Sylvia Borrelli, as Cynthia's sister; and to Jaclyn as Cyndi.

The more Meczyk rambled on, the more disorganized he became. On the crucial issue of what David said when told that Jaclyn had been found, Meczyk's tangled syntax was barely comprehensible:

"One time, I should say, at the very end again, they said when we found her body, and David after being repeatedly grilled, repeatedly asked questions by them, a prolonged period of time, said, 'I suppose you want me to cry now.' And I misspoke before. He never told him they found the body. So when he said, 'I suppose I should cry now'—why, ladies and gentlemen? You will see from the evidence because he was angry, he was fed up."

Meczyk made only passing reference to whether an intruder could have entered the Dowaliby home through the basement window. "I ask you to pay very close attention to it," he said. "You will be convinced beyond a reasonable doubt that an intruder wanted to go through that window." Having thus shifted the burden of proof to the defense, he dropped the subject.

O'Brien had begun with a bang, Meczyk with a whimper.

Standing stiffly at a podium in front of the jury box, Lawrence Hyman dryly dissected the case against Cynthia Dowaliby.

"Despite the police and their belief that it was only Cynthia and David Dowaliby who could have committed this crime," said Hyman, "you will hear evidence that there is an individual by the name of Perry Hernandez, and this individual, almost a year to the date, crawled through the window of the home of David and Carline MacRand, in the early-morning hours.

"And you will hear evidence that Perry Hernandez went into that home for one purpose, and that was to remove a six-year-old girl while her parents lay asleep, while her brother slept no more than twelve inches from her."

Hernandez, Hyman continued, carried Rory MacRand to Cal-Sag Channel in Blue Island, less than a mile from where Jaclyn's body had been found.

"What the police said could not have happened—that anybody could crawl through a window and take a child out—was disproved by this heinous predator, Perry Hernandez."

Hyman said that the evidence "the state will literally pile in front of you does not at all reflect any involvement" of Cynthia in Jaclyn's death.

Cynthia, he said, had made no inconsistent statements and "cooperated as much as she could" in the investigation.

"You will hear how the police took blood from her, how they took hair from her, how they took her fingerprints, how they took all this evidence, and you will hear that it is all negative," he said.

Hyman concluded, "I submit to you, ladies and gentlemen, that Cyndi Dowaliby is not guilty and that the state will not be able to show anything but that."

After a break for lunch, the prosecution called its first witness, Victoria Verble, a blond-haired, blue-eyed girl who was one of Jaclyn's closest friends.

The purpose of calling her was to prove an essential element of every murder case—that the victim had been an actual, living person.

For the prosecution, Victoria was ideal for the task. A little girl, more effectively than anyone else, could bring the tragedy of Jaclyn Dowaliby to life in the courtroom.

Victoria was examined by George Velcich, who, after several introductory questions, asked her, "Now, Vicky, do you remember the last time you saw Jaclyn Dowaliby?"

"It was on a Friday."

"Do you know what Friday that was?"

"No."

"Did anything happen the next day?"

"She was missing."

"Vicky, where was it that you last saw Jaclyn?"

After some prodding, Vicky recalled that she and Jaclyn were playing outside on the afternoon of the Friday in question.

Velcich then showed her a photograph of Jaclyn and asked, "You recognize the little girl shown in that photograph?"

"Yes."

"Who is that?"

"Jaclyn Dowaliby."

She was then shown a photograph of the former Dowaliby home and asked whose it was.

"Jaclyn Dowaliby's house," she said.

"Your honor, I have no further questions of this witness," said Velcich.

There was no cross-examination.

The second prosecution witness was Michael Healy, the man who had been with Ann Dowaliby the night Jaclyn disappeared.

Under direct examination by Patrick O'Brien, Healy testified that on September 9 he had been partying with some friends at the Eldorado Restaurant.

He said that Ann Dowaliby joined him "after midnight." They had drinks and talked, leaving the Eldorado at about 4:30 A.M. on September 10.

O'Brien asked, "At the time you left the restaurant with Ann Dowaliby, was she intoxicated?"

"Yes."

"And how would you describe your condition?"

"I was drunk also."

"Once you left the restaurant, where did you go?"

"To my place."

"How did you get there?"

"My vehicle."

A few moments later, O'Brien asked, "When you got to your house, who went into the house?"

"Ann and myself."

"Did you leave your house sometime that morning on Saturday?"

"Yes," Healy said, explaining that he drove Ann back to the Eldorado at about 9:15 A.M.

"What happened when you got to the Eldorado parking lot?"

"I dropped Ann off and I left."

On cross-examination, Hyman asked only one question, which had no apparent purpose: "Before Ann Dowaliby left your home, did she make any phone calls to anyone?"

"Not that I believe," Healy answered.

The next prosecution witness was Ann Dowaliby. Since she was considered hostile to the prosecution, George Velcich was permitted to ask her leading questions, which normally are allowed only on cross-examination.

After establishing that she was David Dowaliby's mother and that she had lived with the family in Midlothian at the time of Jaclyn's disappearance, Velcich asked, "Would it be correct to say that Jaclyn Dowaliby was not your natural granddaughter?"

"That's correct," she answered.

"Would it be correct that Jaclyn Dowaliby was the daughter of Cynthia Dowaliby, and later was adopted by your son, David, after they were married?"

"Yes, that's correct."

Velcich then asked who owned the home.

"I did."

"And were the defendants paying rent to you?"

"They were giving me money towards a down payment."

"And ma'am, what part of the house did you live in?"

"The lower area."

"Would that have been the basement?"

"Yes."

Velcich asked Ann what time she left home on Friday, September 9, and she said it was about 10:30 P.M.

Velcich made no effort to account for the period between ten-thirty and "after midnight," when Healy testified he met Ann at the Eldorado.

"When you left your home that night," Velcich continued, "which door did you exit from?"

"The rear door."

"And did you customarily use the back door?"

"I used both doors."

"Well, did you come in the front door, ma'am?"

"Sometimes, yes."

"Isn't it a fact that you did not have a key to the front door?"

"That's right."

Since Ann could not have opened the door, the implication of this line of questioning was that an innocent father would have checked on Jaclyn immediately when he found it ajar.

Next, in an effort to support Patrick O'Brien's suggestion that discipline might have led to Jaclyn's death, Velcich asked if Jaclyn misbehaved before she was sent to bed on September 9.

"She danced a little bit in the living room," Ann replied.

"Well, ma'am, was Jaclyn a brat that night?"

"No."

"Was she a typical seven-year-old who refused to mind her parents that night?"

"No."

"Didn't you tell investigator Walsh that she was a brat that night?"

"No, I did not."

"Did you tell investigator Walsh that she was a typical seven-year-old who refused to mind?"

"Refused to mind me. Not her parents. She minded them very well."

"Did you tell investigator Walsh about how you punished Jaclyn?"

"Yes, sir, I did."

"Did you tell him that you spanked her?"

"Yes, I did."

Velcich asked whether Davey ever played with a rope.

"Yes, he did," Ann said.

Showing her an evidence bag containing the rope found around Jaclyn's body, Velcich asked, "Does the rope look like the rope that Davey used to play with?"

"No, it doesn't. It looks like a different rope."

Velcich reminded Ann of her conversation with Assistant State's Attorney Norma Reyes and Blue Island Police Chief Paul Greves on October 28, 1988, and asked if they had shown her a rope.

"Yes," she said.

"Does this look like the rope that you saw that day?"

"It looks like the one they showed me."

Velcich asked if she had told Reyes and Greves that the rope looked like "the type of rope" with which Davey played.

"Yes."

"After Jaclyn disappeared, did you see the rope that Davey used to play with anymore?"

"No, I didn't."

Despite Ann's resistance, Velcich had succeeded in leaving the impression that the rope that killed Jaclyn might well have come from the Dowaliby home.

Daniel Franks conducted the cross-examination. After eliciting that Ann voluntarily went to the Blue Island police station on October 28, he asked, "And one of the things they showed you was a rope, isn't that right?"

"Yes," she said.

Franks asked if the rope they showed her was similar to the rope Velcich had shown her a few minutes previously.

"It was in a smaller bag."

"How much of the rope did Chief Greves show you when he brought out the rope?"

"He just showed me the bag with the rope visible inside and coiled up."

"So, could you tell when you saw the rope coiled up how long it was?"

"Not really, no."

"How long was the rope that you saw Davey playing with?"

"It was ten to twelve feet at the most."

Franks then uncoiled the rope, stretching it from the witness stand past the jury box, and asked, "Was the rope Davey played with as long as this rope?"

"No, that's much longer than the one he played with."

"Were you ever shown the rope in that condition unrolled?"

"No."

Franks noted that it was almost twenty-six feet long.

There was a long pause while all eyes in the courtroom were drawn to the presumed murder weapon, lying on the floor.

Neville finally broke the silence, "Why don't you remove that from the floor?"

"Be happy to, judge," Franks replied, confident that he had made his point.

The final prosecution witness of the day was investigator Thomas Walsh, who was called to rebut Ann's denial that Jaclyn was behaving like "a brat" on the night of September 9.

Calling Walsh's attention to his September 12 interview with Ann, O'Brien asked, "Did you ask her how Jaclyn was behaving?"

"Yes, sir."

"And what did she say?"

"She said she was a brat, like any typical seven-year-old, and that she was refusing to mind."

"Was that placed in your notes?"

"Yes, sir."

On cross-examination, Daniel Franks asked, "Officer Walsh, the notes that you made reference to were just some handwritten, scribbled notes that you wrote on a pad of paper, correct?"

"Yes, sir."

"It's not in an official report?"

"No, sir."

"And you don't recall every word, obviously, that Ann Dowaliby said to you a year and a half ago, do you?"

"No, sir."

"You were asking her questions and she volunteered the fact that she does spank Jaclyn at times?"

"Yes, sir."

"And at the time she was talking about spanking Jaclyn she was also saying that Jaclyn was a typical seven-year-old who can act like a brat, isn't that right?"

"Yes, sir."

Franks said nothing else.

On redirect, O'Brien directed Walsh's attention to a line in his notes that said, "The night she went to bed," and asked him to read what followed.

Quoting from the notes, Walsh said, "Brat. Typical seven-year-old. Refused to mind."

On recross, Franks asked Walsh about an S-shaped mark that appeared in his notes between the words "The night she went to bed" and the word "Brat."

"That's just a doodle to stop that particular phrase," Walsh said.

"Okay," Franks said, "so your notes read, 'The night she went to bed.' Then you have your doodle. Then we have a new subject, 'Brat. Typical seven-year-old. Refused to mind.' "

Franks's point was that because of the doodle, the "Brat" reference did not specifically refer to Jaclyn's behavior on the night of September 9.

The point was largely lost, however, when O'Brien objected to the compound question, and Neville sustained the objection.

Franks then asked, "You have a phrase 'The night she went to bed,' period. Is that correct?"

"No," Walsh answered, backtracking from his previous answer.

Franks asked, "And you said you had your doodle, indicating a new phrase then. Is that correct?"

"It's a continuation of another phrase."

"Well, what is the doodle for?"

"It's just a habit I got into when taking notes."

"You indicated before that that is a new subject matter and that's why you put the doodle there. Is that correct?"

O'Brien objected, "That's not his answer."

Neville sustained the objection.

Franks then asked, "You have written down, 'Brat. Typical seven-year-old. Refused to mind. Spank. She has.' Is that correct?"

"Right," Walsh said emphatically, having comfortably returned to what he had said on direct examination.

After Walsh was excused, Neville told the jury, "It is likely there will be some publicity about what occurred in this courtroom today. There is no one in a better position to know what happened here than you are. I would ask you not to read anything about this case and, if anything comes on about this case while you are watching TV, I would ask you to turn it off."

As the jurors left, television crews in the lobby were feeding live reports to their stations for the early news.

Channel 7's Dick Johnson and Channel 5's Paul Hogan saw the day's events rather differently.

Johnson reported: "Cynthia Dowaliby wept, clutching the hand of her husband, David, while prosecutor Pat O'Brien said there are some things in this courtroom that bind us tighter than hand-holding. The defendants are bound together by a chilling secret that they murdered Jaclyn Dowaliby and then covered it up."

Hogan featured the apparent holes in the prosecution's case, saying that it appeared "loaded with circumstantial evidence but weak on physical evidence." The prosecution, he said, "didn't even hint at a possible motive for the crime."

MANN TAKES THE STAND

With Everett Mann on deck, the leadoff prosecution witness on the second day of the trial was the secretary of the league in which David Dowaliby bowled.

The purpose of calling David L. Urewicz, a forty-one-year-old salesman, was to establish that Dowaliby had been in Blue Island the night Jaclyn disappeared.

Urewicz testified that the bowling league opened its 1988 season at the Anchor Bowl on Friday, September 9, and George Velcich asked whether Dowaliby had been there that night.

"Yes," said Urewicz.

"Where is Anchor Bowl located?"

"In Blue Island."

Velcich asked Urewicz to step down and approach an easel holding a large map of the south suburbs, including Blue Island. At Velcich's direction, Urewicz circled the location of the Anchor Bowl with a blue marker. The circle extended to the Islander Apartments, where Jaclyn's body had been found.

On cross-examination, Ralph Meczyk asked, "Would you characterize David Dowaliby as being in good spirits that night?"

"Sure," said Urewicz.

"He was getting along with all the fellows?"

"Oh, yeah."

"Paying attention to his bowling game?"

"As much as we all do."

"And David is a regular bowler in the league?"

"Yes."

"As far as you know, well liked by everyone in the league?"

"Oh, yeah."

There was not the slightest hint in Urewicz's answers that David Dowaliby could have been on the verge of committing murder on the night of September 9.

As Meczyk returned to the defense table, Patrick O'Brien called Everett Mann to the stand.

A look of dread swept Meczyk's face. "Oh, boy, oh, boy," he said with a gasp. "This is it. Here we go."

O'Brien calmly led Mann through the questions they had rehearsed at the Markham courthouse several days earlier.

Mann testified that after getting off work at 10:30 P.M. on September 9, he went to see "a friend of mine, Miss Latricia Wood."

"You were married at the time?" O'Brien asked.

"Yes," Mann said.

After spending "a very brief time" at Latricia Wood's house, Mann said, they went to a park for about two hours. Then he took her home and headed for the Islander Apartments.

As he made a U-turn into a parking space behind his building, he saw headlights come on near the middle Dumpster (a few feet from where Jaclyn's body was found).

"What did you then do?" O'Brien asked.

"I stopped my car and looked at the lights."

"What did you observe that car do?"

"I observed that car slowly pulling forward."

"Could you tell us what that car looked like?"

"It appeared to be a dark-colored, late-model, midsize car."

"Was anyone inside the car?"

"I did see one head, yes."

"Were you able to make out any features of this person?"

"Yes."

"What was that?"

"It appeared to be a large nose."

"Could you tell if the person was a man or a woman?"

"It seemed like a man."

"What did the car most resemble in make and model?"

"Most resembled a late seventies model Malibu Classic."

After the car disappeared into a driveway between two buildings, Mann said, he went inside and went to sleep.

Six days later, Mann continued, two police officers came to his home, had a brief conversation, and left. O'Brien did not ask what Mann told those officers. To do so would not have been helpful to the prosecution; the officers' report indicated only that Mann saw an unfamiliar "dark-colored car near the middle Dumpster."

O'Brien asked whether two other officers interviewed him a short time later and showed him photographs of five men.

"Yes," Mann said.

"And what did they ask you when they showed you these photographs?" O'Brien asked.

Mann said they asked whether any of the men looked familiar.

"And what did you say?"

"Yes."

"And could you tell us what it was about any of those photographs that looked familiar?"

"The nose structure."

O'Brien showed Mann a cardboard display containing the photographs and asked, "Is the person you picked out whose nose structure resembled the one of the person you saw on the tenth shown in there?"

"Yes."

Mann identified photo number four: David Dowaliby's. Following O'Brien's instructions, Mann placed an X and his initials on the cardboard under David's photo.

O'Brien asked Mann about photographs of four vehicles he was shown at the Blue Island police station on September 28.

Mann responded that he had been shown photos of one car, one pickup truck, and two vans. The jury was not told that all of the photos were of vehicles driven by the Dowalibys—Cynthia's Malibu, David's Ford pickup, and David's employer's vans.

"With regard to the photograph of the car," O'Brien asked, "what kind of car was it that you were shown?"

"Chevy Malibu Classic."

"And what were you asked about that car?"

Mann said they asked whether the car looked familiar.

"What did you say?"

"I said it resembles the car, the shape of the car I saw that night."

O'Brien asked the color of the car.

"It was light blue."

"And the car that you described, you described it how?"

"As a dark-colored car."

"How is it that you described the car as dark-colored?"

"Well, the lighting in the parking lot wasn't that great, so a light-colored car could pass for dark under the circumstances."

"No further questions," said O'Brien.

Mann had not come close to identifying David Dowaliby, thus defying Ralph Meczyk's expectation; there had been no canard.

Meczyk asked for a short break, but Neville denied it.

Flustered, Meczyk lunged into a series of stumbling questions about Mann's background, beginning with his time in the Air Force.

"You were placed in a military occupational speciality school to be an air policeman, am I right?" Meczyk asked.

"No," Mann answered.

"You didn't start as an air policeman and were pulled out after a few weeks of training in law enforcement?"

"No."

"Isn't it true that you were originally placed—I'm sorry, I'll back up. You didn't start out as an air traffic controller, did you?"

"No."

"What did you start out as?"

"I was listed as a special security police officer, but I was put—"

"Please, Mr. Mann," Meczyk interrupted. "Maybe you didn't understand my question."

Neville interjected, "Mr. Meczyk, I do not allow lawyers to conduct examinations that control a witness. If you ask a question, let the witness finish."

"I will," Meczyk said.

"Thank you," Mann said to the judge. "I was put on standby status."

Meczyk asked, "Your enlistment, then, was for—I'm sorry, let me back up again. So after basic training, you were not immediately assigned to air traffic school, but to a police training school, is that right?"

"No, I was assigned to standby status."

Meczyk ran through a series of redundant questions about Mann's discharge, drawing objections, which Neville sustained.

Meczyk then asked, "Mr. Mann, while you were in the military, you also underwent psychological testing?"

O'Brien objected. His reason was implicit: Neville had ruled before the trial that Mann's psychological tests were not relevant.

"Sustained," said Neville.

Undaunted, Meczyk resumed, "Mr. Mann, as a result of the psychological testing—"

O'Brien leaped to his feet with an objection.

"Sustained," Neville snapped.

Meczyk then questioned Mann about his efforts to become a police officer.

"You also took the psychological tests to be a Chicago patrolman?" Meczyk asked.

"Yes," Mann answered.

"Judge, could we approach?" said O'Brien, exasperated.

Neville excused the jury.

"I thought there was a ruling with regard to psychological testing, since it couldn't be connected to credibility," said O'Brien.

"So did I," said Neville.

"Goes to motive to say he has been rejected from the police and he keeps trying again," Meczyk argued. "I was not going to get into the MMPIs. I was going to follow your ruling to the letter."

O'Brien started to ask a question, but before he could complete the thought, Meczyk interrupted him.

"I'm only going to say this to you once more," Neville scolded Meczyk. "Wait your turn. Everybody gets their chance. I get a chance to talk, state gets a chance, and you get a chance. Wait your turn."

Turning to O'Brien, Neville said, "Make your statement."

"This is attempting to get through the back door what he couldn't get in the front door," O'Brien said.

"Mr. Meczyk, it doesn't make any difference why he was rejected," Neville said. "By bringing in the psychological tests you are in fact—"

"It shows he never has any chance," Meczyk blurted out, interrupting the judge.

"Mr. Meczyk," Neville exploded, "shut your mouth until I'm finished. It is so simple to be polite. It is so difficult to deal with someone who talks over you."

"I'm sorry, your honor," Meczyk said.

"The psychological tests are irrelevant," Neville said. "The reason for the rejection is not pertinent. I sustained the objection twice. Next time, you're in contempt."

"Very well, your honor," said Meczyk.

"Let's go," said Neville, and the jury was brought back into the courtroom.

"Mr. Mann," Meczyk asked, "isn't it true that when this case is over, you hope that the prosecution will write you a letter or make a recommendation to the Chicago Police Department?"

"No," Mann replied.

"Mr. Mann, isn't it true that you would like to have a letter from someone like Cecil Partee?"

"No."

"And you know who that is, do you not?"

"Yes, I do."

"That's the state's attorney of Cook County."

"This is terrible," O'Brien angrily interjected. "I'm going to object to this on behalf of Mr. Partee."

Neville warned Meczyk that he might be going too far, but Meczyk continued, "Mr. Mann, isn't it also true that you would like to have a letter from someone like Jeremy Margolis, who is the director of the Illinois State Police?"

Without waiting for O'Brien to object, Neville said, "State's objection is sustained. Get on to something else."

Meczyk asked a series of questions about Ralph Styer, Mann's Air Force sergeant who owned a 1976 Chevrolet Malibu. Mann testified that his familiarity with Styer's car helped him identify the car he saw in the Islander Apartments parking lot.

To discredit the identification, Meczyk tried to show that Mann had claimed that the cars were identical, when in fact they were strikingly different. That should have been simple enough. Meczyk had tape-recorded a February 1989 interview in which Mann had indicated that they were "the same exact" cars. Photographs proved that was not true. However, in broaching the subject in his cross-examination of Mann, Meczyk made a disastrous factual error—and the point was lost.

Referring to the February interview, Meczyk asked, "And I showed you photographs, two photographs, I'm sorry, let me back up, three photographs, while we were in the restaurant?"

"Yes," answered Mann, apparently not recalling that Meczyk had shown him only a photo of Cynthia's Malibu.

Meczyk continued, "And two of the photographs were photographs of Ralph Styer's automobile, is that right?"

Mann appeared confused, and gave an indefinite answer; in fact, Meczyk had not shown him photos of Styer's car.

Suddenly Meczyk realized his error. In an effort to extricate himself, he said, "Mr. Mann, I made a mistake. I didn't show you those photographs at the restaurant, did I?"

"I object," O'Brien said. "He's impeaching himself."

"No, I made a mistake," Meczyk said.

Neville asked the lawyers to approach the bench for a sidebar—a conversation out of the earshot of the jury, reporters, and spectators.

"What's going on?" Neville demanded.

"I didn't have Styer's photographs until after the conversation," said Meczyk. "I'm sorry."

Neville was incredulous. "You led the witness through a whole series of questions!" he declared.

"Well, unless he wants to say I showed him the photographs," Meczyk sputtered. "It's true, I never showed them to him. If he wants to admit to them, that's fine, but I never showed him those photographs."

"I'm going to excuse the jury," said Neville. As the jurors filed out of the courtroom, Neville instructed Mann also to leave the courtroom.

"Is it my understanding that you just asked this witness about a number of photographs, saying that you showed them to him in a restaurant, and now you want to tell me that you didn't?" Neville asked.

"That was my mistake," Meczyk admitted.

"How would you suggest that we clear this up?" Neville asked.

"I can simply go on the record and say that I made the mistake and continue on with the cross-examination, that's all," Meczyk offered. "My mistake was I legitimately thought I had the photographs with me. I'm being very honest. That's why I came forward."

"I find that hard to believe," said Neville.

"It wasn't done intentionally," said Meczyk.

"Regardless of why it was done, the issue now is whether you should be allowed to take advantage of your own misdeed in order to confuse the witness," Neville said. He instructed Meczyk to "clear up for the witness what is going on."

When Mann returned to the stand, Meczyk told him, "Mr. Mann, I made a mistake. When I saw you at the restaurant in February of 1989, I only brought along one picture, do you recall that?"

"Yes," Mann answered.

"We talked about the automobile that you said you saw the person drive on February 14 in Blue Island, right?" Meczyk asked.

"Objection," said O'Brien. "February 14 misstates the evidence."

The correct date of Mann's identification was September 10.

Neville ordered Meczyk to restate the question.

"I'm sorry," said Meczyk, "September 14."

"Objection, September 14 also misstates the evidence," said O'Brien.

Neville sustained the objection.

"Mr. Mann," Meczyk resumed, dropping his reference to a date, "we discussed the automobile that you said you saw in Blue Island that night when you were coming home?"

"Correct."

"And we discussed the automobile that your sergeant had in the military?"

"Correct."

"Mr. Mann, when we were at the restaurant, you told me that the cars looked the same, right?"

"Correct."

"That they were *exactly* the same, right?"

"Chevy Malibu Classics," Mann replied, dodging the question.

Without pressing further, Meczyk asked Neville for permission to show the photographs to the jury.

"Denied," said Neville.

Meczyk had run right into a stone wall of his own making. Not only had he failed to discredit Mann's identification; worse, by bringing up Styer's car, he had provided a plausible reason why Mann could have recognized a Malibu.

Realizing that he was floundering, Meczyk took a moment to confer at the defense table with Daniel Franks, who had scrawled out a brief series of questions designed to underscore Mann's uncertainty.

Asking Franks's questions, Meczyk elicited that seventy-five yards separated Mann from the car he had seen.

"That was three quarters of a football field away?" Meczyk asked.

"Correct," Mann said.

Meczyk, following Franks's script, next inquired about the photo spread from which Mann had picked David's photograph.

Mann said, as he had on direct examination, that the spread consisted of frontal photographs.

"So whoever was driving that car, you could only see a side view of that individual, correct?" Meczyk asked.

"Correct," Mann replied.

"You also told the officers that you couldn't tell if this person was black or white, correct?"

"Correct."

"And all you said you could see was a silhouette, correct?"

"Correct."

Having exhausted Franks's questions, Meczyk concluded by zeroing in on the false address Mann had used in applying to work for the Chicago Police Department in 1987.

"You lied on that application, did you not?" Meczyk asked.

"Correct," said Mann.

Although he was living in Blue Island, Mann admitted, he had put a Chicago address on the application.

Meczyk also forced Mann to admit that he had used the same false address on his voter registration form and driver's license application.

"And the reason you kept separate addresses, Mr. Mann, is because you wanted to be a Chicago police officer, am I right?" Meczyk asked.

"No," said Mann.

Meczyk ended the cross-examination without making the point that Chicago police applicants must live in the city.

* * *

As Everett Mann left the stand, Patrick O'Brien turned to George Velcich and grinned. With more than a little help from Ralph Meczyk, the prosecutors had gotten far more from Mann's testimony than they had expected.

David Dowaliby shook his head in disbelief. Mortified by Meczyk's cross-examination of Mann, he and Cynthia began discussing the possibility of having Daniel Franks replace Meczyk as lead counsel.

Richard Neville was befuddled. For more than a year, he had been led to believe that Mann had positively identified David Dowaliby. Now he wondered what Mann actually had seen.

After lunch, the jurors boarded a chartered bus for Midlothian and Blue Island.

George Velcich led them on a tour of the Dowaliby home, which the new owners were remodeling. Some of the wallboard had been taken down, and fist marks were visible on the walls of Davey Dowaliby's former bedroom.

The jury then visited the Islander Apartments—in broad daylight. Velcich walked them to the spot where Jaclyn's body had been found. He pointed out the middle Dumpster, the building in which Everett Mann lived, and the driveway through which Mann claimed the midsize car left the parking lot in the early-morning darkness of September 10.

Neville asked the jury to board the bus, invited the lawyers aboard, and gave the jurors final instructions for the day. He cautioned them not to begin making a decision until they had heard all the evidence.

Referring to the reporters and camera crews filming the bus at that very moment, Neville added, "It should be obvious that something's going to be on TV. It is best, as I told you before, for you not to watch TV because I don't know what will be said about what we did here, but you know better than anybody else what happened. Same goes for newspapers."

Neville, who planned to participate in a judicial conference on Thursday and Friday, April 12 and 13, recessed the trial until the following Monday.

* * *

"Star witness identifies Dowaliby by his nose," said a headline over a story by Matt O'Connor in Thursday's *Chicago Tribune.*

"David Dowaliby was identified in court Wednesday by the nose on his face—and nothing more—as the man who was seen the night of his daughter's disappearance near where her body eventually was found," O'Connor wrote.

Calling it "one of the more unusual identifications" ever made in a Cook County criminal case, O'Connor reported that Everett Mann had testified that Dowaliby's "nose structure" resembled that of a man he had seen from seventy-five yards away.

"You couldn't see Jimmy Durante's nose from that distance," O'Connor quoted an unnamed observer as saying.

Although prosecutors had "characterized Mann's eyewitness account as a strong identification" before the trial, O'Connor noted, Mann was much less certain on the witness stand.

"Under direct examination by prosecutors," said the story, "Mann conceded he was not sure whether the nose he saw belonged to a man or a woman, or to a black or white individual."

The long break in the trial gave the Dowalibys time to review their situation.

David told Ralph Meczyk that he was upset with the cross-examination of Everett Mann.

Meczyk apologized, attributing the problem to nervousness.

"I'm thinking of going with Dan Franks," David said, to which Meczyk, his ego wounded, replied, "If you want him as your attorney, take him as your attorney."

David backed off, telling Meczyk, "Well, maybe Dan can do more questioning of the witnesses."

Meczyk said that would be possible, and David did not press him further.

For David, the conversation triggered a mixture of emotions—concern for Meczyk's feelings and fear that a drastic change at this stage might do more harm than good.

Daniel Franks, while more articulate than Meczyk, had entered the case late and lacked Meczyk's command of the facts.

David's best hope was that Meczyk would hit his stride when the trial resumed.

A PRODUCTIVE PROP

Towering over the defense table when the Dowalibys and their attorneys arrived in the courtroom on Monday, April 16, was a full-scale mock-up of the Dowalibys' basement wall and window.

The window swiveled inward, like the one in the home. At the base of the exhibit were the metal towel rack, the small plywood table, and various household items that investigators had found beneath the window on September 10, 1988.

The seven-foot-high mock-up would be used during the testimony of several upcoming witnesses and become a powerful symbol of the prosecution's central contention—that no one could have entered the home without disturbing the items below.

The exhibit would remain in the courtroom until the jurors retired to deliberate, when it would be removed for them to examine.

* * *

At the opening of the day's proceedings, Judge Neville announced that Davey Dowaliby would not be permitted to testify. As expected, Neville ruled that Davey had no knowledge relevant to the period when the crime occurred.

After the jury was seated, Patrick O'Brien called his first witness of the day, Erin Bell, the Dowaliby neighbor who had told police that Davey occasionally had been unsupervised.

On direct examination, Bell testified that at about 3:00 P.M. on September 9, 1988, she had seen Davey "crossing the street by himself" to visit her son, Kyle. Bell added that at about 6:00 P.M. Jaclyn came to her house to get Davey. That was the last time Bell saw Jaclyn alive.

On September 12, two days after Jaclyn disappeared, Bell said, Davey came to her home by himself between 11:30 A.M. and noon. About a half hour later, David called to check on Davey.

On September 16, the Friday after Jaclyn was found, Davey again appeared at the Bell home and spent part of the day. The following week, Bell said, she saw Davey in the neighborhood about a half dozen times. He was alone some of those times, but at other times was accompanied by an adult.

The point of this testimony was that if the Dowalibys believed a kidnapper was on the loose, they would have watched Davey more closely.

Bell also testified that shortly before 10:00 A.M. on September 10, the morning Jaclyn was reported missing, she saw David and Davey on 148th Place.

"At the time that you saw David Dowaliby, the defendant, how did he look?" O'Brien asked.

"Calm, concerned," Bell replied.

O'Brien ended his examination without directly asking whether Bell considered the Dowalibys lax in the supervision of their children, but Lawrence Hyman, inexplicably, proceeded to make the point for him on cross-examination.

"You considered the Dowaliby children to be somewhat unsupervised, did you not?" Hyman asked.

"Yes, I did," Bell replied.

Hyman did not ask if it were possible, as members of the

family contended, that someone was keeping an eye on Davey from the picture window of the Dowaliby home.

Instead Hyman asked, "Isn't it a fact that David and Cyndi had asked both yourself and Sue Haseman to watch Davey while they were at the wake of their daughter?"

"I never talked to Dave and Cyndi," Bell replied.

Other members of the Dowaliby family actually had made the arrangements with Bell, but Hyman did not elicit that fact.

Instead, Hyman concluded the cross-examination with a series of questions that led nowhere.

He asked the distances between the homes and driveways on the Dowalibys' block, whether there were "nooks and crannies" where children might hide, whether Bell had seen the Dowalibys' broken basement window, and whether Cynthia was barefoot when Bell saw her on September 10.

Bell, for what it was worth, estimated the distances, confirmed that there were places where children might hide, and said she had not noticed the basement window or whether Cynthia was barefoot.

The next prosecution witness was Jackie Guess.

On direct examination by George Velcich, Guess explained that her son James had married Cynthia shortly after she had become pregnant with Jaclyn. Soon after Jaclyn was born, they were divorced.

Guess testified that she had continued to see Jaclyn, who occasionally had spent the night at her home.

"Do you remember the last time that Jaclyn stayed over at your house?" Velcich asked.

"Yes, it was in the middle of August," Guess answered, breaking into tears.

"Ma'am, do you need some tissue?" Velcich offered.

"I'm all right," said Guess.

Guess continued that the last time she had seen Jaclyn was the week before she disappeared, when Guess had brought photos of her other grandchildren to the Dowaliby home.

At about 10:00 A.M. on September 10, Guess said she had been waiting on customers at Wag's when Cynthia called.

"What did she say?" Velcich asked.

"She said that Jaclyn was missing. Was Jim in town?"

"What did you say?"

"I told her I would be right there."

When she arrived, an officer asked her about James. She said that he was in prison in Florida.

A little later, Guess said, she went home. That evening the FBI arrived.

"Did they search your home?" Velcich asked.

"Yes."

"Did you allow them to do that?"

"Sure."

"Did they ask to speak to any other members of your family?"

"They spoke with my husband, and they spoke with my son Tim. Tim was at the Park Avenue Restaurant. I told them where he was, and they went and talked with him."

On cross-examination, Ralph Meczyk established that Jackie Guess had never told David or Cynthia that James was in prison.

Meczyk then asked about Timothy Guess: "He works at the Parkside Restaurant in Harvey, is that right?"

"Park Avenue Restaurant," she corrected him.

"Park Avenue Restaurant," said Meczyk. "I am sorry."

Meczyk asked several questions designed to portray Timothy as an alternative suspect to the Dowalibys. In the process, however, Meczyk both confused the time frame of Jaclyn's disappearance and suggested a possible alibi for Timothy.

"Between five in the morning and sometime in the late evening hours of September 9, as far as you know, Timothy Randall Guess was working as a busboy at the Park Avenue Restaurant in Harvey, correct?" Meczyk asked.

"Well, sometimes he worked there and sometimes he just went there," the witness answered, thereby indicating that Timothy's routine was consistent with his alibi.

"Mrs. Guess," Meczyk asked, "is it true that from time to time he would pick up a waitress named Margaret Murphy?"

"Yes, sometimes he would," Guess answered.

"Margaret Murphy, you knew, lived at—"

O'Brien quickly objected, asking for a sidebar.

Neville ordered the lawyers to approach the bench, and O'Brien demanded to know the relevance of where Margaret Murphy lived. Meczyk said that she lived at the Islander Apartments and that Timothy often picked her up and dropped her off there. "That's hearsay," said O'Brien. "How does she know what Tim Guess was doing if she's not with him?"

Meczyk said he was entitled to ask whether Jackie Guess had told her son not to go to the Islander Apartments after Jaclyn's body was found.

Neville said Meczyk had a right to ask that.

O'Brien continued to argue that the testimony would be hearsay, but Neville said, "Apparently he is only going to ask what she told him, which is okay. He can do it."

Back before the jury, Meczyk asked Guess, "There came a time, after Jaclyn was found murdered, that you told your son not to pick up Margaret Murphy at the Islander Apartments where she lived, correct?"

"Right," Guess answered.

Meczyk then asked her about Timothy's mental problems, and Guess replied that Timothy was a paranoid schizophrenic and took medication for that condition. On occasion, she said, Timothy had wandered off and no one heard from him for days.

"To change the subject," Meczyk continued, "you told police that to the best of your recollection Jaclyn was well treated by David and Cynthia Dowaliby?"

"As far as I know," she said.

Meczyk's final question was, "Where Jaclyn's body was found was about a building away from where your son, Tim, picked up the waitress, Margaret Murphy, am I correct?"

Without waiting for an objection, Neville instructed the jury to disregard the question; Guess only had hearsay knowledge of where Jaclyn's body had been found.

On redirect examination, George Velcich asked, "At any time was Tim aware of where Jaclyn lived?"

The defense did not object, although the question called for hearsay.

"No," Guess answered.

"Did Tim know Jaclyn's last name?" Velcich continued.

"Objection to what Tim knew, your honor," Meczyk shouted.

Neville called the lawyers to the bench and asked why they were asking so many questions about Timothy.

"Tim Guess is a possible suspect," Meczyk declared.

"That is news to me," said Neville. "This is the first time I have heard about it. If that is what the defense position is, and that is part of their defense—"

"It raises reasonable doubt," Meczyk interrupted, adding, after a silence, "I am sorry to interrupt you."

"Ralph, if you don't keep your mouth shut, I am going to ban you from these conferences," Neville snapped. "When I'm talking, out of common decency, you ought to keep your mouth shut."

"I apologize," said Meczyk.

"This is not a debate," said Neville.

"I accept your rebuke," said Meczyk.

Returning to the subject at hand, Neville ruled that since Meczyk had initiated the questions about Timothy Guess, the prosecution was entitled to pursue the issue further.

"If you open the door," Neville told Meczyk, "then you live with the consequences."

Back before the jury, Velcich repeated the question about whether Timothy knew where Jaclyn lived.

"No," the witness answered.

"Did you ever tell Tim Jaclyn's new last name?"

"No, I didn't."

Velcich had no further questions.

Lawrence Hyman conducted a recross examination. After a few perfunctory questions, he started to ask about James Guess's alleged attempt to snatch Jaclyn when she was an infant: "In 1981, that was the same year that Jimmy Guess was arrested for going through the window of the Borrelli apartment—"

O'Brien objected. Hyman's question called for hearsay. It also misstated the facts—James Guess had not been arrested, and the incident had not occurred at the Borrellis' apartment, but at the Malias' single-family home.

Neville sustained the objection.

Hyman tried a different tack, asking, "Your son Jimmy, after the separation between himself and Cyndi, tried to see his daughter, did he not?"

"Yes," Jackie Guess answered.

"Did he see her by trying to go through a window?"

"No."

"Did he ever try to get into an apartment in Harvey where Cyndi and her mother lived?"

"I will object," O'Brien said. Once again, the question called for hearsay.

"Objection is sustained," Neville ruled.

Hyman dropped this line of questioning, thus failing to establish why it would have been natural for the Dowalibys to suspect James Guess of taking Jaclyn.

Hyman next asked, "To the best of your knowledge, you do not know that your son Tim knew where the Dowalibys lived?"

"No," she said, "he did not know where they lived."

The answer reinforced the point that, only a few minutes earlier, Meczyk had objected to the prosecution making.

Guess was excused.

As she left the courtroom, the defense and prosecution stipulated that James Guess was in prison between September 9 and 14 and remained there at the present time.

The prosecution then called Sally Crowley, the Midlothian Police Department dispatcher who had taken David's call the morning of September 10. The purpose of her testimony was to establish the authenticity of a tape recording of the call.

After she so testified, George Velcich played the tape for the jury. The tape revealed no hint of panic in David's voice and showed that he mentioned the break-in before he said that his daughter was missing—points that, the prosecution would argue, were incriminating.

Next the prosecution called John Del Cason, the sheriff's policeman who had built the mock-up of the basement wall and window. He testified that the window in the exhibit was of the same manufacture as the one in the home and that all of the measurements were true to the original.

Meczyk conducted a brief cross-examination that seemed to serve no purpose other than to flatter Del Cason. "I compliment you on your carpentry skills," said Meczyk.

What Meczyk neglected to establish was that the exhibit was incomplete: It showed neither the ground outside nor the interior wall.

Without the ground or the interior wall for support, it would be extremely difficult for someone to get through the window without disturbing the items below, as jurors would learn—by attempting it themselves.

The next prosecution witness was Donald Woodark, the policeman who was first to arrive at the Dowaliby home.

On direct examination, Patrick O'Brien asked Woodark to describe David and Cynthia's demeanor that morning.

Cynthia was "extremely upset, pacing back and forth, crying," Woodark said, but David was "calm from the time I first encountered him at the house until the time I left."

Immediately after arriving, Woodark testified, he briefly examined the broken window from the outside, noticing that the screen had been ripped from left to right and that broken glass covered the ground and window ledge.

Woodark quoted David as saying that he had found the front door open at about 8:00 A.M. and was "positive" that he had bolted it the previous night. David added that he had installed the bolt because Jaclyn once had gone out without permission, Woodark said.

Woodark continued that he obtained a description of Jaclyn from David and radioed it to the Midlothian Police Department so it could be put out immediately on the police radio network.

Then, Woodark said, he went back to the broken window and picked up several pieces of glass, looking for blood and other possible clues. At one point, he said, he noticed Davey trying to touch the glass and told him not to touch anything.

Woodark said that he next went to the basement, where he used a flashlight to examine the scene.

O'Brien asked, "On the wall itself, underneath the window, did you see any marks or defects on that wall?"

"Yes, sir," Woodark said.

"Could you tell us what that was?"

"Directly below the window, I found a smudge, just an indeterminate mark on the wall."

After parting the curtains on the window, Woodark said, he noticed "an even layer of dust on the inside window ledge."

O'Brien showed Woodark an interior photograph of the window. Carefully avoiding asking whether the photograph showed any dust, O'Brien instead asked whether it showed "the area" where Woodark had seen dust.

"Yes, sir," said Woodark.

O'Brien asked him to circle the area of the photograph where he had seen the dust, and Woodark circled the window ledge.

At O'Brien's request, Woodark then pointed out the corresponding area on the mock-up of the basement window.

"Nothing further," said O'Brien.

Ralph Meczyk began the cross-examination by calling Woodark's attention to a report he filed on September 27, forcing Woodark to admit that the report said there was a "scuff mark"—not an "indeterminate" mark—on the basement wall.

Meczyk then directed Woodark's attention to the interior photo of the basement window and asked, "You circled, did you not, the ledge, and you stated that you can see dust over that, am I correct?"

"Objection," said O'Brien. "That is not what he said about the picture. He said he saw dust when he was in the room."

Without waiting for Neville to rule, Meczyk resumed, "You just circled the area where you said you saw dust?"

"Yes, sir," said Woodark.

"You can see that in this photograph?"

"Yes, sir."

"Isn't it true, sir, that there is a reflection from the window, from the outside onto that sill, that is not dust?"

"That is possible, but there was dust there."

Meczyk and Woodark were talking past each other. Meczyk was challenging Woodark's ability to see dust in the photo, but Woodark was not saying that he saw dust in the photo—only that the photo showed the ledge on which he originally had seen dust.

Meczyk had so feared a surprise corroboration of the presence of dust that he was determined to read it into Woodark's testimony, regardless of what Woodark actually said.

Then, in an effort to discredit a statement that Woodark had not made, Meczyk asked whether the photo "also" showed a reflection cast by the sun onto the window ledge.

"It is very possible," Woodark replied.

Drawing Woodark's attention to his inspection of the basement on September 10, Meczyk asked, "You state that when you parted the curtains, you noticed an even layer of dust?"

"Yes, sir."

"That was a very astute observation you made. In your mind, when you saw the dust across the inside sill, that told you that no one could have gotten through the window, am I right?"

"That is what I thought."

Calling Woodark's attention to his initial report, Meczyk asked, "There is a box provided at the bottom, and it says 'method of entry.' You wrote down broken basement window, east side, did you not?"

"Yes, sir."

"You stated five times in your report that entry was made through the broken window, correct?"

"Yes, sir."

"Now, Officer Woodark, show us in your report that you made at the time where it states that the dust on the inside window ledge is undisturbed."

"It is not there, sir."

"That, of course, is an important fact, is it not?"

"Now I believe it is, yes, sir."

"But seventeen days after that report, you wrote the supplementary report, right?"

"Yes, sir."

"You wrote that report after you had conferred with your boss, Chief Fischer, am I right?"

"Yes, sir."

"He told you to write a second report, did he not?"

"Including all the detail that I could think of."

"But an important detail was left out of your first report, correct, the dust?"

"Yes, sir."

In a brief redirect examination, Patrick O'Brien showed Woodark his September 27 report and asked, "Do you talk about the dust in that particular report?"

"Yes," said Woodark.

At O'Brien's direction, Woodark read a sentence from the report to the jury: "Dust on window ledge undisturbed."

"Did you notice if there was anything disturbed underneath the window?" O'Brien asked.

"No," Woodark answered. "Nothing appeared to be."

As Donald Woodark stepped down, Judge Neville declared a ten-minute recess.

While Cynthia was in the women's room, David puffed on a cigarette and chatted with Daniel Franks in the hall.

Seeing them talking, Ralph Meczyk asked to speak privately with David.

"If you want to replace me with Dan Franks, just go ahead and do it," Meczyk whimpered.

"Ralph, I was just talking to him for a second," David said appeasingly.

David later said that the exchange inhibited him from further discussing a greater role for Franks in the trial.

For the moment, however, David had a more pressing concern: Cynthia's emotional stability.

In the courtroom, she clung to David's arm with both hands, sometimes sobbing audibly.

With each witness, she seemed to come more unglued.

Next on the stand was Colleen Jones-Godin, a neighbor who had had two conversations with David Dowaliby that the prosecutors wanted her to relate.

According to Jones-Godin, the first conversation occurred the day before Jaclyn's body was found, when she encountered David and his next-door neighbor Robert Tolbert in front of the Tolbert home.

On direct examination, George Velcich asked, "What was the first thing that was said?"

Jones-Godin answered, "I told David how sorry I was about Jaclyn being missing and that I was praying for her every day."

"When you said that to David Dowaliby, what was his answer?"

"He said, yeah, it was really hard at first, but it gets easier day by day."

"Was Jaclyn still missing at that time?"

"Yes."

The second conversation, according to Jones-Godin, occurred two days after Jaclyn's funeral and one day after the police searched the Dowaliby home.

Jones-Godin testified that she encountered David outside the Dowaliby home and asked, "How are you all holding up over here? I saw the search that was going on yesterday."

"Only in America," Jones-Godin quoted David as responding.

After a pause, David added that the police "ain't got nothing on me," Jones-Godin said.

The testimony was damaging to the Dowalibys because it portrayed David as callous when he should have been worried, and as flippant when he should have been in mourning.

Judge Neville later would confide that he found Jones-Godin's testimony about the first conversation particularly damaging to the defense. "It was the one statement attributed to David that could not be explained innocently," Neville said.

On cross-examination, however, Daniel Franks raised doubts about Jones-Godin's credibility, forcing her to acknowledge that she had failed to mention either conversation to police for more than five months.

Franks also elicited testimony helpful to the Dowalibys concerning an incident that Jones-Godin witnessed on September 10, when the Dowalibys claimed they were searching for Jaclyn.

Jones-Godin testified that she was on her front porch with several children, including a young girl who was selling pizza for a school project, and that, when Cynthia Dowaliby saw the girl from behind, she exclaimed, "Jaclyn!"

Under prodding by Franks, Jones-Godin acknowledged that when the girl turned around, Cynthia "looked disheartened."

The final witness of the day was FBI Agent Steven Kashirsky.

On direct examination by Patrick O'Brien, Kashirsky described the initial investigation, making it sound quite thorough. It included interviewing neighbors, searching surrounding areas, checking the whereabouts of James Guess and other possible suspects, and canvassing hospitals, hotels, motels, and bus terminals, he said.

After a discussion with Daniel McDevitt on September 11, Kashirsky said, he inspected the basement, looking for points where an intruder might have entered other than through the broken window. He said he found an unlocked window on the north wall of the basement overlooking the backyard.

Kashirsky continued that on September 14 he received a call at the Dowaliby home from McDevitt, who told him a body tentatively identified as Jaclyn had been found.

Kashirsky said that he went to the scene, later returning to the Dowaliby home, where he spoke with Ann Dowaliby.

"Tell us what occurred," said O'Brien.

"I advised her that I wanted to get the recording device and the tapes, along with the log, and she refused to let me into the house," Kashirsky said. The suggestion was that the Dowalibys had been uncooperative with the authorities.

On cross-examination, however, Daniel Franks established that the family had been cooperative earlier. "You and your men were in that house from September 10 to September 14 with total and complete access to every part of that house, isn't that correct?" Franks asked.

"That is correct, sir," Kashirsky answered.

Franks, his voice rising, then asked, "They didn't tell you, you can't go into this room, or look in this box, or go up on the roof, did they?"

"Not that I am aware of," said Kashirsky. He conceded that the Dowalibys permitted the tapping of their telephone, gave fingerprints and blood samples, and allowed officers to take the family's medical records.

Finally, he acknowledged that Ann Dowaliby subsequently had returned the FBI recording device and logs.

When Kashirsky was excused, the jury was dismissed for the night, after an admonition not to read newspapers or watch television reports about the case.

"Where's the evidence?" Channel 5's Paul Hogan asked his colleagues in the criminal court building press room.

"My sources tell me it's coming," said Channel 7's Dick Johnson.

Hogan just shook his head.

That evening, the Channel 7 and Channel 5 coverages were so different that viewers might have wondered if Johnson and Hogan were covering the same trial.

Johnson's live story for the early news on Channel 7 led with Donald Woodark's testimony. Johnson told viewers that when Woodark arrived at scene on September 10, "he found all of Cynthia and David Dowaliby's relatives arguing."

If true, that certainly would have made the family look bad, but in fact Woodark had said nothing of the sort.

On the later news, Johnson abandoned the argument angle and focused instead on Colleen Jones-Godin's testimony. "She told the jury she was perplexed by two statements made by David Dowaliby when she offered her sympathies," Johnson reported, although Jones-Godin had not testified that she was "perplexed."

The Channel 7 report also contained an erroneous assertion by the anchorman that prosecutors soon would present evidence that fibers had been transferred between Jaclyn's bedspread and the trunk liner of Cynthia's Malibu.

The latter inaccuracy occurred because Channel 7 failed to check a report by the City News Bureau, a wire service, that fiber transfer had occurred; actually, no fiber transfer had occurred, as the state's expert would testify.

Hogan, in sharp contrast, began his live report, "It's been another day of strictly circumstantial evidence."

The prosecution, said Hogan, suffered "a blow" when Judge Neville ruled that Davey Dowaliby was too young to testify.

"Police witnesses are now taking the stand, attempting to show why they don't believe that the Dowalibys' home was broken into by an unknown intruder," Hogan reported. "The focus of the testimony is a mock-up of the basement window of the home."

Referring to Woodark's testimony that there was a scuff mark on the wall beneath the window, Hogan concluded, "That would seem to indicate that somebody *did* come through there."

PIECES OF A MOSAIC

Over the next four days—Tuesday, April 17, through Friday, April 20—Patrick O'Brien and George Velcich kept building their case like a mosaic, fragment by fragment.

Anticipation was high among reporters covering the trial that the prosecution would produce some dramatic bit of evidence at any moment, but none would come.

Daniel McDevitt—the leading man of the investigation, the star grand jury performer—played only a bit part in the trial.

On direct examination, McDevitt explained how he came to head the task force and described the search for Jaclyn in detail. He said that scores of leads were checked during the investigation, and suspects were pursued systematically until all except David and Cynthia Dowaliby were eliminated.

So thorough was the investigation, said McDevitt,

that officers even were assigned to search Midlothian garbage trucks for evidence that might have been thrown away.

On cross-examination, Ralph Meczyk sparred with McDevitt over how diligent the investigation had been.

"You and your brother officers learned that an Everett Mann had been contacted, correct?" Meczyk asked.

"Yes, sir," McDevitt replied.

"At that point you stopped investigating all other leads, isn't that correct?"

"No, sir."

"At that point, the Dowalibys were the only suspects, isn't that correct?"

McDevitt denied that the Dowalibys were the only suspects after Mann was interviewed but acknowledged that the task force focused primarily on them.

Meczyk then tried to show how sloppy the investigation had been by asking McDevitt what had happened to pieces of rope that had been seized from the home of a Dowaliby neighbor.

"I don't recall right offhand, sir," McDevitt answered.

"If I told you those ropes were lost, would you take my word for it?"

"Probably not, sir."

"But those ropes were to be tested, were they not?"

McDevitt contended that testing them was unnecessary because they did not look like the presumed murder weapon.

"But you do not have those ropes, do you?"

"No, I do not."

In a brief final exchange, Meczyk tried to establish that investigators initially targeted the Dowalibys in the mistaken belief that the basement window had been broken from the inside.

Meczyk failed to make his point, however, because he ignored a basic rule of evidence—that a witness can testify about what other persons said or did, but not about what they thought.

Instead of asking whether Hayden Baldwin had told McDevitt that the window might have been broken from inside,

Meczyk asked, "All of the investigators *thought* that the force came from the inside going out, correct?"

"Objection!" shouted Velcich.

"Sustained," said Judge Neville.

Meczyk could have rephrased the question, but he gave up, asking nothing further.

John Waters, present in court for the first time, glared at McDevitt as he strode from the witness stand. Waters could no longer counter his archrival's moves.

Patrick O'Brien called FBI Agent Alfred Hardman to testify about David Dowaliby's allegedly incriminating statements.

Hardman told the jury about David's "lie" about kissing Jaclyn good night and his "I didn't do it" response when asked if he knew where Jaclyn was.

O'Brien then asked Hardman about David's reaction to the news that his daughter's body had been found.

"He asked if it was in a field," Hardman said.

"What else did he ask?"

"He asked if we were sure it was Jaclyn, and then he asked if she was alive. I told him no, she was not alive, and he said that he thought we were lying just to get him to confess. And then he said, 'I guess you guys think I ought to cry now.' "

"And did he cry?"

"No, he did not."

FBI Agent Timothy Eley testified that Cynthia Dowaliby had told him that she rather than David normally disciplined Jaclyn.

If the jury believed that Jaclyn might have died when discipline got out of hand—the only motive ever offered by the prosecution—Eley's testimony suggested the likelihood that Cynthia would have been responsible.

Eley's only other function as a prosecution witness was to identify the rooms of the Dowaliby home on a diagram. At George Velcich's request, Eley wrote "Defendants" on David and Cynthia's bedroom.

Lawrence Hyman conducted a brief cross-examination, focusing on Cynthia's reaction to the news that Jaclyn was dead.

"She burst into tears and was horrified at what had happened," Eley acknowledged. "She did in fact collapse."

State Police Officer Nancy Dollarhide testified that she had assisted in the arrest of Cynthia Dowaliby.

Patrick O'Brien asked Dollarhide to identify Cynthia in the courtroom, and Dollarhide pointed her out, describing her as "the lady in the blue dress with the gold chain."

Dollarhide then testified that the contents of Cynthia's purse were inventoried at the Blue Island police station after her arrest. It contained "some handwritten letters," Dollarhide said.

Dollarhide also identified mug shots of Cynthia, which were shown to the jury. Mug shots have a way of making people look guilty, and Lawrence Hyman objected that they were irrelevant and "extremely prejudicial," but the judge overruled the objection.

Dollarhide testified that she had spent about an hour with Cynthia after the arrest. "She was not crying or upset," said Dollarhide. "She appeared angry or hostile."

On cross-examination, Hyman asked Dollarhide to identify a pink card that police had found in Cynthia's purse. It was a Mother's Day card, which Jaclyn had made at school. It said, "Mom, my love for you just grows and grows. Love, Jaclyn."

Dollarhide said she had no recollection of the card.

On redirect examination, O'Brien asked if Cynthia's purse had contained a pair of children's underpants.

"Yes, sir," Dollarhide said.

On recross examination, Hyman tried to establish that Cynthia was carrying the underpants to give them to the psychic Linda Petrine, who had told Cynthia that an intimate garment would be helpful in divining what had happened to Jaclyn.

"Isn't it a fact," Hyman asked, "that Cynthia told you she had the underpants because she was going to see a psychic?"

"No, sir," said Dollarhide.

* * *

Jennie Hahn, a forensic serologist with the Illinois state police, testified that bloodstains had been found under seven of Jaclyn's fingernails.

"Were you able to type that blood?" George Velcich asked.

"Yes, I was," said Hahn. "I was able to determine that it was Type O."

"That would be consistent with Jaclyn Dowaliby's blood?"

"Yes, sir."

Hahn testified that Cynthia and Davey also were Type O, while David was Type A.

Velcich then asked Hahn about stains on Jaclyn's pillow, and Hahn replied that there were two small stains of Type O blood.

"That is consistent with Jaclyn Dowaliby's blood, is that correct?" Velcich asked.

"Yes, sir, that is," Hahn answered.

Velcich did not ask Hahn about the age of the blood.

Instead he changed the subject, asking Hahn about tests she had conducted on the white panties found near Jaclyn's body and on rectal and vaginal swabs taken at the autopsy.

Hahn said both the panties and the swabs tested negative for blood and semen.

Ralph Meczyk began the cross-examination by asking whether a hair had been found on the rope found around Jaclyn's neck.

"Well, there was more than one hair that I believe I recovered from the rope," said Hahn.

"You recovered actually three hairs, am I correct?" Meczyk asked, although Hahn's report had said there were only two.

"Yes, sir," Hahn responded, not catching the error.

After eliciting that "two of the hairs" were consistent with Jaclyn's, Meczyk then asked about the remaining hair.

"I identified it as Negroid," Hahn answered.

In an effort to suggest that the latter hair might have been Perry Hernandez's, Meczyk asked if it could have come from someone of Mexican descent.

"Someone of Mexican descent may have some Negroid characteristics, but not very much," Hahn answered.

Meczyk then elicited that there was no evidence of fiber

transfer between the trunk mat of the Malibu and Jaclyn's nightgown or the white panties.

Turning to the faint bloodstains on Jaclyn's bedspread, which Velcich had mentioned on direct examination, Meczyk inexplicably asked, "You cannot really wash out blood?"

"You can if you do it properly," said Hahn, who added that washing in cold water would remove traces of blood from fabric. Hahn's answer was detrimental to the defense, and Meczyk heightened its impact by immediately asking whether Hahn had found blood on Jaclyn's Lady Lovely Locks sheets.

"No, I did not," Hahn answered.

Referring to the fingernail clippings, Meczyk asked, "When you tested those, you discovered Type A blood, is that correct?"

Only a few minutes earlier, on direct examination, Hahn had testified that the blood was Type O; David's blood was Type A. By mixing up the types, Meczyk raised the possibility that the blood beneath Jaclyn's nails could have been David's.

Fortunately for Meczyk, Hahn promptly corrected him, saying that the fingernail blood was Type O.

"I'm sorry, Type O?" Meczyk asked.

"Yes, that is correct," Hahn answered.

"Type O would exclude David Dowaliby, who is Type A?"

"Yes, sir, that is correct."

Meczyk then turned to the bloodstains on the pillow. Hahn acknowledged that one of the stains, the lighter of the two, was old. Noting that the second stain was darker, Meczyk asked if that meant that it was even older.

"No, just that it was darker," Hahn answered.

Without asking about the age of the second stain, Meczyk returned to the Malibu trunk mat, asking, "You did find several hairs that were visually similar to the victim's head hair?"

"Yes, sir," she testified.

Thus Meczyk raised the specter that Jaclyn's body had been transported in the Malibu—why else would her hair be on the trunk mat?

)avid and Cynthia Dowaliby at their 1983 wedding. *[Courtesy Dowaliby family]*

Jaclyn Dowaliby in her kindergarten photograph. *[Courtesy Dowaliby family]*

Davey Dowaliby a few weeks before his sister was murdered and he was taken from his family by police. *[Courtesy Dowaliby family]*

avid and Cynthia with Jaclyn in 1988. *[Courtesy Dowaliby family]*

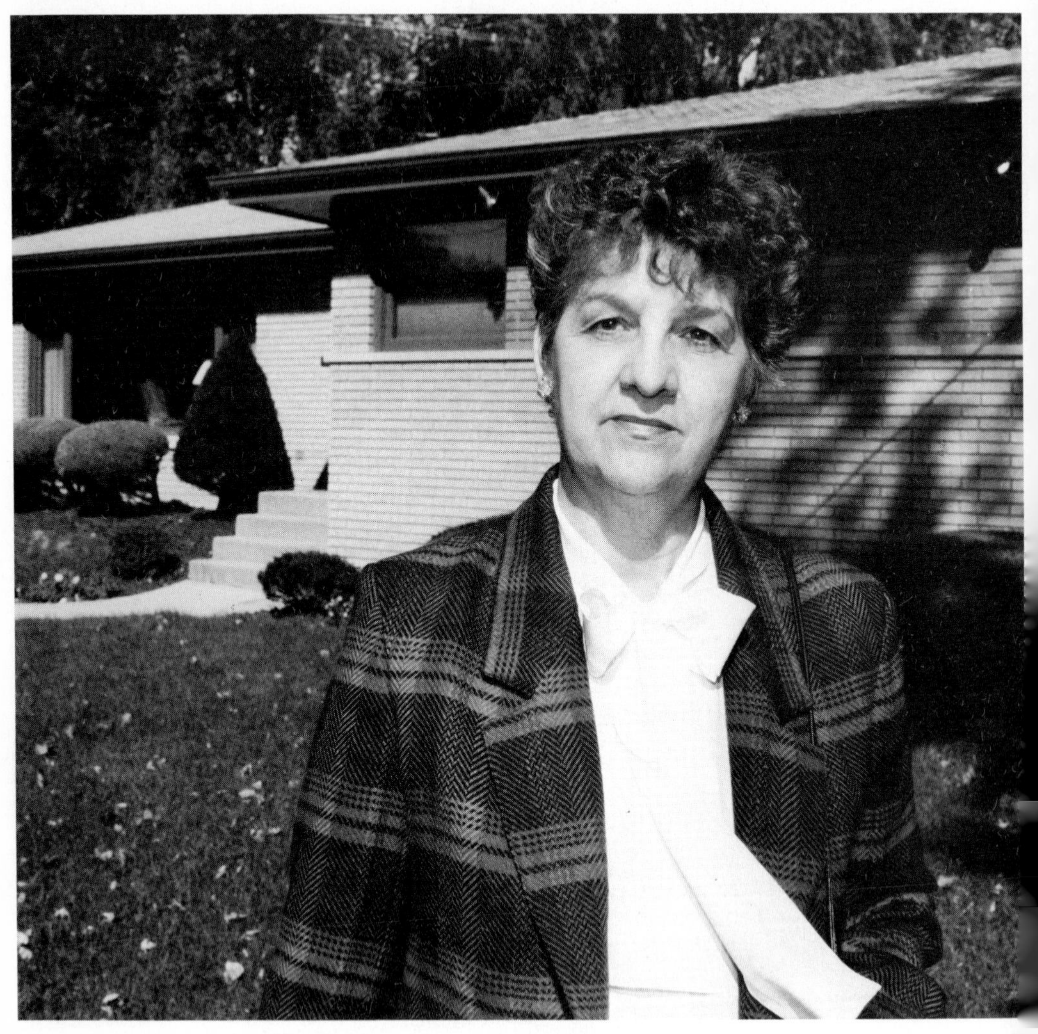

Ann Dowaliby, David's mother, in front of her Midlothian home, which she sold to help pay her son and daughter-in-law's legal expenses. *[J. Carl Ganter]*

Leaders of the investigation—Blue Island Police Chief Paul Dennis Greves, right, with Illinois State Police Captain Daniel S. McDevitt. *[Courtesy WMAQ-TV]*

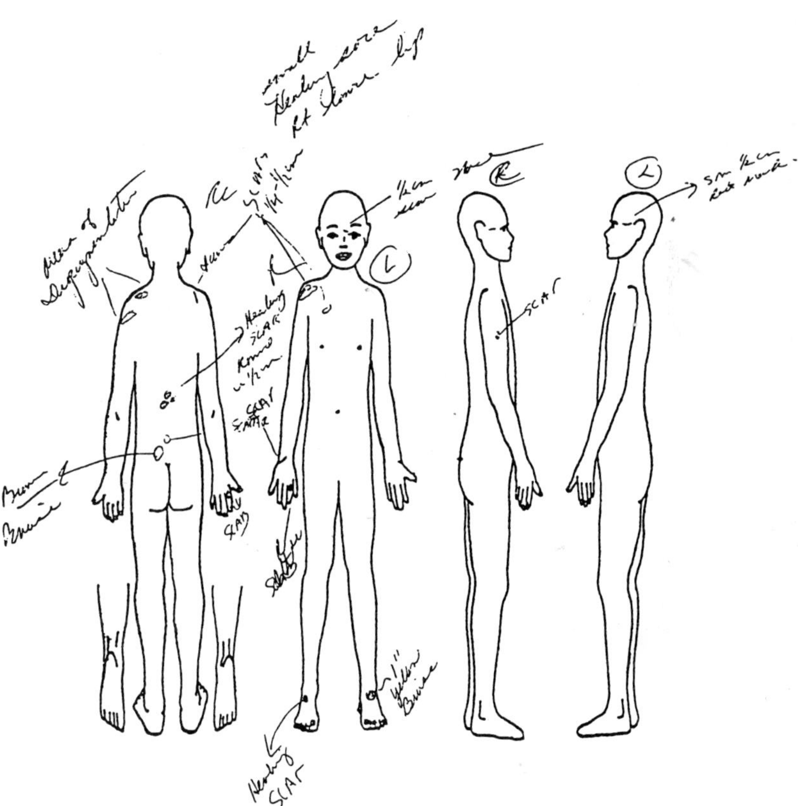

The chart prepared by Mount Sinai Hospital's Dr. Sharon Ahart purporting to indicate that Davey Dowaliby had been physically abused and possibly sexually abused. Dr. Ahart later resigned her position as part of a Mount Sinai reorganization in the wake of the Dowaliby case. *[Courtesy Cook County Circuit Court, Juvenile Division]*

Chicago Police Department photographs taken the same day that Dr. Ahart prepared the chart, showing that each of the "abuse marks" she identified either did not exist or was exaggerated. *[Courtesy WMAQ-TV]*

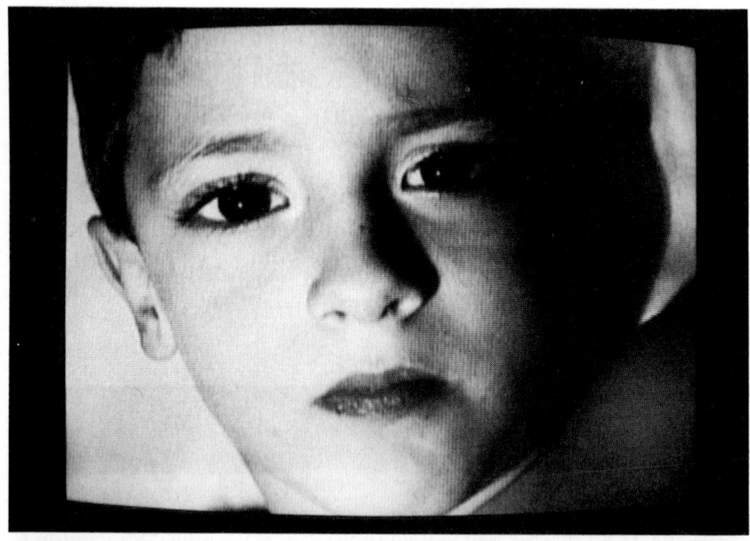

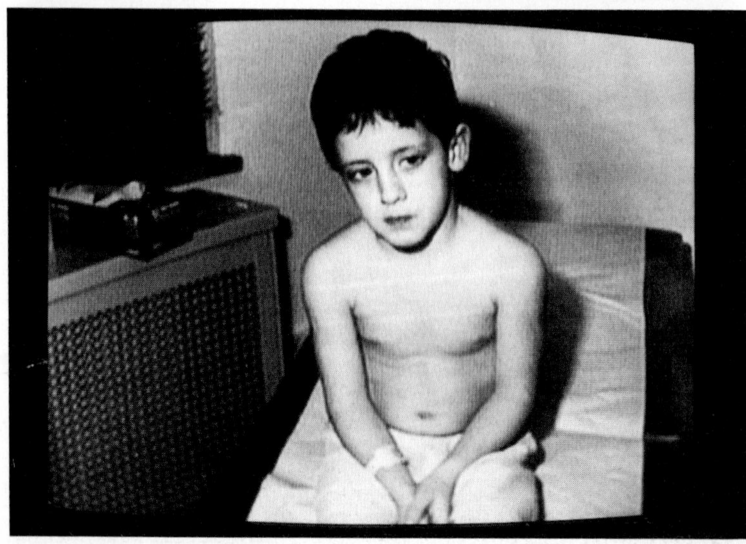

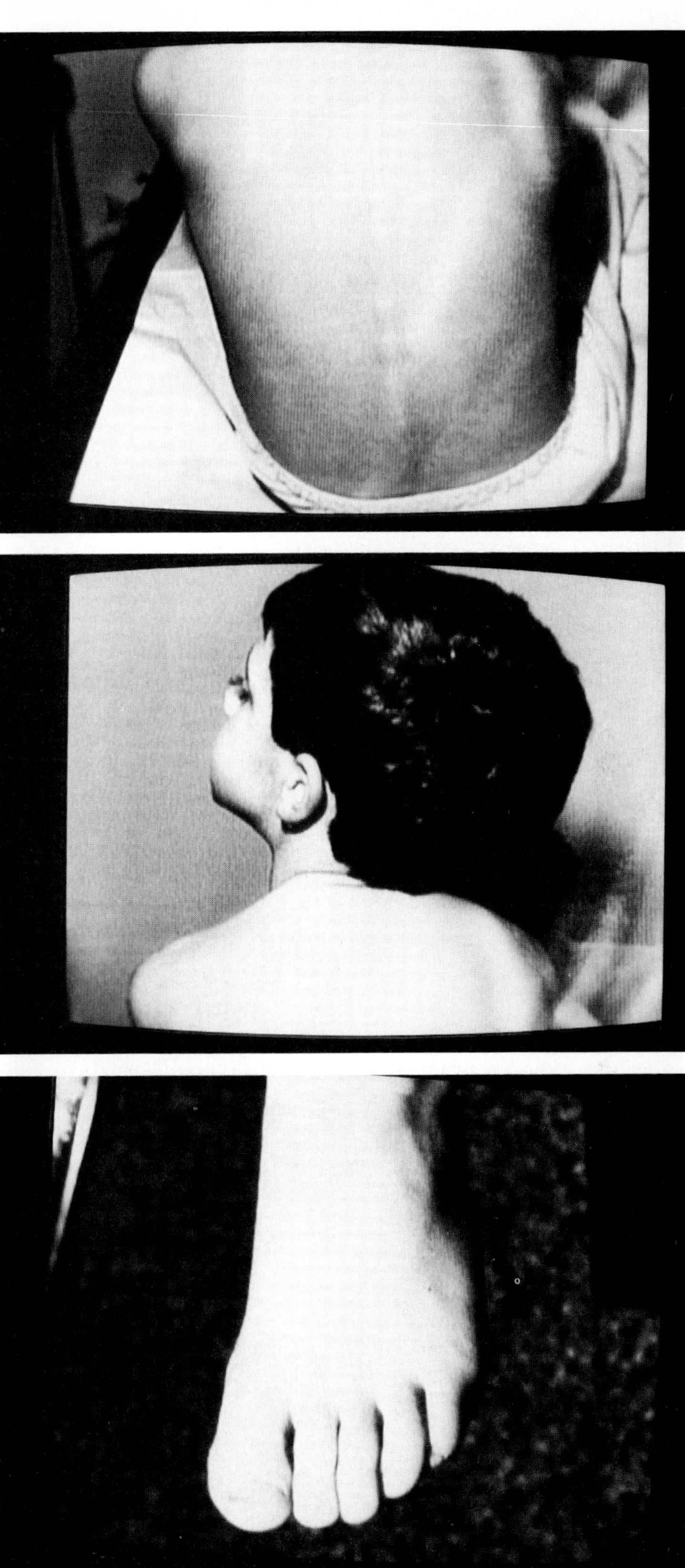

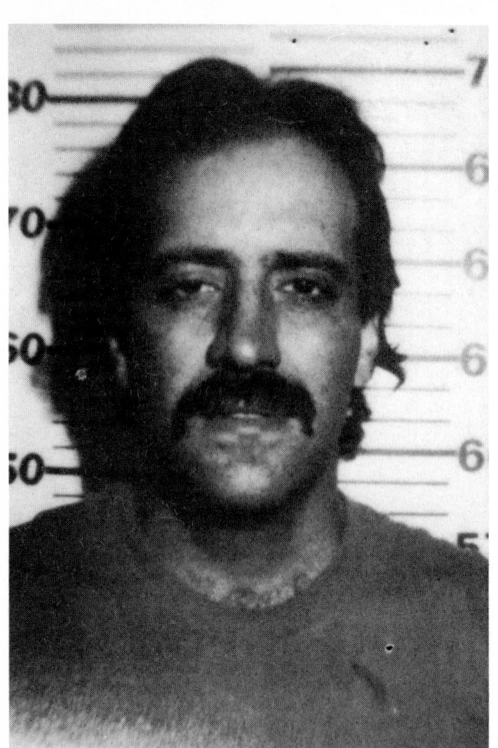

Mug shot of David Dowaliby taken in 1988. *[Courtesy Cook County Department of Corrections]*

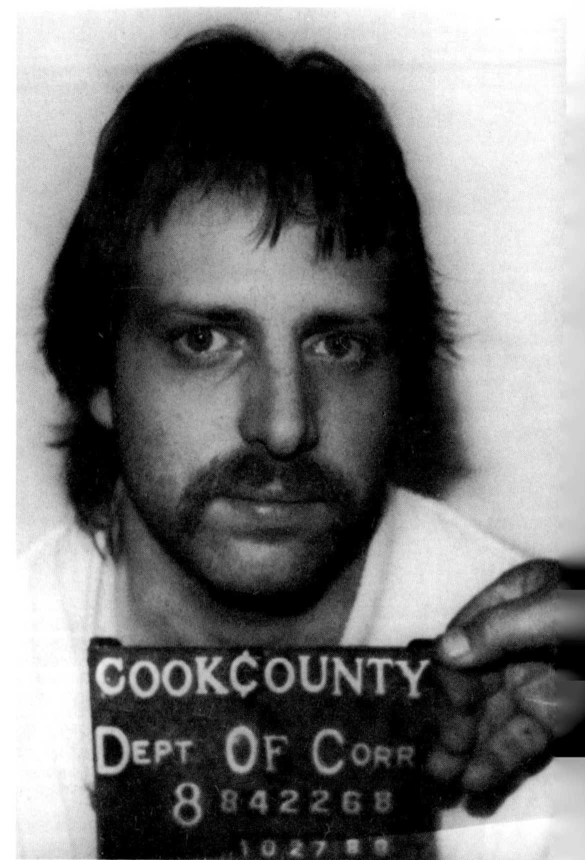

Mug shot of Roy Padecky taken in 1988. *[Courtesy Cook County Department of Corrections]*

Detective for the defense—John Waters a few months before he died of cancer in 1990. *[Courtesy Charlotte Waters]*

The Dowaliby trial team (clockwise from the top)—Daniel Franks, Lawrence Hyman, and Ralph Meczyk. *[Courtesy* Chicago Daily Law Bulletin*]*

Perry Hernandez, who admittedly abducted a sleeping child from her bed not far from the Dowaliby home, was never questioned by police about Jaclyn's murder. *[Loren Santow]*

Richard M. Daley campaigning for his third term as Cook County State's Attorney. On the advice of a political aide and against the advice of several career prosecutors in his office, Daley ordered the Dowaliby case to proceed. *[Loren Santow]*

Prosecutor Patrick O'Brien, who carried out Daley's order, with co-prosecutor George Velcich. *[Courtesy WMAQ-TV]*

Cook County Circuit Court Judge Richard J. Neville presided over the Dowaliby trial. *[J. Carl Ganter]*

David Dowaliby at the Stateville Correctional Center, Joliet, Illinois. *[J. Carl Ganter]*

ynthia Dowaliby, right, with Freedom Committee members Beverly Robinson, t, and Julie Schedin, center, in 1990. *[J. Carl Ganter]*

Channel Five's Paul Hogan exposed the sloppy police investigation and misleading grand jury testimony that led to the indictment of Cynthia and David. *[J. Carl Ganter]*

Writers Rob Warden, left, and David Protess. *[J. Carl Ganter]*

Jenner & Block's Robert L. Byman handled David Dowaliby's appeal *pro bono. [Kathy Richland]*

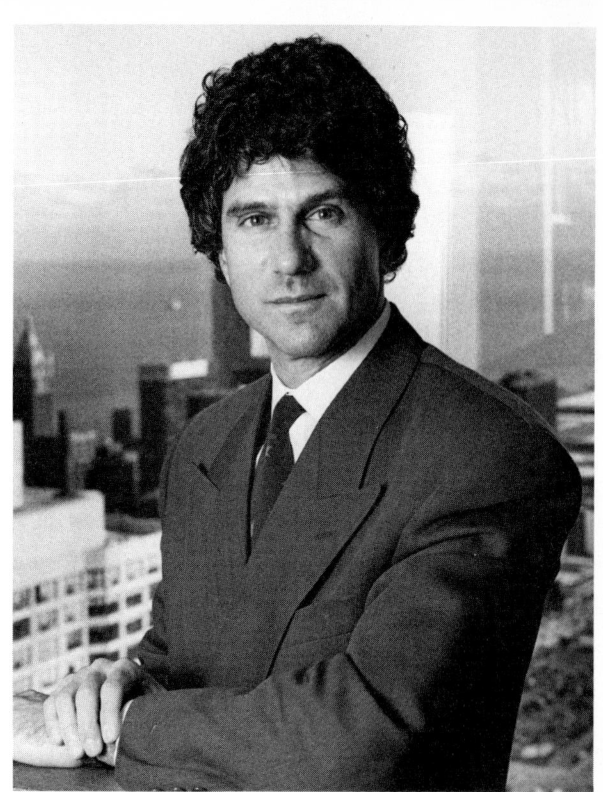

vid and Cynthia Dowaliby surrounded by reporters outside the Stateville
rrectional Center following his release from prison. *[J. Carl Ganter]*

David Dowaliby with his children, Carli and Davey, on the day of his release from Stateville prison. *[J. Carl Ganter]*

Timothy Guess, Jaclyn's paranoid schizophrenic uncle. *[J. Carl Ganter]*

Having introduced such an idea, Meczyk tried to undo the damage with a series of confusing questions about "the doctrine of hair transference."

Capitalizing on Meczyk's tactical error, Velcich asked on redirect examination whether Hahn had compared the hairs on the trunk mat to Jaclyn's own head hairs.

"Yes, I did a visual examination," Hahn answered.

"Did you find Jaclyn's hairs and the hairs on that mat to be consistent?"

"Yes."

Ralph Meyer, a state police forensic microscopist, testified that the Negroid hair found on the rope could not have come from Perry Hernandez—eliminating the doubt left by Jennie Hahn.

Meyer also testified about his analysis of the fiber evidence and the broken basement window. Although his testimony on these matters was exculpatory—entirely unhelpful to the prosecution—it was better for Patrick O'Brien to elicit it in a low-key fashion, minimizing its impact, than to allow the defense to raise it.

"Did you receive on a slide certain fibers which were taken from a black car mat?" O'Brien asked.

"Yes, I did," said Meyer.

"And did you also receive certain fibers which were taken from a bedspread?"

"Yes, I did."

"Did you make a comparison between those two slides?"

"Yes, I did."

"What did you find?"

"I did not observe any fiber transfer between the mat and the sheet."

Channel 7's Dick Johnson winced; his station had incorrectly reported that the prosecution would present evidence that there had been fiber transfer—an error the station would never apologize for or retract.

Shifting the focus of the testimony to the window, O'Brien asked, "Were you also requested to do certain examinations regarding the direction of force on the broken window?"

"Yes, I was."

"What were you able to tell regarding direction of force?"

"The window was broken from the outside of the house going into the house," Meyer answered.

Channel 5's Paul Hogan shook his head in disgust. He felt ashamed, he later confided, that he had been taken in by Daniel McDevitt's off-the-record claim that the window had been broken from the inside. Meyer's testimony, said Hogan, led him to suspect that the Dowalibys were being railroaded.

Hayden Baldwin testified that he had worked for the Illinois state police for twenty years and had processed more than a thousand crime scenes.

On the morning of September 10, Baldwin said, he was assigned to process a crime scene at 3636 West 148th Place in Midlothian, the Dowaliby home. He said he arrived at 12:12 P.M. and gave "a cursory exam" to the broken basement window.

"As you approached the window could you tell us what you observed?" Patrick O'Brien asked.

"On the inside of the window were two cobwebs, one up on each corner of the inside window," Baldwin answered. "On the windowsill was a layer of dust."

"Could you tell us what was located underneath the window?"

Baldwin said there were a cardboard box, a plywood counter, and a metal towel rack, on top of which were several items.

"Were any items on the floor?"

"No, they were not."

O'Brien asked if there were "footwear impressions" on the metal stand or boxes, and Baldwin said there were not.

Turning to Jaclyn's room, O'Brien asked, "Was there any bedding on the bed, when you saw it?"

"Just the mattress pad itself and two or three pillows," Baldwin answered.

O'Brien asked whether Baldwin had found fingerprints.

Baldwin said that he found latent prints on two of the pieces of broken glass outside the window and on some of the glass that remained in the frame. He added that he checked for prints on the front door, the door to Jaclyn's room, and the lock of the basement window, but found only "smear marks"—overlapping prints unsuitable for testing.

Baldwin continued that he processed the torn window screen for fingerprints, hair, and fibers, but found none. He explained that he did not take the screen or broken glass on September 10, but returned three days later and removed the window frame and "what I could recover from the broken glass."

"The broken glass that you collected, where did you actually collect that from?" O'Brien asked.

"I collected that from a paper bag that was full of trash inside the basement bedroom," Baldwin said.

On cross-examination, Ralph Meczyk asked, "When you process a scene, you follow a certain protocol, is that right?"

"That is correct."

"You were trained to follow that protocol when you attended the field officers' training program back in June of 1979, right?"

"No, that is not correct."

"You did attend the program in 1979 called a field officer's training program when you became an evidence technician?"

"No, that is not correct. I attended a program, but it has nothing to do with being a crime scene technician."

"You also learned about the protocol while you were at the basic supervisor's school in October of 1980, correct?"

"No, that is not correct."

"You, of course, then were trained sometime during your career in the steps of processing a scene, right?"

"That is correct."

Meczyk dropped the subject and asked about Patrolman Donald Woodark's disturbance of the glass and other evidence.

Baldwin conceded that the Dowaliby home "was not a virgin crime scene" when he arrived.

Meczyk then turned to Baldwin's contention that he had seen dust on the interior ledge of the basement window, asking, "When you came upon this very, very significant clue, you made a note of that, did you not?"

"Not at that time, no," Baldwin replied.

"There came a time when you did make a note of that, correct?"

"That is correct."

"Did you preserve those notes?"

"No, I did not."

"Where are those notes today?"

"They are destroyed."

"Why did you destroy them?"

"The crime scene report was completed."

"Is there another reason why you destroyed them?"

"No."

"Is there a policy in your department that says you have to destroy your notes?"

"No."

In an effort to discredit that answer, Meczyk brought up another case in which Baldwin had testified that it was his practice to destroy his notes after writing a report. Asked why, Baldwin had answered, "There is no need for the notes, plus it is a bureau policy."

Meczyk asked Baldwin, "You were asked that question and you gave that answer, didn't you?"

"That is correct," Baldwin said.

Meczyk thus had caught Baldwin in an inconsistent statement, but in the process also had allowed Baldwin to offer a rationale for destroying the notes.

Meczyk then turned to Baldwin's crime scene report dated October 6, 1988, asking, "Your report does reflect that you noticed dust on the interior ledge of the Dowaliby residence?"

"That is correct," Baldwin said.

"Your notes also reflected that, did they not?" Meczyk continued.

"Yes," Baldwin responded, reinforcing his contention that the original notes and the later report were consistent.

Meczyk instructed Baldwin to step down and approach the mock-up of the basement window. Directing his attention to the interior ledge, Meczyk asked, "It is true, is it not, that when you noticed this dust, you ran your finger horizontally across this ledge?"

"No," said Baldwin.

"Did you run your finger across that?"

"Eventually."

"When you did run your finger across it, did you notice the contrast between the dust and the mark that your finger left?" Meczyk asked, explicitly acknowledging the presence of dust.

"Yes, I did," Baldwin answered.

"Did you notice any splinters on the inside of that ledge?" Meczyk continued.

"Splinters?"

"Broken glass splinters."

"There may have been a minute amount, but nothing large."

Meczyk asked several questions about what Baldwin had done to preserve evidence of the dust, forcing Baldwin to acknowledge that he had done nothing in that regard.

Meczyk's final exchange with Baldwin pertained to the bolt lock on the front door.

"You did not even attempt to dust that lock, did you?" Meczyk asked.

"Yes, I did," Baldwin replied.

Meczyk seemed taken aback. Although Baldwin had testified only minutes earlier that he did dust the bolt for fingerprints, Meczyk somehow anticipated a negative answer, hoping to expose Baldwin's maladroit evidence-gathering effort.

That purpose would have been served if only Meczyk had asked the same question about Jaclyn's room, or the rear door, or the patio door, all of which Baldwin indeed had failed to dust.

After a pause, sounding puzzled, Meczyk asked, "You did dust the bolt?"

"Yes, I did," Baldwin repeated.

"I have nothing further," said Meczyk.

On redirect examination, O'Brien asked only two questions.

"Did you see the dust on the inside window ledge in the Dowaliby home?"

"Yes, I did."

"Did you see any disturbance on the rack below the window?"

"No, I did not."

On recross examination, Meczyk asked Baldwin whether he checked for dust on the box beneath the window.

"Yes, I did," said Baldwin.

"You did?"

"Is that in your crime scene report?"

"No, it is not."

"That box, from your wonderful recollection that you now have, that box—"

O'Brien interrupted, "I am going to have to object."

"I will withdraw that," said Meczyk.

Judge Neville intoned, "Rather than withdraw it, Mr. Meczyk, let me say this: I have asked you once not to make extraneous statements. I think they are improper. Don't do it anymore."

"I accept your rebuke, your honor," said Meczyk, who then asked, "Sergeant Baldwin, that box appeared to have stress marks on it, did it not?"

"Yes, it did."

"Nothing further," said Meczyk.

In a brief redirect examination, O'Brien asked, "Sergeant, does it appear that somebody jumped five feet from the window ledge onto that box?"

"Definitely not," said Baldwin.

"Objection, your honor," said Meczyk. "That is not something he can answer."

"Objection overruled," Neville said.

"Definitely not," Baldwin repeated.

T. Scott Hendricks, one of the first FBI agents to arrive at the Dowaliby home, was called to establish that the hallway floor between the bedrooms was hardwood.

The point was that hardwood floors made it more likely that the Dowalibys would have heard an intruder.

* * *

As Cynthia Dowaliby wept, eight-year-old Sarah Haseman testified that she and Jaclyn often had played with dolls in Jaclyn's bedroom.

George Velcich asked her, "Did you ever notice that she didn't have any sheets on her bed?"

"She always had sheets on her bed," Sarah answered.

To reinforce Erin Bell's claim that Davey Dowaliby was not always adequately supervised, Velcich asked about a slumber party Jaclyn attended at Sarah's house in the summer of 1988.

"The next morning when everybody got up, did something unusual happen?" Velcich asked.

"Yes. Davey, Jaclyn's brother, came to my back door and he wasn't wearing anything but a T-shirt."

"Was he wearing any pants?"

"No."

On cross-examination, Daniel Franks asked if anyone had helped her practice her testimony.

"Yes," she said, "George and the guy next to him."

Karen Williams, a recordkeeper for Illinois Bell Telephone Company, was called to document the various telephone calls that were placed from the Dowaliby home the morning of September 10.

Testifying from company billing records, Williams said that the first call was made at 9:46 A.M. to the home of Michael and Sylvia Borrelli. Other calls were made at 9:52 A.M. to the Haseman home, at 9:57 A.M. to the Guess home, at 10:06 A.M. to Wag's (the restaurant where Jackie Guess worked), at 10:25 A.M. to telephone information, and at 10:26 A.M. to the Midlothian police.

Sylvia Borrelli, the wife of Cynthia's oldest brother, testified that she and Cynthia had planned to start a ceramics class on the morning of September 10.

A few minutes before 10:00 A.M., Borrelli related, she received a call from Cynthia, who said that "she was not going to make it to the ceramics class, that her mother-in-law was not there, she had been on a binge, and that she did not have a sitter that day."

"Did Cynthia Dowaliby tell you that she was going to wake the children up?" George Velcich asked.

"No," Borrelli answered.

Velcich reminded her of a conversation she had on September 22, 1988, with FBI Agent Steven Kashirsky, and asked, "Didn't you tell Agent Kashirsky that just before Cynthia Dowaliby finished the conversation she said that she was going to wake up the children?"

"He asked me if Cyndi mentioned the children, and I said that I assumed they were sleeping."

"Did you tell him that Cynthia Dowaliby told you that she was going to wake up the children?"

Lawrence Hyman objected, "I think this witness has answered that question."

"Overruled," said Judge Neville, clearing the way for Velcich to press hard for an answer more to his liking.

"Did you tell Agent Kashirsky that Cynthia Dowaliby told you that she was about to wake the children up?" Velcich demanded.

"I assumed that she was going to wake the children up," Borrelli said.

"Do you understand my question?"

"Yes."

"Did you tell Agent Kashirsky that Cynthia told you she was going to wake up the children?"

"No."

"You did not tell that to the agent?"

"Not that I can remember."

"During that conversation with Agent Kashirsky, did you tell him that Cynthia did not mention the children by name but that she was going to wake the children up? Did you say that?"

"I assumed that she was going to wake them up."

"But did you *tell* Agent Kashirsky that Cynthia said she was going to wake them up?"

"Yes."

"You *did* tell that to Agent Kashirsky?"

"Yes."

The exchange left Borrelli in tears and the jury with the possible impression that she was lying to protect Cynthia.

The cross-examination, conducted by Hyman, did little to restore Borrelli's credibility.

Hyman asked, "Mrs. Borrelli, did you tell the FBI agent that Cyndi told you she was going to wake up the children?"

"No, I did not."

"Tell the jury what you did tell him."

"I told him that I assumed that the children were sleeping because he kept asking me about the children. He asked if she mentioned anything about the children. I said no."

Velcich asked on redirect examination, "Do you remember my asking you whether Cynthia said that she was going to wake up the children? Do you remember answering that question, 'Yes'?"

"Yes," she said.

"That is what you said in court a few minutes ago, right?"

"Yes."

Michael Chatman, who discovered Jaclyn's body, followed Sylvia Borrelli to the stand.

Chatman testified that he arrived home from work at about 5:45 P.M. on September 14 and, after parking beside the Dumpster at the rear of the lot, noticed "a very strong odor." As he stepped into the weeds, he said, he saw a small body partially covered, with its head face up and an arm visible.

Cynthia Dowaliby burst into tears, burying her head in her husband's arms, and then collapsed. David and a deputy sheriff carried her into the hall, where the three of them remained until Chatman left the stand.

After the interruption, George Velcich asked Chatman what he did when he saw the body.

Chatman said that he went inside and called the police.

Velcich asked Chatman to step down and approach a map showing a large area of the southwest suburbs. Velcich gave Chatman a red pen and asked him to place an X next to the location of the body.

It was the same map on which a previous witness, David

Urewicz, had drawn a circle around the Anchor Bowl. Because of the scale of the map, the locations appeared to be quite close.

The jury would never be told that the apartment complex and the bowling alley were on opposite sides of Cal-Sag Channel—and linked only by a circuitous route.

Gary Johnston, a Blue Island police corporal, testified that he was the first officer to arrive at the scene after Michael Chatman's call.

He said that when other officers arrived, the location of the body was secured with yellow crime-scene tape, thirty feet in each direction.

Jeffrey J. Koleczek, who lived two houses east of the Dowalibys, testified that he had seen Davey Dowaliby playing with rope on several occasions.

George Velcich showed Koleczek the rope found with Jaclyn's body and asked, "How does this rope compare to the rope you saw David Dowaliby playing with?"

"It's the same type of rope."

"After Jaclyn was missing and later found murdered, did you ever see Davey playing with the rope anymore?"

"No."

On cross-examination, Lawrence Hyman asked, "Can you say that this is the rope that you saw Davey playing with?"

"No."

Thus Koleczek contradicted the police report claiming that he had identified the rope as the one with which Davey played—a report on which Patrick O'Brien had based his public assertions that the murder weapon came from the Dowaliby home.

The final witness for the prosecution was Dr. Robert Stein, the Cook County medical examiner, who had performed the autopsy on Jaclyn.

Before Stein began his testimony, there was an in-chambers hearing to determine whether the prosecution would be permitted to show the jury color slides and photographs of Jaclyn's corpse.

Lawrence Hyman argued that the slides and photographs were "not probative or relevant" to any facts in the case and that showing them in court would inflame the passions of the jurors.

"These photos are beyond gruesome," Ralph Meczyk added. "If there is any probative value at all to the photographs, the prejudice here outweighs it. When the victim is a young child, that brings out natural emotions in all people."

George Velcich responded that the slides and photographs were probative of the time of death.

"Is Stein going to testify to any approximation of the time of death?" Judge Neville asked.

"He is not Quincy, to say what hour it is, but he can tell us whether it is consistent in a time period," Velcich replied.

"Does he need all these photographs with this heavy maggot infestation to get to that point?" Meczyk interjected.

"Gruesome events have occurred, and that is why gruesome photos come into evidence," Neville responded. "There are all types of gruesome. Gruesome is a word you have chosen to use. It just looks to me like a body being eaten away by maggots. Whether that is gruesome or not to you, it is not gruesome to me."

"But when they see these pictures, whatever passions they have, that will inflame the jury," said Meczyk.

"I do not agree with you," said Neville. "I do not think that is what these photographs do."

Neville ruled that seventeen slides and seventeen eight-by-ten prints made from the same slides could be shown to the jury, but he excluded eight others because they were similar to the seventeen allowed into evidence.

The lawyers and Neville then went into the courtroom. David and Cynthia were not present. When the jurors filed into the courtroom moments later, Neville explained:

"Mr. and Mrs. Dowaliby have asked to be excused from the courtroom for the next witness, and I have excused them. The medical examiner is about to testify. He will use photographs and slides taken during the autopsy. Some of these are distasteful. I have ruled that they are probative of the issues in this case. They are not shown to you to cause any prejudice."

On direct examination by George Velcich, Stein testified that in his thirteen years as medical examiner, he had performed more than a thousand autopsies, including Jaclyn Dowaliby's.

"Doctor," Velcich asked, "did the child's body appear to have been decomposed consistent with having been dead approximately five and a half days?"

"Considering the temperature and the humidity, I would say yes," Stein answered.

Since the autopsy was on September 15, five and a half days placed the time of death at about the time Everett Mann saw the Malibu-like car pull out of the Islander Apartments parking lot.

Stein said he was reasonably certain that Jaclyn died of ligature strangulation, since a rope had been wrapped twice around her neck. He added, however, that decomposition of the body made it impossible to rule out other causes; nor could it be determined whether she had been sexually molested.

"There were maggots all over the neck, mouth area, and also in the region of the shoulders and arms," Stein said. "The face was completely black because of drying. The eyes were missing, and they were completely destroyed and digested by the maggots."

Stein provided a possible explanation for the Negroid hair found on the rope: It was the practice of his office to destroy maggots with insecticide before an autopsy, and the person who applied the insecticide was African-American.

Velcich showed Stein photographic prints of the seventeen autopsy slides, asking if they "truly and accurately show the way Jaclyn Dowaliby appeared during the course of your autopsy."

"They do," said Stein.

Velcich then asked Stein to approach a screen that had been set up facing the jury. The courtroom lights were dimmed and the slides were shown as Stein described what they showed.

Of the seventeen slides, two were particularly gruesome—one showing Jaclyn's head, the other her genital area. Of the latter, Stein told the jury: "Note the thousands and thousands of maggots. Now, after the maggots were cleaned away, you have the labia, the remnants of it, and this is all dead necrotic tissue, as well as the area surrounding it."

In a brief cross-examination, Hyman asked if Jaclyn might have been dead only four days at the time of the autopsy—placing the death after the event witnessed by Everett Mann.

"It could be four, it could be six, it could be eight," Stein answered.

As Stein left the courtroom, Judge Neville recessed the trial until Monday, April 23, when the prosecutors would rest their case.

"Have a nice weekend," the judge cheerily told the jury.

In a live report from the criminal court building, Paul Hogan called the photographs "graphic and stomach-wrenching.

"It was clear the jurors were shocked by the display," Hogan said. "One woman covered her eyes, another her mouth. All of them winced at times.

"If the prosecutors intended to shock the jury with this tactic, they succeeded, leaving the jurors over the weekend with some very vivid and perhaps inflammatory images to ponder."

IN THE DARK

"Now it's the defense's turn in the Dowalibys' trial," said a headline in the Monday, April 23, *Chicago Tribune.*

"The state's case against Cynthia and David Dowaliby all but ended Friday without a bombshell piece of evidence," wrote Matt O'Connor. "Perhaps worse yet for the prosecution, what had been considered its single strongest piece of evidence—a positive identification of David near where his daughter's body was found—turned out to be less than billed."

Although the thrust of the story was favorable to the defense, it contained a potentially prejudicial disclosure—that David had a "slight criminal record, involving relatively minor narcotics offenses more than a decade ago."

O'Connor speculated that David's lawyers might advise him against taking the stand because it could clear the way for prosecutors to inform the jury of his marijuana convictions.

"If the jurors found out about David's drug convictions, their view of the clean-cut man who frequently consoles his grieving wife in court could change somewhat," the story said.

When prejudicial information appears in the press during a trial, defense lawyers often ask the judge to poll the jurors to find out if any of them had read it. The Dowalibys' lawyers, however, decided against such a course, reasoning that asking about the article might backfire by calling attention to it.

At the outset of Monday morning's court session, Ralph Meczyk told Judge Neville that the Dowalibys felt that the subject "would be best to be left alone at this time."

Neville agreed. "It may do more harm to bring it up than not," he said. "We'll just leave it as it is."

Judge Neville and the lawyers spent Monday morning in chambers, while reporters waited impatiently in the courtroom.

Behind Neville's closed doors, the defense lawyers presented motions for directed verdicts of acquittal. Ralph Meczyk said that the defense preferred to argue the motions in chambers, and Patrick O'Brien said that was fine with him.

"Let's argue them right now," said Neville.

Motions for directed verdicts are common in criminal cases. They are an important safeguard for the accused, designed to force judges to test the sufficiency of the evidence and reduce the risk of capricious guilty verdicts by juries.

Defendants seldom prevail in such motions, however, because the legal standard is high: To direct a verdict, a judge must view the evidence in "the light most favorable to the prosecution" and conclude that no "rational" jury could find it sufficient to prove guilt beyond a reasonable doubt.*

---

* In circumstantial cases, in many states, the defendant is entitled to an acquittal unless the evidence presented by the prosecution excludes every reasonable hypothesis of innocence. That used to be the law in Illinois as well, but the Illinois Supreme Court raised the burden for

Daniel Franks argued the motion on behalf of David. The defense team agreed that Franks had a better chance than Meczyk of prevailing, since the relationship between Meczyk and Neville had steadily deteriorated and, by now, was barely civil.

Franks focused on three contentions: First, the alleged dust on the windowsill had been neither preserved nor contemporaneously noted. Thus there was no credible evidence ruling out the possibility of an intruder. Second, the statements that the prosecutors contended showed guilty knowledge on David's part could be interpreted innocently. Third, the only "direct evidence" against David was unworthy of belief—the purported identification of a nose by Everett Mann from seventy-five yards away in a dark parking lot on a moonless night.

"The only real evidence or theory would be that the defendant somehow had the opportunity and, therefore, he must be guilty," Franks told Neville. "That kind of suggestion should not be considered by this court as coming close to meeting the prosecution's burden of proof.

"The state has propounded no motive in this case," Franks added. "They have propounded no theory as to how it happened. They haven't even propounded the location where this terrible crime occurred.

"Your honor, I don't believe they've given you enough evidence to sustain their burden. I don't believe that this case should continue, and I think that your honor should direct this case out and find the defendant not guilty."

"State?" said Neville.

"Your honor, I would only argue briefly," said Patrick O'Brien. "One of the propositions the state feels the evidence has shown is that there was no entry through that broken window. Through David Dowaliby's own statements, there

---

defendants in a series of cases between 1986 and 1989. The applicable standard in cases when the sufficiency of the evidence is challenged became whether a rational trier of fact, construing all of the evidence in the light most favorable to the prosecution, could find the defendant guilty beyond a reasonable doubt. See *People* v. *Eyler,* 133 Ill. 2d 173 (1989).

was no other way for entry to be made. It is not only the dust that belies that, but the undisturbed items under the window.

"We also feel that the evidence has shown that the rope that was recovered from Jaclyn Dowaliby's neck circumstantially is in fact the rope that Davey Dowaliby played with.

"We have a situation where when the police come to the residence and look in the bedroom, there are no sheets on the bed. There were clothes all around. There is Type O blood on the pillow on the bed.

"Although there is no trace evidence of transfer between the car mat and the bedspread, a witness did say that there were hairs in the trunk which were similar to Jaclyn Dowaliby's.

"The circumstantial identification by Everett Mann of a late-seventies Chevy Malibu, though it is not a positive identification of the driver, was an identification of a male driving the car in the lot at two to two-fifteen in the morning.

"There are statements made by David Dowaliby, some of which show lies, one of which admits withholding evidence.

"Respectfully, we would ask your honor to deny the motion for a directed finding as to David Dowaliby."

"Well," Neville said, "I'm obligated to take the evidence in the best light for the state, which means that I can't accept all of Mr. Franks's arguments because he wants me to make factual findings. The state believes no one came through that window. That's a factual issue the jury will have to decide.

"The jury is going to have to decide what, if any, use to make of both Everett Mann's identification and the rope.

"I agree with the defense that there is not a lot of direct evidence against David Dowaliby, but there is significant circumstantial evidence, and his case is going to the jury."

Lawrence Hyman then argued the motion for Cynthia Dowaliby, contending that no "*rational* trier of fact" could find her guilty.

"Is that with a capital R?" Neville asked.

"That's with emphasis added," Hyman retorted.

Hyman contended that there was "no true circumstantial evidence" against Cynthia—no inconsistent statements and no testimony placing her "or her nose structure or her head structure" near the Islander Apartments.

If Neville granted a directed verdict of acquittal for Cynthia, Hyman said, "I would consider it, and I think the legal community would consider it, a brave statement to make—that prosecutions of this nature should not be brought."

"Mr. Prosecutor?" Neville asked.

"Judge, first of all," said O'Brien, "I don't think I'll talk about the legal community and brave statements, as if it's some kind of hammer over a judge's head, as if there's some set of lawyers or judges out there who somehow have to be appeased."

O'Brien conceded that there was less evidence against Cynthia than against David, but contended that some of the evidence applied to both: "They share the fact that the house was closed, and that there was no indication of entry. The broken window was a statement by both defendants. The rope is similar to both defendants'. The bedroom from which Jaclyn Dowaliby is taken is adjacent to a bedroom shared by both."

O'Brien added, "Some statements which are an attempt to conceal the crime can be used against both—the person who says it and the coconspirator. David Dowaliby has Davey coming into the bedroom at eight in the morning, and at nine forty-six Sylvia Borrelli is being told by Cyndi Dowaliby that she has to get the kids up. Obviously, from the statement of David, one child is already up. And, from the state's position, the other child is already gone, and the defendants know where that is."

Neville asked Hyman if he wished to add something.

"In no way did I mean to imply that you should be swayed by the outside legal community," Hyman said. "I doubt that someone of your character and constitution would be."

Hyman then addressed O'Brien's conspiracy argument, saying, "If in fact Mr. O'Brien attempts to show that the defendants' statements are conspiratorial in nature, he first had to show a conspiracy, and I don't think that was done here."

Neville nodded in apparent agreement.

After a pause, however, he said that he would hold off ruling on Cynthia's motion until he had a chance to review several prosecution exhibits.

He then expressed concern about the possible prejudicial effect that would occur if the news media reported that he had denied David's motion but had not yet ruled on Cynthia's.

"No one should indicate to the press what has occurred," he said. "It would be reported. I hope the jury doesn't read the papers, but it would be best if it weren't made noticeable."

The lawyers agreed to keep the secret.

The group then went into the courtroom, and Neville apologized to the jury for the delay. After O'Brien formally rested the prosecution case, Neville recessed court for lunch.

To Neville's dismay, however, Rosalind Rossi, covering the trial for the *Chicago Sun-Times,* asked the court reporter for a transcript of the morning's in-chambers proceedings.

The court reporter relayed Rossi's request to Neville, prompting him to call the lawyers into his chambers again before the start of the afternoon session.

Neville suggested that they stonewall Rossi and say, for public consumption, that he would not rule on the motions for directed verdicts until just before the closing arguments. "I will say in open court that those motions are entered and continued," Neville proposed. "That's not exactly what the record is, but I think it's the fairest way to do things."

Both sides agreed.

"I'm comfortable doing it this way," Neville said. "I expect that you will just make your motions and then the state can object, and I'm going to enter and continue it, okay?"

Both sides again agreed.

The group then returned to the courtroom, where Meczyk and Hyman, following the script orchestrated by Neville, made motions for directed verdicts of acquittal. Neville announced that he would rule on the motions "at the close of all the evidence."

He already had made up his mind on Cynthia's motion, he

said later, but for now he wanted to keep everyone in the dark.

Following Neville's plan, the defense would proceed with its case—for both defendants.

The first defense witness was Holly Deck, the Dowalibys' former next-door neighbor to the west.

Ralph Meczyk asked her if, on the afternoon of September 9, she had "noticed anything in the Dowalibys' backyard."

Deck said she had seen sheets on the clothesline. "One of the sheets was like a little girl's sheet," she said. "It had a picture of a girl with long blond hair on it."

The answer suggested that Jaclyn's Lady Lovely Locks sheets indeed had been washed that day, as Cynthia had claimed.

That night, Deck continued, she awoke at 2:10 A.M., noting the time on her digital alarm clock, and went to the kitchen to get a glass of water. She said she looked out of the window and noticed that the street, which earlier had been filled with cars because of a Tupperware party, now was virtually empty.

"All of the cars were gone, except for one," she said.

"That one car you said was still there, did you recognize it?" Meczyk asked.

"Yes," she said. "It was a blue car that Cyndi drove."

"Did you ever see David Dowaliby drive that car?"

"Very rarely."

"Was there anything unusual about the way it was parked?"

"Yes, it was overhanging their driveway approximately a foot." Deck thus placed the Malibu in front of the Dowaliby home at the same time Everett Mann had made his sighting behind the Islander Apartments.

When she learned that Jaclyn was missing, Deck said, she joined in the search. A little later, she saw Cynthia standing beside the broken window "jumping up and down, very upset."

Deck also testified that between eleven and midnight on

September 9, her four dogs were barking at her side door, which faced the Dowaliby home.

"Was that unusual for your dogs?" Meczyk asked.

"Yes, very unusual," Deck answered. "They usually bark that nasty when there's a stranger around."

"Did you ever observe the way that your dogs acted when the Dowalibys were outside?"

"Yes."

"Would you tell us how the dogs behaved?"

"They liked them. My Chihuahua, the meanest one, absolutely adored Jaclyn."

"Did anyone go outside to see why the dogs were barking the way that they were barking?"

"Yes."

"Who was that?"

"My husband."

"As far as you know, did he see anything?"

"Judge, I'm going to object," O'Brien interrupted. "Is her husband alive and well?"

"I ask Mr. O'Brien, don't make statements in front of the jury," Meczyk angrily responded. "The question so far is, if she knows based on her knowledge."

"I object," O'Brien persisted.

"Sustained," said Neville.

Meczyk's final question was, "While you lived in Midlothian, did you socialize with David and Cynthia?"

"No, we really didn't have that much in common," Deck said. "We had no kids."

George Velcich conducted the cross-examination, first establishing that the dogs had barked only briefly and that she saw nothing unusual.

Velcich then tried to shake her testimony about the Malibu.

Referring to her statement that she saw it overhanging the driveway at 2:10 A.M., Velcich asked, "You remember that very clearly, is that right?"

"Yes," Deck answered.

"Now, do you remember that the day after Jaclyn was reported missing, some FBI agents came to your home and talked to you?"

She said she did.

"And you didn't tell them about looking out your window at two-ten in the morning, did you?"

"No."

"That's because it wasn't important, was it?"

"They didn't ask."

"When was the first time that you told anybody that you looked out your window at two-ten in the morning?"

"In January of 1989."

"Where were you when you told this person?"

"Mr. Meczyk's office."

"In Mr. Meczyk's office?"

"Yes."

"You didn't tell that to the FBI, did you?"

"No."

Velcich then ran through a series of questions about the fact that he and another assistant state's attorney had interviewed her in September 1989.

She acknowledged that she had not said anything at that time about seeing the car.

Turning to the sheets on the Dowalibys' clothesline, Velcich asked Deck if she recalled the last time before September 9 that she had seen laundry on the line.

"I don't really remember," Deck answered.

"When was the next time after September 9 that you saw any laundry on the Dowalibys' clothesline?"

"I didn't really pay any attention."

"Now, obviously, you have a memory of the laundry on September 9 because it's important, is that correct?"

"Yes."

"Now, again, was it Mr. Meczyk who told you that it was important that you see some laundry in the backyard?"

"No, I just remember seeing a sheet because it's one I had never seen before. It just stood out."

"The day that you did talk to Mr. Meczyk in his office with Cynthia Dowaliby there, how did you get there?"

"I drove with Cyndi."

"Didn't Cyndi Dowaliby ask you to be a witness for her?"

"Well, yeah."

On redirect examination, Meczyk asked, "When Mr. Velcich and the other prosecutor visited you, did they ask if you saw Cyndi's car that night?"

"No," said Deck.

"If they had asked you that, what would you have answered?"

"I would have told them that it was there."

After a short recess, Dr. Henry Lee, chief forensic scientist for the Connecticut State Police, was called to testify about the Dowalibys' broken window.

Lee had been retained by the defense early in the investigation, while Daniel McDevitt was telling any reporter who would listen that the window had been broken from the inside.

When the report by the prosecution expert, Ralph Meyer, later established that the window had been broken from the outside, disproving McDevitt's theory, Lee's usefulness to the defense had largely evaporated.

Nonetheless, if for no other reason than that the Dowalibys had paid Lee $3,000 plus expenses to conduct experiments with similar windows, the defense called him to testify.

On direct examination by Lawrence Hyman, Lee agreed with Meyer that the force that broke the window came from outside.

"Did a good job," Lee said of Meyer.

The only thing that Lee added to Meyer's testimony was that, in tests with similar windows, Lee had found that large pieces of glass tended to remain in the frame when the glass was broken.

The point was that the large pieces of glass that Hayden Baldwin had found on the ground outside the Dowaliby home might have been "picked out" after the window was broken—presumably to enlarge the opening enough for an intruder to reach through and unlatch the locking mechanism.

Lee said that he conducted four videotaped experiments involving the breaking of windows similar to the Dowalibys'. The videotape of one of the experiments, in which the window was smashed with a crowbar, was shown to the jury. No large pieces of glass fell opposite the direction of the force.

On cross-examination, Patrick O'Brien asked Lee if he ever invited experts from other states to lecture in Connecticut on forensic topics.

"Yes, sir," Lee answered.

"And just recently, was Hayden Baldwin one of the persons who was called to lecture?"

"Yes, sir."

As Lee stepped down, Neville recessed the trial for the day.

The defense was not off to an auspicious start.

THE HERNANDEZ DEFENSE

As Perry Hernandez waited in a detention area behind the courtroom on Tuesday, April 24, the child he had abducted was called to the stand.

Rory MacRand, now seven years old, testified that she lived in Blue Island with her parents and four siblings.

After establishing that the crime had occurred on September 1, 1989—a year after Jaclyn Dowaliby had vanished—Daniel Franks asked, "Did something unusual happen during the nighttime?"

"Yes," she replied.

"What happened, Rory?"

"I got stoled."

"You got stoled. Did a man come into your room?"

"Yes."

"And what did he do with you?"

"He took me out of my bed."

"How did he do that, Rory?"

"Like this," she said, indicating with her arms that he scooped her up.

"And did he carry you in some way?"

"Yes."

"Where did he carry you?"

"Down the stairs and out the side door."

"Now what were you wearing at that time, Rory?"

"Pajamas."

"Did you have anything on underneath your pajamas?"

"Yes."

"What did you have?"

"My underpants."

"Now, did this man take you anywhere?"

Rory said he carried her through a trailer court to a place beneath a railroad bridge on Cal-Sag Channel.

"Did he take your nightgown off?" Franks asked.

"Yes."

"And did he take your panties off?"

"Yes."

"Now, at that point, Rory, some bad things happened to you, isn't that right?"

"Yes."

"I'm not going to ask you about any of that, okay?"

"Hmm, hmm."

"Did you stay with this man the whole night?"

"Yes."

"Now, when the sun came up, were you able to see his face?"

"Yes."

"What did he look like?"

"He looked like the person across the alley."

Franks elicited that when Hernandez let her go, she walked home and told her mother what had happened.

"What did your mom say?" Franks asked.

"She didn't believe me," Rory answered.

Rory said that she showed scratches and bruises on her back and buttocks to her mother, who called the police. Rory said the police took her to a hospital and then to the police station, where they showed her "the bat cave."

"What's the bat cave?" Franks asked.

"It's just a little room, and it has a window, and there's people standing around with numbers on them."

"And did you see anybody when you were inside of this bat cave that you recognized?"

"Yes, the person who lived across the alley."

Franks showed her a photograph and asked if she could identify it.

She said it was a picture of "Perry."

"What did he do to you?"

"He stoled me."

"I have nothing further," said Franks.

On cross-examination, Patrick O'Brien asked, "Rory, the person who stole you is Perry Hernandez, is that right?"

"Yes."

"And the week before Perry stole you, you saw him looking at you in the yard, is that right?"

"Yes."

"How many times had you seen Perry before he stole you?"

"Three times."

"When Perry took you to the bridge, did you tell him that you thought you knew him?"

"No."

Changing the subject, O'Brien asked, in a reference to Jaclyn's room, "The bed that you were sleeping in upstairs, did that have sheets on it?"

"Yes."

"After you got home, you showed your mom some of the scratches and bruises that happened to you, is that right?"

"Yes."

"Could you see those yourself?"

"No."

"But your mom could see them, is that right?"

"Yes."

"I have nothing further, thank you, Rory."

On redirect, Franks asked only one question: "Rory, did the man who stole you come through the kitchen window?"

"Yes."

Rory's mother, Carline MacRand, testified on direct examination that she was sleeping upstairs in a room adjacent to Rory's bedroom on September 1, 1989, and that the family dog slept nearby.

Daniel Franks asked what happened when Rory told her that a man had taken her out of the house.

"I didn't believe her at first, and I told her to go down and watch TV," MacRand answered, adding that Rory soon returned and told her that the TV was not working.

"What did you do?" asked Franks.

"I went downstairs and tried it, but we didn't have any power," MacRand said. "I went to the basement and found that the main switch had been shut off, and I turned it back on."

"After that, did you go anywhere else?"

"I went into the kitchen, and I found silverware and tomatoes all over my floor, and the kitchen screen had been taken out. Then I woke up my husband, and we called the police."

"When the first officer came, did you have a conversation?"

"Yes, we told him what had happened."

"What was his response?"

"He was shocked."

The officer called for assistance, including paramedics who took Rory to the hospital, MacRand said.

Referring to police and hospital personnel, MacRand continued, "They didn't believe us at first, until word came that her underwear had been found under the railroad bridge."

Franks then showed MacRand a photograph of Perry Hernandez and she identified it, saying that he lived across the alley from her home.

On cross-examination, Patrick O'Brien zeroed in on the differences between the MacRand and Dowaliby crimes. He began with several questions about the silverware and tomatoes that had been knocked onto the kitchen floor and MacRand's discovery that the electricity had been turned off.

Then he asked, "Was the kitchen window broken?"

"No, the window wasn't broken," MacRand said.

"You found something on the hamper on the first floor, is that correct?"

"Yes, sir—a package of cigarettes."

She added that the cigarettes were Newports and that no one in the home smoked that brand.

"Now, the night of September first, you didn't discipline Rory before you went to bed, did you?" O'Brien asked.

"No."

"Objection," said Franks.

"Overruled," said Judge Neville.

"When you talked to the police," O'Brien resumed, "you didn't lie to them about when you last saw her, did you?"

"Objection!" shouted Ralph Meczyk.

"Let me see the lawyers for a minute," said Neville.

The lawyers approached the bench and, in a low voice, Neville asked O'Brien, "What's the purpose?"

O'Brien said that since the defense had attempted to show similarities between the MacRand and Dowaliby crimes, "I believe we are entitled to show the differences."

"You asked to put this in to show similarities," Neville told Meczyk. "They are entitled to show dissimilarities."

Meczyk agreed that the prosecution was entitled to show physical dissimilarities but that it was improper for O'Brien to imply that the Dowalibys had disciplined Jaclyn.

"And I'm going to overrule you," said Neville.

O'Brien resumed, asking MacRand, "When the police came to investigate, you didn't lie to them about the last time you had seen your daughter before she went to bed, did you?"

"No."

"Was there an open suitcase on her bed when you went to sleep on September first?"

"No."

"On September second, when you got up, did you find any of your doors open?"

"No."

"The dog that you have in your house, that dog didn't appear to bark at anyone, is that correct?"

"No, she is pretty quiet."

O'Brien asked how often she had seen Hernandez when he lived across the alley.

"Quite a bit," MacRand answered.

O'Brien then established that MacRand had met several times with Meczyk.

"And during one of those times, Mr. Meczyk gave you money, is that correct?" O'Brien asked.

"He gave it to my daughter when he was leaving," MacRand said.

"And that was approximately thirty dollars?"

"Something like that, yes."

On redirect examination, Franks asked, "Why did Mr. Meczyk give you that money, if you know?"

"Because we don't have very much, and he wanted the children to buy something for themselves," she answered.

"And isn't it true that the police questioned your husband about his whereabouts the night of September first and second?"

"Yes, they did."

"And didn't they question your husband before they found those panties?"

"Yes."

On recross examination, O'Brien drew MacRand's attention to an October 13, 1989, conversation with Meczyk in the presence of a court reporter.

From the transcript, O'Brien quoted this exchange:

MECZYK—"Was your husband ever questioned about Rory's abduction?"

MACRAND—"No, but they said they were giving him funny looks."

MECZYK—"Did they ever accuse him of the abduction?"

MACRAND—"Not that I know of."

"Do you remember being asked those questions and giving those answers?" O'Brien asked.

"Yes," MacRand acknowledged.

"And now that you've talked to the defense attorneys

more and they've given you the thirty dollars, has your testimony changed?"

"Objection, your honor!" yelled Meczyk.

"Sustained," said Neville.

"No further questions," said O'Brien.

Blue Island Detective Joseph Kosman, who had been involved in both the Dowaliby and MacRand investigations, was the next witness. He had recovered Rory MacRand's underpants near Cal-Sag Channel.

Daniel Franks asked Kosman to step down and approach a large map on an easel in front of the jury box. Kosman marked the location of the MacRand home, the point where he found the panties, and the spot where Jaclyn Dowaliby's body had been found the previous year; he said that the MacRand assault occurred "about a mile" from where Jaclyn's body was found.

Kosman said that he was involved in the arrest of Perry Hernandez on September 5, 1989, and was present when Rory identified Hernandez in a lineup.

Then, at Franks's request, Hernandez was led into the courtroom.

Wearing prison fatigues, his hands and legs in irons, Hernandez walked in front of the jury.

Cynthia and David's faces froze. "Cynthia had a look of absolute fright," Paul Hogan said later. "David's teeth were clinched, and he stared daggers at Hernandez."

Jurors, however, could not see the reactions because their view of the Dowalibys was obscured by the map.

Hernandez turned, facing the witness stand, as Franks asked, "Officer Kosman, do you see in court at this time Perry Hernandez?"

"Yes, I do," Kosman answered.

"I have nothing further with Mr. Hernandez," Franks said.

"Mr. Hernandez, thank you, you can leave," said Neville.

On cross-examination, O'Brien asked Kosman a series of questions about the scene at the MacRand home, again emphasizing how it differed from the scene at the Dowaliby home.

Referring to Rory's bedroom, O'Brien asked, "Did you observe sheets that were still on that bed?"

"Yes, I did."

O'Brien asked Kosman to step down and approach the map. Kosman pointed out the location of Hernandez's home in relation to the MacRands'.

"It would be into almost the dot that was on the MacRand house," Kosman testified, the point being that Hernandez was a neighbor of the MacRands but lived several miles from the Dowalibys.

On redirect examination by Franks, Kosman testified that the kitchen window of the MacRand home had been left open the night Rory was taken.

"So entrance was made by taking off the screen and going through the window, which was open, is that right?" Franks asked.

"Yes."

"There was no glass to push away from the windowsill when entry was made, is that right?"

"Yes, that's correct."

"There were just tomatoes to push away when he came through the window, isn't that correct?"

"Yes."

On recross examination, O'Brien asked, "So when Hernandez entered the MacRand house, he chose an unlocked, open window?"

"That's right," said Kosman.

"Hernandez didn't go to the window closest to the street, choose a locked window and break it, did he?"

"No, he didn't."

Franks rose again and asked, "That window is substantially above the ground, isn't that right?"

"Yes."

"So the individual who took that screen off had to do some climbing to open that screen, take it off, put it down by the ground, and then enter that window, isn't that right?"

"Yes."

* * *

The next witness was Perry Hernandez's girlfriend, Julie Oster.

Oster testified that Hernandez stayed at her Midlothian apartment occasionally in September 1988.

Lawrence Hyman asked her to step down and put her initials at the location of the apartment on the map. It was just a few blocks from the Dowaliby home.

Hyman elicited that Oster and Hernandez had frequented a Blue Island tavern on the edge of the Islander Apartments complex; Oster located the tavern on the map.

On cross-examination Patrick O'Brien established that Hernandez did not have a car at the time he was staying with Oster; his car had been demolished in an accident shortly before Hernandez began staying with her.

Oster acknowledged that she had spoken with defense lawyers several times, including on October 18, 1989, when she met Ralph Meczyk at his office.

"Did he ask you about money?" O'Brien asked.

"Yes."

"And did you tell him that money would be nice?"

"I believe I probably did."

"But you did not get any money, is that correct?"

"I did not."

On redirect examination, Hyman asked if Oster had a car when Hernandez was staying with her.

She said she did.

"It was a Chevrolet, was it not?" Hyman asked.

"Yes," Oster said.

On recross examination, O'Brien asked, "Did Perry Hernandez drive your car in September of 1988?"

"No."

Court adjourned for the day, with Neville's usual admonition to the jury to avoid news coverage of the trial.

"The Dowaliby defense team is trying to turn the tables on the prosecutors by implicating another man in the crime," Paul Hogan reported on the evening news.

Other news stories drew the same conclusion.

The defense strategy going into the trial had been to use

Hernandez mainly to show that a child could be abducted from her home in the middle of the night while her parents slept.

As reporters saw it, however, the jury was being asked to choose: Did Perry Hernandez kill Jaclyn, or did David and Cynthia?

GRAVE IMPORTANCE

The news media took on a new role in the case on Wednesday, April 25, when lawyers for the *Sun-Times* and Channel 5 challenged Judge Neville for shutting reporters out of portions of the trial.

"We are faced with a situation of grave importance to the press and the Constitution that mandates them to serve it," Lawrence R. Levin, representing the *Sun-Times,* told Neville.

Levin, as well as Carol Anne Been, representing Channel 5, complained about both the secrecy surrounding the motions for directed verdicts and Neville's use of sidebar discussions out of reporters' earshot "to determine important rulings."

They told Neville that he had violated the First Amendment, as interpreted by the U.S. Supreme Court in *Richmond Newspapers* v. *Virginia*. The Court's decision required that criminal trials be public, absent a specific finding by the trial judge of "an overriding interest," such as the right to a fair trial.*

Neville was on precarious legal ground, the lawyers contended, because he had failed to identify any overriding interest in the Dowaliby case.

Levin sounded apologetic for raising the issue. "We fully appreciate that your honor has not intended to violate the First Amendment," he said, "but rather your honor has attempted to assure a fair trial."

"It was never my intent to preclude anyone from having information," said Neville. "It was merely a matter of what time they would hear it. I have only closed one transcript."

"Well," said Levin, "it's my unfortunate duty to tell you that I don't think you're meeting the Constitution."

Neville promised to read the relevant case law and rule the next day on whether reporters could have a transcript of the arguments on the motions for directed verdicts.

He added, however, that he would continue to exclude reporters from sidebars. Since they had not attended sidebars during the prosecution case, he said, the jury might draw an unwarranted inference from a sudden change in procedure.

"Then I have no choice but to appeal," said Levin.

Backing off, Neville offered a compromise, saying that he would either provide prompt transcripts of sidebars or, out of the presence of the jury, state in open court what had occurred.

"Thank you," said Levin.

"Okay, thank you," said Neville.

As Levin and Been left, Neville asked, "Anybody have anything else?"

---

*The Supreme Court's decision was 7 to 1, with Justice William H. Rehnquist dissenting and Justice Byron R. White not participating. Each member of the majority submitted a separate concurring opinion. Justice John Paul Stevens wrote in his often-quoted concurrence that "an arbitrary interference with access to important information is an abridgment of the freedoms of speech and of the press protected by the First Amendment." See *Richmond Newspapers* v. *Virginia*, 448 U.S. 555 (1980).

"There is another matter we would like to deal with in chambers," said Ralph Meczyk.

"In chambers?" Neville asked.

"Yes," Meczyk said.

"We can't do that anymore," Neville said sarcastically.

He called a recess and went into his chambers—alone.

When court reconvened a few minutes later, the defense launched an attack on the prosecution theory that Everett Mann had seen David Dowaliby in his wife's car at the Islander Apartments parking lot.

Five witnesses were called in the counteroffensive, which was topped off by the jury's second visit to the parking lot—this time at night, with lighting conditions similar to those described by Mann.

The first of the five was Ralph Styer, Everett Mann's former Air Force sergeant.

Ralph Meczyk asked Styer if he recalled Mann serving under him at Altus Air Force Base, Oklahoma, from 1975 to 1977.

"No, sir, I don't," Styer replied.

"In July of 1976, while you were stationed at the Altus Air Force Base, did you purchase a new automobile?"

"Yes, I did."

"Would you please tell us what make it was?"

"It was a Chevrolet Malibu Landau Classic."

"What year was it?"

"Nineteen seventy-six."

"What color was it?"

"It was red."

"Was it a two-door or four-door automobile?"

"It was two-door."

Styer then identified two photographs of that car, the ones Styer had sent to Meczyk at the request of John Waters. Meczyk asked Neville's permission to show the photographs to the jury, but Neville said he wanted to hear the cross-examination first.

George Velcich cross-examined only to clarify a point that Meczyk had left unclear.

"Mr. Styer," Velcich asked, "it is your testimony that Everett Mann wasn't in the Air Force at the time you were, or you just don't remember?"

"I don't remember him being assigned to me."

Neville then permitted the photographs of Styer's car to be shown to the jury, but the defense never explicitly made the point that his two-door 1976 Malibu Landau bore little resemblance to Cynthia Dowaliby's four-door 1980 Malibu Classic.

The next two witnesses were Eileen and Brian Anderson, who had hosted the Tupperware party across the street from the Dowalibys on the night of September 9, 1988.

Eileen Anderson testified that her mother-in-law arrived for the party shortly after 7:00 P.M.

Ralph Meczyk asked, "What happened after her arrival?"

"I went to let another guest in," she said. "When I opened the door, I saw Cyndi Dowaliby pulling up. I watched her, because my mother-in-law had taken Cyndi's usual parking place and there wasn't much room left for her to park. I kept an eye on her, just to see that she didn't tap my mother-in-law's car."

"Did you notice anything unusual about the way that Cyndi Dowaliby parked her car?"

"Yes. Because there wasn't that much room for her to park, the nose of her car was overhanging the driveway."

Brian Anderson, Eileen's husband, testified that he also had seen Cynthia park that evening, adding that at about 8:00 A.M. the next day, he went outside to wash his car and noticed the blue Malibu still "hanging over the driveway."

In cross-examinations of the Andersons, Velcich elicited that they recalled seeing Jaclyn in the car when Cynthia parked but that neither recalled seeing Davey.

Cynthia had told police during the investigation that both children were with her when she parked the car after returning from Kentucky Fried Chicken.

Velcich also established that neither of the Andersons had seen the car between 2:00 and 2:30 A.M. on September 10—the time pertinent to Mann's testimony.

Following the Andersons to the stand was Ralph Meyer,

the forensic expert who earlier had testified for the prosecution. Meyer's colleague Jennie Hahn had testified that "several" hairs found in the trunk were visually consistent with Jaclyn's head hair. In examining the same hairs, however, Meyer had found only one consistent with Jaclyn's.

Meczyk's purpose in recalling Meyer was to cast doubt on the competence of Hahn's analysis. However, in the process he exaggerated the validity of Meyer's finding concerning the lone hair in question.

"Only one hair *matched* Jaclyn Dowaliby's standard, am I correct?" Meczyk asked.

"That is correct," Meyer answered.

The question and answer left the impression that Jaclyn's hair indeed had been found in the trunk of the car that allegedly was used to transport her body to the Islander Apartments.

Actually, forensic science was not capable of matching hairs; Meyer only had found, as his report plainly stated, that the hair was "similar" to Jaclyn's—not that they "matched."

The fifth and final witness called to cast doubt on Mann's testimony was James O'Connor.

O'Connor, the brother of David Dowaliby's best friend, Gene O'Connor, testified that he had bowled in the league with David and that they regularly had gone together to the Anchor Bowl. It was their habit to take Interstate 57, the fastest route.

"When you drove to the Anchor Bowl on I-57, would you ever go near the Islander Apartments?" Daniel Franks asked.

"No," said O'Connor.

On cross-examination, George Velcich established that the Islander Apartment complex was clearly visible from I-57. O'Connor also acknowledged that he had met several times with Ralph Meczyk but had refused to meet with an investigator from the state's attorney's office.

After O'Connor left the courtroom, Neville took the lawyers into his chambers—shutting out reporters—to discuss the jury's impending excursion to the Islander Apartments.

In chambers, Meczyk asked Neville to expand the itinerary to include a "drive-by visit" to the Dowaliby home, which the jury had seen only in daylight during the prosecution case. A night visit, Meczyk argued, would show that the broken basement window was a logical entry point for an intruder; although the window was near the street, it was not illuminated.

O'Brien objected to returning to the Dowaliby home, contending that the next-door neighbors, Robert and Mary Tolbert, might have changed the lighting outside their home to diminish the illumination. The prosecution had attempted to interview the Tolberts about the lighting, O'Brien said, but they had refused to cooperate.

Meczyk responded that the area could not be darker than it had been when Jaclyn disappeared. Any change, he said, could "only help the state by having brighter conditions."

"That is a foolish argument, and I don't accept it," Neville scoffed, ruling that the visit to the home would not be allowed.

"This is over the defense's vigorous objection," said Meczyk.

"No, it isn't," said Neville. "It is a denial of your request. That's what it is."

"We have a vigorous, vigorous objection," Meczyk persisted.

"I understand," Neville said wearily.

"I know you're getting tired of this," Lawrence Hyman interjected, "but if we find out what neighbors they tried to talk to, we can make them available."

"I don't need you to make anybody available," Neville snapped. "If you told them not to talk to somebody—"

"I didn't tell them," Hyman interrupted.

"No one told them," Meczyk quickly added.

"I think you are playing with me now," Neville said, "and based on that, I am convinced that my ruling is correct."

Neville then asked if the prosecution had any problems with the planned visit to the Islander Apartments.

George Velcich said he objected to an experiment that the defense wanted to conduct in the parking lot.

Neville asked what the experiment was.

"Mr. Franks will be wearing Groucho glasses with a large nose," said Meczyk.

Neville summarily rejected that idea.

He said that the jurors would stand where Mann had parked his car and, as a point of reference, the defense could direct their attention to the middle Dumpster—with no props.

When the judge and the lawyers returned to the courtroom, Rosalind Rossi, of the *Sun-Times*, asked Neville, "Are you going to let us talk to you?"

"Yeah," said Neville, ascending to the bench. "I like to be higher, so I get proper depth."

"Judge, we're asking for no bond on them," Velcich joked, pointing to reporters who had amassed at the bench.

"No bond on this whole group?" Neville asked with mock severity.

"Take us away, great story," one reporter quipped.

Dispensing with the levity, Neville asked Rossi, "What do you want to say, Roz?"

"About half an hour ago, the judge and attorneys for this proceeding had a meeting in chambers, and I'm objecting that discussions were held outside of the press's earshot," she said.

"Okay, well," said Neville. "It was an attempt to figure out how to do this at the scene, and I have come out and told the press what we expect of them, and that's what we discussed."

Neville said nothing about the dispute over the defense request to visit the Dowaliby home.

Paul Hogan joined in Rossi's complaint.

"Okay, the objection is noted," Neville said, "and we'll attempt not to do things without your knowing about them."

A short while later, the judge, jurors, and lawyers boarded a bus for the ten-mile trip to the Islander Apartments, where Meczyk pointed out the middle Dumpster and led the group to the spot where Mann parked at 2:00 A.M. on September 10, 1988.

Neville asked the television crews to turn off their lights, and the group stood silently in the dark for a few moments before boarding the bus for the return trip to the courthouse.

After the usual admonition to avoid newspaper and television coverage, Neville recessed the proceedings for the night.

Neville later confided that when the television lights were extinguished, he could see nothing seventy-five yards away.

"It was like the Black Hole of Calcutta," he said.

The defense called only three more witnesses before resting its case on Friday, April 27.

The first was Michelle Goldrick, David Dowaliby's younger sister, who had gone to the Dowaliby home the evening of September 9 to look at clothes that Ann Dowaliby had purchased earlier that day for Goldrick's four-year-old daughter, Marissa.

When she arrived at about 7:00 P.M., Goldrick testified, she immediately went downstairs with Ann to look at the clothing, and Cynthia and Jaclyn soon joined them.

"What did Jaclyn do at that time?" Daniel Franks asked.

"Jaclyn was watching us take the clothes out of the bag," Goldrick answered, "and she was making comments, 'Isn't that pretty?,' 'Oh, I like that,' 'That's really nice.' "

After a few minutes, Goldrick said, Jaclyn went upstairs and returned with "a very pretty red and white Christmas dress."

"And did she say anything then?" Franks asked.

"She said, 'Isn't this dress pretty? I want to give it to Marissa, so she can wear it for Christmas.' "

A little later, Goldrick continued, everyone went upstairs to the living room, where "the children played with toys, and danced and ran around."

"At some point," Franks asked, "did Jaclyn Dowaliby do something?"

"She went up and whispered something in Cyndi's ear," Goldrick said.

"At that point, what did Jaclyn and Cyndi do?"

"Cyndi and Jaclyn both got up and left the living room."

"Did you see Jaclyn again after that?"

"No, that was the last time."

When Cynthia returned to the living room, Goldrick said, she asked her what Jaclyn had whispered.

"What did Cyndi say?" Franks asked.

"She said that Jaclyn wanted to look at the Christmas Wish Book to find gifts for people," said Goldrick. "I thought that was sweet because she was thinking about Christmas so early."

Goldrick added that David Dowaliby came home at about 9:45 P.M. and she left shortly afterward.

"Michelle, do you know what happened to that dress that Jaclyn showed you?" Franks asked.

"She was buried in that dress," Goldrick answered.

Franks also asked Goldrick about September 14, the night Jaclyn's body was found.

Goldrick said that she had been at the Dowaliby home when David returned following his five-hour interrogation at the Midlothian police station.

"What did David do as he came into the house?" Franks asked.

"He looked for Cyndi," Goldrick replied.

"How did he act?"

"His eyes were real wide, and he had a look of disbelief on his face. As he came over and sat down by Cyndi, he was crying."

In a brief cross-examination, George Velcich asked whether Jaclyn had welcomed David home with open arms on September 9.

Goldrick said that she had not.

"Are you aware," Velcich continued, "that Cynthia Dowaliby told the FBI that Jaclyn welcomed her father with—"

"Objection!" Franks shouted. He asked for a sidebar, at which he pointed out that Goldrick had no way of knowing what Cynthia had told the FBI.

If Velcich were allowed to ask the question, it would suggest to the jury that Cynthia had lied to the FBI about the last time David had seen Jaclyn; it also might affect Judge Neville's ruling on Cynthia's motion for a directed verdict.

Neville sustained Franks's objection.

Velcich asked nothing further.

The next defense witness was Linda Petrine, the psychic. Neville had ruled that she could not testify about her "psychic feelings" but only about what she said or did.

On direct examination, Lawrence Hyman asked Petrine her occupation.

"I am known as a psychic," she proclaimed.

Hyman then asked about her visit to the Dowaliby home on the night of September 12, 1988.

Petrine said she first visited the basement and then Jaclyn's room, where "I told David that I felt that Jaclyn would be found strangled."

"Will you tell the members of the jury what you told David Dowaliby about a body in weeds?" Hyman asked.

"I saw three to four feet of weeds that were like grass, kind of yellowish-green in color," she answered.

"Can you say whether those weeds were in a field?"

"I saw they were in a field, yes, I did."

In an effort to explain the underpants found in Cynthia's purse when she was arrested, Hyman then inquired whether Petrine had asked Cynthia for anything of Jaclyn's.

Petrine said she had requested an item of Jaclyn's clothing and a sample of her writing or drawing. Before leaving the home, Petrine said, Cynthia gave her a coloring Jaclyn had made for a Disney World contest but did not give her any clothing.

After Jaclyn's funeral, Petrine continued, she spoke with Cynthia on the telephone to arrange another meeting and again asked for a piece of clothing, but they never were able to get together.

On cross-examination, referring to Petrine's visit to the Dowaliby home, Velcich asked, "The purpose of you being there was to assist in finding Jaclyn, right?"

"Yes, it was," she answered.

"You knew that the police were looking for Jaclyn?"

"Yes."

Turning to what Petrine had told David, Velcich asked, "When you gave Mr. Dowaliby this information, did you tell him not to tell the police where he got that information?"

"No."

"You never told him to lie to the FBI, did you?"

"No."

Referring to Cynthia and the article of clothing, Velcich asked, "You didn't ask her for underwear, did you?"

"I told her that generally underwear is usually something that families give us."

"Well, you didn't ask her for underwear, did you?"

"Not specifically."

On redirect examination, Hyman asked whether Petrine had told David that the police could be present for their September 12 discussion.

"Yes, I did, I actually requested that," Petrine answered.

"And the police chose not to be there?"

"The police chose not to be there."

"And when you suggested that Cynthia bring something, you believed that underwear is something close to an individual?"

"Yes, I did."

The final defense witness was Mary Tolbert.

Before beginning the direct examination, Hyman explained to the jury that Tolbert was deaf and that he would be standing right next to her so she could read his lips.

Tolbert testified that she had noticed printed sheets hanging on the Dowalibys' clothesline both in the morning and late afternoon of September 9, but she could not recall whether they had a Lady Lovely Locks design.

Tolbert said that she went out that evening, returning at about 11:00 P.M.

Hyman asked her to describe the lighting conditions on the block at that time.

"Our block is very, very dark," she said.

On Saturday, September 10, she said, she left for work at about 6:15 A.M. and drove past the Dowaliby home, noticing that Cynthia's Malibu was parked "by the driveway." She said she could not recall whether the car was overhanging the driveway.

On cross-examination, O'Brien established that the last time she noticed the Dowalibys' sheets was at 3:00 or 4:00 P.M. on September 9. Then he asked if, when she took her own sheets down from the line, she made her daughter's bed. "I don't know," she said.

"Well," O'Brien asked, "did you let her go to sleep that night without sheets?"

"No," Tolbert said.

He asked her if she knew where Cynthia's Malibu was at 2:00 A.M. on September 10.

"No, I was in bed," she answered.

The only other evidence presented by the defense came in the form of stipulations—statements agreed to by both sides and read to the jury—indicating what two investigators would have said if they had been called to testify.

The first stipulation pertained to Midlothian Detective Neal Cauuwe, who would have testified that on September 12 Cynthia Dowaliby gave him a Sears catalog—the Wish Book referred to in testimony and police reports.

Neville allowed Franks to show only the front of the catalog to the jury. Several gift items inside had been circled, but there had been no testimony that Jaclyn had drawn the circles.

The second stipulation pertained to an interview that FBI Agent Jonathan Newcombe conducted on September 11 with Colleen Jones-Godin, who had been a prosecution witness.

According to the stipulation, if Newcombe had been in court he would testify that Jones-Godin had told him that on the morning of September 10, 1988, a young girl was selling pizza in front of her home. The girl had her back to the street when David and Cynthia yelled "Jaclyn!" from the corner.

"When the young girl turned and looked at them, they looked disheartened," the stipulation said. "When Jones-Godin later heard of Jaclyn's disappearance, she was sure her parents thought the girl selling pizza may have been her."

Outside the presence of the jury, Judge Neville announced his decision on the previous day's motion by the *Sun-Times* and Channel 5.

He said he would release the transcript of the proceedings on the motions for directed verdicts, and that anyone who wanted a copy could order it from the court reporter. Neville also said that he would make transcripts of sidebar discussions available to reporters at the end of each court day's session.

Lawrence Levin, the *Sun-Times* lawyer, asked Neville whether in future trials—"if you ever had a case like this again"—he would permit reporters to attend sidebars.

"If I'm lucky," Neville retorted, "I won't have a case like this again."

The next morning's *Sun-Times* carried a major story about the testimony of psychic Linda Petrine.

Buried in the story was the news from the liberated transcript—Judge Neville's doubt about the sufficiency of the case against Cynthia Dowaliby and his denial of a directed verdict for David Dowaliby.

The newspaper's defense of the First Amendment was extolled in a separate story that included nothing of the substantive content of the transcript.

"This," proclaimed *Sun-Times* lawyer Lawrence Levin, "is a victory for the reading public of Chicago."

ACCOUNTABILITY

As the end of the trial approached, the defense team faced a decision fraught with danger—whether to call the Dowalibys to testify in their own defense.

If David and Cynthia did not take the stand, their silence might be taken as an indication of guilt. If they did take the stand, they might make a poor impression and lose a case that otherwise could have been won, based on reasonable doubt.

While the Dowalibys had persuaded their lawyers of their innocence, it could be quite another matter to persuade the jury, in the intimidating atmosphere of a courtroom, under stringent cross-examination. Any mistake on the stand—the slightest appearance of frustration, hesitancy in answering a question, the shift of eyes away from the jury at the wrong moment—could cost the Dowalibys dearly.

Another risk, feared by Meczyk from the beginning, was that David's appearance on the stand might explode some unpredictable "bombshell."

Meczyk called John Waters at home and told him that the prosecutors "could be waiting to tear David apart." According to Waters's notes, Meczyk was worried that putting David on the stand would clear the way for the prosecutors to bring up his marijuana convictions. Worse yet, Meczyk told Waters, the prosecutors might call Melvin and Laverne Buckley to testify that David had smoked marijuana at the Islander Apartments.

Neither the convictions nor the Buckleys' testimony could be used as direct evidence against David, but the judge might allow the prosecutors to use either or both to impeach David's credibility. Even though the convictions were minor and the Buckleys' observations had been discredited both by police and by Waters, their possible impact on the jury was incalculable.

As a result, the defense team considered putting Cynthia on the stand without David. That idea was quickly rejected, however, because the jury might infer that David was hiding behind his wife.

At the last minute, Meczyk sought advice from colleagues in the criminal defense bar, whom he found sharply divided on whether his clients should be called.

One of the city's best-known defense lawyers, Edward M. Genson, at first urged Meczyk to call the Dowalibys to testify. "When parents are charged with murdering a child, the presumption of innocence is gone," said Genson. "The jury won't be sympathetic unless they deny the crime."

Genson changed his advice, however, after inquiring about what the defense had done to prepare the Dowalibys to testify. "Prepping" important witnesses, particularly defendants, should include at least one rigorous dry run, such as the prosecution had done with Everett Mann. Ralph Meczyk and Lawrence Hyman had twice begun to prep the Dowalibys, but the efforts were waylaid by the chaos that had beset the defense throughout the trial.

When Meczyk acknowledged that there had been no dry

run, Genson told him, "Well then, you've made your decision by default. You can't put them on. It's too late."

Meczyk also sought the counsel of Channel 5's Paul Hogan, who demurred, explaining that it would be inappropriate for a journalist to offer legal advice.

Ultimately Meczyk decided simply to lay out the pros and cons for the Dowalibys and leave the decision to them.

The Dowalibys had little trouble making up their minds.

"We felt that the prosecution hadn't proven its case," Cynthia said later, "so we didn't think we needed to testify."

David said that he had seen his statements to police twisted beyond recognition and feared that the prosecution would do more of the same.

The Dowalibys also said that they were strongly influenced by the case of Sandra Fabiano, a south suburban nursery school operator who, in a headline-grabbing case the previous year, had been acquitted of child sexual abuse without testifying.

"Sandra Fabiano didn't take the stand and she won," said David. "That seemed the way to go."

When court convened on Friday, April 27, Ralph Meczyk and Lawrence Hyman stood side by side facing the jury.

"Ladies and gentlemen, David Dowaliby rests his case," said Meczyk.

"Ladies and gentlemen, Cynthia Dowaliby rests her case," said Hyman.

Juror Phyllis Halvorsen gasped audibly. Her jaw dropped, and she glared at the defendants, shaking her head.

Other jurors seemed stunned.

Judge Neville asked if the prosecution wished to present any rebuttal evidence.

"Yes, sir, we do," said Patrick O'Brien.

The prosecution offered three brief rebuttal witnesses.

Two of these had been baby-sitters for the Dowalibys in 1987 and 1988; their sole purpose was to testify that they had never seen Jaclyn's bed without sheets.

The third was Assistant State's Attorney Anthony

Calabrese, who was called to discredit Holly Deck's contention that she had noticed Cynthia's Malibu in front of the Dowaliby home at 2:10 A.M. on September 10.

Calabrese testified that he and George Velcich had interviewed Deck in 1989. She told them at that time that she had been asleep from 1:00 A.M. to 9:00 A.M. on September 10, 1988, Calabrese said.

"Did she ever tell us that she woke up and looked at her alarm clock and saw it was two-ten in the morning?" Velcich asked.

"No, she never said that," Calabrese answered.

"Did she ever tell us that before going back to her bed she looked out her window and noticed Cynthia Dowaliby's blue Malibu parked in front?"

"No, she never said that, either."

Velcich also asked whether Deck had said anything about her relationship with the Dowalibys.

"She said that she would socialize frequently with Cynthia Dowaliby after the arrest," Calabrese answered.

On cross-examination, Ralph Meczyk established that O'Brien and Velcich, as supervisors in the state's attorney's office, held power over Calabrese's promotions and assignments.

Meczyk then asked Calabrese whether he and Velcich had asked Deck specifically if she had seen the Malibu in front of the Dowaliby home around the time Jaclyn disappeared.

"Specifically, that question?" Calabrese responded.

"That question," said Meczyk.

"No, sir, I did not," said Calabrese.

Judge Neville recessed the trial for the weekend, leaving Cynthia Dowaliby dangling over the fate of her motion for a directed verdict of acquittal.

Lawrence Hyman pleaded with Neville to end Cynthia's uncertainty before the weekend, but to no avail.

"Larry, what's the big deal?" Neville asked. "I think it's reasonable to do it Monday."

* * *

On Monday, Judge Neville again delayed his ruling on Cynthia Dowaliby's motion, devoting most of the day to deciding which of the 239 trial exhibits could be taken into the jury room.

The rulings on the exhibits were entirely favorable to the prosecution, producing fractious exchanges with the defense lawyers.

Neville held that the jury could have and hold the morgue photographs, which the defense branded "offensive," "gruesome," and "inflammatory."

Over defense objections, Neville ruled that the jury could study interior photographs of the Dowaliby home, showing damaged walls with no known connection to Jaclyn's murder.

Likewise, Neville said the jury could examine Jaclyn's pillow with the bloodstains that, a prosecution forensic expert had conceded, predated Jaclyn's disappearance.

In contrast, Neville held that the jury could not see the Sears Wish Book in which, the defense contended, Jaclyn had circled possible gifts for her family. "Who put the evidence in that Jaclyn Dowaliby marked those pages?" Neville taunted.

"Judge, we don't know who marked the pages, but we also don't know where the blood came from on the pillow, and that is in," Daniel Franks countered.

"There is testimony that the blood on the pillow matches Jaclyn Dowaliby," Neville said. "There's no evidence in the record about who made these markings in the book."

Lawrence Hyman pointed out that the forensic analysis only showed that the blood was Type O. "It could have been Cyndi's," he said.

"I don't disagree with that," Neville said, "but at least there's some evidence to indicate what it is."

"But there's evidence here, too, judge," said Franks, referring to the Wish Book. "It corroborates exactly what Jaclyn was doing that night, and it's been testified to."

"Overruled, not to go to the jury," said Neville.

Lost in the brouhaha was the prosecution mock-up of the Dowalibys' basement window. It would be rolled into the jury room without objection.

* * *

Monday's proceedings also featured a significant skirmish over whether Judge Neville should instruct the jury that David Dowaliby could be held responsible for Cynthia's acts, and vice versa.

The prosecutors, who were concerned that Neville might acquit Cynthia before her case went to the jury, desperately wanted "accountability" instructions. Their case had been based on the premise that the Dowalibys committed the crime together. Accountability instructions would allow the jury to continue to view the case that way, even if Cynthia were acquitted.

Specifically, Patrick O'Brien wanted Neville to give the jury two such instructions:

First, that a person is legally responsible for the conduct of another when "he knowingly solicits, aids, abets, agrees to aid, or attempts to aid the other person in the planning or commission" of a crime.

Second, that a person "who is legally responsible for the conduct of another" may be convicted for an offense committed by the other, even though that individual is "not before the jury."*

In arguing for the instructions, O'Brien acknowledged, "We cannot show which of the defendants is aiding or abetting the other, but our theory is that the only two people who could have committed this crime are the defendants. That has been our theory because of the house being locked."

The defense vehemently objected to O'Brien's proposed instructions, insisting that there were no facts in the case to

---

*The first proposed instruction was a standard jury instruction, derived directly from an Illinois statute. The second proposed instruction deviated from a standard instruction by including the words "not before the jury." The standard instruction is faithful to the following statutory language: "A person who is legally responsible for the conduct of another . . . may be convicted . . . although the other person . . . *has not been prosecuted or convicted, or has been convicted of a different offense or degree of offense, or is not amenable to justice, or has been acquitted.*" Ill. Rev. Stat., Chap. 38, Sec. 5-3.

support them—neither direct nor circumstantial evidence that one defendant "aided" or "abetted" the other.

Daniel Franks told Neville, "The admission by Mr. O'Brien that he does not have any evidence whatsoever as to who did what, or how it happened, I think is one that you have to rely on."

Referring to O'Brien's references to the prosecution "theory," Franks added, "Theories are not what this case should be about. It should be about evidence."

Neville said, "Well, it appears to me that for the state to get this instruction in, they have to show some evidence of one of the words which are required in the instruction."

Turning to O'Brien, Neville asked what evidence supported giving the instruction.

"As to the murder, obviously we're talking about something where the only witnesses are the people in the house," O'Brien said. "As to the concealment of homicidal death, it's our theory that David Dowaliby deposited Jaclyn's body in Blue Island, while back at the house, the sheets were taken off the bed. The person who hung up the sheets was Cynthia Dowaliby. Those sheets could not have come off the bed without her actually doing it."

"All I can say, judge," Hyman interjected, "is that this is the wildest of speculations. It's certainly not evidence of aiding or abetting."

"I'm going to hold off ruling on this," Neville said, promising to resolve the controversy the next day, after finally announcing his ruling on Cynthia's fate.

Facing an empty jury box, the Dowalibys awaited Judge Neville's arrival on Tuesday, May 1.

The courtroom was packed with reporters and spectators, most of the latter being the defendants' family and friends, including John and Charlotte Waters.

Everyone rose as Neville entered with customary haste, his black robe flowing behind him.

"Cynthia and David Dowaliby," said the clerk, officially opening the session.

"Ready to argue the motions for directed findings?" Neville asked the lawyers.

Patrick O'Brien indicated that he would stand on the arguments that had been made in chambers at the close of the prosecution case.

"Your honor, I will stand on my argument also," said Ralph Meczyk.

"Mr. Hyman," said Neville.

"The only thing I would ask again is that the court consider the law," said Lawrence Hyman. "This is an issue of law, not an issue of fact to be determined by the jury. In the light most favorable to the prosecution, there is nothing which shows any of the elements charged in the indictment. I would ask the court to make a directed finding as to Cynthia Dowaliby."

"Well," Neville began, "I spent extensive time going through all the notes that I have and studying transcripts of the attorneys' arguments."

Cynthia leaned forward, rising slightly in her chair, her gaze fixed on the judge.

"It is my position," Neville said, "that there is sufficient evidence for David Dowaliby's case to go to the jury."

There was no reaction in the courtroom, since journalists had reported the denial of David's motion the previous week.

"As to Cynthia Dowaliby," Neville continued, "I have looked at all of the evidence which has been presented by the state relative to both the charge of murder and concealment of a homicidal death, and I am, as a legal matter, ruling that there is insufficient evidence for her case to go to the jury.

"Therefore, Cynthia Dowaliby's case is discharged, and she is released from the courtroom."

Applause broke out as the Dowalibys and many of their supporters leaped to their feet. Cynthia and David momentarily embraced.

"Thank you, your honor," said Cynthia, choking back tears.

John Waters turned to his wife, smiling. "We're halfway there," he said.

Neville announced that the closing arguments in David's

case would begin in fifteen minutes. Meanwhile, he asked lawyers to meet with him—privately.

In chambers, Neville advised the lawyers that he planned to keep the jurors in the dark about Cynthia's fate. "It is my intention to tell them that they are only going to decide David's case and that they are not to be concerned about why they are not hearing Cynthia's case," he said.

Neville did not explain his reasoning to the lawyers.

Later, however, he explained that he was concerned that if the jurors knew that he had acquitted Cynthia but not David, the jurors might think that he believed David guilty.

Having made up his mind to acquit Cynthia at the close of the prosecution case, Neville said, he chose to delay the announcement so that the jury would have less time to speculate about her absence from the defense table.

Neville said he realized that delaying the announcement might affect the lawyers' strategies for the remainder of the trial, particularly the defense decision on whether to call Cynthia to testify. Consequently, Neville attempted to send the lawyers subtle signals that he would acquit her—by nodding approvingly, for instance, during her lawyer's argument for a directed verdict.

The defense missed the message. (Meczyk had told John Waters that there was "no way" that Neville would throw out both charges against Cynthia. "Ralph thinks he's ball-less," Waters wrote in his notes.)

The prosecutors got the message, however, leading them to propose the accountability instructions allowing David to be convicted for the actions of someone "not before the jury."

Now, in Neville's chambers, the lawyers resumed their debate over those instructions.

Patrick O'Brien argued that David could be accountable for Cynthia's acts despite her acquittal. He cited a 1980 Illinois case, *People* v. *Grice,* in which a woman distracted a sales clerk while another woman stole clothing. The woman who took the clothes got away, but the accomplice was convicted of theft—on the grounds that she aided and abetted the actual thief.

Daniel Franks argued that the facts in *Grice* were significantly different from those in the Dowaliby case. In *Grice,* he noted, there had been eyewitness testimony that the defendant aided and abetted another person in a crime. In the Dowaliby case, he said, there was no evidence of aiding and abetting; in fact, the only person David could have abetted had just been found not guilty.

"The state has proven nothing that Cyndi did that had anything to do with this crime," Franks said. "To suggest now that David is somehow accountable for what she did, when they did not show what she did, is totally inconsistent and improper. Your honor has ruled as a matter of law that Cynthia Dowaliby is in no way culpable—"

"I didn't rule that she was in no way culpable," Neville interrupted. "What I ruled was that there was insufficient evidence for her case to go to the jury."

Neville said that the jury was entitled to draw inferences from the limited circumstantial evidence against Cynthia, including removing Jaclyn's sheets and calling Sylvia Borrelli, and to conclude that David was accountable for those acts.

Accordingly, Neville ruled, the accountability instructions would be given exactly as requested by the prosecutors.

"We object strenuously," Franks protested.

"Overruled," said Neville. "Let's go."

David Dowaliby could be convicted of aiding and abetting his wife in a crime—of which she stood legally innocent.

THE HEART OF MIDLOTHIAN

Judge Neville and the lawyers returned to the courtroom, where the jurors joined them moments later for the dramatic finale to the three-week trial.

"You see that David Dowaliby sits before you, and Cyndi Dowaliby does not," Neville told the jury. "You will not be deciding the case of Cynthia Dowaliby."

Several of the jurors craned their necks, searching the courtroom with their eyes, finding Cynthia among family members in the second row of the spectator section.

"You are not to take into consideration the fact that you are not deciding her case," Neville continued. "You should not hold the fact that she is not there for or against David Dowaliby. You are to listen to the arguments of the lawyers and my instructions and decide his case based on the facts as you find them and the law as I give it to you."

George Velcich, dressed in a dark gray suit, white shirt, and conservative striped tie, rose to present the first closing argument, a customary function of the junior member of the prosecution, leaving the rebuttal argument to the senior member.

In every detail—demeanor, dress, body language—Velcich exuded confidence and reason. He spoke in measured tones, rich with simplicity and clarity, and with an illusion of spontaneity that was in fact the product of meticulous preparation.

"In the last month since you first came into this courtroom you have learned a lot of things about a neighborhood in Midlothian," he began. "One of the most important things you learned was about a little girl. Her name was Jaclyn Dowaliby. She was seven years old in September of 1988, as her little playmate, Vickie Verble, told you."

Holding up Jaclyn's kindergarten photograph, Velcich told the jury, "Jaclyn Dowaliby looked like this. She had long brown hair and beautiful blue eyes. She liked to ride her bike up and down the streets where she lived. She liked to giggle and laugh. She liked to squeal when she was tickled, and she liked to play and run and have all the fun that she could have as a child."

After a dramatic pause, Velcich continued, "During the last month, you have also learned that something terrible happened to Jaclyn Dowaliby. She was taken away from her friends, from the good and decent people who were close to her, from all of us. She was taken away, the evidence has shown you, by the two people she expected to protect her—by this man and by his wife."

That was the first of numerous references that Velcich, and later Patrick O'Brien, would make to the alleged guilt of the legally innocent Cynthia.

Cynthia scornfully shook her head, glaring at her accuser.

"David Dowaliby is here, and Cynthia Dowaliby was here, because of what they did," Velcich continued.

Then, cutting through the legal jargon, he laid the groundwork for the jury to understand the accountability instructions: "The first thing you know from common sense is that criminals don't always commit their crimes alone. Criminals often work in pairs, and each one has a different role to play."

He continued, "You know from your experience that one man may distract a woman while another one takes her purse. You know that one person may sit outside as a getaway driver as someone goes in and robs a bank. Under the law, they work together and each one is guilty for what happened throughout the crime.

"If you find that David Dowaliby drove Jaclyn's body in the trunk of that Malibu while Cyndi Dowaliby washed the sheets, they're guilty of those acts together."

Daniel Franks objected, "Mr. Velcich is stating that Cyndi Dowaliby's guilty, and I think that's inappropriate."

"The jury understands that they are deciding David Dowaliby's case only," said Neville. "I don't think it's confusing. Go ahead, Mr. Velcich."

"So ladies and gentlemen," Velcich resumed, "when the judge instructs you, you will see a phrase that says 'or one for whose conduct he is legally responsible.' That means that you can apply whatever Cynthia Dowaliby did to whatever David did.

"His honor will tell you that we have to prove that the defendant, or one for whose conduct he's responsible, performed the acts which caused the death of Jaclyn Dowaliby, whether those acts were choking her with that rope, or in a fit of anger slapping her and causing some other fatal injury to her that we couldn't find because of her condition.

"We also have to prove that the defendant, or one for whose conduct he's legally responsible, either intended to kill her or knew that his acts created a strong probability of death or great bodily harm.

"In other words, if this started out as a fit of anger and they knew that if they hit her hard enough she could die, even if they didn't intend that she die—"

Ralph Meczyk interrupted, "There's no evidence of that at all!"

"The jury will have to decide if that's a proper inference from the evidence," said Neville.

Velcich continued, reinforcing his point: "Even if they didn't intend for her to die, but knew that she could die, they are guilty of murder. There's no requirement that we prove that this crime was premeditated. There's no requirement that we prove a motive. We don't have to prove that it was sexual assault, or that it was a discipline situation.

"People like *them* kill children for lots of reasons, and we can't be held responsible to know what *he* intended or what *she* intended at the time that Jaclyn breathed her last breath."

Velcich pointed at David with a flourish, and walked almost into the spectator section to jab his finger at Cynthia.

Leading into a summary of the evidence, Velcich noted that in some cases there are eyewitnesses, in some there are confessions, and in some there is circumstantial evidence. "At first glance," he said, "circumstantial evidence may not appear to prove anything, but it's just as good as an eyewitness, just as good as a confession."

"Judge," Franks interrupted, "I'm going to object to his suggestion that circumstantial evidence is like a confession. That's a misstatement of the law."

"Overruled," said Neville. "Go ahead."

"The case hasn't been a big bombshell of an eyewitness," Velcich conceded. "It hasn't been a big confession that you might have expected to hear.

"We're asking you to do a difficult job, to look at these pieces of evidence, at all the circumstantial evidence, and if you do that, you will come to the conclusion that these individuals killed Jaclyn Dowaliby.

"Our best witness, of course, would have been Jaclyn, but they took her away from us. Davey was in that house. We would have liked to hear what he had to say, but he's too young and too immature to tell us what he knew about this case."

There was no objection, even though Velcich had distorted the reason that Davey had not testified; Neville had held simply that Davey had no relevant information about Jaclyn's death.

Velcich then spun a theory about what happened after Jaclyn was sent to bed on September 9, 1988.

It was "possible," he said, that instead of going to sleep, Jaclyn wanted to play with her dolls, that she refused to stay in her room, and "because of that, the defendants chose to do something to restrain her."

Lifting the evidence bag containing the rope, Velcich continued, "We don't know that they used this rope—"

"Judge," Franks interrupted, "I don't think the state should be allowed to speculate wildly."

"Overruled, go ahead," said Neville.

"Ladies and gentlemen," Velcich said, "we know that this rope, which turned up around her neck, was connected to the Dowaliby house. Ann Dowaliby was shown that rope and she said it looked like the very rope that Davey played with. A neighbor testified that he saw Davey with that rope."

"That was not the evidence," Meczyk objected.

Without waiting for Neville to rule on the objection, Velcich backed off, saying, "Well, it looked like the same rope."

"Thank you," said Meczyk.

"Obviously," Velcich resumed, "we can't tell you absolutely that it is the same rope, but what's interesting is that when Jaclyn disappeared, so did the rope that Davey played with."

Velcich allowed that the prosecution could not prove "exactly how it was that Jaclyn died" because "this poor little girl's body was eaten by maggots, severely decomposed—and you saw those pictures."

Although "we don't have all the evidence to tell us what happened to Jaclyn Dowaliby," he said, Dr. Robert Stein, the medical examiner, had testified that death could have resulted from a head injury without any fractured bones. "I suggest, based on what Dr. Stein told you, that this child was killed as a result of discipline or some kind of angry strike or hit," Velcich said, slamming his fist into the palm of his hand.

"Ladies and gentlemen, after Jaclyn died in that house, the defendants had some decisions to make," Velcich went on. "They didn't want to be caught. It was risky to take the body out of the house, but it was a lot riskier to leave her in, so they decided that they would move her.

"Everett Mann told you that on the same night that Jaclyn died, he happened to be coming home to his apartment in Blue Island. He told you that he looked over and he could see that car. He was familiar with that kind of car, a Chevy Malibu Classic, and he was able to see the nose of the driver. Nobody ever told you that Everett Mann made a positive identification; it's not possible to make one at that distance under those lights.

"Everett Mann told you as best he could what he saw. We are not asking you to believe Everett Mann all by himself. We are asking you to look at all the evidence and decide whether it was in fact the blue Malibu that David Dowaliby had that night."

Velcich claimed that Mann's testimony was corroborated by the fact that one of the hairs found in the trunk of the Malibu was "like" Jaclyn's hair.

Next Velcich offered a theory about what happened when David came home after dumping the body. He claimed that David or Cynthia selected the window leading into Ann's room to break so that Ann would discover it when she came home. However, Ann stayed out all night, thwarting the plan. Thus the Dowalibys had to pretend to discover the window themselves.

When Ann finally came home, Velcich said, "They sent her down to look. They told her, 'Jaclyn's not here, why don't you look downstairs?' "

Franks objected that there was no such evidence, but Neville overruled the objection.

"Ann screwed up," Velcich resumed. "She went into her room, and guess what, she missed the glass, so they had to try again. They suggested that she look around again. Finally, Cynthia walked over to the window that they both knew was broken and put on a show of discovery.

"She started to cry, and the police were called. You heard the tape of David Dowaliby's voice, a fellow who claims that he's been looking for his daughter for forty-five minutes, a fellow who claims that he loved his daughter. He calmly says, 'There's been a break-in, and my daughter's missing.' Is that what you would have said? Which is more important—the break-in or the daughter?

"So at that point they decided to let the world know about Jaclyn's disappearance, but it wasn't going to be the truth."

The Dowalibys came up with the "phony alibi" that James Guess might have taken Jaclyn, Velcich said. If David were innocent, he would have looked for Jaclyn when he discovered the front door ajar, Velcich asserted.

Turning to the police investigation, Velcich said, "It was logical, it was thorough, and it was as hard a job as any police officers have ever had."

Pointing to David, Velcich declared, "The evidence says that the police cared more about that little girl than he did."

The police had been skeptical, Velcich said, because they had noticed the "even layer of dust" on the windowsill and because they had caught both parents in lies. Thus the police returned to the house and removed the broken window.

"You've seen the junk that was under the window," he continued. "Nothing was disturbed. Nothing was crushed. Nothing was knocked over. This is circumstantial evidence that suggests nobody came in that window, but there's more."

Walking over to the prosecution mock-up of the basement window, he said, "You've got this window right here. This is built to specifications."

Noting that the mock-up would be in the jury room during deliberations, Velcich offered a challenge: "I suggest, ladies and gentlemen, that, if you find that you can crawl through that window without disturbing any of the dust, then you have to find that somebody broke into that house."

He quickly added, however, that he was confident the jury would find it impossible to go through the window without rubbing the ledge or disturbing the objects beneath it.

"If you find that is impossible, then you know that the house was sealed tight as a drum, and that no one else could have killed Jaclyn Dowaliby, and that they are guilty," Velcich said, pointing both to David and Cynthia.

Velcich concluded, "During the course of this trial, the defense has tried to suggest that it was Perry Hernandez who broke into this house and took Jaclyn. But Perry Hernandez left clues all over the MacRand house. In the Dowaliby house, though, there's not a trace that anyone else was ever there.

"Our case, then, ladies and gentlemen, is an accumulation of all of those things. Those people wanted you to have their lies and their contradictions and their cover-ups, and they didn't want you to have evidence like the dust on the windowsill and Jaclyn's hair in the trunk. We have all of those things.

"I suggest to you that you look carefully at all this evidence because this matters a lot. There was a little girl killed, a little girl who liked to play, and a little girl who liked to laugh and shout, a little girl whose voice you won't hear anymore, a little girl whose voice was stilled by silence.

"They silenced Jaclyn. They kept her from us. Don't let them silence the truth."

After excusing the jury for lunch, Neville ordered Lawrence Hyman to approach the bench. The prosecutors already had left.

Neville said that Cynthia Dowaliby had been communicating with the jury through facial expressions, by shaking her head, and "looking plaintively."

"She opted not to testify," Neville said. "It is inappropriate for her to communicate with the jury now. If she does it again, I will order her out of the courtroom."

Hyman said that Cynthia had a First Amendment right to shake her head.

Since the prosecutors were not present, Neville temporarily broke off the discussion.

After lunch, he called the attorneys into his chambers and told them what he had said to Hyman before the recess.

"Mr. Hyman said that Cynthia Dowaliby—who was sitting at the second row, at the end, looking at the jury and crying and nodding her head 'no' through the argument—has a First Amendment right to communicate with the jury," Neville said.

Hyman protested, "I did not say she had a First Amendment right to communicate with the jury."

"What did you say, Mr. Hyman?" Neville asked.

"I think she has a First Amendment right to certainly shake her head," he said.

"She is out of the courtroom," Neville snapped, like an umpire ejecting a player from a game. "That is the First Amendment right she has got. It is an insult to me to tell me she has a right to communicate with the jury."

"Well, I never indicated that to the court," Hyman pleaded.

Neville's face turned beet red. "You tell me what your response is about this bullshit First Amendment right," he thundered. "What First Amendment right has she got as a spectator in the courtroom during closing argument?"

"I agree with the court," said Hyman, backing down, "that she cannot communicate with the jury."

"That's my point," said the judge.

"No one in the family should," Hyman said, deferentially. "I have advised everybody that all they can do is sit there. They have no right to make any gestures or sounds."

"I want that on the record, in front of everybody," Neville said, "because if it happens again I am going to throw them out."

"Fine," said Hyman.

"You don't murder your daughter because she wanted to play with dolls," Ralph Meczyk began. "That is basically what the state is telling you."

Meczyk said that the prosecution had failed to present "a scintilla of evidence" to show "why normal persons like David Dowaliby and his wife, Cynthia, would go to bed and wake up the next morning accused of the most heinous murder a human being can ever be charged with, the murder of their child.

"Why did it happen? There is no reason why, and that is a reasonable doubt, ladies and gentlemen."

Meczyk contended that the police "started out with a popular misconception—and that popular misconception was child abuse, the parents."

He quickly added, "I am not condoning child abuse, but in the context of this case it is on everyone's mind, and it was on the minds of the police when you had the break-in at the Dowaliby home.

"You had an intruder go through the window while the parents were sleeping and remove the child from the house. To the police, that was absolutely preposterous, but, almost a year to the day later, you had a monster like Perry Hernandez go through a window into the MacRand home in Blue Island, and no one was awakened in the house. How could it happen? It happened.

"We also know from the MacRand case, from what Carline MacRand told you, that her husband was accused first by the police, but then the Dowaliby case came to mind and there but for the grace of God, too, went David MacRand.

"You heard about Captain McDevitt's task force. The majority of leads in this case, who were they targeted to? The Dowalibys. That is who they had zeroed in on."

Meczyk said that McDevitt's task force had been like a "freight train that couldn't be stopped—nothing could derail it, except now, I hope, ladies and gentlemen, you will."

Meczyk said that the authorities seemed to have had some trouble deciding what manner of man they were prosecuting —whether he was "the devious David, or David the dunce— David the dummy."

Said Meczyk: "Look at the two Davids you have here. When you have a David who is so smart, a master criminal, you cannot by the very same token have a David who is so dumb, who makes terrible, terrible mistakes in this supposed cover-up.

"You have a David who is so clever that he breaks the window from the outside because he knows that the forensic scientists will be able to show how the window was broken.

"Then you have the dumb David. What does the dumb David do? He has all of the time in the world to go into the basement and knock over the towel rack, knock over the shelf, but, of course, dumb David does not think of that.

"He has the intelligence, the craftiness, David the devious, to break the window in that way, yet he is dumb, dumb as a box of rocks, because he does not go in and mess up Ann's room.

"You have another David the devious. After he goes to Blue Island, he has the intelligence to come back and park exactly in the same spot. On the other side of the coin, there is David the dunce, who forgets to put the sheets back on—the crafty, evil, criminal genius forgets something as glaring as the sheets."

Turning to the mock-up of the window, Meczyk continued, "We know that the window was broken from the outside. We know that the impact did not break out the entire glass. What was left was a hole, and we also know the bottom portion held that glass in tightly. That glass had to be picked clean by the intruder.

"Why choose this particular window? After all, some of the other windows were in fact unlocked. It is true, except the question is, how would the intruder have known that? There were screens on every single window. The intruder would never have known that those windows were unlocked.

"I say to you that the intruder picked this window for a very, very good reason. There are no lights on 148th Place. That is a very, very dark street.

"There is still more. The entire Dowaliby residence was surrounded by a fence. An intruder would not want to go into the backyard because, if he was caught, he would have to jump over that fence, so the best place for an intruder to go into that house is actually that window.

"There is more. Mr. Velcich makes the argument that for David the devious to use that window is perfect—because that is the window to his mother's apartment. She would be the first one to discover this. If he is that smart, why is he so dumb as to rely on Ann Dowaliby when he knows she is a drunk?"

Meczyk then turned to the purported dust on the windowsill. Referring to Hayden Baldwin's failure to preserve evidence of the dust, Meczyk said, "I asked about notes, and uh-huh, our clever sleuth sees the dust, but is it in his notes? I asked him, where are your notes? They are destroyed."

The dust, said Meczyk, was "the single most important clue, the single most important piece of evidence pointing the finger at the Dowalibys," yet Baldwin failed to photograph it.

"He talked about cobwebs," Meczyk added. "Would you like to see a photograph of the cobwebs? It does not exist."

Reminding the jurors of their night visit to the Islander Apartments parking lot, Meczyk branded Everett Mann's identification testimony a "preposterous lie."

"You couldn't see seventy-five yards away," Meczyk said. "You would be lucky if you saw fifteen feet away."

Mann had invented his story, Meczyk charged, in the hope that the prosecutors would help him obtain a law enforcement job. "Well, we know who Everett Mann is now," said Meczyk. "Everett Mann has a motive for telling his little lie."

In a bizarre digression, Meczyk said that Mann's testimony reminded him of a story:

"Before my dad died, I used to take him, my wife, and my kids, and drive to Wisconsin or Indiana to find a restaurant or an inn on Sundays. Invariably my father would always order one thing. He would order the beef stew.

"So we finally find this lovely little place. I think it was outside Fond du Lac. We go to an inn, and on the menu is beef stew, but the waiter comes by with a beautiful plate of chicken. My dad said, 'I think I am going to order the chicken.' I turned to my wife and said, 'He is not going to order the chicken. He is going to order the beef stew.' Of course, I was right. He ordered the beef stew.

"He put his fork into the first piece of meat, and he started to gag. He spit it out. He said, 'This is terrible. It is rancid,' called the waiter over, and said, 'Send it back. I don't want it.' "

Meczyk then told the jury, "Same with you. What are you supposed to do? It's just like the beef stew. Eat this whole story? If one piece is rotten, the rest is rotten."

Changing the subject, Meczyk held up a photograph of the interior of the trunk of Cynthia's Malibu, saying, "Maybe

Cyndi Dowaliby can be condemned for being a lousy housekeeper. She does not clean the trunk of her car very well."

Referring to the one hair found in the trunk that was similar to Jaclyn's hair, Meczyk called it "Jaclyn's hair."

"Big deal, so what?" he said, pointing out that Jaclyn's hair could have arrived there in any number of innocent ways.

"As long as we are on the topic of hair," Meczyk continued, "what about the Negroid hair found on the rope used to strangle Jaclyn Dowaliby? You cannot dismiss it."

Although that hair could not have come from Perry Hernandez, he said, neither could it have come from David Dowaliby. "The same evidence that excludes Perry Hernandez, excludes David Dowaliby," Meczyk said.

"I suppose everyone wants to hear about the sheets," Meczyk continued. "Well, we know about Cynthia Dowaliby's day, the ninth of September. She had worked all day. Her day was busy.

"So we should condemn her and condemn him, and send them to prison—send him to prison because his wife didn't have time to change the sheets?"

Since the prosecutors had no evidence, Meczyk said, they were appealing to the jurors' emotions. "They will show you a picture of a really beautiful young child," he said. "The next picture they will show you is an obscene photograph of her body.

"Please don't go by those pictures. Go by the evidence, by what you have seen and heard. You have heard they were a good family. The child was well cared for, no evidence of abuse, no nothing. Why all of a sudden do you kill your child? That is reasonable doubt."

In closing, Meczyk told an old, obscure story, the story of Effie Deans. Pregnant out of wedlock, Effie fell asleep after giving birth to a son. The midwife kidnapped and sold the baby, telling Effie he had died. When Effie was seen in public without her child, she was charged with murder and convicted by a jury, only to be exonerated years later when her son was discovered living.

Like the case against Effie, Meczyk said, the case against the Dowalibys was tenuous and circumstantial. Like Effie, the Dowalibys claimed they were asleep when their child was taken.

Effie Deans was fictional, Meczyk said, the protagonist in a novel by Sir Walter Scott, published in 1818. In a stunning coincidence, Midlothian, Illinois, had been named after the county in Scotland where Sir Walter had set his story.

"Oh, the title of the book?" Meczyk asked rhetorically. "The title is *The Heart of Midlothian.*"

Waving a copy of Scott's weighty work, Meczyk told the jury, "It comes back today. I ask you not to make the same mistake as that jury. Remember Effie Deans. I beg of you, I plead with you, please acquit David Dowaliby because this man is not guilty."

Now it was Patrick O'Brien's turn.

"There is no easy way to present this to you," O'Brien began. "Your first instinct as parents is to say it couldn't be David Dowaliby and Cynthia Dowaliby. That is understandable. The problem is, it can't be anyone else.

"This is not about David Dowaliby's nightmare, about his disgust, about his problems. The focus on David Dowaliby is misplaced. This is about Jaclyn's nightmare. This is about the thing done to her, about what she suffered.

"Counsel, in a dramatic moment, held up a book and said, isn't it strange that the book that I'm referring to is called *The Heart of Midlothian*? There was one heart from Midlothian on the night of the ninth and into the morning of the tenth, and it ended up in a field in Blue Island.

"There is not an answer between the pages of that book that will tell you anything more about this case. This is a mystery, as I said at the start, but a mystery created by the defendant, David Dowaliby, and his wife, Cynthia.

"They stand up and call it reasonable doubt. You can equally call it chutzpah."

O'Brien then attacked the defense interpretation of the evidence, focusing on the psychic Linda Petrine. "In this case, God help us, we have had everything," he said. "Linda Petrine tells us what David Dowaliby supposedly is thinking after being told about Jaclyn's body and he asks, 'In a field?'

Who can tell us what David Dowaliby is thinking? Who can tell us?''

Meczyk objected, because O'Brien's remark was an implicit reference to David's exercise of his right not to testify.

Neville overruled the objection.

O'Brien resumed, answering his rhetorical question, ''The stepfather, the 'heart of Midlothian,' made of stone that day.''

Countering Meczyk's charge about Everett Mann's motivation for testifying, O'Brien said, ''The only attorney in this case who has done anything to a witness with regard to giving them something is Mr. Meczyk. Mr. Meczyk gave Carline MacRand money.''

Meczyk interrupted, ''I am proud of it, your honor, and not ashamed!''

Spectators burst into laughter.

''Good, good,'' said O'Brien. ''I am not surprised he is proud of it.''

He continued, ''Jaclyn cannot be a witness because she is dead.'' Then he, like Velcich, asserted that ''Davey can't be a witness because he has been held to be too young to testify.''

Turning to Meczyk's juxtaposition of ''devious David'' and ''dumb David,'' O'Brien said, ''We are not saying that David Dowaliby is smart at times and stupid at times.''

Breaking the window from the outside, for example, indicated neither genius nor stupidity, O'Brien asserted; it would have made little sense to break it from the inside, since there was a screen on the outside that had to be removed first.

O'Brien, thus, had discredited the theory that originally led Daniel McDevitt to believe in the Dowalibys' guilt—the theory that the window had been broken from the inside. The irony was lost on the jury, however, since the theory had not been brought out during the trial.

Pointing to the mock-up of the window, O'Brien told the jurors, ''Now, I don't know if you're going to try climbing through this window when you get back in the jury room.''

In case they did, he advised them to keep in mind: ''When you are moving about and trying to get your legs into position, you are directly underneath the sill on the outside, and you don't leap through the window like some kind of long-jumper. Your knees are underneath that sill. Your feet are kicking up the leaves because you are trying to get your body through."

He emphatically added, "Nobody came through that window. It didn't happen."

O'Brien then picked up where Velcich had left off on the prosecution theory of how the crime occurred, speculating that Jaclyn had been tied to her bed.

Holding up the rope, he said, "This is the rope that was around Jaclyn's neck, not tied, but wound twice, not a rope that was five feet long that could be bound at both ends to strangle a child, but a twenty-six-foot rope."

He pointed out that it would be unusual to use a rope of such length to strangle a child, "but if you are going to bind her and have loose ends at either side of the bed—"

Franks objected, "There is absolutely no evidence that that occurred."

"That is an inference the jury will have to make," said Neville.

O'Brien concluded by asserting that "David Dowaliby tried to hide his stepdaughter, Jaclyn, in the weeds, in a field, in back of Blue Island. When the case was being investigated, he tried to hide behind his lies. When the case pointed to him on the fourteenth, cooperation stopped.

"During this trial, he has tried to hide behind Perry Hernandez, Tim Guess, and, yes, even Rory MacRand.

"Jaclyn deserved more. We all deserve more."

Judge Neville read more than twenty pages of instructions to the jury. Among them were the definitions of first-degree murder (intentionally killing someone or performing acts that "create a strong probability of death or great bodily harm") and concealment ("the performing of some act or acts for the purpose of preventing or delaying the discovery of a death by homicidal means") and, of course, the accountability instructions.

Neville also instructed the jury that David was entitled to the presumption of innocence, and the fact that he did not testify "must not be considered" in arriving at a verdict.

"You are to apply the law to the facts and in this way decide the case," said Neville.

The jurors retired to deliberate at 5:00 P.M.

Copies of the jury instructions and more than two hundred trial exhibits, including the prosecution mock-up of the broken window and the towel rack, were removed to the jury room.

An hour later, Paul Hogan began a live report, "Shielded by friends and family tonight, David and Cynthia Dowaliby went home, but, as they left, they still seemed stunned by another unusual twist in this unusual trial."

He was referring to Cynthia's acquittal, which he called a "commentary on the weakness of the state's case."

"As the couple cried and embraced in the courtroom, they knew the jury would get to judge David," said Hogan. "The difference between the case against Cynthia and David Dowaliby boils down to one witness—a man of disputed credibility who says he saw someone who looked like David Dowaliby near the scene where the girl's body was found.

"The judge is required to view this witness and all of the state's evidence in the best possible light for the prosecution, so he could not acquit David Dowaliby."

The report included Cynthia's first public comment on the case, recorded minutes before Hogan went on the air.

She said eleven words:

"I'm waiting for David's acquittal. I feel fine. I'm very happy."

Judge Neville left the courtroom for an evening workout at the East Bank Club, taking a beeper in case there was a verdict.

He later described his thoughts on the closing arguments.

"George Velcich," he said, "was brilliant. He wove the circumstantial evidence in the case into a cohesive pattern. Pat O'Brien did the right thing, keeping the rebuttal argument short, staying out of the way."

In contrast, Neville said, "Ralph Meczyk got lost in the forest and didn't see the trees. It was a failure of style. He was prepared—he put in a lot of time on the case—but he didn't get across his points well."

Neville said he had no clue about how the jurors viewed the case.

"I was just hoping they'd reach a verdict," he said.

WINDOW TO A VERDICT

The room where the jury retired to judge David Dowaliby was drab yellow, appointed with a potted plant, a broken water fountain, and a long table with twelve hard chairs. There was an ashtray on the table and a no-smoking sign on the wall; the jurors quickly agreed that the latter was an ornament.

The first task was selecting a foreperson—a job for which Phyllis Halvorsen had been campaigning from the beginning, using her southern charm, telling the others, "Call me P.J."

Since no one else was interested—two jurors whose names were suggested declined—Halvorsen was chosen by acclamation.

"Guilty, guilty, guilty," was her first pronouncement in her official leadership capacity.

Juror Evelyn Roda, a west suburban homemaker, physician's wife, and mother of three, seconded

Halvorsen's view, and a few of the others nodded in agreement.

However, about half of the panelists expressed doubts, pointing out that not even the prosecutors had claimed that Jaclyn died at David's hands. Patrick O'Brien, in fact, had suggested that Jaclyn's death might have been an accident—perhaps caused by Cynthia. If that were true, was David guilty of first-degree murder?

There was general confusion over what had happened to Cynthia. The best guess was that she had been acquitted, but no one knew for sure. Maybe a mistrial had been declared in her case or, as one juror put it, "there might have been some weird legal development that we don't understand."

The jurors also were confused by Neville's instructions regarding Cynthia. After her abrupt departure from the case, Neville had said, "You are not to take into consideration the fact that you are not deciding her case." The accountability instructions, however, said that David could be held responsible for the acts of a person "not before the jury," which could only mean Cynthia.

This perceived paradox was particularly troubling to several women jurors, who had become infatuated with Neville and assumed that any misunderstanding must be their fault.

George Velcich, who also had attracted his share of admirers, had further bewildered the jury by continuing to point an accusing finger at Cynthia after Neville declared her out of the case.

Ralph Meczyk, whom jurors had viewed as a "Columbo-like character" with an intentionally distracting style, had done nothing in his closing statement to clarify the legal definitions of either murder or accountability.

After two and one-half hours of grappling and gossiping, the jury adjourned until the next morning, retiring to an area hotel.

The first day's deliberations had ended without a single juror arguing that an intruder killed Jaclyn.

On Wednesday, May 2, David and Cynthia Dowaliby fretted away the hours drinking coffee and smoking cigarettes in the public cafeteria on the second floor of the criminal court building.

Reporters congregated in the press room a floor below, setting up a table and microphones where the defense lawyers bullishly had agreed to speak—right after the not guilty verdict was returned.

Meanwhile, on the sixth floor, Phyllis Halvorsen led the jury through a bit-by-bit, exhibit-by-exhibit review of the evidence. Halvorsen, along with Richard Chmela and Evelyn Roda, put a guilty spin on almost every tidbit.

Other jurors, principally Linda Wisniewski, Joyce Jaske, and Anna Marie Pulcini, offered possible innocent explanations of the evidence.

As the day wore on, however, the voices of reasonable doubt were stilled by an increasingly vocal and growing majority led by Halvorsen.

The majority coalesced around questions about the Dowalibys' actions on the morning of September 10.

When David found the front door ajar, why didn't he look in on Jaclyn? A guilty person, several jurors reasoned, would know she was not there.

When Jaclyn still was not up at 9:30 A.M., why didn't either parent check on her? "A kid that age doesn't sleep that late on a Saturday," one juror said.

Were the telephone calls too close together for the Dowalibys to have conducted the thorough search that they had claimed? "It almost looks like the calls were planned," another juror said.

As the discussion turned to other evidence, Chmela recalled noticing holes in some of the walls of the Dowaliby home.

"Yes, they jumped right out at you," said Halvorsen, who pulled photos of Davey's room from a stack of exhibits, noting apparent fist marks. "This was a house of great violence."

Chmela also pointed out that Davey's room locked from the outside. He speculated that this might mean either that Davey had been locked in the room as punishment or to prevent him from seeing what went on in the house late at night.

Several jurors nodded in agreement.

All of the jurors found it curious that police had found Jaclyn's room in disarray, since several witnesses had testified that it normally was neat.

A dispute arose over Jaclyn's sheets, however. Roda contended that the removal of the sheets was part of a cover-up, while Wisniewski and several other women jurors countered that there was nothing unusual about children sleeping on unmade beds. "Oh, come on," Halvorsen responded incredulously, "do you believe it was just coincidence that Jaclyn disappeared the same night that they didn't make the bed?"

Several jurors supported Halvorsen and Roda, contending that if there had been an innocent explanation for the removal of the sheets, the Dowalibys should have taken the stand to provide it. "If you're not guilty, you should say so," said one juror. Another chimed in, "If you have something to hide, then you don't take the stand."

Even Wisniewski agreed with that.

Since the jury had not heard from the Dowalibys, they were left to judge their appearance and demeanor.

"David's eyes were very shifty," said Roda. "With some of the witnesses, particularly one of the baby-sitters, his eyes got real wide. He looked petrified, like she might say something horrible was going on in the house."

Chmela said, "Cynthia started out looking foxy, but someone must have told her to try to look more normal. The handholding seemed like an act."

"She cried at all the right times," insisted Halvorsen.

Several of the other women thought the Dowalibys' behavior was understandable, however. One said that the case reminded her of *A Cry in the Dark,* a popular movie based on the true story of a woman wrongfully accused of murdering her child. Noting that the mother in the movie cried intermittently, like Cynthia, while her husband was supportive, like David, the juror mused, "What if we find him guilty and are proven wrong later, like in the movie?"

"This isn't a movie," Halvorsen said, scoffing.

Another issue regarding a possible cover-up was Everett Mann's credibility. Several jurors rejected Ralph Meczyk's contention that Mann had testified to further his law enforcement ambitions, since Mann had not sought the limelight but had been "discovered" by police. These jurors were impressed that he had offered evidence even though he was out with another woman.

Others insisted that Mann could not have seen what he claimed. One juror, referring to the night visit to the Islander Apartments, said, "I could barely make out the Dumpster."

Halvorsen asserted that she could see "at least a hundred yards in the parking lot." When a juror questioned that, Halvorsen added, "Well, I'm farsighted."

In the midafternoon, the discussion focused on whether it would have been possible for an intruder to have entered the Dowaliby home through the basement window without disturbing the towel rack or other items beneath it.

Jurors quickly rejected Perry Hernandez as a suspect, since there was no mess in the Dowaliby home comparable to the one that Hernandez had left at the MacRand home.

Halvorsen argued that the MacRand case in fact discredited the defense claim that an intruder had taken Jaclyn. "When you break into a home, you leave evidence," she said. If there had been an intruder at the Dowaliby home, Halvorsen claimed, at least the towel rack would have been dented.

To test that assertion, juror Felix LaGioia volunteered to try to climb through the prosecution mock-up of the Dowalibys' basement window—as Velcich and O'Brien had suggested. LaGioia, a wiry 5 feet, 7 inches tall and weighing 130 pounds, figured that he had the best chance of getting through the window and avoiding the towel rack.

Since the mock-up was on stilts, LaGioia placed a chair atop the jury table to simulate the ground outside the actual window. As he climbed on the chair, however, it began to wobble. "Get down from there!" one of the women shouted. "You'll get hurt!"

LaGioia moved the chair to the floor and, with considerable difficulty, wiggled through the window and dangled above the towel rack. His legs flailed as he tried to avoid crashing down on the rack until two other male jurors finally rescued him.

Chmela then decided to give it a try. He was by far the tallest juror, standing 6 feet, 2 inches and weighing almost 200 pounds. As he made it partially through the window, one of his feet struck the rack and bent it slightly, causing considerable consternation among the other jurors. He pulled himself out before causing more serious damage to the evidence.

The jurors concluded that if neither the smallest nor the largest juror could perform the feat, then it simply could not be done. The experiment was a turning point in the deliberations.

Having ruled out an intruder, the question became who killed Jaclyn: David or Cynthia? Halvorsen, believing from the fist marks on the walls that David was a violent man, argued that he had committed the murder. Four other women jurors doubted that David did it. They believed it more likely that Jaclyn had died from "overdisciplining" by Cynthia.

One juror suggested that they ask Neville to clarify the extent to which they could consider Cynthia. Others rejected that idea, however, pointing out that Neville had said that they should rely on their own judgment.

The jury adjourned for the night, agreeing to review Neville's instructions more carefully the next day.

When the jury reconvened for the third and final day, everyone agreed that it was unlikely that either David or Cynthia had killed Jaclyn without the other's help or knowledge.

Chmela outlined on a piece of paper the four remaining scenarios—that David and Cynthia together had killed Jaclyn; that Cynthia had killed Jaclyn but that David had aided in some way, such as giving Cynthia the rope to tie Jaclyn to the bed; that Cynthia had killed Jaclyn with David's knowledge, while David did nothing to stop the crime; or that David committed the murder with Cynthia's help or knowledge.

Under any of the scenarios, Chmela argued, David was guilty of murder—"Our instructions say so." Halvorsen and Roda voiced complete agreement, while some of the other women continued to question whether it would be right to convict David of first-degree murder unless the jury could be certain that he was directly responsible for Jaclyn's death.

Waving the instructions, Chmela impatiently declared, "We didn't make up the rules. Our job is to follow them."

The holdouts gradually fell silent. When there was no longer any vocal opposition, Halvorsen asked for a show of hands to see where everyone stood.

The vote was unanimous: David was guilty of murder.

Halvorsen then asked for a vote on whether he also was guilty of concealment. It was 10 to 2 for conviction, with the dissenters focusing primarily on Everett Mann's credibility.

The majority quickly won over the holdouts by reading the definition of concealment: "the performing of some act or acts for the purpose of preventing or delaying the discovery of a death by homicidal means." It was not necessary to believe that Mann saw David in order to believe that David had at very least delayed the discovery of Jaclyn's death.

After the jurors signed the verdict forms, some of them with shaky hands, Halvorsen rang a buzzer three times to inform the court personnel that a verdict had been reached.

It was 2:50 P.M.

Sitting in the cafeteria, David Dowaliby was working on a crossword puzzle and Cynthia was fidgeting with a rosary when their lawyers told them that the jury had reached a decision.

David and Cynthia walked to the courtroom, arm in arm, trying unsuccessfully to mask their trepidation with an air of confidence.

As they parted, Cynthia hugged and kissed David.

"I love you," she said.

Cynthia took her seat next to her sister Julianne in the second row on the defense side of the courtroom. Peggy O'Connor and Mary Malia, seated in the same row, held hands, as Cynthia silently prayed with her rosary.

David, sitting at the defense table with his lawyers, searched the jurors' faces for any hint of the outcome but could discern nothing. He had waited twenty months for this moment but hardly could bear waiting ten seconds more.

"Has the jury reached verdicts?" the judge asked.

"Yes, we have, your honor," replied Phyllis Halvorsen.

Halvorsen handed a stack of papers—the verdicts—to the court clerk, who passed them to the judge. Neville read them to himself, betraying nothing of their content.

As the judge handed the verdicts to the clerk to be read aloud, David's thoughts flashed to a dream he had had the night before: A locomotive thundered toward him. There were two tracks abreast. He sat on one and felt only a gust of wind as the engine roared past.

Then the dream began again. This time, though, a ghostly, deformed hand came out of a cloud. It pulled a rusty switch, and the engine splattered him across the face of eternity. He awoke trembling, breathing heavily, his sheets wet from sweat.

Now, in the courtroom, reality intruded. The clerk solemnly read the verdicts: "We, the jury, find the defendant, David Dowaliby, guilty of first-degree murder. We, the jury, find the defendant, David Dowaliby, guilty of concealment of a homicidal death."

Pandemonium erupted. "Oh, my God, no!" a woman spectator shouted. "How can this happen?" a man cried out.

David looked at Cynthia, his eyes wide, but their eyes did not meet.

"How can you do this?" Cynthia shouted at the jury. "I can't believe this. This is unbelievable."

Neville slammed his gavel to quell the outburst, but the commotion did not subside. Exasperated, he turned to the jury: "We are going to have some questions for you, but first I am asking you to go back to the jury room."

When the jury was gone, Neville appealed for silence. "We have yet to poll the jury," he said. "I cannot do that if there is a disturbance which makes it impossible for the jury to pay attention. If you are unable to control yourselves, then you should step out."

The crowd gradually fell silent, and the jurors returned.

Addressing each by name, Judge Neville asked, "Were these and are these your verdicts?"

Each answered affirmatively, although Linda Wisniewski hesitated before finally replying, "Yes, your honor."

"Judgment is entered on the first-degree murder and concealment of a homicidal death," Judge Neville said, "guilty verdicts."

Neville immediately revoked David's bond and set sentencing for June 4.

David stood frozen before the judge.

"Come this way, sir," a deputy sheriff ordered, taking David into custody.

Cynthia was allowed to remain briefly with David in a holding area near Neville's chamber where they clung to each other and sobbed.

Meanwhile, Neville took the jurors into his chamber to thank them for their service. A juror asked, "What do you think about the verdict?"

"I think it's great that you reached a verdict," Neville said. "I understand how difficult your job was, and now I think maybe you understand what I do every day."

"We won't be talking about judges being overpaid," one juror quipped.

David and Cynthia, their lives shattered, heard the judge and jurors burst into laughter.

Before leaving the courthouse for the last time, the jury met separately with the prosecutors and defense lawyers.

The jurors wanted to know from the prosecutors what facts had been kept from them during the trial.

George Velcich told them that David had been convicted of two drug offenses and that a triple-beam scale had been found in a search of the Dowaliby home.

"We figured something like that," said Richard Chmela.

Velcich told the jurors that it was up to them whether to make public statements about the case, but emphasized that "you don't have to talk to the media or anybody else."

The jurors agreed among themselves that they would not comment to reporters.

In their meeting with defense lawyers, the jurors indicated that there had been no decisive piece of evidence in the trial.

Lawrence Hyman asked if the jury would have convicted Cynthia as well as David.

The answer was yes.

Television stations interrupted their regular programming for live reports on the verdict.

Paul Hogan called the outcome "a stunning upset victory for the prosecution—in effect a split decision that finds David Dowaliby guilty, but one in which the judge said there wasn't enough evidence to allow Cynthia's case to go to the jury."

When the verdict was announced, said Hogan, "David stared at Cynthia in horror."

Dick Johnson, standing a few feet away, characterized that same stare as "a look of anger."

While Hogan and Johnson were still on live, the prosecutors appeared for an impromptu news conference.

"The jury's verdict is an enormous victory for Jaclyn Dowaliby and all of the children like Jaclyn who have only the system to protect them," declared Patrick O'Brien.

Hogan asked O'Brien, "How can you have one parent guilty and one not guilty?"

"As Judge Neville indicated by his decision, there was less evidence against Cynthia Dowaliby," O'Brien responded. "It doesn't mean she's innocent."

"Does it bother you that Cynthia Dowaliby walked out of this courtroom a free woman?" Hogan persisted.

"Certainly it bothers us that she is going home," O'Brien said, "but if Jaclyn can't have full justice, at least there's a measure of justice for her."

Ralph Meczyk and Lawrence Hyman trudged into the lobby a little later.

Asked about O'Brien's contention that Cynthia was guilty despite her acquittal, Hyman retorted, "I don't think there should be any question as to Cynthia Dowaliby's innocence."

Meczyk, near tears, choking on his words, told reporters,

"When someone is charged with a crime as heinous as killing their child, reasonable doubt goes right out the window."

Later, Meczyk lamented the defense decision not to exercise peremptory challenges against Phyllis Halvorsen and Richard Chmela during jury selection.

Referring to Halvorsen, Meczyk said, "Clarence Darrow used to say that you can't trust church people on a jury. We obviously should have followed that advice."

Without Halvorsen and Chmela, Meczyk added, the verdict might have been different.

With them, he said, "It was the jury from Hell."

Sheriff's deputies led Cynthia out of the courthouse through a back door, literally lifting her off the ground as they fled pursuing reporters.

As she climbed into a waiting car, a reporter shouted, "Do you think you got a fair trial?"

Cynthia was too numb to answer, but Ann Dowaliby angrily responded: "Absolutely they did not get a fair trial. It was biased because of the media. The prosecutors did their job and you did yours—to put out false information, to print lies without facts."

After the car sped off, reporters quickly reassembled in front of the courthouse, just in time to catch the jury's exit.

"We're tired," said Phyllis Halvorsen. "We're just too tired to talk."

Reporters quickly gathered other reactions.

Ronald Patterson, David's boss, said, "I can't believe what I heard today. I'm just distraught, and I can't believe it. I will stick with Dave just as long as it takes."

That sentiment was echoed by other Dowaliby supporters, including their former next-door neighbor Robert Tolbert.

State's Attorney Cecil Partee said that "the evidence as we saw it indicated that both of them should have been found guilty," but the jury verdict showed that "the system works."

At City Hall, Mayor Richard Daley told reporters, "I would like to compliment the fine prosecutors, Pat O'Brien and the others. The investigators did a very thorough job. A lot of people doubted the investigation and doubted the indictment, but those professional trial lawyers did an outstanding job."

Dick Johnson obtained an exclusive interview with Daniel McDevitt. Johnson asked McDevitt to comment on a report from an unnamed source that jurors had attempted to crawl through the mock-up of the basement window.

"You can't do it," said McDevitt. "You can't get through it unless you're somehow able to levitate. You can't get through that window without leaving a trace."

On camera, Johnson asked McDevitt to respond to Ann Dowaliby's charge that the investigation and trial were unfair.

McDevitt held up Jaclyn's photo, looked directly into the camera, and told Johnson, "That this beautiful seven-year-old girl is dead, that's unfair."

At 5:00 P.M., Ralph Meczyk called the bedridden John Waters, who already had heard the verdict on television.

Meczyk told him that the jury would have convicted Cynthia, too.

In an unsteady hand, Waters wrote a single word on his notepad: "unbelievable."

SILENCES BROKEN

The day after the verdict, Phyllis Halvorsen, the jury foreperson, broke her promise of silence, granting an exclusive interview to the *Chicago Tribune.*

"In a surprise disclosure, Halvorsen said photos of the interior of Dowaliby's house revealed signs of what she called 'great violence,' " Matt O'Connor wrote in the May 4 *Tribune.* Fist marks through doors and dry walls "jumped out at you" in the photos, Halvorsen was quoted as saying.

"Prosecutors had never pointed out the damage," said the story, "but the inference the jury apparently drew was that only a hotheaded father could have done that kind of damage, a father with the kind of temper that could result in a killing."

Halvorsen told O'Connor that the jury had become convinced that there had been no intruder when jurors were unable to climb through the mock-up of the basement window without disturbing the items beneath it. She also said that the jury credited Everett Mann's testimony because, as a married man out with another woman, he had "a lot to lose" by coming forward.

The jury, said Halvorsen, had been unmoved by Cynthia Dowaliby's tearful outbursts during the trial—"Her crying was at all of the right moments.

"I think we probably would have convicted her."

On Sunday, May 6, Cynthia Dowaliby, clutching a photograph of Jaclyn and David in a heart-shaped frame, faced reporters en masse for the first time, appearing at a press conference in Ralph Meczyk and Lawrence Hyman's office in the Loop.

With the lawyers at her side, Cynthia proclaimed in a steady voice, thick with emotion, "My husband and I are innocent. We would never harm our daughter. We're very loving parents."

Looking squarely at television cameras, she said, "Someone out there knows something. We beg them to come forward. It's time to come forward."

Channel 7's Dick Johnson touched off a biting exchange by asking why she and David had decided to stop cooperating with police.

"We never decided that, Mr. Johnson," Cynthia snapped. "When I found out my daughter was dead, I collapsed and other family members and then our lawyers took over."

Johnson asked her to respond to Phyllis Halvorsen's statement that, as he paraphrased it, "Jurors thought your sobbing was staged."

"They weren't sitting in my seat," Cynthia said. "They weren't talking about their child."

Asked by another reporter about the fist marks that the jurors had noticed, Cynthia said they were many years old and had not been repaired because the family could not afford it.

Channel 5's Paul Hogan asked about David.

"He's numb," Cynthia said. "His heart has been ripped out. There's been a great injustice here, but we're going to fight for him, for our family. We'll never stop, and he knows that."

Friends and family members packed Hope Christian Reformed Church in Oak Forest on Saturday, May 12, for a prayer service for David Dowaliby.

Standing in front of a banner proclaiming, "Dave and Cyndi, we all love both of you! We have always believed in you," Mary Malia took the microphone.

"I am Jaclyn's grandmother," she said. "God sent us a rosebud on May 17, 1981. She flowered into a beautiful little girl. In September 1988, she was robbed of life and every ounce of dignity by the most heinous, despicable person on the face of this earth.

"I demand the case be reopened. Jaclyn's horrible death must not go unavenged. Someone knows what happened to her, and I pray for them to come forward. And I pray to Jaclyn, our little saint in Heaven, to comfort us during this time. It's been twenty months since her death, and we have had no time to mourn."

After the service, a group of the Dowalibys' supporters, several of whom had not known them before Jaclyn disappeared, gathered to form a "Freedom Committee."

Led by Peggy O'Connor, the members decided to meet weekly to work for David's release and provide emotional support to Cynthia. They started a newsletter, ordered red T-shirts bearing the slogan "Stop Injustice—Free David Dowaliby," and made red and white macramé bracelets, vowing to wear them until David was freed.

Committee member Trisha Rickard's family posted a $10,000 reward "for information leading to the arrest and conviction of Jaclyn Dowaliby's killer."

Handmade "Free Dave" signs began to appear in the windows of homes and cars in Midlothian—to the dismay of the police, who put the Freedom Committee under surveillance.

At Northwestern University's Medill School of Journalism on May 15, Cynthia Dowaliby and Ralph Meczyk joined an off-the-record panel discussion on media coverage of high-profile cases.

David Protess, a professor at Medill, had invited them eleven days earlier, after hearing Ann Dowaliby on the radio blaming journalists for the jury verdict.

The discussion, which had been planned for several weeks, also featured Sandra Fabiano, the south suburban nursery school operator recently cleared of child sex abuse, and Melanie Kosar, a futures trader accused of fraud in a high-profile FBI sting investigation. Protess had publicly criticized the media's role in the Fabiano and Kosar cases*—a factor that weighed in Meczyk and Cynthia's decision to join the discussion.

In anticipation of Cynthia's appearance, more than seventy Medill students and faculty members jammed a seminar room designed to hold forty.

Meczyk began by giving an example of the danger of talking to the news media. He said that a prospective prosecution witness, an entomologist who had analyzed the maggots on Jaclyn's body, had destroyed his credibility before the trial by talking on the radio about faking evidence.

"Sorry, Cyndi," said Meczyk, interrupting his description of how maggots devour a cadaver. Panelist Sandra Fabiano shook her head, watching Cynthia struggle to maintain her composure until Protess finally cut off Meczyk's gruesome soliloquy.

Cynthia then responded to questions in a soft voice, which was easily heard in the dead silence of the room. Tears streamed down faces in the audience as she told of her shattered life, the pain of losing one child and the separation

---

* As a *Chicago Lawyer* contributing editor, Protess had helped prepare an article on the Fabiano case ("Witch Hunt," October 1988). He had received a Peter Lisagor Award for Exemplary Journalism from the Society of Professional Journalists for three articles on the commodities fraud investigation; "Commodities Investigation—The Story Behind the Story," *Chicago Lawyer* (March 1989); "In the Pits," *Chicago Lawyer* (May 1989); "Did the Press Play Prosecutor in an FBI Sting Investigation?" *Columbia Journalism Review* (July–August 1989).

from her husband and her other children, of being destitute, and of losing her home.

She said that it had been frustrating to pass television cameras each day during the trial, constrained from speaking on the advice of counsel, and then to watch reports that made her appear guilty.

"Was any reporter fair to you?" a student asked.

"Paul Hogan," she said in unison with Sandra Fabiano.

After the discussion, Cynthia and Fabiano went into Protess's office. When Protess joined them, he found Fabiano maternally embracing Cynthia, who was in tears. Inviting them to sit down, Protess asked Fabiano if she could offer Cynthia advice on what to do next.

"If you don't have full confidence in your lawyer, find another one," Fabiano said. "This is your life and your husband's that you're fighting for now."

David Protess sat at his desk, emotionally drained from the discussion and the poignant scene in his office.

Protess had followed news coverage of the case since Jaclyn's disappearance and—based on reports that "eyewitnesses" had placed David Dowaliby at the Islander Apartments—had assumed the Dowalibys guilty before the trial.

During the trial, as the eyewitnesses evaporated and the news coverage suggested that the remaining evidence was weak, Protess had assumed that Cynthia and David would be acquitted. When the guilty verdict was returned against David, Protess was surprised, but thought perhaps there had been evidence that the news media had failed to report.

As soon as Cynthia left Northwestern, Protess called Paul Hogan to ask his view of the case and to let him know that Cynthia and Sandra Fabiano had paid him a compliment. Protess had worked with Hogan on various investigative projects and respected his judgment.

"The prosecution's case was as shaky as it looked," Hogan told Protess. "We reported all of the damaging evidence."

Hogan added, however, that he had not made a judgment about the Dowalibys' guilt or innocence. "I don't know what happened in that house," he said, "but I'd sure like to find out."

Hogan said he had been trying to persuade the defense lawyers to release their files on the case and to make David Dowaliby available for an interview, but they had refused.

"I don't know if they're hiding something, or if they just don't know what's in their clients' best interest," Hogan said, "but if the Dowalibys are innocent, now's the time to let it all hang out."

Protess told Hogan that he planned to send Cynthia a thank-you note and might say in it that he was interested in writing about the case for a newspaper or magazine. If Hogan approved, Protess would add that Hogan wanted to interview David on camera.

Hogan enthusiastically agreed.

It was the beginning of a long partnership.

Cynthia Dowaliby received David Protess's letter on Saturday, May 19, and promptly called him at his home.

Protess, who could tell from her tone that she was depressed, asked, "Are you okay?"

She said the days since the panel discussion had been rough. John Waters had lapsed into a coma after his long bout with cancer. On Thursday, Jaclyn would have turned nine years old. On Friday, Cynthia had seen David for the first time since the verdict more than two weeks earlier, but the visit had lasted only fifteen minutes and they had not been allowed to touch.

David now was in maximum-security isolation at the Cook County Jail, where he had been moved after ten days under routine psychiatric observation in the jail hospital. He had been permitted neither reading material nor television and, because of overcrowding, he had to sleep on the floor.

After the visit, Cynthia said, she had sat in the car for several minutes, "feeling like a widow." Sitting there, she contemplated how their lives had come to this and realized that their public silence had been "a terrible mistake."

She and David were in a quandary about what to do now; they had been "burned" by the media and were worried that if they spoke out, journalists simply would seek a response from prosecutors and the mudslinging would continue.

They thought Paul Hogan might treat them fairly, but at the moment they had a more pressing problem than public relations—they had to decide who would handle the appeal.

Ralph Meczyk had recommended two lawyers, Cynthia Giachetti and Mary Ellen Dienes.

"My wife's a lawyer," said Protess. "I could ask her to check them out if you like."

Cynthia said she would appreciate that, and they agreed to speak again the following week.

When the conversation ended, Protess told his wife, Joan, "I think the Dowalibys have an incredible story, and I want to tell it. How would you like to help them out on the legal end?"

"I know just the person to call," said Joan. "Bob Byman."

Robert L. Byman, a partner at Jenner & Block, one of Chicago's largest law firms, was primarily a corporate lawyer, but also knew his way around the criminal courts. He had handled two murder cases—one successfully against Patrick O'Brien.

Joan Protess and Byman had been on opposite sides of a civil case, and she had been impressed by his legal acumen; she hoped that he would take the case, or at least provide a reliable assessment of the kind of help that David Dowaliby needed.

Byman knew Cynthia Giachetti by reputation, which he said was excellent, but was unfamiliar with Mary Ellen Dienes. He offered to "check around," adding that there was a possibility that Jenner & Block would handle David's appeal *pro bono*—in other words, without charge.

Joan Protess thought that was an exciting possibility. Jenner & Block's *pro bono* program recently had been rated tops in Chicago by *American Lawyer* magazine. Equally important, she thought, Byman had a caring attitude and a gentle demeanor that would be helpful in guiding the Dowalibys.

Joan immediately related her conversation with Byman to

her husband, who was at Channel 5, talking with Paul Hogan about how to advance the Dowaliby story.

As it turned out, Hogan and David Protess had just been on the telephone with Lawrence Hyman, whom they found uncooperative.

"Look, you work for a wealthy media company," Hyman had told Hogan. "How much do you think it would be worth?"

"We don't pay for stories," Hogan replied.

When Protess had said that he was interested in free-lancing an article about the case, Hyman snidely replied, "How much could you get for something like that?"

"Not much," said Protess, "but it could help your clients."

After they got off the phone, Hogan told Protess, "If we're going to do this story, we've got to get past Larry and Ralph."

"With Jenner & Block in the picture," said Protess, "maybe we won't need them."

Lawrence Hyman warned Cynthia Dowaliby to stay away from Paul Hogan and David Protess, telling her, "They don't care about you. They don't care about Jaclyn. They just want a story."

Cynthia nonetheless continued to talk on the telephone with Protess. Each conversation was longer than the preceding one, and Protess grew increasingly interested in her story.

However, she insisted that everything she said was "off the record." She fretted that publicity might adversely affect her husband's sentencing, which Judge Neville had postponed until July 9, and harm the slim chance that he might overturn the jury verdict before sentencing.

"All the more reason that you should speak out now," Protess responded. "After July ninth, it might be too late."

Cynthia, however, would not budge.

On May 23, Hogan and Protess decided that they might have better luck confronting Cynthia face to face.

Hogan tried to call Cynthia at home, planning to go there, but learned from her mother that she was at her lawyer's office. Protess proposed intercepting her as she left the office.

"You mean kidnap her?" said Hogan. "Let's do it."

They jumped into Hogan's car and raced to Meczyk and Hyman's office, parking illegally across the street beside City Hall. When Cynthia had not appeared half an hour later, Hogan impatiently called her mother on his car phone and learned that she had "just left" to go to a nearby bank.

"They must have gone out the side door," Protess said.

The bank was the wrong way down a one-way street, so Protess ran there. He caught Cynthia and her sister Julianne just as they were leaving. "This isn't a coincidence," he said. "Hogan's with me, and we need to talk."

Protess veritably shoved the women into Hogan's backseat, and they went to a cocktail lounge a few blocks away.

Over drinks, Protess and Hogan made their pitch. Protess wanted a personal account of the case from the Dowalibys and those who knew them, while Hogan wanted an exclusive, on-camera interview with David Dowaliby.

"Larry's holding your story hostage for money," Hogan told her.

Cynthia was furious that Hyman wanted money for the story, but she remained concerned that speaking out might lead to a new attack by the prosecutors.

"If David grants the interview, I won't talk to the prosecutors," Hogan assured her. "They've already had their say." Protess added that he was interested in writing "the untold story" of the case, not in having the lawyers on either side rehash the evidence.

Cynthia was interested, but remained skeptical of Protess and Hogan's motives.

In the hope of demonstrating that his interest transcended the story, Protess excused himself, called Robert Byman from a pay telephone, and asked if he had given further thought to representing David Dowaliby.

If the Dowalibys wanted him to, Byman said, he would ask Jenner & Block's Pro Bono Committee to authorize him to take the case, but added, apologetically, "It might take some time to jump through the bureaucratic hoops."

"I'm with Cynthia Dowaliby right now, and I'll suggest that she call you," said Protess.

He returned to the table and told Cynthia what Byman had said. Cynthia had never heard of Jenner & Block, but she knew what *pro bono* meant. Grateful, she promised to talk to her husband both about Byman and about telling their story.

Hogan and Protess dropped them off in the Loop, assuming that they would go home. Cynthia, however, had a different plan.

She stormed into Meczyk and Hyman's office and chastised them for telling her to stay away from Hogan and Protess.

"You were wrong to keep these guys from us," she declared. "You were wrong about a lot of things."

Cynthia Dowaliby called David Protess on Sunday, May 27, and said that she had decided to talk to him on the record. After the resulting article appeared, she said, David would decide whether to grant an interview to him and Paul Hogan.

Cynthia and Protess scheduled their interview for later that week. In the meantime, Protess realized that he needed a coauthor with knowledge of the trial. Since Hogan's contract with Channel 5 prevented him from working for another medium, Protess turned to one of his former students, Mary Ann Williams, who had covered the trial for *New City*, a Chicago weekly newspaper.

Williams enthusiastically agreed to work with Protess, saying that the Dowalibys' story had not come out at the trial, partly because they had not testified and partly because Ralph Meczyk had done a "horrible job" in the courtroom.

Protess and Williams agreed that the best outlet for their story would be the *Chicago Tribune* because of its prestige and circulation of more than seven hundred thousand.

Protess, however, had a problem at the *Tribune*. During the past year, he had blasted its coverage of an FBI probe of the futures industry, accusing the newspaper of unfair and inaccurate reporting. At one point the *Tribune*'s financial editor had tried to get the dean of Medill to silence Protess, only to discover that he had tenure.

Hoping that he was not persona non grata everywhere at the *Tribune*, Protess called Charles Leroux, editor of its features section, Tempo. Leroux assured Protess that his "baggage" would never get in the way of an important story at the *Tribune* and asked how soon he and Williams could deliver copy.

"Give us ten days," said Protess.

"Terrific," said Leroux, "but don't try to go much beyond her personal account. This is a feature story, not an investigative piece." He added that the *Tribune* would pay $450 for the article.

To prepare for their interview with Cynthia, Protess and Williams spoke with the Dowalibys' relatives, former neighbors, David's employer, Jaclyn's teachers, and various trial witnesses. Virtually all expressed faith in the Dowalibys' innocence.

Protess and Williams were particularly struck that two neighbors reported trusting Cynthia so much that they regularly had asked her to baby-sit—after Jaclyn's murder.

Teachers described Jaclyn as "well cared for" and "lovely." Without exception, neighbors said that the Dowalibys never so much as yelled at the kids. "If there was a problem with their parenting," said one, "it was that they were too nonchalant."

Ronald Patterson, David's boss, described him as reliable and even-tempered. "I'm holding his job open for him," said Patterson.

On May 31, Cynthia appeared for her interview in a conference room at Medill. She brought an album of family photographs—David with Jaclyn at a Brownie Valentine's Day dance, David with Jaclyn on a fishing trip, David with Jaclyn accepting a trophy at a father-child bowling tournament, and David with his arm around Jaclyn in the last family portrait before she disappeared.

Cynthia described her hysteria during the days that Jaclyn was missing, how David had held her together after Jaclyn's body was found, her dreams about Jaclyn, and her horror at Davey being taken from her. She mentioned that she had sought counseling through a support group for parents of murdered children, only to be told, in so many words, that the group was not for parents who had murdered their children.

The interview lasted three hours and, at the end, Cynthia said with a sigh, "I've held this inside for two years, and now I feel like I'm ready to burst."

Moved by Cynthia's obvious emotional pain, Protess and Williams embraced her as they parted.

They had all they needed for their *Tribune* article, but sensed that there was a bigger story to tell.

When Protess and Williams presented their story to the *Tribune,* it ran more than ten thousand words. The editors decided to break it into two parts, playing both on the front page of Tempo.

The first part, covering events from Cynthia and David's romance through their arrest, appeared on Sunday, June 10. It was accompanied by an eight-column color photo of Cynthia by J. Carl Ganter, a Medill student. "Cynthia Dowaliby's story," said the headline, although more than a score of sources were quoted.

The second part, published on June 11, covered the period from the arrest to the present. Its headline proclaimed, "Having Her Say: When Her Daughter Was Slain, Cynthia Dowaliby's Ordeal Had Just Begun."

An editor's note, which preceded each installment, began: "Cynthia Dowaliby is in an unimaginable situation. A jury has decided that her husband, whom she loves and supports, killed her daughter. A judge has acquitted her of the same murder charges. Nonetheless, she faces a lingering public suspicion that she somehow was involved in the death.

"Instructed by her attorneys not to testify in court or to speak in detail to the press, she now tells her side of the story.

"The most unfathomable tragedy of all, of course, would be if neither he nor she had done anything wrong. That, she says, is precisely the case."

Out of concern that the article was too favorable to the Dowalibys, the editor's note concluded with a caveat: "What follows is not an attempt to deal comprehensively with the evidence presented by both sides in this case. It is simply Cynthia Dowaliby's story."

The morning that the second part of the *Tribune* series appeared, Paul Hogan called David Protess.

"Are you ready for this?" Hogan asked. "Somebody's leaking the Mount Sinai Hospital records on Davey."

"Who's doing it?" Protess inquired.

"I'm not sure," said Hogan, "but he called before he sent them, and he clearly was a cop."

"Are you going with it?"

"No way. The documents are incomplete, and they're the medical records of a juvenile. There's some damaging stuff in there, though—a chart claiming that Davey was covered with bruises when they brought him to Mount Sinai."

"Shit."

"I'm going to try to talk to the Dowalibys' lawyers about it, but you can put it in the bank that somebody's going with this story."

Dick Johnson was out of town, but Channel 7 led that evening's early newscast with an "exclusive" story by reporter Chuck Goudie about the leaked hospital report.

As the chart flashed on the screen, Goudie told viewers, "This medical chart, obtained for the first time by Eyewitness News, shows seventeen suspected abuse marks. The principal diagnosis by Dr. Sharon Ahart: physical abuse of Davey by Cynthia; the secondary diagnosis: possible sexual abuse."

Cynthia Dowaliby and her lawyer in the juvenile case, Janet Trafelet, struck back swiftly.

At a press conference the afternoon after Chuck Goudie's report, they released more than two dozen Chicago Police Department photographs, showing Davey Dowaliby's naked body from every angle.

The photographs had been taken without Dr. Sharon Ahart's knowledge just hours after she examined Davey. They showed that most of the marks identified by Ahart did not exist and that the others had been significantly exaggerated—the product of prejudice instilled by police briefings of the Mount Sinai staff, Trafelet charged.

Channel 5 broadcast a live report from Trafelet's office by Paul Hogan, who said that the photographs revealed that Davey had nothing more than "the kind of marks that kids get" and characterized the leaking of the Mount Sinai report as "illegal."

Hogan's report included a tearful retort from Cynthia. "This," she said, "is the kind of stuff we've put up with from the beginning—the worst nightmare parents can be put through."

Undeterred, Goudie seized on the press conference as an opportunity to rehash the hospital report, which he said "documents" the abuse marks.

A Channel 7 video bite from the press conference showed him indignantly asking Trafelet, "How do you explain those photos in light of the hospital documents that show a doctor-prepared report indicating bruises, wounds, et cetera?"

"The photographs speak for themselves," said Trafelet.

Later, when questioned by *Sun-Times* TV/radio reporter Robert Feder, Goudie acknowledged, "I was merely the conduit for putting the information on the air." He claimed that his reports were justified by his concern for "the future that that kid has."

"That's how Goudie tried to explain away the dippy decision by his station," wrote *Sun-Times* columnist Dennis Byrne, who blasted Goudie for "conduit ethics" and "an automaton-like approach to his trade."

David Dowaliby, now on the offensive and increasingly confident of David Protess and Paul Hogan, agreed to his first interview.

Ralph Meczyk insisted on being present, even though the Dowalibys had decided that he would play only a bit part in the remaining legal proceedings. With Jenner & Block undecided about taking the case, the Dowalibys had asked Daniel Franks to argue posttrial motions and assist Mary Ellen Dienes in handling the appeal.

For Meczyk, the forthcoming media exclusive would be a

last quest for glory. He responded by cutting Franks and Dienes out of the interview—by not telling them about it.

The interview was conducted by Hogan, cameraman Hal Bernstein, Protess, Mary Ann Williams, and photographer J. Carl Ganter, on June 27. The location was the room that once housed the electric chair at Cook County Jail.* To get there, the journalistic entourage took the last walk of the condemned, passing a sign inspired by *The Wizard of Oz:* "You're not in Kansas anymore."

The journalists hoped that their subject would be unaware of the history of the setting. After warmly greeting them, however, David asked, "Know what used to be in this room?" Pointing to the chair in which he would sit for the interview, he added, "With my luck, it was probably right on that spot."

Despite his good humor, David looked gaunt and pale, having lost twenty pounds since the trial and having steadfastly shunned the sunlight of the jailyard. "I won't go outside until I'm really free," he said.

Meczyk had tried to set up rules for the interview, but his client summarily brushed them aside. "There's nothing I don't want to answer," said David.

The interview lasted more than two hours. "The only thing I did wrong was that I didn't wake up and save my daughter," David said. "My daughter would expect me to be her hero and to save her, but I couldn't save her. I wish to God I woke up that night, but I didn't. I'm guilty of that. If that's why I was here, I could accept it."

He cried at several points as he spoke of Jaclyn, whom he described as "sweet" and "beautiful."

"Whoever did this to her was an animal," he said.

He spent a good deal of time explaining his alleged inconsistent statements and why he had not testified at the trial. Despite repeated interruptions by Meczyk, he talked about his personal use of marijuana, acknowledging that he

---

* Last used in 1962, when James Dukes was executed for the murder of two police officers. Illinois now uses lethal injection.

smoked it at poker games and parties and occasionally sold small quantities to fellow workers.

"I'm not a drug dealer," he said. "I'm a normal parent. I had a wife and children, and to me, they were the most important things in my life."

He attacked Everett Mann's credibility, saying, "At 2:00 A.M., it's pretty dark, and seventy-five yards is a long way. I don't know if he has bionic eyes or what."

Because of "law enforcement leaks to the media," he said, he and his wife were "guilty until proven innocent." He added, "Because the other side was talking and we weren't, they were getting across a lot of evidence that they couldn't back up in court. We weren't coming back in our defense, so the public felt we must be guilty."

He displayed no animosity toward the jury. "Those jurors are just human beings," he said. "I'm not about to blame them for everything that has happened to us. If I did, they would have to be all the way down on a long list."

He said he was thankful that Judge Neville "had stuck his neck out" to acquit Cynthia. "I couldn't be happier that my wife is home," he said. "If I had to make a choice between me and her, I would choose to sit here. I don't know if I could survive, knowing that she was in jail."

Asked about the future, he said with a sigh, "I have to face up to the possibility that I could be in jail for the rest of my life. It's very hard to accept, but it's not the worst thing that ever happened to me. What happened to my daughter was the worst."

After the interview, Protess lingered for a few minutes before David was escorted back to his cell.

"I believe you're innocent," Protess said. "My remaining doubts are gone, and I'll do everything I can to get you out. That's a promise."

MILESTONES

At almost the exact moment that David Protess made his promise to help clear David Dowaliby, John Waters died.

The June 29 *Tribune* carried an obituary headlined, "John Waters, former detective and police academy instructor."

It quoted his daughter Julie as saying, "He was tough but really nice. He kept in contact with many people after he arrested them and they went to prison. He felt many of them had just fallen on hard times. They often came back and thanked him."

The family chose not to mention Waters's role in the Dowaliby case, out of fear that the police hierarchy might retaliate in some way.

At Waters's wake, Cynthia Dowaliby joined scores of police officials to pay their last respects.

"I think I know how you feel," Cynthia told Charlotte Waters.

They embraced.

"I know you do," the widow said softly.

Meanwhile, David Protess wrote to the twelve jurors, telling them that David Dowaliby had broken his silence. He asked them to watch for *Tribune* and Channel 5 coverage of the interview, adding that he would contact them for reactions.

Protess and Mary Ann Williams's article was headlined, "Dowaliby: I Didn't Kill Jaclyn—'I Wish to God I Woke Up That Night, but I Didn't.' " It ran eighteen hundred words, beginning at the top of the *Tribune*'s local news section. Channel 5 found the interview sufficiently compelling to carry it as a three-part series, which included home video of Jaclyn somersaulting in front of her house and splashing in a backyard pool with Davey.

On the July 4 weekend, after the stories appeared, Protess drove across Cook County, visiting the home of each juror. Some slammed doors in his face, while others talked freely about the jury deliberations, explaining why they believed that the Dowalibys—both of them—were guilty.

At the twelfth home, however, Protess heard a different story. "I haven't slept a night since the trial," juror Linda Wisniewski said. Although she would not say whether she thought the verdict was right or wrong, she confided that she was uncomfortable about the way the jury had arrived at its decision. "Anyone who raised doubts was shouted down by Phyllis Halvorsen and her supporters," she said.

Referring to defense motions to overturn the verdict, scheduled to be heard the next week, Wisniewski added, "I think Judge Neville is a really fair man. Let's wait and see what he does." She agreed to speak with Protess again after the motions were decided.

"This trial was based on unfair inferences and half-truths," Daniel Franks told Judge Neville in open court on Monday, July 9. "The facts and the truth were lost."

Analogizing the prejudice against the Dowalibys to "racism, sexism, fascism, and McCarthyism," Franks argued that Neville should acquit David Dowaliby notwithstanding the jury verdict.

Behind Franks in the courtroom sat women of the Dowaliby family and the Freedom Committee dressed in bright red and white to symbolize, they had proclaimed to the press, "courage and innocence."

Journalists filled the jury box, directly facing Ralph Meczyk and David Dowaliby at the defense table.

David wore a baggy gray suit, his weight loss creating an illusion that his clothes had grown since the trial.

In contrast, Neville looked fit and tan, having recently returned from scaling the highest peak in Europe, Mount Elbrus in Soviet Georgia.

Franks spoke for more than an hour, dissecting the prosecution evidence bit by bit, insisting that it fell far short of proof beyond a reasonable doubt.

At the conclusion, his voice rising in the otherwise still courtroom, he said, "Your honor, I'm asking you to do something that's more challenging than climbing a mountain. It's not a physical challenge, it's a challenge of leadership and intellectual honesty.

"If you look at this case, stripped of the unreasonable inferences and conjecture by the state, I don't think you can say the words 'David Dowaliby is guilty of murder.' Judge, in the name of justice, I'm telling you this: He is innocent."

Patrick O'Brien offered the briefest of rebuttals. Scoffing at Franks's rhetoric, he said, "Sometimes attorneys in their egos believe that arguments decide cases." Since Neville had found that the evidence was sufficient to submit to the jury, O'Brien said, it would be inconsistent to hold differently now.

Neville, while crediting Franks for articulating his argument "superbly," promptly agreed with O'Brien. Noting that the defense had demanded a jury trial, he said, "I don't think it's appropriate for me to second-guess twelve people."

After a break for lunch, just before Franks was to present a motion for a new trial based on procedural grounds, Ralph

Meczyk called a surprise witness to the stand—Kathy Farley, a south suburban resident who had contacted Meczyk after reading David Protess and Mary Ann Williams's *Tribune* articles.

On direct examination, Farley testified that on September 10, 1988, two Hispanic men in a car asked her for directions while she was jogging near Blue Island. She said that she noticed a "fuzzy white blanket" covering something in their backseat. Later that day, after hearing that a little girl with a blanket was missing, "I started thinking that it could have been her under the blanket," she said.

Farley said that she considered reporting the incident at the time but had been reluctant to get involved. When she heard sometime later that a witness had reported seeing David Dowaliby at the Islander Apartments, she assumed that Dowaliby was guilty and that her observation had been unrelated to the crime.

She testified that Meczyk had shown her "several photographs of different suspects" and that she believed that one of those might have been the passenger in the car. It was a photo of Perry Hernandez. Farley acknowledged that her identification was uncertain, "a five on a scale of one to ten."

Meczyk also had shown her a photo of Jaclyn's bedspread, she added, but she was "not sure" whether it was the one she had seen.

In a dramatic gesture, Meczyk took Jaclyn's Lady Lovely Locks bedspread from an evidence bag and unfurled it onto the courtroom floor in front of Farley.

"Is there any difference between this blanket and the blanket that you saw?" Meczyk asked.

"There was no pattern on the one I saw," said Farley.

"Anything about the texture?"

"The one I saw was more fuzzy."

Farley was excused after a brief cross-examination, and Neville called a recess during which Cynthia Dowaliby told Daniel Franks that the reverse side of Jaclyn's bedspread matched the witness's description.

Meczyk had shown Farley the wrong side.

When court reconvened, as part of his motion for a new

trial, Franks presented a hastily prepared affidavit from Cynthia noting that "the other side of the bedspread is white and fuzzy from wear and repeated washings."

"Well, I wasn't in control of how the witness saw it or why it was shown to her in any special way," said Neville, ruling that Farley's testimony was insufficient to justify a new trial.

"Ralph fucks up again!" Paul Hogan wrote in a note that he passed to Protess.

For the next two hours, Franks detailed thirty-three alleged trial errors, including the accountability instructions, the admission of the gruesome photographs of Jaclyn's body, the exclusion of evidence of similar crimes, and the psychiatric testimony pertaining to Everett Mann.

Neville complimented Franks for his "extensive" and "well-done" motion but unhesitatingly denied it.

"I don't believe there is evidence which was improperly presented, or new evidence which had been brought forward, which would make it appropriate for me to grant a new trial," he said. "Sentencing is set for ten-thirty tomorrow morning."

Police, FBI agents, and a contingent of Patrick O'Brien and George Velcich's colleagues from the state's attorney's office appeared in Judge Neville's courtroom the next morning.

Before sentencing, there was a brief hearing on aggravating and mitigating circumstances that might affect the length of the sentence.

Three witnesses were called by each side.

O'Brien's first two witnesses testified that David Dowaliby had sold them marijuana.

On cross-examination, Ralph Meczyk elicited that the quantities David had sold were tiny and that he had made no profit.

The third prosecution witness was the officer who had found the triple-beam scale in the Dowalibys' bedroom.

Meczyk got the officer to acknowledge that the scale was found in a closet, that there was no drug residue on it, and that no drugs were found in the Dowaliby home.

The first defense witness was Ronald Patterson, David's

employer, whom Meczyk instructed, "Tell us in one word what David's most outstanding quality to you was."

"Trustworthy," said Patterson.

Deborah Spears, a Dowaliby baby-sitter now living in South Carolina, testified, "Jaclyn would tell me the smallest things."

"Would she tattletale on her brother?" Meczyk asked.

"Yes," Spears answered.

"Did she ever tattletale on her daddy or mommy?"

"She only expressed love. She told me how beautiful her mommy was and how nice her daddy was."

The final witness was Jaclyn's maternal grandmother, Mary Malia, who was asked by Meczyk, "Did David ever have any terms of endearment towards his daughter?"

"All the time," she answered. "He held her. He would read to her. He would play with her. He was and is a good father."

"Mary—"

"Ralph," she interrupted, "who would want this murderer apprehended more than me? Would I sit here today if I felt that she met with harm in that house? Jaclyn was murdered, and somebody out there knows something. Please don't carry that guilt with you. Let the world know what happened."

She swung around in the witness chair and, looking Neville directly in the eye, said, "David belongs with us, belongs with his children and his wife. There's a life to go on and it just is destroyed at this point."

"Do you want to say anything else, Mary?" Meczyk asked.

"No," she said.

When she left the stand, George Velcich asked Neville to impose "a substantial sentence."

"Yesterday his lawyer claimed that this trial was something like the McCarthy era or fascism," said Velcich. "This case isn't about the McCarthy era, judge, and it isn't about Nazi Germany. To trivialize those events is a mockery of this court."

Waving Protess and Williams's *Tribune* article, Velcich continued, "I have an article here that shows the kind of person

David Dowaliby is," said Velcich. "He says that he's never sold drugs since he was seventeen,* and we've shown otherwise today. If he's willing to lie about that, is there any question that he would lie to everyone about what he and his wife did in the dark of the September night to a fragile little girl?"

Glancing at Paul Hogan, Velcich added, "We can see Jaclyn on television, doing somersaults on the sidewalk and playing in her swimming pool. No sentence that you can issue can ever bring her back, but what you can do, judge, is give this community a sense of the enormity of their conduct."

Meczyk responded, "No matter what you do, your honor, it's not going to matter to David Dowaliby because in his heart of hearts he's always going to feel guilty of one thing—guilty because he slept through the night.

"The best that they had to offer today was that he sold a nickel bag to a coworker, no better than the evidence that the jury heard—flimsy, nothing evidence like dust, pardon the pun.

"I suppose people come before you every day and beg your forgiveness. Well, David Dowaliby can't do that. That isn't arrogance. He just didn't kill his daughter. Whether you give him ten years or you give him a thousand years, it's not going to matter, because what's happened to him is his nightmare. The time isn't really going to matter."

Neville asked David if he had anything to say.

David trudged to the bench. Referring to the lawyers, he said, "There's just one thing they couldn't tell you, because they didn't know who Jaclyn was. Your honor, Jaclyn was beautiful. She was charming. She was warm. She was pure. She was giggly. She was bubbly. She was soft, and she was innocent. She had a right to live, your honor, so who can kill an innocent child—an animal, a monster, a degenerate? It's

---

*The article did not quote David Dowaliby as saying that he had never sold drugs since he was seventeen, but rather as saying, "When they took the blood and urine tests the day after Jaclyn was missing, they came up negative. There was no marijuana, no cocaine. I'm not a drug dealer. I'm a normal parent." *Chicago Tribune,* Chicagoland section (July 2, 1990).

not me, your honor. I did not kill my daughter. I loved her, and I will love her forever in my heart."

"Okay, you can have a seat," said Neville, indicating that he was ready to pass sentence.

Pointing out that the sentencing range for first-degree murder was set by state law at twenty to sixty years, he said that neither the maximum nor the minimum seemed appropriate.

David Dowaliby, he observed, had been described as "a good, honest, and trustworthy man who was promoted at his job and who was thought to be a good, stable family person. I think he is entitled to consideration for those factors in his life."

On the other hand, he said, "This case involved the murder of a child. For minimum sentences, you have to show mitigation in committing the crime itself. Unfortunately, we do not know why this happened. We do not even know how this happened."

After noting that there was no legal requirement that the prosecution prove either motivation or method, he continued, "We have a system that takes twelve people who have no ax to grind, who have sworn to reach a verdict untouched by events outside this courtroom. I believe that the jurors in this case did this to the best of their ability."

Looking sternly at David, he said, "The jury has concluded that you killed your daughter and concealed her death.

"You are sentenced for the first-degree murder of Jaclyn Dowaliby to forty years in the Illinois Department of Corrections and for the crime of concealment of a homicidal death to five years, consecutive, for a total of forty-five years."

David dropped his head and closed his eyes.

The courtroom was still.

Breaking the silence, Franks asked for bond pending appeal.

"Appeal bond denied," said Neville.

A deputy sheriff led David past the journalists sitting in the jury box.

"Where he's going," one reporter said to another, "he'll need plenty of Vaseline."

* * *

As Cynthia Dowaliby prepared to go downstairs to answer the questions of waiting reporters, David Protess told her, "I'm not joining that pack. I'll say good-bye here."

Embracing her, he said, "This case isn't over, and it won't be until David's home with you."

In fact, however, Protess had no idea what to do next.

In frustration, he indulged in a futile gesture—flashing his middle finger to the prosecutors as they left.

RETRIAL BY TELEVISION

The day after David Dowaliby's sentencing, David Protess met juror Linda Wisniewski for lunch.

She was not hungry.

As tears streamed down her face, she declared, "I don't believe this man murdered his daughter. It wasn't even his daughter, and I bet he loved her more than anybody. That's the feeling I had."

Protess, who was taking notes, asked if he could turn on a tape recorder.

She nodded affirmatively.

"You have reasonable doubt that David Dowaliby is guilty of murder, don't you?" Protess asked.

"Yes, I do," she said in a pained voice. "When they read the verdict and said that David Dowaliby was guilty of murder, I don't know why I didn't go into a seizure, or why I didn't say 'not guilty.' Afterwards I felt, 'God, what happened here? Why didn't I say something?' And he's convicted of a murder that I don't believe he did."

Sobbing uncontrollably, her voice cracking with emotion, she continued, "If I was the one person who said, 'I'm not sure,' I could have caused a mistrial. Then they would have had to have another jury, and now this man doesn't have a chance.

"I'll be dead by the time he gets out of jail."

Wisniewski said that she and three other jurors who shared her concerns had lacked the courage to stand up to Phyllis Halvorsen and the majority.

"It was hard to argue with them," she said, "especially when the Dowalibys didn't testify and after our experiment with the mock-up. When it came down to a vote, I just caved in."

Protess told Wisniewski that he would like to write her story for the *Tribune.*

She asked if she could see the story before publication.

Protess said that the newspaper had a policy against that, but suggested a compromise: He would transcribe her tape-recorded remarks, show her a transcript, and allow her to approve the verbatim quotations that he would use in the article.

On July 16, Protess took the five-page transcript to her home. She read it, made minor changes, and signed each page.

Protess drafted an article and took it to the *Tribune* but found the editors unreceptive. "We've decided to cover future developments in the Dowaliby case only with our own reporters," said Gene Quinn, *Tribune* suburban editor.

"But your reporters didn't get this story," Protess replied.

"It doesn't matter," Quinn rejoined. "It's too controversial to have an outsider write it—especially someone who has a point of view on the case."

Protess next approached the *Chicago Sun-Times.*

"We're going to cover only the developments that occur in court in this case," said Editor Dennis A. Britton.

Protess turned to Paul Hogan at Channel 5.

After listening to the tape, Hogan said, "That's news any way you cut it. I'll do the story, and credit you as the source, if Wisniewski will go along with that."

After initial hesitancy about having her photograph and emotion-filled voice broadcast, Wisniewski agreed.

Hogan's July 19 story included comments by Albert Alschuler, a jury expert on the faculty of the University of Chicago Law School, who called Wisniewski's recantation "shocking and unusual." However, Alschuler added that a juror recantation, by itself, would not be sufficient to overturn the verdict.

"But that's exactly what juror Linda Wisniewski would like to happen," Hogan said on camera.

The story ended with Hogan quoting her as saying, "I have to live with this forever. I don't know if I'll ever sleep again."

On the evening that the Linda Wisniewski story aired, Peggy O'Connor, president of the David Dowaliby Freedom Committee, called David Protess at Channel 5.

"I just heard that there's been another kidnapping in Midlothian," said O'Connor. "I don't have a name or address, but it's supposed to be a little girl, and it happened in the middle of the night."

"Jeezus," said Protess. "We'll get on it."

Paul Hogan asked an assignment editor to check with the Midlothian police, who flatly denied the rumor.

Taking the police at their word, Protess and Hogan temporarily dropped O'Connor's lead and focused instead on another angle—official misconduct in the Dowaliby case.

Two members of Channel 5's investigative unit, Douglas Longhini and Marsha Bartel, had obtained the complete law enforcement file on the case, including the grand jury transcript and other previously secret official reports.

Comparing the transcript with the official reports, Longhini and Bartel concluded that Captain Daniel McDevitt and Assistant State's Attorney Dean Morask had presented grand jury testimony "that proved to be false or never materialized at trial."

The station then retained Samuel "Skip" Palenik, a nationally known forensic expert, to review the physical evidence reports. Palenik concluded that law enforcement agencies had badly botched the case—destroying evidence that might have proved whether there had been an intruder at the Dowaliby home and that might have linked a specific culprit to the crime.

More important, however, Palenik said that the Illinois crime laboratory's fiber tests established with "virtual certainty" that Jaclyn's body had not been transported in the trunk of Cynthia Dowaliby's Chevrolet Malibu.

In addition to the law enforcement file, Channel 5 had obtained a box of John Waters's materials, including his complete investigative notes—eight full legal pads—and the long-lost videotape showing the Dowalibys' former neighbor Robert Tolbert easily climbing through their basement window.

For the Channel 5 investigators, the Tolbert tape disproved the prosecutors' contention that no one could have gone through the window without disturbing the items below.

Channel 5 scheduled three reports on the findings for late July, but a startling development would upstage the series.

Peggy O'Connor called David Protess at home on Saturday morning, July 21, to report that one of her neighbors had further information about the Midlothian kidnapping that the police claimed had not occurred.

The neighbor wished to remain anonymous and would not reveal the source of the information, but said that the victim lived "just off 145th Street, not far from where the Dowalibys lived."

Protess called the Channel 5 assignment desk and asked an editor to check again with the police. Again, the police emphatically denied that there had been a kidnapping.

Suspicious, Protess went to a library and photocopied, from a criss-cross telephone directory, the names, addresses, and numbers of everyone in that section of Midlothian.

Through four hours of calling, Protess learned that a kidnapping indeed had occurred and that the victim was a young girl, Jenny Balchristie. The Balchristie family lived six blocks from the former Dowaliby home.

Protess went to Midlothian the next morning, hoping to interview the Balchristies, but they were on vacation.

Neighbors confided that the Balchristies had hoped to keep the incident quiet to protect their daughter's privacy. Since the neighbors were concerned about their own children's safety, however, Protess easily persuaded them to break the silence.

Protess called Paul Hogan, who joined him in Midlothian with a camera crew. While police continued to deny that the crime had occurred, Protess and Hogan pieced together the story.

Jenny was seven years old and bore a striking resemblance to Jaclyn Dowaliby. While Jenny's father was at work the night of July 14–15, an intruder had entered the Balchristie home through the window of a bedroom in which Jenny's mother was sleeping, tiptoed past her and three of Jenny's siblings, and carried her away, wrapped in her bedspread, sound asleep.

The intruder had taken Jenny to a nearby field, sexually assaulted her, and let her go. She had found her way home and awakened her mother, who called police. Jenny then had been taken to Mount Sinai Hospital for treatment.

Hogan called Midlothian Police Chief William Fischer at home, telling him, "Your police department has been lying to my television station. Tell me what happened here, or I'm going to go on the air tonight and call you a liar."

Fischer reluctantly acknowledged that the kidnapping had occurred. The earlier denials had been intended only to protect the Balchristie family's privacy, he said, adding that there was no link between the Balchristie and Dowaliby crimes.

"How do you know?" Hogan asked.

"Because Jenny Balchristie wasn't murdered," said Fischer.

Hogan broke the story live on the 10:00 P.M. news from the parking lot of the Midlothian police station, saying, "This abduction story is remarkably similar to the one told by David and Cynthia Dowaliby."

When Protess returned home, Cynthia Dowaliby called.

"You know what?" she said. "Jenny Balchristie's mother runs a fitness center. Jaclyn went there a lot with me the summer before she disappeared."

At 8:00 A.M. the next morning, Monday, July 23, the Midlothian police station's parking lot resembled a scene from *Bonfire of the Vanities.*

Among the first to arrive were camera crews from five television stations and virtually every reporter who had covered the Dowaliby trial.

A dozen Freedom Committee members followed, wearing their red shirts emblazoned, "Stop Injustice. Free David Dowaliby," and passing out hastily prepared leaflets describing the similarities between the Balchristie and Dowaliby cases.

Midlothian residents spontaneously appeared, carrying handmade signs saying such things as, "No more cover-ups" and "Who's stealing our children?"

Cynthia Dowaliby held an impromptu news conference, declaring, "I'm outraged that our community wasn't told about this. We need to be able to secure our homes."

At one point, Erzebette Sziky showed up to demand a full investigation to determine if there was a link between the Balchristie crime and the unsuccessful effort of an intruder to snatch her daughter, Nicole, the night before Jaclyn disappeared.

Daniel Franks pushed his way through the crowd to serve a subpoena on Chief Fischer for the Balchristie file, finding that the police had locked the station.

When Captain John Bitten opened the door a crack to accept the subpoena, the crowd booed and hissed.

"Why the cover-up?" a reporter shouted over the din.

"The family wanted to keep it private so as not to harm the girl more," said Bitten. "They didn't want it to turn into something like what happened to the Dowalibys."

Bitten then slammed the door.

The clamor continued over the next three days, with television stations carrying regular live updates from the Midlothian police station parking lot.

Paul Hogan had dropped out of the pack to put the final touches on Channel 5's investigative series.

The first installment, blasting the law enforcement investigation, was broadcast on July 26. "It is police mistakes that make this case an ongoing mystery," said anchor Carol Marin in introducing the exposé.

Hogan then said, "After going through thousands and thousands of documents, our investigative unit concludes that police made so many errors that it's now impossible to determine through physical evidence who killed Jaclyn Dowaliby."

The next day, the Midlothian police announced that a suspect had been arrested and charged with the kidnapping and sexual assault of Jenny Balchristie.

Chief Fischer identified the suspect as Mark Melcher, asserting that there was "physical evidence" linking Melcher to the crime and—almost gleefully—that he had been in prison when Jaclyn Dowaliby disappeared.

Jenny Balchristie's abductor could not have been Jaclyn's killer—assuming, that is, that Fischer had nailed the right man.

David Protess had shared details of the Jenny Balchristie abduction and the Linda Wisniewski recantation with Daniel Franks, whom he regarded highly. Protess believed, however, that the Dowalibys' interests would be better served by a large law firm and encouraged the Dowalibys to meet with Robert Byman.

After Cynthia Dowaliby visited Jenner & Block's sleek offices at One IBM Plaza (designed by the renowned Ludwig Mies van der Rohe), and after Robert Byman visited David Dowaliby at the squalid county jail, there was a tentative meeting of minds.

If Jenner & Block said yes, David Dowaliby would say yes.

Before the deal could be struck, however, Byman had a problem to overcome. The case failed to meet two points of the firm's *pro bono* criteria: that the client could not secure able private counsel, and that the case provide an educational experience for young associates.

On the first point, although the Dowalibys were broke, Daniel Franks and Mary Ellen Dienes were able and willing to handle the appeal and defer their fees. On the second point, Byman, an experienced partner, wanted to handle the case principally by himself.

Despite misgivings about skirting the *pro bono* criteria, Jenner & Block's Executive Committee bowed on August 5 to Byman's passionate desire to take the case and his promise that younger associates could handle some aspects of the appeal. The vote was 4 to 3.

Byman immediately called Cynthia, who was thrilled with the news. To her, Jenner & Block was "just like *LA Law.*" The next day, David signed a letter asking Jenner & Block to represent him—with mixed feelings, out of loyalty to Franks and Dienes.

By the end of the day, however, the deal would be derailed by yet another astonishing development: The Illinois Appellate Court, acting on a motion filed by Dienes, agreed to free David pending the appeal.

The Appellate Court order, which restored the $500,000 bond that had been in effect before the guilty verdict, was virtually unprecedented in a murder case.*

The vote was 2 to 1. While the majority did not explain its decision, Justice Dom J. Rizzi later would say that David Dowaliby had met the three standards for an appeal bond: He was not a danger to the community, or a risk to flee, and there was substantial likelihood that he would prevail on appeal.

Since the courts were closed by the time the state's attorney's office received the bond order, prosecutors rushed to

---

* The most recent release of a defendant on bond pending appeal of a Cook County murder conviction had been in 1971. That defendant, Dr. John M. Branion, Jr., an African-American physician found guilty of murdering his wife, jumped bond and fled to Africa. He was apprehended in Uganda in 1983 and returned to Illinois to serve his sentence. See Rob Warden and Patricia Haller, "An American Nightmare/The Ordeal and Odyssey of John M. Branion, Jr.," *Chicago Lawyer* (November 1987).

Mary Ellen Dienes's office to serve notice that they would seek a stay from the Illinois Supreme Court the next morning. Dienes agreed not to try to spring David before then; at any rate, Judge Neville's signature was necessary to secure David's release, and it was doubtful that Dienes could obtain it at that late hour.

Meanwhile, Daniel Franks went to the county jail to give David Dowaliby the good news.

"Now, are we your lawyers or not?" Franks asked David.

"You're my lawyers," David replied, apologizing for signing on with Jenner & Block.

"See you tomorrow—on the outside," Franks told David.

David promptly tried to reach Cynthia, but she was not at home. He called Peggy O'Connor, screaming, "Peg, I'm coming home! Tell Cyndi!"

He packed his belongings.

When Cynthia heard the news, she told Davey, who jumped with joy.

The next morning, Daniel Franks and Cynthia Dowaliby went to Judge Neville's courtroom to secure his signature, assuming that it would be perfunctory.

Neville thought otherwise. He refused to sign anything until the Supreme Court decided whether to review the Appellate Court's action.

At that very moment, Dienes and Renee G. Goldfarb, chief of the state's attorney's Appeals Division, were meeting with Supreme Court Justice William G. Clark, who seemed ready to rule on the spot. Goldfarb wanted to avoid that, knowing that Clark was the most liberal of the seven-member court.

"Your honor," said Goldfarb, "I would ask that you defer our motion for the entire Supreme Court to consider."

"Do you mean to say that I don't have the authority to act on this motion by myself?" Clark responded.

"I'm only saying that there is a substantial issue raised by this order," she said, "and I think it's appropriate for the entire court to hear us on this."

Undaunted, Clark asked Dienes, "Are you ready to proceed?"

"I would like a couple of hours to prepare a written response to the state's motion," Dienes said.

"Well then, I have no choice but to issue a temporary stay of the bond order," said Clark.

The momentum of the Appellate Court order had been halted by default.

That afternoon, Clark deferred the matter to the entire court.

The next day, the court, neither explaining its ruling nor specifying how the individual justices voted, reversed the Appellate Court order.

David Dowaliby would stay in jail until his full appeal would be decided—more than a year later.

Jenner & Block was back on the case.

On Monday, August 13, David Protess and Paul Hogan met Robert Byman for the first time in person. He had blue eyes, naturally bushy hair, and a quick wit.

The three hit it off from the start, confessing over breakfast that they had become obsessed with the case—"Dowalibized," Hogan called it.

Now in their midforties, enjoying success with its outward trappings—Protess and Byman sported Porsches, Hogan a BMW—they had lost some of their youthful idealism. The Dowaliby case rekindled a fire they had felt in the sixties.

Protess was near tears as he described how Cynthia Dowaliby had been forced to tell her son that his father, in fact, was not coming home. Protess had a son, Benjamin, born five days before Davey Dowaliby. When Protess himself was that age, living in Brooklyn, he had been horrified when the government orphaned two young boys by electrocuting their parents, Julius and Ethel Rosenberg.

Protess saw the Dowaliby case as a means to come to terms with the past by helping correct an injustice in the present. He also wanted to involve his students, hoping they might someday pursue similar stories.

Hogan relished the role of watchdog. Hardly anything bored him more than covering criminal cases with predictable and justifiable outcomes. Dowaliby was different, offering a chance to expose the abusive exercise of state power.

Byman, inspired at an early age by *Perry Mason*, rarely had the opportunity to represent an innocent man—which he thought should be every lawyer's highest calling. He had gone to law school precisely to defend a client like David Dowaliby.

"When I solve the crime," Protess told Byman jocularly, "I'll come up to you in court and whisper the killer's name."

"And I'll broadcast it exclusively," added Hogan.

While their motives differed, the three had a common goal: to create a climate of public and legal opinion that would reverse David Dowaliby's conviction.

HARD TIMES

For the time being, David Dowaliby had only one request of Robert Byman: "Bob, get me to a real prison so I can hold my wife and kids."

Since his conviction, he had been denied physical contact with his family. Cynthia, Davey, and Carli were allowed a brief, noncontact visit each Friday at the county jail, during which they were separated from David by thick Plexiglas.

Byman asked for a medium-security prison, but the Illinois Department of Corrections sent David to Stateville, a maximum-security institution near Joliet. Stateville housed more than two thousand prisoners, all convicted of violent crimes. Its most famous resident was mass murderer Richard Speck.

When Byman expressed concern about David's safety to the state's attorney's office, George Velcich sarcastically asked, "Who's going to protect the other inmates from David Dowaliby?"

Prison officials had a different attitude. They assigned David to a wing known as X House, one of the safest places in the institution. It housed a small group of older men who posed so little danger to other prisoners that their cells were unlocked except at night.

David took a job for fifteen dollars a month in the prison supply room and, realizing that he was likely to be at Stateville for quite some time, forsook his vow not to go outside until he was free. X House had its own yard and indoor recreational area, where its residents pretty much could come and go as they pleased, segregated from the general prison population.

More important, David was permitted twelve hours of contact visits each month. Cynthia visited once a week.

At the beginning, Davey and Carli came with her, which required the presence of a family member or friend approved by the Department of Children and Family Services. (Although the children were living with her at her mother and stepfather's condominium, Cynthia still could not be alone with them because the child-abuse allegations had not yet been resolved.)

After several weeks, Cynthia reluctantly cut back on the children's visits to shield them from the realities of prison. Prisoners in the visiting areas sometimes were shackled for disciplinary reasons, and Davey had become despondent from imagining his father being treated in that way. On one visit, the children saw a prisoner fornicating with a female visitor while guards looked the other way.

To communicate with his children, David began writing stories for Cynthia to read to them at bedtime. One grew into an adventure novel, seven chapters long, about three young heroes—Davey and his cousins, Matthew and John. By popular demand, David wrote a longer sequel.

David also channeled his anger about being behind bars into poetry, titling his seminal effort "Good Morning America":

Good morning America
Land of the free

Freedom for all
Except for me.

A nation so great
Strengthened through time
Your justice lies hanging
Like a leaf on a vine.

Good morning America
Home of the brave
My life in your hands
You could not save.

Proud country of ours
So many do hail
Can an innocent man
Be sent to jail?

Good morning Miss Liberty
Standing so proud
Your eyes are closed
Your dreams in a cloud.

The time has come
Old lady of lore
Lay down your torch
And gather your sword.

Strike hard and fast
No time for haste
Already, liberty
Shows a dying face.

Good morning America
Land of the rich
You've lost my respect
You son-of-a-bitch.

As Robert Byman began legal research for the appeal, David Protess, thinking it unlikely that Jaclyn had been her killer's only victim, assembled a cadre of journalism students to explore possible links with similar crimes throughout the country.

Within a few weeks, Protess and the students identified more than a dozen recent cases in which girls aged five to eight appeared to have been abducted by strangers from their beds in the middle of the night. Several had been murdered or were still missing. Others had been released alive.

Only the Balchristie and MacRand abductions had occurred in the Chicago area. Protess decided to investigate those cases himself, assigning students to look into the others.

After obtaining police reports on the Balchristie case and interviewing the victim's mother and the lawyer representing Mark Melcher, the man charged with the crime, Protess wondered if police once again had rushed to judgment.

Melcher had a smooth complexion and wore Coke-bottle-thick glasses, but Jenny had told police that her attacker had a "bumpy" face and was not wearing glasses. Although Jenny had been inches from her abductor's face, she had been unable to identify Melcher's photograph.

Melcher denied committing the Balchristie crime, and there was nothing in his record to suggest that he might be a pedophile; he had been in prison for a date rape.

Most stunning, Melcher and Balchristie were Caucasian, but police had found a Negroid hair on Jenny's pillow. A Negroid hair also had been found on the rope in the Dowaliby case.

Melcher's lawyer, William F. McGlynn, told Protess that he would request court permission for an independent analysis of the fingerprint evidence and a comparison of the Negroid hairs. McGlynn said, however, that his request would have to await completion of pretrial discovery months later.*

---

* The independent analysis was never done because Mark Melcher pleaded guilty to the crime in August 1991, *People* v. *Melcher*, Cook County Circuit Court No. 90 C 6-60943. In a 1992 interview with David Protess, Melcher said that he had suffered an alcoholic blackout and did not remember committing the crime. He said he assumed that he must have committed it because he was told that his fingerprints had been found at the scene, although he never saw the fingerprint report.

Meanwhile, checking on the MacRand case, Protess obtained a copy of Perry Hernandez's signed confession. Taken with the other evidence, the confession left no doubt that police had the right man in that case. The only question in Protess's mind was whether Hernandez also had murdered Jaclyn Dowaliby.

Unbeknownst to Protess, as he was pursuing the connections, a prisoner had informed prosecutors that he in fact had overheard Perry Hernandez confess to the Dowaliby crime.

Gerald Baumann, a convicted armed robber, had written to *Chicago Sun-Times* reporter Rosalind Rossi after reading a May 7 article quoting Cynthia Dowaliby's plea for information that would help exonerate her husband.

In mid-February 1990, while he was awaiting transfer from Cook County Jail to a state prison, Baumann wrote, he had noticed Perry Hernandez in the jailyard talking with a group of prisoners who were members of the Latin Kings street gang.

Baumann claimed to have heard enough of the conversation to determine that Hernandez was seeking the gang's protection. A guard broke up the gathering, but Hernandez continued talking with one of the gang's leaders, "Lefty" Ortez.

Ortez, according to Baumann, mentioned Cynthia Dowaliby's name. Then, apparently referring to television reports suggesting that Hernandez might have murdered Jaclyn, Ortez asked, "Did you do what they say you did on TV?"

"I tried to break in through a window, but was making too much noise, so I went around the house and went inside through an open door," Hernandez responded, according to Baumann.

Ortez then allegedly said, "We're going to have to put you

He said that he pleaded guilty in exchange for a forty-year sentence after he was threatened with a sixty-year sentence if found guilty at trial. With Melcher's cooperation, Protess renewed his effort to obtain the evidence for independent analysis as this book went to press.

on hold"—apparently referring to Hernandez's request for the Latin Kings' protection.

"I hope what I told the cops about me being with a girl that night sticks up," Baumann quoted Hernandez as saying.

Reporter Rossi promptly answered Baumann's letter and, in mid-May, tape-recorded an interview with him at Joliet Correctional Center. After hearing his story, Rossi told Baumann that she would contact him again soon and that he might become a witness for David Dowaliby.

When Baumann had not heard from her after David Dowaliby's sentencing on July 10—which Rossi covered for the *Sun-Times*—Baumann wrote her again.

Rossi wrote back that she was trying to check his story with "Lefty" Ortez.

In early August, hearing nothing further, Baumann wrote her once more but received no reply. Finally, on August 11, he wrote to the prosecutors, mentioning his correspondence with Rossi.

Ten days later, Assistant State's Attorney Joseph Kazmierski interviewed Baumann and wrote a memo to Dowaliby prosecutor Patrick O'Brien. "In response to a question as to why he contacted Rosalind Rossi," said the memo, "Baumann stated that he didn't like seeing someone in jail for something he didn't do. Baumann did not expect anything in return."

On September 7, Assistant State's Attorney Anthony Calabrese interviewed Baumann, who repeated details of the story he had told to Rossi more than three months earlier. Calabrese also wrote a memo to O'Brien.

O'Brien finally informed Jenner & Block of Baumann's allegations three weeks later.

Rossi's silence continued.

"Is Baumann credible?" David Protess asked when Robert Byman told him of Perry Hernandez's alleged confession.

"I'm going to talk to him," said Byman, "but I don't see how Hernandez could have gotten in through an open door. The doors were all locked."

"Not the patio door," said Protess. "I asked Cyndi about

that, and she said the kids were opening it all day and no one remembered locking it. The cops didn't even dust it for prints."

"If Hernandez went in through the patio door," Byman mused, "that would explain why the stuff under the window wouldn't have been disturbed."

Byman asked Protess to keep the alleged confession quiet, adding, "Of course, Rossi already has the story, but it looks like she's not doing anything with it."

"Yeah," said Protess. "I can't believe she watched David Dowaliby get sentenced to forty-five years without telling the defense or at least the judge about it."

If Baumann had requested confidentiality, Protess said, Rossi's silence might have been justified. Baumann, however, evidently wanted the story told—why else would he have contacted Rossi in the first place?

"I think Rossi has an ethical problem here," Protess added.

"Journalism ethics—isn't that an oxymoron?" Byman scoffed.

Protess asked a longtime journalistic cohort, Rob Warden, what he thought of Rossi's role in the matter.

Warden had been the editor and publisher of *Chicago Lawyer,* an investigative publication that, over the previous decade, often had criticized the media for proprosecution biases. Having sold *Chicago Lawyer* the previous summer, Warden now was issues director for Jack O'Malley, a Republican in a heated campaign to unseat State's Attorney Cecil Partee.

Warden knew Rossi from covering the case of Gary Dotson, a young man whose rape conviction had been called into question by the recantation of the alleged victim. In that case, Warden told Protess, Rossi had been a conduit for prosecutors, only to be embarrassed when forensic tests proved Dotson innocent.*

Questioning Protess's reference to Rossi's "silence," War-

---

* For a discussion of the Gary Dotson case and other wrongful convictions, see Rob Warden, "Guilty Until Proven Innocent," *Chicago Times Magazine* (January–February 1990).

den said, "I doubt that she was silent. She would have told her prosecutor pals. She just wouldn't have told the defense."

Protess said he would check that angle, and Warden agreed to discuss the Dowaliby case further after the November election.

On October 24, in an interview with Robert Byman and two other Jenner & Block lawyers, Gerald Baumann confirmed what he had told Rossi and others and said he would be willing to testify. After trying unsuccessfully to interview "Lefty" Ortez and Perry Hernandez, Byman prepared a motion to overturn David Dowaliby's conviction based on Baumann's promised testimony.

Byman agreed that Protess could tip Paul Hogan to the story if Hogan would agree not to broadcast it until the motion was filed. Hogan accepted that condition and went to Joliet to interview Baumann on camera.

"Prove to me that you're not lying," Hogan began.

"Why would I stick my neck out in order to help somebody I don't even know?" Baumann answered, adding that prosecutors were unhappy that he was coming forward and that the defense had nothing to offer him.

Hogan also contacted Hernandez, who refused to discuss Baumann's allegation. However, Hogan secured an on-camera interview with Hernandez's lawyer, Ronald Rodger. For the first time, Rodger acknowledged that Hernandez had no alibi for the hours surrounding Jaclyn's disappearance.

To preserve Hogan's exclusive for Channel 5's October 31 evening news, Byman quietly filed the motion on the Baumann evidence late that afternoon with Judge Neville.*

The next morning, Byman appeared before Neville to schedule a hearing. Seeing his jury box filled with reporters, Neville rolled his eyes; only Patrick O'Brien and George Velcich seemed less pleased than Neville to be there.

In tones flat with futility, O'Brien and Velcich objected to

---

* For most purposes, a trial court loses jurisdiction thirty days after the verdict. However, it retains jurisdiction for ten years over petitions involving newly discovered evidence. See Illinois Code of Criminal Procedure, Sec. 122-1.

holding a hearing, which Neville, after resolving scheduling conflicts among the lawyers, set for December 18.

At Channel 5's studios that afternoon, Protess asked investigative reporter Peter Karl a favor—to call Rosalind Rossi, with whom Karl was friendly. Protess wanted Karl to find out whether Rossi had privately told the prosecutors about Baumann before David Dowaliby's sentencing.

Outraged that Rossi might have done that, Karl agreed.

When asked directly, Rossi would not say if she had discussed the matter with anyone.

"Roz," said Karl, "just tell me that you didn't talk to them —deny it right now—and I'll drop it."

After a ten-second silence, Karl ended the conversation.

The same day that Robert Byman filed the motion before Judge Neville, he also moved on another front: the Appellate Court.

Byman and three other Jenner & Block lawyers—J. Kevin McCall, Daniel Lynch, and Terrence J. Truax—filed a seventy-four-page appellate brief seeking the outright exoneration of David Dowaliby based on insufficiency of the evidence.

The brief argued that the cases against David and Cynthia had been legally identical and, consequently, that Neville should have tossed out both cases at the same time. It also called on the Appellate Court to nullify the indictment, alleging that it had been obtained "through false and misleading testimony."

After elaborating on the alleged trial errors that Daniel Franks had raised before sentencing, the brief concluded:

"The state did not prove that David Dowaliby committed —and he did not commit—any crime. The conviction was obtained as a result of error, passion, and prejudice, not evidence."

Speaking at a fund-raiser organized by the Freedom Committee, Robert Byman boldly predicted victory.

"We're going to win complete vindication, not just a new trial," he said in a calm, deliberate voice. "I promise."

Cynthia was not so confident.

"Byman's brilliant," she told David Protess, "but I've lost faith in the system. It will take a miracle to free David."

Cynthia Dowaliby's life was complicated by financial woes.

The fund-raiser had yielded only a few hundred dollars. Pridefully refusing to go on welfare or take money from her "tapped out" family, she had been reduced to selling her belongings at garage sales to raise money.

Living with her mother and stepfather in a cramped condominium, Cynthia had to sleep on the living room couch, while Davey and Carli shared the only spare bedroom.

Cynthia told Joan Protess that she considered returning to work, but was concerned that her absence would be too upsetting for her children. She also expressed fear that whoever took Jaclyn might take Davey: "When he goes to school in the morning, I worry about him until the minute he comes home."

In the midst of this, Lawrence Hyman was clamoring for money. The Dowalibys had paid Hyman and Ralph Meczyk $55,877, but Hyman wanted $53,399 more "to cover expenses."

Cynthia disputed the amount, and said that she could not pay it in any event. Although she recently had received a refund from David's bond, most of that had been borrowed. In Cynthia's view, the lenders had first claim to the money.

When Hyman called and threatened to sue her for the cash, Cynthia slammed down the receiver.

Hyman then sent a revised bill, suddenly demanding $500,000 "for professional services in preparation and trial."

A month later, Hyman sued—for the more modest $53,399.

Robert Byman agreed to handle her defense—*pro bono.*

He informed Hyman that Jenner & Block would file a response to the suit that would disclose the $500,000 bill, which Byman called "unethical."

On December 4, Hyman withdrew the suit.

That was his final legal action in the Dowaliby case.

* * *

Gerald Baumann was better on TV than on the witness stand.

On December 18, under oath in Judge Neville's courtroom, he repeated the story of Perry Hernandez's "confession" exactly as he had told it to Robert Byman and Paul Hogan.

Then George Velcich took over, casting considerable doubt on Baumann's veracity.

Velcich first elicited a possible motive for Baumann to lie—to get himself moved to more comfortable confines. In fact, Baumann had won a transfer to a medium-security prison by claiming that he had been threatened by the Latin Kings after Hogan's story aired.

More devastating, Velcich pinned Baumann down on the date that he claimed to have overheard Hernandez talking to "Lefty" Ortez in the jailyard: February 15. Baumann said he recalled the date because it was four days before his birthday. Velcich then introduced a jail record indicating that the yard had been closed to prisoners on February 15 because of inclement weather.

Byman called witnesses who testified that Baumann had told them the same confession story, showing consistency over time. Byman also called David's mother, Ann Dowaliby, who testified that she had not checked the patio door before she went out the night Jaclyn disappeared, raising the specter that an intruder could have entered the home in a manner consistent with Baumann's testimony.

Following Ann, in a moment of drama, Byman called David Dowaliby to the stand. Byman had two reasons for wanting David to testify. First, David was prepared to say that he had not checked the patio door before going to bed. Second, David's willingness to take the stand would help dispel any notion that his failure to testify at trial had been a sign of guilt—a message that Byman wanted to send to the appellate judges.

David, wearing a bright yellow prison jumpsuit and a gold crucifix around his neck, stood to be sworn.

Patrick O'Brien leaped from his chair to object, arguing that David had nothing to say that he could not have said at the trial, when he had chosen to remain silent.

Byman countered that David's testimony should be allowed, since Baumann's statement raised a new possibility—that entry had been made through an open door rather than through the broken window.

Neville sustained O'Brien's objection, saying that the defense had had every opportunity at the trial to have David discuss alternative points of entry; it was too late now.

"Do you want him on the stand for any other reason?" Neville asked Byman.

"Not unless somebody else wants to ask him a question," said Byman. "We are happy to let him answer."

There were no takers, and David was escorted by a deputy sheriff back to the defense table.

After brief summations by Byman and O'Brien, Neville denied the defense motion to overturn the jury verdict. He said, "It would have been impossible for Mr. Baumann to receive the information he says he received on the date he received it in the manner that he said he received it."

Neville thereupon dispatched David back to Stateville.

The Hernandez defense had failed again.

"We have suffered many defeats in this courtroom," Cynthia Dowaliby told reporters after the hearing. "No matter what the courts do, we'll never rest until the killer is caught."

To that end, she announced that the Freedom Committee had established a toll-free hot line and urged anyone with information about the case to call.

As Cynthia left the courthouse, reporters asked Patrick O'Brien what he thought of the hot line.

"Will she call it herself and finally confess to the crime?" O'Brien responded.

O'Brien's offhand remark was featured prominently on that evening's newscasts.

Cynthia swiftly counterattacked, branding O'Brien's comment "slanderous" and demanding that he be fired.

The next morning, reporters scrambled to find O'Brien's new boss—Republican State's Attorney Jack O'Malley, who had trounced Democrat Cecil Partee in the November election.

Channel 5's Paul Hogan was the first to corner O'Malley, who had promised during the campaign to make the state's attorney's office the fairest prosecutor's office in the country.

Hogan demanded to know if O'Malley thought that O'Brien had been fair to Cynthia Dowaliby.

"What Pat O'Brien said was regrettable and inappropriate," O'Malley responded. "When a defendant is acquitted, we accept the decision of the court. That is the way the criminal justice system works, and I have impressed that upon Mr. O'Brien."

As a side effect of the controversy, the Freedom Committee's hot line number—1-800-328-DAVE—was flashed repeatedly on television screens across the Chicago area.

Among those who saw it was a man who had hung out at the Islander Apartments around the time that Jaclyn vanished.

DOUBLE TAKE

The Freedom Committee hot line was cluttered with crank calls—some placed anonymously from the Blue Island police station, evidently unaware that their telephone numbers were automatically recorded.

One message, however, was from a young man who said, "I thought you might like to know that David Dowaliby has a look-alike." The caller identified himself as Raul Velazquez and left a number.

Intrigued, David Protess called Velazquez, who explained that his message referred to Roy Padecky, a painter who lived and worked at the Islander Apartments.

"I saw David Dowaliby on television right after he was arrested," said Velazquez, "and I told a friend of mine, 'Man, that dude looks just like Roy.' "

Velazquez speculated that Padecky easily could have been mistaken for Dowaliby.

Padecky often invited friends to late-night parties in the apartments he was painting, Velazquez said, adding that he had attended one such affair "right around" the time of Jaclyn Dowaliby's murder.

Velazquez agreed to meet Protess the next morning and point out the apartment where he had attended the party.

Protess invited Rob Warden to go along. In the weeks since Jack O'Malley's election, Warden had been infected with the same fascination that had drawn Protess, Paul Hogan, and Robert Byman to the case.

When Protess and Warden arrived at the apartment complex, Velazquez pointed to a third-floor apartment in the building at 1900 Canal.

"Are you sure?" Protess asked.

"I'm positive," said Velazquez. "My brother used to have an apartment in the same building."

Of the eighteen buildings in the complex, this one was nearest the Dumpster where Jaclyn's body had been found.

"What kind of car did Padecky drive?" Protess asked.

"It was a light-colored, midsize car, I think either a Chevy or a Pontiac," Velazquez answered.

Velazquez knew that a witness had claimed to have seen David Dowaliby near the Islander Apartments. However, he seemed surprised when Protess explained the importance that officials had attached to a midsize car and that particular Dumpster.

Protess and Warden thanked Velazquez for his help and set about trying to locate Roy Padecky.

Eileen Blaylock, manager of the Islander Apartments, told Protess and Warden that Padecky had moved to a nearby suburb, but she could provide no address or telephone number.

Although Protess and Warden were unable to find a public record of Padecky's whereabouts, they did unearth two significant police reports.

One showed that Padecky had been involved in an automobile accident before Jaclyn disappeared; his car, which sustained minor damage, was a light green midsize 1981 Pontiac—virtually identical in body style to a 1980 Chevrolet Malibu.

The other report showed that Padecky had been arrested and booked at Cook County Jail for marijuana use a month after Jaclyn's murder. That meant that Padecky's mug shot would have been taken at about the same time as David Dowaliby's.

Protess and Warden hatched a plan: to obtain the mug shot and show it to Everett Mann.

In the first week of the new year, 1991, State's Attorney Jack O'Malley gave Cynthia Dowaliby a belated Christmas present, publicly promising to drop the child abuse allegations.

"This is a big victory," said Janet Trafelet, Cynthia's lawyer for the juvenile case. "The state couldn't prove the abuse allegations. Rather than lose them, they dismissed them."

Trafelet asked Judge Robert Smierciak to schedule a hearing to resolve the custody case, and Smierciak set it for March 5.

Before the hearing, however, fate intervened, causing O'Malley to renege on his promise.

Trafelet arranged for Cynthia to take psychological tests, which are routine in custody matters. The psychologist Trafelet chose was Edward Joseph Michaels, of Children's Memorial Hospital in Chicago.

Cynthia and Michaels were anything but fast friends. They had trouble arranging meeting dates, and both acknowledged that they failed to establish rapport.

Michaels gave Cynthia Rorschach and MMPI tests, which she struggled to complete, becoming flustered when Michaels pressed her for answers.

Michaels wrote a report saying that Cynthia was "defensive," exhibited "overcontrolled hostility," and "might be capable of explosive violence."

Trafelet had no choice but to turn over Michaels's report to the state's attorney's office, where it was promptly passed to Patrick O'Brien.

Jack O'Malley, despite his harsh criticism of O'Brien for the hot line flap, had rejected Cynthia's demand that O'Brien be fired. Instead, O'Malley had promoted him to chief deputy state's attorney.

Now O'Brien was in a position to use the juvenile proceeding as a forum to accuse Cynthia once again of murdering Jaclyn.

On March 5, 1991, reporters expected to cover a brief, routine hearing that would end in an easy victory for Cynthia.

They were stunned when Patrick Walsh, a hard-nosed young protégé of Patrick O'Brien, opened with blazing rhetoric on the first day of what would drag into a six-day hearing.

"Cynthia Dowaliby leads a secret life," Walsh began.

Jabbing his finger at Cynthia, he declared, "We will prove that she is capable of uncontrolled violence and rage and that she covered up information about Jaclyn's death.

"We also will show that Davey was physically and sexually abused by his mother, and we will ask the court to name a private guardian for Davey and Carli and not return custody to Cynthia."

To make the case, Walsh said he would rely on the defense's own psychologist, Edward Michaels, and the Mount Sinai reports.

Janet Trafelet retorted that the state's attorney's office was engaging in a "personal vendetta" against Cynthia, whom she called "a fit and capable parent."

Noting that Cynthia's mother, Mary Malia, already had temporary custody of the children and that Cynthia was living in the Malia home, Trafelet vowed to prove that "the children are thriving."

The defense was asking only that legal custody be returned to Cynthia so that she could be alone with her children, said Trafelet.

Robert Byman, who had joined Catherine Ryan as counsel to David Dowaliby in the juvenile case, also made a brief opening statement, accusing Walsh of grandstanding for the press to undermine the appeal of David's murder conviction.

Assistant State's Attorney Revelle Peritz, second-chairing Walsh, called the first witness: Michaels.

After leading Michaels through a description of the tests he had administered to Cynthia, Peritz asked him to relate his "most striking observation."

"My most striking observation is that Cynthia had a great deal of difficulty completing the tests," he said with a thud.

Peritz asked him to be more specific.

"Well, she had trouble seeing anything in the inkblots," Michaels answered, referring to Cynthia's Rorschach test.

The answer produced titters among the spectators.

Peritz then asked for his professional opinion about the other test results.

"My opinion is that she's a very angry woman," he said. "Most of the time, her anger is under very good control. However, she has the profile of someone who, from time to time, will lose control of her anger."

"Would small children be at risk if she lost control?"

"They could be, if her anger exceeds the controls."

Trafelet and Byman objected that the answer was speculative, and Judge Smierciak ordered it stricken from the record.

"Would Cynthia benefit from psychotherapy?" Peritz asked.

"Calls for speculation, your honor," Byman objected. "That's like asking a car salesman if someone would benefit from buying a car."

Smierciak, smiling, sustained the objection.

Peritz rephrased the question: "Does Cynthia Dowaliby require psychotherapy?"

"No," said Michaels.

Trafelet and Byman conducted short cross-examinations in which they elicited admissions that Michaels had not established rapport with Cynthia and that rapport was important in conducting valid tests.

Michaels also acknowledged that the test results could be skewed by anxiety and that Cynthia had been extremely anxious in taking the tests because she knew that custody of her children could hinge on the outcome.

"So what you're saying," Byman asked, "is that you suspect that Cynthia Dowaliby has a bad temper?"

"Yes," said Michaels.

"But you have no clinical data or observations to support that she's ever lost her temper?"

"That's right."

Next on the stand was Mount Sinai's Dr. Sharon Ahart, who on direct examination by Walsh repeated her original charges that Davey Dowaliby had been physically and perhaps sexually abused.

Ahart testified that she based her conclusions on her physical examination of Davey and on psychological tests administered by the Mount Sinai staff.

Catherine Ryan conducted the cross-examination. A nun and former prosecutor of child sex abuse cases, Ryan had been instrumental in establishing Mount Sinai's Pediatric Ecology Unit. Now, she believed, the PEU had turned into a cash cow, with a financial incentive to find abuse.

Ryan began by establishing that the PEU was a money-making arm of the hospital and that Davey's five-day stay in the PEU was predicated upon a finding of abuse; without such a finding, Ahart acknowledged, Davey would have been assigned elsewhere.

Next, Ryan confronted Ahart with the photographs that Chicago police had taken of Davey.

Noting that the photos did not show the marks and bruises that Ahart claimed to have seen, Ryan asked, "Do you think that they just disappeared?"

"I can't say," Ahart answered.

Asked if the photos were "true and accurate depictions" of Davey on the day she examined him, Ahart responded, "That is clearly Davey. I know the photos were ordered, but I cannot say that they accurately depict him on that day."

Turning to the question of sexual abuse, Ryan asked, "Your report says that you cannot rule it out, but can you rule it in?"

"No," said Ahart.

After Ahart acknowledged that Davey had no scarring, lacerations, fissures, or loss of perianal tissue—conditions often associated with sexual abuse—Ryan asked, "Would you say the probability of sexual abuse was high or low?"

"I would say there is a low probability," Ahart said.

"Did Davey cry for his parents in the five days he was at Mount Sinai?" Ryan concluded.

"Constantly," Ahart responded.

The next state witness was Noel Kalinowski, who had interviewed Davey at Mount Sinai while Assistant State's Attorney Dean Morask and Assistant Public Guardian Jeanette Volpe watched through a two-way mirror.

On direct examination by Walsh, Kalinowski repeated what her written report had said—that Davey had indicated, by pointing to pictures in a book, that Cynthia had spanked Jaclyn with a broom, a belt, and a rope.

On cross-examination, Trafelet asked, "Did Davey ever *say* that his mommy hit Jaclyn with a broom, a belt, or a rope?"

"No," Kalinowski acknowledged.

Trafelet then showed Kalinowski the actual page from the book that she had used during her interview with Davey. It was covered with scribbling, which Kalinowski said was Davey's.

"Do you see any marks indicating that he pointed to any objects?" Trafelet asked.

"No, but I remember that he pointed," said Kalinowski.

"Which object did he point to first?"

"I can't recall."

"Which object did he point to second?"

"I can't recall."

Kalinowski also acknowledged that before she ever met Davey, the police had told her that his parents were murderers and child-abusers.

The final state witness, Dr. Demetra Soter, added an astonishing element of confusion to the proceeding.

While Dr. Ahart had voiced certainty about physical abuse, but not sexual abuse, Soter thought it was the other way around: She was "uncertain" whether Davey had been physically abused but believed that he "had been sexually abused by his mother."

Soter acknowledged that she had reached her conclusion

solely on the basis of the Mount Sinai reports, without interviewing Davey or Cynthia or examining the records kept by Davey's private pediatrician.

Byman asked Soter if she would have more confidence in her diagnosis if she had interviewed at least Davey.

"Yes," said Soter.

The state offered nothing further, conspicuously failing to call Dean Morask, who had told the grand jury that he had observed Davey pointing to the broom, belt, and rope—testimony crucial to the Dowalibys' indictments.

Robert Byman called David Dowaliby as the first defense witness, once again making the point that David had nothing to hide. Since this was David's first opportunity to take the stand in the custody matter, prosecutors could not object, as they had at the Baumann hearing, that he had waived his right to testify.

Byman asked only one question: "Did you or your wife ever physically or sexually abuse your children?"

"No," David answered emphatically.

Patrick Walsh rose.

"Would you tell us the truth if you did?" he asked.

"I would tell the truth about anyone who did that to my kids," David replied.

Walsh asked nothing further in what would be the state's one and only cross-examination of David Dowaliby.

The defense next called Reid Schwartz, a psychologist who had been Davey Dowaliby's therapist for the past two years.

Over the objection of Patrick Walsh, Judge Smierciak ruled that Schwartz could testify as an expert on child abuse.

On direct examination by Janet Trafelet, Schwartz testified that there was "absolutely no indication" that Davey ever had been either physically or sexually abused.

"He has very positive views of his mother and father," Schwartz said. "When I began seeing him, he was afraid to go to sleep, fearful that he'd be kidnapped. Cynthia was instrumental in getting the treatment off the ground. Since resuming living with his mother, he has improved tremendously. His nightmares are gone. His fears are gone. His depression is gone."

Schwartz added, "Davey relishes his big brother role toward Carli. He is very protective toward her, and he's good about sharing things with her."

Asked if he had any hesitation about Cynthia having custody, Schwartz said, "Davey and Carli are completely safe with her."

On cross-examination, Patrick Walsh elicited that Cynthia sometimes joined in Davey's therapy sessions, and asked if Schwartz thought that she was a "very angry person."

"Sure she's angry," said Schwartz. "She's suffering from tremendous grief and loss."

Judge Smierciak then asked if Davey had ever reported being struck by his parents.

"Davey said that his parents don't hit him, that when he's punished he's given time-outs," Schwartz answered.

The next defense witness was Barbara White, a social worker at Children's Memorial Hospital and a member of the state's attorney's Task Force on Mass Child Molestation. She had evaluated Davey and Cynthia at the request of the Department of Children and Family Services.

White, who had spent fifteen hours with Cynthia and reviewed Edward Michaels's test results, described her as "a warm, loving mother who is able to set limits but is not rigid."

Based on an interview with Davey and a review of his pediatric records, in addition to his Mount Sinai records, White described him as a "developmentally normal" child with only one wish in life: "for his father to be home."

Charlotte Wenzel, Davey's therapist at Hephzibah, where he had gone after Mount Sinai, followed White to the stand. She testified that Davey had exhibited no signs of abuse, calling him "a warm kid who was active but not aggressive."

Wenzel added that Davey's parents had been "very cooperative" during his stay at Hephzibah. As David and Cynthia prepared to leave after one visit, she said, Davey shouted, "I hate you!" Said Wenzel, "Abused kids don't take that risk."

Wenzel continued that Davey was angry at police "because

they lied to him when they told him that he would go home soon."

Davey once told her, fancifully, that the doctors at Mount Sinai had gagged him and tied him to a chair. "I never want to go back there," she quoted him as saying. "I never want to see those doctors again."

Next up was Assistant Public Guardian Jeanette Volpe, who had observed Noel Kalinowski's interview with Davey at Mount Sinai. She testified that at no time did Davey point to any objects in the book that Kalinowski showed him.

"I was looking straight at him, and he wasn't paying attention to her questions," said Volpe. "In fact, he was trying to ignore her. He was just scribbling on the page."

Asked if anyone else had observed the interview, she said that prosecutor Dean Morask had been present for part of it.

As Volpe left the stand, Judge Smierciak asked the prosecutors why he had not heard from Morask.

"His wife's in labor," Revelle Peritz claimed.

"For how many days?" Smierciak inquired—the hearing now being in its fourth day.

Peritz shrugged.

If Morask really had seen Davey point to a broom, belt, and rope, he could be called to corroborate Kalinowski and undermine Volpe.

Morask, however, would not be called.

Later, David Protess and Rob Warden obtained records revealing that Dean Morask's child had been born on March 7 —the day before Peritz had claimed that Mrs. Morask was in labor.

Cynthia Dowaliby took the stand on the final day of the custody hearing.

Janet Trafelet asked her first about Edward Michaels and the Rorschach test.

"I felt I was doing the test wrong by the way he treated me," Cynthia said. "He kept asking if I could see more. I felt he expected more than I could see."

When Trafelet asked about drug use, she acknowledged that when she was younger she had smoked marijuana "three or four times a year" and once had used cocaine. She added that she had insisted that David remove his marijuana stash to the garage because she did not want it in the house with the children.

"My kids mean everything to me," she said. "Having custody of them would give us the freedom that we don't have now—the freedom to pick up and go, and not be constantly watched. It would help me be a normal parent again."

Patrick Walsh rose. "Miss Witness!" he boomed.

Cynthia flinched, and Robert Byman objected, "Your honor, Mr. Walsh is being offensively rude. He knows Mrs. Dowaliby's name."

"He can conduct the cross-examination this way if he wants, but that's going to be his problem," said Judge Smierciak.

Walsh hammered Cynthia with questions about her "history of drug use," eliciting only that she had begun smoking marijuana when she was seventeen and had last smoked it in 1987.

When Walsh turned to her disciplining of Jaclyn, Cynthia responded that, not believing in corporal punishment, she had deprived Jaclyn of television for misbehaving.

Walsh asked if Davey had "lied" at Mount Sinai about playing games with her and others naked.

"He was fantasizing," Cynthia said.

Dissatisfied, Walsh rephrased the question, again using the word "lied."

"Her testimony was that he was fantasizing," the judge interrupted. "That's not the same as lying."

Asked if she believed she needed psychological therapy, Cynthia replied, "I believe I should have counseling for my bereavement over losing Jaclyn and my separation from David."

The final witness was Dr. Alan Ravitz, a child psychiatrist at the University of Chicago.

Ravitz testified that he had diagnosed or treated more than one thousand physically or sexually abused children.

After meeting twice with Cynthia and after reviewing both Michaels's report on her and the Mount Sinai reports on Davey, Ravitz said, he found "no evidence of psychopathology in Cynthia, nothing in her personality that would prevent her from being a good parent."

Michaels, said Ravitz, had used "an invalid protocol" to evaluate Cynthia and had "arrived at conclusions that weren't warranted by the data."

When asked if he had found Cynthia "guarded," he replied, "If I were Cynthia Dowaliby, I would be guarded, too, given the way she has been treated by people over the last few years."

Davey Dowaliby's psychological symptoms, Ravitz said, were "normal, considering the traumatic events in his life. They do not suggest abuse. Rather, my diagnosis is separation anxiety brought about by the police taking him out of his home."

Referring to the police photographs taken of Davey at Mount Sinai, he said, "No way was this child physically abused. I have a four-year-old who doesn't look as good."

Patrick Walsh argued, in closing on March 11, that the evidence showed that there was a "Dowaliby code of silence" involving the murder of Jaclyn and the abuse of Davey.

"You must understand the code and how it was pierced," Walsh told Judge Smierciak. "It wasn't pierced by David Dowaliby, who went down for the murder of his daughter. It wasn't pierced by Cynthia Dowaliby, who hid behind David and now hides behind people like Barbara White and Reid Schwartz. It was pierced by a little boy, Davey Dowaliby, and by the statements he made to Dr. Sharon Ahart and others."

He added, "Cynthia couldn't hide behind Edward Michaels because he gave her objective tests. He was able to see through her lies."

The testimony showed Cynthia to be "defensive, guarded, and withholding because she has a terrible secret—the secret that she tries to cover up to this day," Walsh argued.

Catherine Ryan countered, in the main closing argument for the defense, that the evidence overwhelmingly showed that Cynthia was "a loving, nurturing parent."

The only evidence to the contrary, she said, were the

Mount Sinai reports, which were prejudiced by police involvement, and Demetra Soter's observations, which were based on the Mount Sinai reports; even Edward Michaels acknowledged that Cynthia did not require psychotherapy.

"A lot of zeroes equal zero," said Ryan.

"Davey has not been allowed to be alone with his mother since the death of his sister three years ago," Ryan added. "Carli has never been allowed to be alone with her mother. It's time to reunite this family. These children should not have to wait another day."

Judge Smierciak ruled on the spot.

Taking strong exception to Walsh's argument, he said, "I did not find Cynthia Dowaliby to be defensive, guarded, or withholding. I found her candid, direct, and unevasive."

Addressing Walsh directly, Smierciak declared, "You stated that there was a code of silence, but I found it noteworthy that you asked neither Cynthia Dowaliby nor her husband any questions about what happened on the night their daughter died."

Turning to the Mount Sinai reports, Smierciak said, "I got the impression that Mount Sinai presumed that there was an abused child and then went looking for evidence to support that assumption."

Assessing the credibility of the prosecution and defense witnesses, he said, "I have to compare the one hundred hours that Dr. Schwartz spent with Davey with Dr. Soter's no hours.

"I conclude that Barbara White, Charlotte Wenzel, and Dr. Ravitz answered all of the issues raised by the state.

"I find that Cynthia Dowaliby is a fit, willing, and capable parent. Granting custody to Mrs. Dowaliby is in the best interests of her children, and it is so ordered.

"It is time for this family to begin healing in earnest."

When Smierciak finished, Robert Byman asked, "Your honor, may the Dowalibys be permitted to embrace?"

Although David and Cynthia had been together in the courtroom for six days, they had been forbidden to touch.

"Motion to hug granted," said Smierciak.

David and Cynthia clung to each other for a full five minutes as spectators applauded.

As the applause subsided, Peggy O'Connor yelled across the courtroom, "You're coming home next, Dave!"

The week after the custody decision, Channel 5 investigative reporter Peter Karl called David Protess at home. It was late, but Karl wanted to see Protess immediately.

"You're not going to fucking believe what I got—a photo of David Dowaliby's double," said Karl.

It was Roy Padecky's mug shot.

Protess pulled David's mug shot from his files; it was the photo from which Everett Mann had identified David—by his nose structure.

When Karl arrived, they held the mug shots side by side.

"It's uncanny," said Karl.

"The main difference I see," said Protess, "is that Padecky's nose is bigger."

As excited as Karl was about the story, newsroom etiquette dictated that he turn it over to Paul Hogan, Channel 5's Dowaliby reporter.

Karl showed the photos to Hogan the next morning. "I think they look alike," said Hogan, "but what matters is what Everett Mann thinks."

However, Hogan and Karl doubted that anyone at Channel 5 could persuade Mann to go on camera. Not only had Mann steadfastly refused to discuss the case with journalists, but he also had become angry when Hogan and Karl had tried to interview him at home for the Channel 5 investigative series.

Protess explained the situation to Rob Warden, who suggested, "How about if I give Everett Mann a try?"

"Nothing to lose," said Protess.

Warden wrote Mann a letter, identifying himself as a legal affairs writer and saying, "I have some information that you may find of interest." He asked Mann to call him, promising him that their initial conversation would be "absolutely confidential."

A few days later Mann called and agreed to meet Warden.

On April 18, 1991, Warden showed Mann the same array of

photos that police had shown him more than two years earlier. Warden then substituted Roy Padecky's photo for David Dowaliby's.

After studying the photos, Mann pointed to Padecky's.

"It's very possible that's who I saw," he said.

Warden asked Mann whether, if the original photo array had included both Padecky's and Dowaliby's mug shots, he would have identified Dowaliby.

"No," Mann answered. "All I saw was a large nose."

After Warden gently questioned Mann about how he could have seen even a nose, Mann offered to take him to the Islander Apartments the following week to demonstrate that it was possible. He agreed that David Protess could come along.

On a dark Saturday night, April 27, Mann stood in the Islander Apartments parking lot and tried to persuade Warden and Protess that he had seen a nose structure from seventy-five yards.

Warden and Protess could barely see the Dumpster at that distance. They tried to conceal their skepticism, but Mann sensed it.

"I never said I was an eyewitness," Mann said with a shrug over dinner at a nearby Ponderosa steak house. "When I read that police had an eyewitness, I thought they were talking about somebody else. What I did see was a midsize car."

Noting that Padecky drove a midsize 1981 Pontiac, Protess asked Mann if it could have been the car he saw.

"The Pontiac and the Malibu are somewhat different," Mann said, "but I don't think I could tell them apart in the dark."

Before the trial, Mann added, he had told Assistant State's Attorney Patrick O'Brien, "Your nose resembles the one I saw."

Protess asked, "If Pat O'Brien's picture had been in the same photo array as David Dowaliby's—"

"I wouldn't have picked out David Dowaliby," Mann said.

After dinner, Mann drove Warden home and signed a statement that concluded, "If either Mr. Padecky's photograph or Mr. O'Brien's photograph had been included in the photo array I was shown on September 16, 1988, I would not have identified David Dowaliby's photograph."

The next day, Warden and Protess returned to the Islander Apartments in the hope of finding a lead on Padecky.

No one knew his current address, but one resident of the complex mentioned that he had run into Padecky recently at a nearby tavern called The Back Door.

Warden and Protess left repeated messages at The Back Door, and Padecky finally called Protess.

Protess said that he wanted to discuss the Dowaliby case, emphasizing that there was no suggestion that Padecky had been involved in the crime. Protess then explained that Everett Mann believed that he might have seen Padecky, rather than David Dowaliby, in the Islander Apartments parking lot.

"That's very possible," Padecky said. "I was in and out of there at all hours, and I always parked in the back."

"Did anyone ever tell you that you look like David Dowaliby?" Protess asked.

"Some people have told me that, but I'm better-looking," Padecky said, chuckling. "I do have a big nose, though."

Protess called Hogan, who broke the story two days later.

"The testimony of Everett Mann was the only significant difference that led a judge to declare Cynthia Dowaliby not guilty and allow a jury to find her husband guilty," Hogan's report began. "Tonight, that crucial piece of the state's largely circumstantial case is gone."

The camera flashed to Rob Warden, who branded Mann's identification of David Dowaliby as "worthless," and then to Robert Byman, who said, "The only real evidence the state had was a so-called eyewitness, who turned out to be a nose witness, and now it turns out that the nose wasn't David Dowaliby's."

Hogan's story was the subject of intense discussion the next morning among the Illinois Appellate Court justices who would decide David's appeal. For them, the story reinforced an impression they already had formed from the legal briefs—that Mann's trial testimony had not been credible.

LONG ROAD HOME

When the Illinois Appellate Court scheduled oral arguments on David Dowaliby's appeal, the demand for seats was so great that Justice Alan J. Greiman quipped, "If we sold tickets, we'd be able to build a new courthouse."

The June 12, 1991, event was moved to the Chicago courtroom of the Illinois Supreme Court for its greater seating capacity, but the crowd still was SRO. For the first time, television cameras recorded a proceeding of the Appellate Court, and portions were carried live on some stations.

David Dowaliby, beginning his second summer in prison, followed the coverage from his sweltering cell; incarcerated defendants are not permitted to attend appellate arguments.

Justices David M. Cerda and Dom J. Rizzi joined Justice Greiman to hear the case. The previous summer,

Cerda and Rizzi had voted to free David Dowaliby on bond pending appeal, only to be reversed by the Illinois Supreme Court.

Since then, Greiman, a liberal former state legislator, had been selected for the Dowaliby panel. He replaced retired Justice William Sylvester White, who had dissented from Cerda and Rizzi's decision on the bond.

"David Dowaliby did not kill his daughter," Robert Byman began. "He does not know who did. Neither David nor Cynthia Dowaliby had a hand in her death, and what is most important this morning, the state did not prove that they did."

Justice Rizzi interrupted, "Before you get into the legal arguments, tell us what you think happened here."

"It is certainly our position that there was an intruder," Byman said, "but it's not our burden to prove that there was."

After Byman described the facts of the case, Justice Rizzi asked, "If the only reasonable inference that you can draw from those facts is that these parents were involved, isn't that sufficient for a jury to believe that they're guilty beyond a reasonable doubt?"

"It is not, your honor," said Byman, arguing that even if it had been clear that David *or* Cynthia had committed the crime, that would not be sufficient to sustain a conviction against either one of them.

"Hold on," said Rizzi. "It could have been both of them."

"Yes, your honor," said Byman.

"So, if it were both, could he be found guilty?"

"Not unless the state *proves* that that happened."

"Right," said Rizzi.

Later, on the same point, Rizzi said, "I guess there's one other alternative here—I guess this crime could have involved Ann Dowaliby, or Cynthia and Ann, excluding David Dowaliby. That's a possibility, isn't it?"

"Sure," said Byman. "I'll give you another alternative."

"I'd like to hear all alternatives that you can think of," said Rizzi.

"Jaclyn could have died prior to David coming home that

night," said Byman. "It could have been Michelle Goldrick, or Ann, or Cynthia. It could have been another family member or somebody else coming in and out of the house who we don't even know about.

"I certainly hope the family doesn't think for one minute that I believe any of these, but if you want alternatives, they exist. The state has not proved that only one person in the world could have done it."

David A. Cuomo, of the state's attorney's appellate unit, argued for the prosecution.

"There isn't any one fact that stands out as a smoking gun," Cuomo began. "It is all of the facts, when considered together, which show that this defendant was proven guilty beyond a reasonable doubt."

Justice Rizzi interrupted, "All right, let's delineate the facts you're relying on. What's the first fact?"

"There are no credible signs of forcible entry," said Cuomo.

"That doesn't prove that David was involved in anything."

"I agree."

"What's the next one?"

"We know for a fact that Jaclyn Dowaliby was alive in the late evening hours of September 9, 1988, and that, from the medical examiner's testimony, she had to have been dead a short time later."

"None of those facts, in my opinion, relates to David Dowaliby."

"I think they do, your honor."

"Well, we have a difference of opinion. Unfortunately for you, I'm deciding the case."

Cuomo took a drink of water and started to say something when Rizzi interrupted again, "Disprove that it could not have been Ann Dowaliby, will you?"

"First of all, she testified that she spent the night—"

"That doesn't disprove it."

Cuomo stammered, "The next day, when she came home, the police smelled liquor on her breath."

"So?" Rizzi said, shrugging. "She was intoxicated. So what?"

Rizzi next asked, "How about Cynthia Dowaliby? Maybe she did it."

"David and Cynthia could have acted together, your honor," Cuomo answered.

"Where's the evidence that they acted together?"

Unable to cite anything concrete, Cuomo offered a theory—that David had canceled his plans to hit golf balls and instead watched cartoons with Davey, while waiting for Ann to come home and discover the broken window.

Insisting that David had lied about why he changed his plans, Cuomo added, "It raises an inference—maybe he'd done something in the night that he had to conceal in the morning."

"In other words," Justice Greiman interjected, "maybe he decided to watch cartoons—or maybe he killed his daughter. That's a big maybe!"

Rizzi then impatiently intoned, "What other evidence, or what other schemes, do you want to get into? How about Everett Mann?"

"His identification is vague at best," Cuomo acknowledged, adding, however, that the car Mann had seen was "consistent with" Cynthia Dowaliby's Chevrolet Malibu.

"There's never been a positive identification of that car," Rizzi retorted. "As a matter of fact, there was testimony that the Malibu was in front of the Dowaliby house at the time."

"I think the jury was entitled to not believe her," Cuomo responded.

"So she lied, too?" Rizzi shot back. "Everybody lied, except who the state called? It's a heck of a case!"

"That sometimes happens," said Cuomo.

"What about the nose identification?" asked Rizzi.

"I admit it's not very persuasive."

"What probative value does it have? It was just a man with a nose."

"Well, it tends to exclude other possibilities. For example, it is significant that he did not see three people in the car—that he only saw one."

"If he had seen three, he would have seen three noses. Would that be probative?"

"Not terribly probative."

"Was Everett Mann's testimony significant enough to convict the defendant?"

"It was important, but it was not critical."

"Well, wait a second. I don't understand that one."

"It's hard to answer."

"I want you to know that I don't see much of a distinction between important and critical."

Cuomo gripped the podium tightly but did not respond.

After a pause, Greiman asked Cuomo to justify showing the jury seventeen photographs of Jaclyn's decomposed body.

Cuomo said that they "helped establish the cause of death."

"These pictures don't show you the cause of death," Greiman said, his voice rising. "They're just gruesome pictures."

Continuing, Greiman inquired, "Do they illustrate the weapon that might have been used?"

"Yes, they do in the sense that they exclude, for instance, a gunshot wound," Cuomo contended.

"No, no, no!" Greiman declared. "You can look at these pictures all day, and you can't tell whether there's a gunshot wound. These pictures barely show a human being, counsel."

Greiman then asked, "Do they shed light on motive?"

"No."

"Do they determine the atrociousness of the act?"

"No."

"So the fact is," Rizzi picked up, "they don't have any probative value."

Rizzi added, "When you give the jury these photographs, it's hard to imagine that they wouldn't have inflamed or aroused their passions—'We're gonna get somebody for this.' "

"I don't believe that happened," Cuomo rejoined.

He then delivered a brief summation in which he argued that the prosecution—"by excluding all the other rational possibilities''—had proved that Jaclyn Dowaliby had been murdered by ''this defendant and his codefendant.''

In a brief rebuttal, Byman told the justices, ''The death of this little girl was a tragedy, but it is perhaps a greater tragedy that her father is now spending forty-five years in prison for a crime that he did not commit and that the state did not prove he committed.''

Cerda glanced at the other justices and, seeing that they had no further questions, announced, ''The case will be taken under consideration.''

Two days later—on Friday, June 14—Justices Cerda, Greiman, and Rizzi held a private ''impressions conference'' on the Dowaliby case. They mused over the Dowalibys' guilt or innocence, concluding what most others had concluded—that the case was an extraordinary mystery.

''I kept waiting for Perry Mason or Jessica Fletcher to step up and tell us what happened,'' said Greiman.

The justices speculated that an intruder could have come through either the broken window or the patio door and that Cynthia or David might have committed the crime.

''What about Grandma?'' Rizzi asked, suggesting that Ann Dowaliby might have come home drunk and killed Jaclyn.

''If a family member killed her, it was probably an accident,'' said Greiman, noting that one of the morgue photos revealed nail polish on Jaclyn's toes. ''She seemed very well cared for,'' he said.

Cerda, who would write the opinion under the Appellate Court's random assignment procedure, turned the discussion to the issue at hand—which was not David's actual guilt or innocence, but whether he was entitled to relief.

The Appellate Court had three options: to affirm the conviction, to grant a new trial, or to reverse the conviction outright.

''This case never should have been prosecuted,'' Rizzi declared, adding that he favored reversing the case outright.

Greiman interjected that there were several grounds for ordering a new trial—''The gruesome photos are enough by themselves''—but shared Rizzi's view that the verdict should be thrown out. Greiman noted that Judge Neville had set a benchmark by acquitting Cynthia. "If she's not guilty, he's not guilty," said Greiman.

Cerda agreed, calling Everett Mann "unbelievable" and David's statements to police "inconsequential."

While the justices took no formal vote, there was a meeting of the minds: The Appellate Court, for the first time in six years, would declare a convicted murderer legally not guilty.*

Also agreeing that the case had Hollywood potential, the justices joked about who might play them—Cesar Romero as Cerda, Danny DeVito as Rizzi, and Sean Connery as Greiman.

When the conference ended, Cerda assigned a law clerk, Jo-Ann Della-Giustina, to draft an opinion that he would revise and circulate to the other justices for comment and further revision. That process would take many months.

Meanwhile, David faced a long, hot summer in prison.

On July 1, David Protess and Rob Warden visited David Dowaliby at Stateville.

Dowaliby said that trouble was brewing at the prison.

Much of the prisoner population of more than two thousand belonged to Chicago street gangs. David was a "neutron," meaning that he had no gang affiliation.

Stateville gang chiefs were rumored to have held a summit meeting in the prison library, after which ominous graffiti began appearing on corridor walls. It said such things as "Kill the warden" and "Kill the police"—meaning guards.

David now shared a cell with three other neutrons in

---

* In 1985, Justice Rizzi authored a majority opinion reversing outright the conviction of Steven Linscott in what was known as "the dream murder case." The next year, the Illinois Supreme Court reversed the Appellate Court, remanding the case for further proceedings. The Appellate Court then ordered a new trial and the Illinois Supreme Court affirmed that decision. *People* v. *Linscott*, 135 Ill. App. 3d 773 (1985), 114 Ill. 2d 340 (1986), 159 Ill. App. 3d 71 (1987), 142 Ill. 2d 22 (1991). In 1992, DNA evidence conclusively established Linscott's innocence, and the Cook County State's Attorney's Office dropped the case.

G Dorm, an honor section of the prison where the cells had lockless doors instead of bars. Fearing that the gangs "had declared open season on neutrons," David said, he and his cellmates had torn strips of sheets to tie their door closed in an emergency.

The prison grapevine had it that whatever the gangs were planning would occur on Monday, July 15.

Protess and Warden, who had arrived at Stateville optimistic from the tone of the justices at the oral argument, left concerned about David's safety.

On Saturday, July 13, two days before the anticipated trouble, a guard in F House, a traditional section of the prison, had disconnected a prisoner's telephone call. The prisoner, a member of the Latin Disciples street gang, then attacked the guard with a prisonmade knife known as a shank. Other guards fired, killing the prisoner and wounding the guard.

The next night, in retaliation for the prisoner's death, seven Disciples took two guards hostage and went on a rampage—in David's G Dorm. The Disciples wore masks. One was armed with an ax, two with five-foot pipes, and four with shanks.

When the rampage started about 7:00 P.M., David and his cellmates carried out their security plan with the torn sheets. Smoke soon began seeping into their cell from mattresses that the Disciples set afire, and David stuffed damp rags around the door.

At about 9:30 P.M. someone shouted, "Everyone who wants out, get out now!"

David untied the strips of sheets, cautiously opened the door, peered into the corridor, and saw a squad of "Orange Crush"—state police in orange riot gear.

By this time the Disciples had hidden their weapons and flushed their masks down toilets. One hostage had been severely beaten with a pipe. Another had suffered slight injuries, and a third, who had hidden under a staircase, had escaped unscathed.

The Orange Crush, armed with shotguns, escorted David and other prisoners into a prison yard, where their hands were bound with plastic straps.

The prisoners were kept in the yard until 5:30 A.M. Monday, July 15, when they were sent to a unit normally occupied by incoming prisoners.

The Dowaliby family had been near hysteria since the initial reports of the riot, partly because the only information that had been released about the slain prisoner was his age—exactly the same as David's.

After finally learning that David was safe, Cynthia, Davey, and Carli rushed to visit him the afternoon of July 15. Cynthia found David exhausted and depressed. He told her that his cell had been ransacked and all of his belongings taken—his clothes, books, television set, radio, and typewriter.

"What else can they take from you?" Cynthia asked, sobbing.

Davey offered his father thirty dollars that relatives had given him for his seventh birthday the previous month.

"You can use it to get a new typewriter, Dad," he said.

The next day, July 16, David Protess called Jo-Ann Della-Giustina, Justice Cerda's law clerk, whom he had met at the oral argument.

Protess knew that, ethically, Della-Giustina was bound to silence about the case. However, he wanted to underscore David Dowaliby's physical peril, in the hope that the Appellate Court would not allow its opinion to languish.

"Could you give me any hint of the timing?" Protess asked.

"I can't tell you that," said Della-Giustina.

"I hope David lives to see his exoneration," said Protess.

"Assuming that he is exonerated," Della-Giustina responded.

Della-Giustina gave no hint that she was at that moment working on a draft opinion that would exonerate David.

In late July, Cerda circulated a slightly edited version of Della-Giustina's work product to Justices Greiman and Rizzi.

The draft opinion accused the prosecutors of repeatedly distorting the trial record in their appellate brief to make the evidence appear more incriminating than it actually had been, concluding that the evidence against David was "improbable, unconvincing, and completely unsatisfactory."

The draft opinion was fifty-nine pages long, forty pages of which were devoted to the facts of the case. The strategy for including so much detail was that, if the opinion should be reviewed by the Illinois Supreme Court, it would be clear that the jury had had no rational basis to convict.

On August 15, Greiman wrote Cerda a memo saying that he agreed with the thrust of the draft opinion but thought the attack on the prosecution "strident."

Greiman noted that the draft opinion failed to point out that "the trial court directed the verdict for Mrs. Dowaliby and that there is nothing more that implicates Mr. Dowaliby than there was for his wife." Thus he tacitly raised a question: Would it be better to blame Judge Neville for sending the case to the jury than to blame the jury for an irrational verdict?

The other justices would consider that question after a Labor Day break.

Thinking that the Appellate Court was more likely to order a new trial than to reverse the conviction outright, David Protess and Rob Warden turned their attention to an issue that might be damaging at a retrial.

Musing about the case over dinner, Judge Neville had told them that only one of the "guilty knowledge" statements attributed to David appeared to have no innocent explanation —neighbor Colleen Jones-Godin's claim that, before Jaclyn's body had been found, David told her, "It was really hard at first, but it gets easier day by day."

Neville could not imagine that an innocent man would have said that while his daughter was missing.

Checking the trial transcript, Protess and Warden noted that Jones-Godin had testified that David made the statement in the presence of Robert Tolbert, who at the time, she said, was helping David Dowaliby board up the basement window.

Protess and Warden contacted Tolbert, who put the statement in a different light. He said that the discussion with

Jones-Godin had occurred not while Jaclyn was missing, but after her body had been found.

Tolbert added that he was certain of the timing because a telephone extension line had been run from his home through the broken window, so that the Dowalibys' telephone could be kept open in case of a ransom demand.

The extension line had not been removed until after Jaclyn's body had been found and, according to Tolbert, it was at least two days after that when he and David had boarded up the window.

Tolbert said he had stood ready to rebut Jones-Godin at the trial but that the defense had failed to call him to testify.

"Incredible," said Robert Byman when Protess and Warden related Tolbert's version. "That mistake will not be repeated if there's a new trial."

Protess and Warden also obtained a document discrediting another "guilty knowledge" statement—that David, when told that Jaclyn had been found, first had asked, "In a field?"

The document was State Police Sergeant Kevin Shaughnessy's deposition, taken in connection with the Dowaliby child custody case and sealed in Juvenile Court files since October 1990. In the deposition, Shaughnessy said that David actually first had asked, "Is she alive?"

Shaughnessy's deposition, by contradicting both Daniel McDevitt's grand jury testimony and FBI Agent Alfred Hardman's trial testimony, would undermine their credibility at a new trial.

In fact, a new trial was no longer under consideration by the Appellate Court. Having already decided before Labor Day to reverse the conviction outright, the three justices now were grappling only with how best to craft an opinion that would withstand a likely appeal to the Illinois Supreme Court.

Justice Rizzi proposed slashing the lengthy statement of facts and getting right to the core of case—to show that, standing alone and taken in the light most favorable to the prosecution, the evidence had been insufficient.

Like Justice Greiman, Rizzi also asserted that the opinion

should focus on Judge Neville's improper denial of David's motion for a directed verdict, rather than on jury error.

Justice Cerda soon agreed.

However, dickering over the wording of the opinion stretched over six weeks, causing Greiman considerable consternation; he quoted the old lament "Justice delayed is justice denied."

Finally, on October 28, the justices settled on a twenty-one-page opinion proclaiming that the prosecution had "failed to introduce sufficient evidence to directly or indirectly link David with Jaclyn's murder."

Said the opinion: "Although there are many unanswered questions, after viewing the evidence in a light most favorable to the state, we conclude that the totality of the evidence is not sufficient to prove David guilty."

The opinion made three basic points about the evidence: First, the prosecution did not prove that David was the only person who had the opportunity to commit the crime. Second, Everett Mann's testimony was "doubtful, vague, and unreliable." Third, the various statements attributed to David, given "their most sinister cast," did not justify a conviction.

"We conclude," said the opinion, "that the trial court erred in denying David's motion for a directed verdict."

Cerda instructed the clerk of the Appellate Court to notify the lawyers and the news media that the opinion would be released at 10:00 A.M. on Wednesday, October 30.

Reporters descended on the clerk's office at 9:30 A.M.

Most predicted that David Dowaliby would be granted a new trial. Only a Channel 7 producer thought that the conviction would be affirmed.

No one had it right.

A deputy clerk called the lawyers into a private room to give them copies of the opinion a few minutes in advance.

At ten on the dot, another deputy tossed a stack of copies across the counter to journalists, who dove for them like sharks in a feeding frenzy.

Robert Byman emerged from the private room, smiling.

"I'm ecstatic," he said. "I just spoke to Cynthia Dowaliby, and all I could hear was screaming on the other end of the line."

Byman said that the next step would be to ask the Appellate Court to release David on bond. (The prosecution had twenty-one days to ask the Illinois Supreme Court to review the case; a bond order was necessary to free David in the meantime.)

As Byman filed his bond motion, Rob Warden, fulfilling a promise he had made to Judge Neville, called him to report what the opinion said.

"They say you erred by not granting David's motion for a directed verdict," Warden told Neville.

"Oh, shit," said Neville.

David Dowaliby heard the news on the radio.

He called the home of his twin sister Rose, where Cynthia and the Freedom Committee had gathered.

David was still on the phone when David Protess and Rob Warden arrived with copies of the opinion.

"Read me the best part," he implored Protess.

"The last line says, 'Reversed,' " Protess told him. "It's unanimous! No new trial!"

Meanwhile, Warden told Cynthia the bad news—that the prosecutors might try to block David's release on bond pending a review by the Illinois Supreme Court.

When reporters and television crews arrived, Cynthia profusely thanked the Appellate Court and her lawyers and made a tearful plea to State's Attorney Jack O'Malley to drop the case. "Please don't continue our pain any further," she said. "Let David come home to his family."

Afterward, Channel 7's Dick Johnson offered his hand to Cynthia, saying, "No hard feelings. It was nothing personal."

She graciously shook his hand.

In another room, Paul Hogan beamed as members of the Freedom Committee smothered him with hugs and kisses.

David Protess drove Cynthia to Davey's school. Davey was just coming out of his classroom for lunch.

"The judges decided!" she told him. "Daddy's coming home soon!"

Davey's eyes grew wide and a smile filled his face as he leaped three feet into his mother's arms.

Although Justice Cerda had written the opinion, some police and prosecutors thought that Justice Rizzi was behind it.

On the prosecution mock-up of the basement window, stored in the state's attorney's office, graffiti anonymously appeared:

"Rizzi sucks donkey dick."

On November 1, two days after the Appellate Court decision, Rob Warden met State's Attorney Jack O'Malley for breakfast.

They had different agendas. O'Malley wanted Warden to return to coordinate issues for his approaching reelection campaign. Warden wanted O'Malley to drop the Dowaliby case. Both would be disappointed.

O'Malley said he planned to announce that morning that his office would ask the Illinois Supreme Court to review the case. He argued that, rather than viewing the evidence in the light most favorable to the prosecution—the proper standard of review—the Appellate Court had retried the case, giving the benefit of the doubt to the defendant.

Warden disagreed that the Appellate Court had done that, adding, "In any case, your office is playing a semantic game with an innocent man's life."

O'Malley would not budge.

Warden said that he could not help in O'Malley's reelection effort. "You can't have an issues director who's sniping at your office over this case," he said.

An hour later, O'Malley told reporters what he had told Warden, adding that his office would oppose David Dowaliby's release on bond. "The jury found him guilty of murder in the first degree," O'Malley said. "I don't think murderers should be out on the streets of Cook County."

Over the weekend, while the Appellate Court's decision on

bond was awaited, David was moved to an isolation cell at Stateville "for his own protection."

"I feel like I'm being punished for being innocent," David told Paul Hogan.

The *Chicago Tribune* agreed with David.

In a Sunday lead editorial headlined "Not Beyond a Reasonable Doubt," the newspaper branded O'Malley's decision to fight bond "politically motivated" and "cruelly unnecessary at this juncture."

The editorial also urged O'Malley and police to "reopen the botched inquiry and redouble their efforts to solve Jaclyn's murder."

The Appellate Court set bond at $400,000 on November 5, but prosecutors sought an emergency stay from Justice Michael A. Bilandic of the Illinois Supreme Court.

Bilandic, a former mayor of Chicago and close political ally of the Daley family, promptly granted the stay, referring the matter to the full seven-member Supreme Court. Bilandic acted without reading any of the legal pleadings, although he said he had followed the case in the news media.

On November 11, Veterans' Day, a holiday for most public offices, the Supreme Court lifted the stay without comment.

David Dowaliby could be free—if he could come up with the bond money and find someone to accept it.

The Dowalibys had $29,000, which was $11,000 short of the amount that had to be posted in cash (10 percent of the $400,000).

David Protess and Rob Warden lent the family $11,000.

Robert Byman persuaded the Circuit Court clerk to process the bond, despite the holiday, and Joan Protess posted it.

However, there was no one at the Illinois Department of Corrections to handle the paperwork.

David Dowaliby would spend one more night in prison.

At 9:06 A.M. on Wednesday, November 13—eighteen months, one week, and three days after her husband's conviction—Cynthia Dowaliby entered the main gate of Stateville.

Five minutes later, she and David emerged arm in arm. They stepped before a battery of television cameras covering the event live, preempting Oprah Winfrey, a *Perry Mason* rerun, and other daytime fare.

"It's hard to believe right now," said David. "I don't feel bitter, but it's never going to end until we find who killed Jaclyn." Referring to Cynthia, he said, "I'm proud of her. She's a real fighter. She never gave up—not for a minute."

Cynthia and David then were driven to a hotel, where they were reunited with their children, family, and friends.

David Protess was asked to give a toast.

Lifting a glass of champagne, he began by wishing the Dowalibys a lifetime of happiness and security.

"It's remarkable that lawyers, journalists, and everyday people came together to make this day possible," he continued. "You represent the best of America—you stood up to be counted when somebody needed you."

After the toast, David Dowaliby clipped from the Freedom Committee members' wrists the tattered red and white macramé bracelets they had vowed to wear until his release.

A few minutes before 6:00 P.M., Cynthia, David, and Davey took leave of the party briefly to grant an exclusive interview to Paul Hogan in a separate room of the hotel.

The interview aired live on Channel 5, to the cheers of viewers in the Dowalibys' suite.

A little later, the revelers left.

While Cynthia waited in an adjoining bedroom, David tucked his children in, holding them until they fell asleep.

On Sunday the Dowaliby family went to church.

After the service they went to St. Mary's Cemetery, where David knelt and placed a wreath on a small gray marble headstone inscribed, "God Bless Our Precious Angel."

Huddled together in the cold, they prayed.

Then David took his family home.

NOT TO BE FORGOTTEN

In the months after David Dowaliby's release from prison, David Protess and Rob Warden resumed the search for Jaclyn's killer.

Picking up where John Waters had left off, they went to see Perry Hernandez at the Pontiac Correctional Center, where he was serving forty-five years for, among other crimes, the kidnapping and sexual assault of Rory MacRand.

Hernandez agreed to break his silence because he wanted "to set the record straight." He emphatically denied murdering Jaclyn Dowaliby, but vividly described how he had abducted six-year-old Rory as she and her family slept in their Blue Island home in the predawn hours of September 2, 1989:

"I broke up with my girlfriend that day and went to a bar to get drunk. I had a few beers and got in a fight with a guy, so I left and went to another bar. I played the jukebox, got more drunk, and finally got thrown out.

"I started to walk home and something clicked in my mind. I went to a house where I knew a little girl lived [the Arias residence]. I tore a screen off, but a light came on. I ducked, and then I took off.

"I went to another house down the alley. I was running. Then the wind hit me, and I thought maybe that was God's way of telling me to stop. Then the wind died down, and I realized what needed to be done.

"I was just going through the motions. I climbed through the window. I was real drunk, and I knocked over some silverware and stuff. It made a lot of noise, but nobody woke up.

"I opened the front door to have a way to escape, and then I went upstairs. When I opened one bedroom door, a dog started barking, so I backed out.

"I went down to the basement and turned off the power. I fell over a washing machine, and I guess I dropped my cigarettes. I went back up and unlocked the back door and kitchen door, so there were three doors open if I had to get out of there.

"I went upstairs again, into a room where two kids were sleeping. The little girl was over by the window. I crept like a cat and lifted her up. She grabbed me around the neck to hold on, and I covered her mouth, in case she tried to yell. I took her out the back door and over by the canal."

Hernandez went on to describe how he molested Rory, concluding, "I didn't mean to hurt her."

Protess and Warden turned the conversation to the Dowaliby case. They hoped that, if Hernandez had killed Jaclyn, he would slip and say something that would betray his guilt—but he held firm.

"I swear I didn't take her," he repeatedly insisted.

However, he acknowledged, "I can't say where I was that night. I just don't remember."

"Did the police question you about it?"

"Never. My lawyer did, but the cops didn't."*

* * *

Looking for other kidnappings that might be linked to Jaclyn's disappearance, Northwestern University students scoured newspaper files and interviewed law enforcement officials across the country.

The students found no apparent connections, but discovered more than forty late-night abductions of children from their beds between 1984 and 1992. Strikingly, the parents often were the initial suspects—sometimes with tragic consequences:

Fairfield, California: Three-year-old Clark Handa, one of five children in a well-known family, was abducted from his bed during the night of August 22, 1984. The next morning, his mother found a ransom note. When no kidnapper contacted the Handa family again, however, the investigation quickly turned to the parents. They eventually were eliminated as suspects. Nearly eight years later, Fairfield Detective Harold Sagam said that police were focusing on "a prime suspect" and acknowledged that by targeting the parents they "lost valuable time along the way." Clark's fate is unknown.

Big Sandy, Texas: Five-year-old Ara Johnson was tucked into her bed by her father on April 2, 1986. At 6:45 A.M. the next day, Ara's mother went to awaken her for school. Ara was gone, along with her corduroy bedspread. The police

---

* Hernandez also denied committing the vicious attack on a woman at the commuter train station in Blue Island mentioned on page 153. Ironically, that was the crime that brought him to public attention, since it was captured on videotape by a security camera. When Protess and Warden compared that videotape (which did not show the assailant's face) with a television news tape of Hernandez made immediately after his arrest, they discovered a startling fact—while Hernandez had a large tattoo on his right arm, the man who attacked the woman in the train station clearly had no tattoo. Hernandez said he had pleaded guilty to the commuter beating only because it was part of a plea-bargain package; it added no additional prison time to his sentences for the other crimes. In June 1992, Paul Greves (by then retired as Blue Island police chief) confided to Protess and Warden that he never believed that Hernandez had committed the Metra crime. "But, what the hell, he pleaded guilty to it," Greves said, adding, "They'll never get the crazy Mexican who really did it."

questioned, but ruled out, the Johnsons as suspects. Ara is still missing.

Lexington, South Carolina: Seven-year-old Jessie Gutierrez vanished from her bed on the morning of June 6, 1986. Her mother found a front window open. Jessie's younger sister said that "a strange man in a big black cowboy hat" had carried her sister away. The mother was questioned, but eventually eliminated, as a suspect. Jessie has never been found.

Serra Mesa, California: Eight-year-old "Alicia" (a pseudonym used by the *San Diego Union*) was abducted on May 8, 1989, by an intruder who entered her home through a window, took her out of her bed as her brother slept nearby, raped her, and put her back. Her father was charged with rape, and prosecutors filed a juvenile petition to remove the children from the home. While he was awaiting trial, forensic tests exonerated him and implicated a man with prior convictions for child molestation. "Sometimes we make inferences that are just plain stupid," the *Union* quoted the judge in the juvenile case as saying.

Reno, Nevada: Seven-year-old Monica DaSilva disappeared from her bed in the middle of the night as her parents and brother slept nearby on September 24, 1990. There were indications that someone had entered the home through a bedroom window, but the parents were interrogated as suspects—one theory being that they had sold Monica for drugs. In October the parents were arrested and charged with using drugs, but the charges were dropped when drug tests proved negative. Meanwhile, the DaSilvas lost their jobs and moved into a homeless shelter. They were eliminated as suspects a year later, when a body found two weeks after Monica disappeared was identified through dental records as hers; the coroner originally had concluded that the decomposition of that body was too advanced for the body to have been Monica's.

In each case, the police targeted the parents based on two assumptions that proved wrong—first, that missing children invariably are taken by family members, and second, that strangers cannot enter homes in the middle of the night and snatch children without awakening their parents.

The Dowaliby case, therefore, appeared to be an aberration only in the lengths to which the authorities went to victimize the parents.

Why did this case go farther than others?

In a word, politics.

The case arose at a seminal point in the career of Richard M. Daley—a prosecutor bent on capturing the mayoral seat that his late father had filled for twenty-one years.

As Daley prepared to begin his mayoral campaign in the fall of 1988, the news media were generating intense pressure for a solution to Jaclyn's murder, but no solution was in sight.

In two meetings with police, the first in mid-October, the second in early November, Patrick O'Brien had declared that there was not enough evidence to charge the Dowalibys.

Although no further inculpatory evidence was developed, Daley ordered the case to proceed as he approached the announcement of his mayoral candidacy. It was a decision made in consort with his chief political aide, Frank Kreusi, and over the objections of several career prosecutors in the office.

Patrick O'Brien would carry out Daley's order.

On November 22, the same day that Daley revealed his intention to run for mayor, the Dowalibys were arrested.

Once Daley had set the criminal justice bureaucracy in motion, it took eighteen months for a trial judge to rescue Cynthia from certain conviction and eighteen months more for the Illinois Appellate Court to liberate David.

The system eventually "worked," but, in the meantime, the Dowalibys were triply victimized—by a killer, by the police, and by politics.

On February 5, 1992, the Illinois Supreme Court—without dissent—denied prosecutors' request to review the Appellate Court's outright reversal of the Dowaliby case.

"The Dowaliby case is over," declared State's Attorney Jack O'Malley—meaning that he would neither appeal to the U.S. Supreme Court nor reopen the investigation. He added that the Appellate Court ruling "sets a dangerous precedent."

Mayor Daley pouted to reporters, "I guess appellate courts can do whatever they want. Maybe we should do away with juries."

Justice Rizzi angrily called a press conference to respond to the current Republican state's attorney and former Democratic state's attorney. "It's the function of the Appellate Court to prevent an injustice," said Rizzi. "This case never should have been prosecuted. It was a waste of taxpayers' money."

Two weeks after the Supreme Court decision, Channel 5 aired a story with an ironic twist.

Paul Hogan disclosed that Captain Daniel McDevitt, who had headed the Dowaliby task force, and his top aide, Sergeant Kevin Shaughnessy, had been suspended by the Illinois State Police—in a child pornography scandal.

Shaughnessy had permitted child pornography tapes, which had been seized in a raid, to be taken from his office and viewed by State Police officers, and McDevitt had covered up the incident.

"What goes around comes around," Hogan commented after the broadcast.

What went around also came around to Dr. Sharon Ahart, whose resignation was accepted by Mount Sinai Hospital in a sweeping reorganization of its hospital's Pediatric Ecology Unit.

Benn Greenspan, who became president of Mount Sinai in late 1991, had made the reorganization a priority in view of the disclosures about the PEU's handling of the Dowaliby case and a second case in which Ahart's diagnosis of sexual abuse appeared to have been unfounded.

Greenspan said that the PEU had been infected with a "missionary zeal" that hampered its objectivity in diagnosing child abuse. The fervor had been unrestrained because the unit lacked checks and balances; unlike other units of the hospital, it had been structured so that all staff members reported only to one person, Dr. Howard Levy.

After an internal assessment of the PEU, Greenspan fired Levy, and twenty-one members of the unit offered to resign. Greenspan asked all but one to remain—the exception being Ahart.

Most of the others did remain to work in a reorganized PEU, in which pediatricians, psychiatrists, social workers, and nurses reported to separate departments, providing external accountability.

When Ahart continued to appear in the PEU after the effective date of her resignation, Greenspan ordered the hospital's security staff to escort her out of the hospital.

On February 21, 1992, the Freedom Committee held its final function—a party for those who had supported the Dowalibys through their ordeal.

More than a hundred well-wishers packed a south suburban VFW hall.

Among the guests was Channel 5's Paul Hogan, who had been named local television's "best reporter" by the Associated Press for his Dowaliby coverage.

Hogan had received another recognition, of sorts—Daniel McDevitt had sent word through an intermediary that Hogan "had better stay out of the south suburbs."

Also at the party was Daniel Franks, who had seriously considered giving up the practice of law after David's conviction. Franks had to leave early to help a client in an emergency, but not before David told him, "I think we would have won at the trial if I had let you take over my defense."

Ralph Meczyk and Lawrence Hyman had not been invited to the party.

Two days earlier, the *Chicago Daily Law Bulletin* had carried a story saying that David's victory had been "bittersweet" for Meczyk because he and Hyman had not received sufficient credit for their work on the case.

"All the investigation was done by us and given to Jenner & Block on a silver platter," Meczyk whined. "We wanted to win so bad that financing the case didn't matter anymore."

The story mentioned neither Hyman's unsuccessful lawsuit against the Dowalibys to collect allegedly unpaid expenses nor a lawsuit that Charlotte Waters had filed more recently against Meczyk. The Waters lawsuit alleged that Meczyk had failed to pay her late husband $5,000 for his investigative work.

Robert Byman was unable to attend the celebration, but called to convey best wishes for the future.

David thanked him for all he had done, asking rhetorically, "How can we ever repay you?"

"I've already been paid—my biggest fee ever," said Byman. "The day you walked out of prison, my three sons jumped into my arms and said they were proud of me. There can be no bigger fee than that."

At the party, David repeated the conversation. "That's the kind of guy Byman is," David said. "He cares more about hugs from his kids than all the money in the world."*

The party reached an emotional climax in the late evening as Peggy O'Connor, who recently had returned to work at the White Castle to help support the family in hard economic times, asked the guests to join hands on the dance floor with David and Cynthia.

Forming a circle, the group joined in the lyrics and swayed to the rhythm of a James Taylor oldie, "You've Got a Friend."

It was the only dance for Cynthia that night. "I can't really celebrate until Jaclyn's killer is behind bars," she said. "Jack O'Malley says it's over, but it will never be over."

Cynthia said that they fleetingly considered suing the police and prosecutors for wrecking their lives.

"Byman tells us it would be hard to win," she said.** "Besides, we've had enough of the legal system."

Cynthia had returned to junior college, taking courses to prepare for a career in nursing.

David was taking classes at the same junior college one evening a week; they drove to class together, as Cynthia's

---

* Jenner & Block had poured more than $250,000 in resources, including eight hundred hours of Byman's time, into the Dowaliby appeal and custody battle.

** Government officials performing discretionary functions enjoy broad immunity from civil liability. See *Harlow* v. *Fitzgerald*, 457 U.S. 800 (1982).

mother baby-sat at her Tinley Park home, where they all still lived.

David had walked out of prison into a major recession, but Ronald Patterson, true to his word, had hired him back. David was working three days a week, spending the rest of his time studying and getting to know his children again.

"Maybe someday," David said wistfully, "we'll buy a home of our own and start a new life." (Later, the Dowalibys did manage to buy a modest home and changed their last name to protect the safety and privacy of their children. News organizations learned the new name, but only Channel 7 disclosed it.)

Amid the revelry of the party, there was anger. "Dave and Cyndi got screwed, just like we all get screwed every day," said the Dowalibys' former next-door neighbor Robert Tolbert. "Our so-called leaders took their life away. Now, who's going to give it back? They never even apologized."

Daniel Verble, another former neighbor, expressed a similar sentiment: "I used to think that this country was straight, but now when I watch the news I'm not sure any of it is true."

Verble also told us, "Others have left our neighborhood because they were afraid, or because they were moving up, but this is where we raised our family. We believe in the community. It has a lot of heart, and we're not going anywhere."

Verble's daughter, Victoria, who had been Jaclyn's best friend, said that she had remained close to Cynthia. Now eleven years old, with long blond hair and bright blue eyes, Victoria had hugged Cynthia earlier in the evening, bringing tears to Cynthia's eyes.

Victoria had been the prosecution's first witness at David and Cynthia's trial, called only to say that Jaclyn had been alive on September 9, 1988.

There had been no cross-examination.

Tonight Victoria talked about Jaclyn.

"I remember the times we rode our bikes up and down the block—we were so happy," she said.

"I still dream about her. In my dreams, we play just like before. Sometimes Cyndi is teaching us how to dance to 'The Greatest Love of All,' Jaclyn's favorite song.

"I'll never forget her—ever."

AUTHORS' POSTSCRIPT

Shortly after the Freedom Committee party, Cynthia Dowaliby called us with a suggestion: Perhaps NBC's *Unsolved Mysteries* would tell the story of Jaclyn's kidnapping in the hope of generating new leads from its vast national audience.

Liking that idea, we contacted the company that produced *Unsolved Mysteries* and spoke with Janet Jones, a researcher. She was interested, but noted that one of the program's goals was to solve crimes; the problem with the Dowaliby case was that the authorities might not investigate new leads.

We offered to investigate them.

After Jones spoke with the Dowalibys and law enforcement officials, she told us that *Unsolved Mysteries* would do the story and turn over any tips both to us and to the State Police.

On November 18, 1992, *Unsolved Mysteries* aired a twenty-minute segment on the case. It featured compelling home video of Jaclyn and ended with an appeal by host Robert Stack for anyone with information to call a toll-free number.

More than fifteen hundred calls flooded the program's telephone lines. Most of the callers merely expressed opinions about the Dowalibys' guilt or innocence, or provided information about other late-night child abductions.

One man who called, however, claimed that an early suspect in the case had given authorities a phony alibi for the night Jaclyn disappeared.

That suspect was Timothy Guess, Jaclyn's psychotic uncle.

The next evening, we contacted the *Unsolved Mysteries* caller, who claimed that Timothy Guess had lied to the authorities when he said he spent the entire night of Jaclyn's disappearance at the Park Avenue Restaurant. The man had limited firsthand information, but named several regular Park Avenue customers who knew more.

In the following days, we interviewed four customers who had been at the restaurant at various times on the night of September 9–10, 1988. They all said that Guess had not been there that night. One claimed that a waitress had told him that the owner of the restaurant, Aristotle Kritikos, had told her to tell law enforcement officers that Guess had been there.

The four customers said they never had been interviewed by the police or the FBI. They had not come forward earlier, they said, out of reluctance to challenge the authorities' publicly stated belief that the Dowalibys were guilty; "we didn't want trouble," as one put it.

Two of the customers also said that, since Jaclyn's murder, Guess repeatedly had said that he could commit murder and get away with it because he was legally crazy. One quoted him as saying after the *Unsolved Mysteries* broadcast, "I've killed before and I can do it again."

In addition, several Park Avenue customers told us that Guess frequently drove a fellow employee, Margaret Murphy, to and from work. Murphy lived at the Islander Apartments—in Everett Mann's building, about seventy-five yards from where Jaclyn's body had been found.

We tracked down Margaret Murphy, who confirmed that,

around the time of Jaclyn's disappearance, Guess drove her almost every day to the Park Avenue and home to the Islander Apartments. Murphy said that she never had been questioned by police, but that prosecutors visited her before the Dowaliby trial and instructed her not to talk to the defense lawyers.

We also interviewed one of the two waitresses who had told the FBI that Guess had been at the restaurant the entire night that Jaclyn disappeared. The waitress, Bonnie Norton, was hospitalized with a life-threatening illness. Speaking through an oxygen mask, Norton clearly said that Guess "wasn't there" that night. She acknowledged that she had told the authorities he was there because Aristotle Kritikos had asked her to say that.

The other waitress, Patricia Nossem, was interviewed by Channel 5 reporters Paul Hogan and Art Norman, with whom we shared our findings. Recanting what she had told the FBI in 1988, Nossem now said that she recalled seeing Guess at the restaurant only briefly, at about 9:30 P.M.

"In good conscience," Nossem said, "I can't say he stayed all night."

She denied, however, that Kritikos had asked her to lie.

When we interviewed Kritikos, he acknowledged that the waitresses and customers who had spoken with us had been at the restaurant the night Jaclyn disappeared, but insisted that Guess had been there, too.

"They're just trying to nail Timmy because he's sick," Kritikos said. "I have known the guy five years, and I never saw him try to hurt anybody.

"I'd just like to save him because he's innocent.

"Timmy's lucky I was here to stick up for him, because sometimes he does run around all night—but not that night. He was here all night long."

Kritikos acknowledged that he and the waitresses "talked together" before the FBI agents arrived, "but I told the girls, whatever you say has got to be truthful."

We met Timothy Guess on Thursday night, December 17, 1992, at a Denny's Restaurant near his home in Harvey. The meeting was arranged by a Park Avenue customer, who told Guess that we were writing a book and wanted to hear whatever he might know about his niece and her family.

The discussion lasted more than five hours.

Guess spoke freely of his mental illness, saying that he had begun "hearing voices" at age six. He had been in and out of mental institutions, had suffered repeated blackouts, and had taken various drugs, legal and illegal, much of his life.

When he was sixteen, he said, he heard "an intense voice" that a spirit helped him put into a pit, where it could not bother him; the spirit had been "a part" of him ever since. The spirit had told him that he would become famous and that his body—"flesh and all"—would live forever.

Telling us his story might fulfill the spirit's promise of fame, he said.

"He'll tell you the truth—always," Guess said. "The spirit gives me psychic powers and never lies."

We asked what the spirit had told him about Jaclyn's murder.

The spirit had told him, Guess said, that Jaclyn's parents had murdered her by tying her to her bed with a rope and that her father disposed of her body.

For more specific details, he added, we could speak directly with the spirit. "My eyes change color," he said. "If they're blue, the spirit's here; if they're green, the spirit's gone."

After we said that his eyes looked blue, Guess assumed a husky voice, which he ascribed to the spirit's presence, and described a series of little-known facts of the crime—that on the night Jaclyn was murdered, the light in her closet was on, but the main light in her room was off; that she was wearing gold pierced earrings and printed underwear; and that her body was placed with her head at an angle to the northeast.

Guess, still speaking in the husky voice, accurately described the layout of the Dowaliby home, which he professed never to have seen. Asked how someone would get to Jaclyn's room, he said, "I walked past Davey's room," quickly adding, "That was the spirit talking, not me. I didn't say nothin'. I just released information."

While Jaclyn was missing, Guess continued, he went to the Islander Apartments parking lot. "Something pulled me there like a driving force," he said, adding that he knew Jaclyn's body was there. He said he was too scared to look at it, and he eventually left.

Soon after Jaclyn's body was found, Guess said, he asked his psychiatrist what would happen to him if he committed a murder. When the psychiatrist asked what prompted his question, Guess said that although he had not murdered Jaclyn, he was worried because the authorities had questioned him about it.

"If you did commit murder," Guess quoted the psychiatrist as saying, "they wouldn't put you in jail. They would put you in the hospital." That, Guess explained, was why he had told the Park Avenue customers that he could commit murder and get away with it.

Guess adamantly asserted that he had been at the restaurant the night of September 9–10, 1988.

Asked why the customers and waitresses would say he was not there, Guess said, "Maybe I was invisible that day. The spirit can help me do that. I was there physically, but no one could notice me."

Perhaps, we suggested, the spirit had killed Jaclyn without his knowledge.

That would have been impossible, Guess said, because "the spirit puts everything he does in my memory bank." While he allowed that the spirit "might be sent by a demon or even the Devil," Guess said that the spirit does not hurt people.

"The spirit liked Jaclyn," Guess said. "He took her over to the Father in Heaven, where she is safe."

Toward the end of the conversation, Guess implored us not to tell anyone about the spirit.

We suggested that he tell the authorities everything the spirit had told him.

"No way," Guess said. "If I told them what I told you, they'd lead me away in handcuffs."

* * *

When the State Police failed to act on the *Unsolved Mysteries* tip, we took our findings to the Cook County state's attorney's office.

We provided sworn statements from Park Avenue customers, tape recordings of our interviews with Bonnie Norton and Margaret Murphy, and a summary of what Timothy Guess had told us.

After reviewing the materials, the state's attorney's office reopened the investigation into the murder of Jaclyn Dowaliby.

The investigation continued as this book went to press.